Hiking
California

by
Ron Adkison

(Formerly *The Hiker's Guide to California*)

FALCON™
HELENA, MONTANA

Falcon Press is continually expanding its list of recreational guidebooks. All books include detailed descriptions, accurate maps, and all information necessary for enjoyable trips. You can order extra copies of this book and get information and prices for the books listed above by writing Falcon Press, P.O. Box 1718, Helena, MT 59624 or calling 1-800-582-2665. Also, please ask for a free copy of our current catalog listing all Falcon Press books. To contact us by e-mail, visit our homepage at http:\\www.falconguide.com.

© 1990 by Falcon Press Publishing Co., Inc.
Helena and Billings, Montana
First Edition published in 1987.
10

Printed in the United States of America.

All text, maps, and photos by the author.
Photos by the author except as noted.
Cover Photo: Larry Carver/Mountain Stock, of the Ansel Adams Wilderness.

Library of Congress Cataloging-in-Publication Data
  Adkison, Ron.
    [Hiker's guide to California]
    Hiking California : formerly, The hiker's guide to California / by
  Ron Adkison.
      p. cm.
    ISBN 1-56044-379-0
    1. Hiking—California—Guidebooks. 2. California—Guidebooks.
  I. Title.
  [GV199.42.C2A25 1997]
  796.5109795—dc21   96-39259
                                           CIP

 Text pages printed on recycled paper.

CAUTION

    Outdoor recreational activities are by their very nature potentially hazardous. All participants in such activities must assume the responsibility for their own actions and safety. The information contained in this guidebook cannot replace sound judgment and good decision-making skills, which help reduce risk exposure, nor does the scope of this book allow for disclosure of all the potential hazards and risks involved in such activities.

    Learn as much as possible about the outdoor recreational activities you participate in, prepare for the unexpected, and be cautious. The reward will be a safer and more enjoyable experience.

ACKNOWLEDGMENTS

Writing a guidebook entails an enormous amount of work—on the trail, on the road, and behind the typewriter. Without the generous help of numerous individuals, this book simply would not be.

My heartfelt thanks are extended to the following individuals who contributed suggestions, corrections, and photos, as well as company on the trail and on the road: John Reilly, Ken Kukulka, John Rihs, Greg Rebitz, Kevin Duck, and Rick Marvin. I also wish to extend my thanks to publishers Mike Sample and Bill Schneider for getting me started on this project, and for suggestions and advice during various stages of the work.

Many thanks to countless government employees for providing valuable information, and for their patience in answering endless questions.

But most importantly, without the unflagging support and generous help of my parents, this book would never have been written, and it is to them that this book is dedicated.

Second Edition

Wild country may change imperceptibly during a human lifetime, but each passing year brings changes to trails and trailheads, access roads, and backcountry regulations.

Thus, keeping a guidebook up-to-date is an endless process. Although far too numerous to name individually, I wish to extend my sincere thanks and gratitude to the dozens of employees of the Forest Service, Bureau of Land Management, and Park Service, for helping me to attain the goal of keeping this guide as accurate and up-to-date as possible. Rising far beyond the call of duty, their generous contributions included reviewing the text, scouting trails, and making important corrections and suggestions to ensure the hike descriptions are accurate and easy to follow.

I would also like to thank my longtime friend and hiking partner, John Rihs, for accompanying me on forays into the East Mojave National Scenic Area.

TREE IDENTIFICATION GUIDE

Douglas-Fir
100-250 ft.

Red Fir
100-150 ft.

Incense-Cedar
100-150 ft.

Live Oak
50 ft.

Redwood
300 ft.

Limber Pine
25-50 ft.

Mountain Hemlock
75-100 ft.

Golden Chinquapin
50-60 ft.

White Fir
125-130 ft.

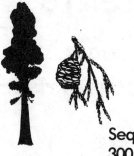

Sequoia
300 ft.

Western
White Pine
or Silver Pine
100-175 ft.

Tan Oak
60-100 ft.

Manzanita
2-15 ft.

Lodgepole Pine
25-80 ft.

Sugar Pine
175-200 ft.

Whitebark Pine
50-60 ft.

Ponderosa Pine
150-180 ft.

CONTENTS

INTRODUCTION 1

UNDERSTANDING THE HIKE DESCRIPTIONS

Map Legend 2
Hikes 3
Trail Markers... 5
Maps 5

BACKCOUNTRY RULES &
WILDERNESS REGULATIONS 7

HAZARDS IN THE BACKCOUNTRY 11

Hypothermia 14
Lightning and Flash Floods 15
Insects... 15
Rattlesnakes 16
Poison Oak 16
Bears 17
Giardia 17
Fires 18
Hiking With Children 19

THE HIKES

SOUTHERN CALIFORNIA

1. Elephant Trees Area...21
2. Borrego Palm Canyon 24
3. Arroyo Seco Creek to Agua Tibia Mountain 26
4. Humber Park to Red Tahquitz 30
5. Palm Springs Aerial Tramway to San Jacinto Peak 33
6. Indian Cove Picnic Area to Rattlesnake Canyon and
   The Wonderland of Rocks 35
7. Indian Cove Nature Trail 37
8. Black Rock Campground to Peak 5195............................ 37
9. East Branch Millard Canyon to Kitching Peak 40
10. Champion Joshua Tree 42
11. Sugarloaf Mountain 45
12. Fish Creek Aspen Grove... 46
13. South Fork Trailhead to San Gorgonio Mountain 48
14. John's Meadow, Anderson Peak 52
15. Ponderosa and Whispering Pines Nature Trail 54
16. Champion Lodgepole Pine.. 56
17. Delamar Mountain 56
18. Cleghorn Pass to Cajon Mountain 59

19. Mt. Baldy Road to Cascade Canyon 60
20. Icehouse Canyon to Cucamonga Peak 64
21. Mt. San Antonio 68
22. Dawson Saddle to Mt. Baden-Powell 70
23. Smith Mountain 73
24. South Fork Big Rock Creek to the Devils Chair 75
25. Twin Peaks 77
26. Sierra Pelona 79
27. Mt. Pinos to Grouse Mountain 81
28. Peak 7416, Pine Mountain 83

MOJAVE DESERT
29. Lanfair Valley to Fort Piute 86
30. Keystone Canyon to New York Peak 90
31. Cima Road to Teutonia Peak 94
32. Kelso Dunes 96

SOUTHERN SIERRA NEVADA
33. Coffin Peak 99
34. Golden Canyon to Zabriskie Point 102
35. Mosaic Canyon 105
36. Wildrose Canyon to Wildrose Peak 108
37. Hell's Gate to Death Valley Buttes 113
38. The Racetrack to Ubehebe Peak 116

BAY AREA
39. Big Falls Canyon 120
40. Pfeiffer Falls, Valley View Loop 123
41. Mt. Carmel 125
42. Pine Valley 128
43. Pinnacles National Monument 132
44. Big Basin Redwoods State Park 135
45. Mt. Wittenberg 138
46. Summit Springs Trailhead to Snow Mountain 140

CENTRAL CALIFORNIA
47. Walker Pass to Morris Peak 145
48. Big Meadow to Domeland 147
49. West Meadow to Stony Meadow, Rincon Trail 152
50. Jackass Peak 154
51. Blackrock Gap to Kern Peak 157
52. Jordan Peak 160
53. Cottonwood Loop 164
54. Alta Peak 169
55. Rowell Meadow Trailhead to Williams and Comanche Meadows 171
56. Big Baldy 175
57. Redwood Mountain Loop 177
58. Onion Valley to Whitney Portal 180
59. Courtright Reservoir to Dinkey Lakes 187
60. North Fork Big Pine Creek 190
61. White Mountain Sampler 193
62. Lake Sabrina to Hungry Packer Lake 198
63. Lake Sabrina to Tyee Lakes 200

64. North Lake to the Lamarck Lakes 202
65. North Lake to Pine Creek 204
66. Rock Creek to Upper Morgan Lake 207
67. Rock Creek to Pioneer Basin 209

NORTHERN SIERRA NEVADA

68. Coldwater Campground to Tully Lake 212
69. Agnew Meadows to Devils Postpile 216
70. Lillian Lake Loop 220
71. Hetch Hetchy Reservoir to Rancheria Falls 224
72. Tioga Road to Ten Lakes.. 227
73. Tioga Pass to Mt. Dana 232
74. Saddlebag Lake to McCabe Lakes 235
75. Green Creek to Summit Lake 239
76. Gianelli Cabin to Upper Relief Valley 241
77. Dardanelles Loop 244
78. Blue Canyon.. 247
79. Sonora Peak 250
80. Desert Creek to Mt. Patterson 253
81. Ebbetts Pass to Nobel Lake 256
82. Schneider Camp to Showers Lake 258
83. Luther Pass to Freel Meadows 261

NORTHERN CALIFORNIA

84. Grouse Ridge to Glacier Lake 264
85. Feather Falls... 266
86. Lakes Basin 270
87. Hay Meadow to Long Lake 273
88. Lassen Peak 275
89. Crags Lake 279
90. Butte Lake to Snag Lake Loop.. 281
91. Tamarack Trailhead to Everett and Magee Lakes........................ 286
92. North Yolla Bolly Mountains Loop... 290
93. Lightning Trailhead to Kings Peak 294
94. Canyon Creek Lakes.. 297
95. Long Gulch to Trail Gulch Loop 301
96. Forest Road 39N48 to Bingham Lake 305
97. Elk Prairie to Fern Canyon and
    Gold Bluffs Beach via the James Irvine Trail............................. 309
98. Kelsey Ridge Trail to Bear Lake, Little Bear Valley 312
99. Shackleford Creek to Summit Lake.. 314
100. Patterson Lake via the Summit Trail 318

A BASIC HIKER'S CHECKLIST 322

IF YOU NEED ADDITIONAL INFORMATION 323

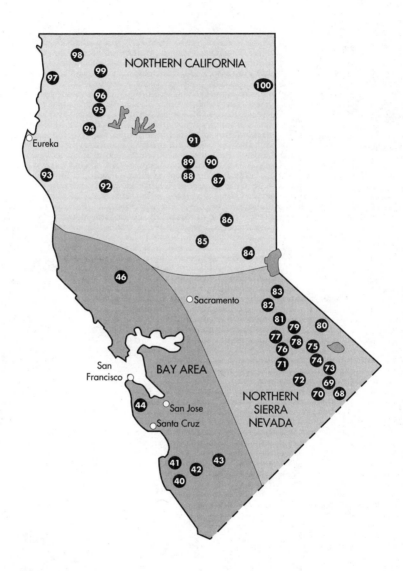

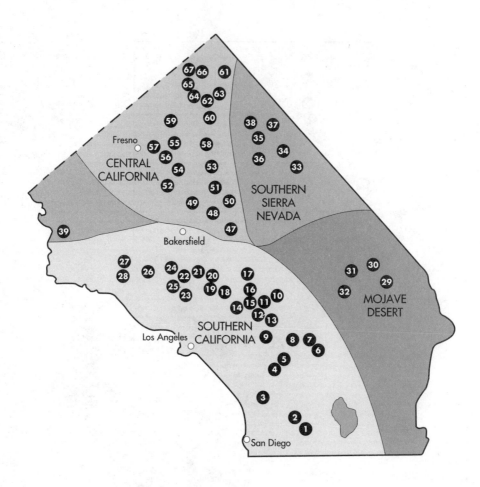

INTRODUCTION

California! The mere mention of the name conjures images of Spanish ranchos, of Franciscan missions, of the Gold Rush, of vast and fertile farmlands, of rugged and spectacular coastlines, of superb, mild weather, of large cities, of parched deserts, and of mountains and wilderness.

California, our nation's most populous state, means different things to each of us, but to hikers it can be expressed in one word—*Paradise!*

Yes, California has it all, and one can hike here in virtually every month of the year. In summer, heat-oppressed lowlanders flee to the cool high country; and as winter tightens its grip, hikers descend into the more hospitable environs of the foothills, the coast, or the desert.

The comparatively slow pace of hikers allows them to experience first hand the changing faces of nature in this incredibly diverse land. Backcountry travelers can revel in the magnificent energy of a high mountain thunderstorm, or enjoy the mellow morning sun reflected on shimmering pine needles. They can spend hours watching fluffy cumulus clouds roll by on invisible rivers in the sky, or experience the excitement of large trout rising to a fly, momentarily interrupting a perfect reflection in glassy water. Hikers are rewarded with the exhilaration and satisfaction of finally scaling mountain crags, where the unspoiled landscape stretches from horizon to horizon, or they are lulled to sleep by the chuckling waters of a clear, cold mountain stream.

Nowhere else in the world does a land of such infinite diversity and contrast exist. From the summit of Mount Whitney, for example, the highest point in the lower forty-eight states, a climber stands within a hundred miles of the lowest point in North America—immediately to the east and more then ten thousand feet below lies the deepest valley on the continent, Owens Valley. Directly across that valley rises the Inyo-White Mountain chain, hosting some of the oldest living things on earth, bristlecone pines. West of Mount Whitney, on the heavily forested western slope of the Sierra Nevada (which, by the way, is the longest unbroken mountain crest in the country) are the largest living things on earth, the giant sequoias. But, as any hiker soon discovers, all this incredible diversity and contrast is not limited to a few well-known features.

Moreover, a hiker who walks these backcountry trails, marveling at the variety of landforms, flora, and fauna, may also journey inwardly—through a wilderness of profound questions—toward deeper insights into the workings of the natural world, where every plant, animal, and rock has its place and function, all seemingly separate but all intricately related.

No single guidebook, of course, could possibly log every potential hike in a state as vast and diverse as California. But each hike described here is itself an introduction to innumerable hiking opportunities nearby, be they trail walks or rugged cross-country scrambles.

As hikers gain the ability, knowledge, and confidence necessary for safe exploration, their backcountry adventures can be limited only by their imaginations. And *Hiking California* can only whet those appetites for exploration in the Golden State—exploration that could, indeed, encompass many lifetimes of adventure.

MAP LEGEND

Interstate	00	Trailhead and Trail of Description	
U.S. Highway	00	Alternative Trailhead	
State Highway	000	Trail	
Forest Road	0000	Cross-Country Route	
Paved Road		River, Creek, Drainage	
Dirt Road	= = = =	Intermittent River or Creek	
Locked Gate		Falls or Rapids	
Bridge		Meadow or Swamp	
Pass or Saddle		Springs	
Power Line		Lakes	
Tunnel		Dry Lakes	
Mine		Glacier	
Building		Depression	
Ranger Station	RS	Peak & Elevation	X 0000
Campground	△		
Picnic Area		Wilderness Boundary	
Ski Lift		Directional Orientation Symbol	N
Map Scale	ONE MILE		

UNDERSTANDING
THE HIKE DESCRIPTIONS

Hikes

For the most part, hike descriptions are self-explanatory. A few points, however, require some discussion to help you get the most from each hiking trip.

Four basic types of hikes are described in this guide: round trips, where you hike to a particular destination, then retrace your route to the trailhead; loop trips, where you hike in on one trail and hike out to the same trailhead via a different route, perhaps retracing as much as one mile of trail; semi-loop trips, where you negotiate a small loop but retrace a portion of your route; and point-to-point or shuttle trips, where you begin at one trailhead and hike out to another, requiring that you hitchhike back to your car, leave another car at the opposite trailhead, have someone pick you up, or divide your group, hiking from opposite trailheads and exchanging car keys in the backcountry.

Elevation gain and loss figures are approximations, accurate within fifty feet. These figures are composites based on altimeter readings. For example, a one-way hike which ascended 1,000 feet, descended 750 feet, ascended another 1,000 feet, and then descended 500 feet would have an elevation gain of 2,000 feet and an elevation loss of 1,250 feet. Especially in rugged terrain, such figures often indicate the strenuous nature of a hike more accurately than would the simple difference between elevation gain and loss (in this example, 750 feet).

For round trips, elevation gain and loss figures are listed for the hike in— you simply reverse those figures for the return trip. For example, if a hiker gains 1500 feet and loses 150 feet for the hike in to a particular destination, the hiker would therefore lose 1500 feet of elevation and gain 150 feet of elevation for the hike back to the trailhead. Only one figure is listed if the hike only gains elevation or only loses elevation from the trailhead to the destination. For example, if the elevation gain figure is listed as "1200 feet," then the hiker gains 1200 feet of elevation from the trailhead to the destination. On the return trip then, the hiker would lose that 1200 feet of elevation going back to the trailhead. Such a listing indicates that a hike is either all uphill to the destination, or if an elevation loss figure only is listed (indicated by a minus sign) then the hike is downhill all the way to the destination.

Occasionally, the text refers to a mountain peak or lake as "Peak 11,071" or "Lake 6730." This refers to unnamed peaks or lakes and indicates the elevation of such a feature.

Season listings are designed to indicate the optimum season in which to take a given hike. Since conditions vary on a yearly basis, however, these listings are certainly not decisive. Thus, for high country hikes, the season indicated is the most snow-and-storm-free period of the year; and for low elevation or desert hikes, the ideal season is the coolest time of year. For some hikes the season indicated is all year—thus, during the "storm season" (from about November through March), you should stay updated on weather forecasts and avoid stormy periods.

3

Hikes are listed as backpack hikes, day hikes, or either. Generally, backpack hikes are those that cover too much distance to be finished comfortably in one day. A backpack hike may also be classified because the attractions of an area, such as fishing or magnificent scenery, make a leisurely pace suitable for a more enjoyable trip.

Hikes classified as strictly day hikes are too short for backpacking or do not have adequate water or campsites available.

Classification of hikes as suitable for either day or backpack hikes indicates that they can be completed in one strenuous day or can be taken at a slower pace, allowing for nights spent camping in the backcountry.

Occasionally, a hike is listed as suitable for backpacking if water is carried along. Packing water, however, is usually practical only for one-night campers or if snow patches are available from which you can melt the water you need. But if lugging pounds of water for miles doesn't sound appealing, remember this: dry camps are usually insect-free, and tend to be more remote and used less than campsites near water. Many solitude-seeking hikers find the advantages of dry camps far outweigh any inconvenience of packing a supply of water. One gallon of water per person for each night at a dry camp is usually adequate.

Hikes listed as cross-country or part cross-country hikes should be attempted only by hikers experienced in off-trail hiking and route-finding. Many of these hikes are straight forward, but some require skills that novice hikers have not yet developed.

A few such cross-country hikes include routes classified as Class 2 or Class 3 routes. Class 2 routes are essentially scrambles over rough terrain, often involving boulder-hopping or scrambling along steep and occasionally unstable slopes—you must use your hands sometimes to maintain balance or latch onto a hold. Most hikers with some cross-country experience should have no trouble on Class 2 routes, but lug-soled boots are recommended.

Class 3 routes entail basic rock-climbing skills where hand and foot holds come into play. These routes are often quite exposed, and the unsteady or

Camping and backpacking aren't necessarily limited to the summer season. With the proper knowledge and equipment, hikers can enjoy the wilderness throughout the year.

novice climber may need to be roped up on Class 3 routes. No hike described in this guide involves Class 3 climbing, but nearby peaks suggested for side trips often do.

Trail Markers

Backcountry hikers occasionally encounter ducks or blazes. Ducks—small stacks of rocks—are most common in timberline or alpine areas, and mark obscure or cross-country routes. Avoid building ducks when traveling crosscountry, however—they are usually unnecessary and always detract from the wilderness experience. Other hikers can find their own way, and you do no one a favor by lining a possible cross-country route with ducks. Hikers who need ducks to lead the way shouldn't be traveling cross-country in the first place.

Blazes, usually the figure "i" carved into the bark of trees, are found along most wilderness trails. Often, blazes are the only clues to the location of an obscure or abandoned trail, and they become invaluable when the trail is buried in snow. Still, individuals should never blaze trees in the backcountry. Keep in mind that most trail signs are semi-permanent fixtures at best, and may be unreliable. The detailed hike descriptions in this guide, on the other hand, will get you where you want to go, trail signs or not.

Maps

Two types of maps are commonly listed in *Hiking California*—United States Geological Survey (USGS) topographic quadrangles and Forest Service maps.

Each national forest is covered by its individual map, which is most useful for locating the general area of a given hike and can be invaluable in trailhead location. The cost of such a map is generally $4.00, and they are available at most Forest Service stations.

USGS topographic quadrangles are preferred by most hikers. These maps have contour lines which help hikers visualize the landscape and identify landmarks and landscape features such as lakes, streams, and peaks.

The 7.5-minute quadrangles usually have contour intervals of forty feet, cover an area of approximately nine miles by seven miles, and are on a scale of 1:24000. (In other words, one inch on the map is equivalent to 24,000 inches on the ground.) The 15-minute quadrangles usually have contour intervals of eighty feet, cover an area of approximately fourteen by seventeen miles, and are on a scale of 1:62500.

Many trails and roads are not depicted accurately on some older topographic quadrangles, but the landscape rarely changes. Maps used in *Hiking California* show the correct location and configuration of trails and roads, and are designed to complement the listed quadrangles.

Topographic maps are available at most backpacking and sporting goods stores, or can be ordered directly from the USGS. Standard topographic quadrangles are currently $4.00 each when ordered from the USGS, with a $1.00 handling charge on all orders under $10. To order, simply list the maps needed in alphabetical order, indicate how many of each are needed, for which state (all maps needed for this guide are California quadrangles), the scale desired, and the price. Send orders to U.S. Geological Survey, Box 25286, Denver Federal Center, Denver, Colorado 80225, or call (800) USA MAPS.

Trailheads listed in this guide vary—some are located alongside major state highways, others are found in very remote "backcountry" locations. Always be sure your vehicle is in good condition, especially if driving to remote trailheads via long dirt roads. Check your brakes, make sure you have plenty of fuel, and carry basic emergency equipment. A shovel, axe, saw, at least five gallons of water, and extra food and clothing should help you deal with a variety of unforeseen problems, and may indeed be your only hope in some remote areas. If you're unsure about road conditions, don't hesitate to check ahead with the appropriate agency.

To locate hikes, use the general location maps in this guide in tandem with a good California road map and Forest Service or Park Service maps.

Crystal clear creeks, lush meadows, and snow-clad granite peaks are all part of the High Sierra experience. Photo by John Rihs.

Finally, remember that you don't need to hike each described route in its entirety or in the described direction to enjoy a particular hiking area. Simply choose an area that appeals to you, and let your ability and desire dictate how far to go or which trail to take. After all, enjoyment is what hiking is all about.

BACKCOUNTRY RULES AND WILDERNESS REGULATIONS

All users of backcountry lands in California have a responsibility to become familiar with and abide by the rules and regulations governing use of those lands.

Some heavily used backcountry areas have specific restrictions regarding the use of campsites, open fires, etc., usually to protect vegetation and to allow damaged campsites to recover from overuse. These specific regulations, attached to wilderness permits, are in addition to the regulations listed below. Visitors should become familiar with all regulations, including those described below, before venturing into California's wilderness backcountry—there is no better way to ensure a safe, enjoyable trip which minimizes disturbance of the land and other visitors.

I. In state park, national park, and national monument backcountry:
• Firearms, loaded or unloaded, are prohibited.
• Pets are prohibited on backcountry trails. Dogs are permitted in national forest wilderness, but are not encouraged. They can pollute water sources, harass wildlife and other hikers, and endanger their owners by leading an angry bear back to camp. If you must bring your dog into national forest wilderness, please keep it under restraint as much as possible, particularly on trails and near other hikers and campers.
• Collection of natural features, such as wildflowers, antlers, and rocks is prohibited. Fishing is allowed under California state fishing regulations, but hunting, shooting, molesting, or disturbing with intent to harm wildlife is prohibited.

II. In national forest wilderness only: Discharging of firearms is permitted in national forest wilderness areas only for emergencies and taking of wildlife as permitted by California game laws. However, some wilderness areas, such as the San Jacinto Wilderness, are also game refuges where firearms are prohibited.

III. In both national forest and national park backcountry:
• Where terrain permits, locate campsites at least a hundred feet from trails, streams, lakeshores, meadows, and other campers. When damaged, fragile lakeshore and streamside vegetation may take generations to recover.

Moreover, campsites located away from water are comparatively insect-free and are often considerably warmer. Carry a supply of water to your camp for drinking, cooking, and washing to avoid continually trampling delicate streamside and lakeshore vegetation.

• Short-cutting switchbacks and walking out of established trails is prohibited. Such short-cutting creates an erosion problem that contributes to the deterioration of the existing trail. Besides, hikers save little, if any, time by short-cutting trails, and the additional energy required to negotiate rugged country makes this practice unproductive.

• Any destruction, defacement, or removal of natural features is prohibited. Avoid disturbing wildflowers, trees, shrubs, grasses, and the like which are important segments of the ecological community. Don't chop, drive nails or carve initials into, cut boughs from, or otherwise damage live trees or standing snags. Damaged trees are vulnerable to insects and disease.

• Pack out all unburnable refuse. Aluminum foil and plastics do not burn, and must be packed out along with cans, bottles, and leftover food scraps—not buried. Many foods carried by backpackers are packaged in airtight foil-lined containers which will not burn—pack them out. And even if buried, leftover food scraps will attract hungry animals. As wild animals become accustomed to eating human food, their natural foraging habits are disrupted, creating problems for future campers at the site.

• Do not litter the trail. Put all trash such as cigarette butts, gum, orange peels, and candy wrappers in your pocket or pack while traveling.

• Stop to smoke. Smoking while traveling is not only hazardous, it is also against the law. Locate a safe spot in a cleared or barren area free of flammable material, such as a large rock or a sandy area. Never crush out a cigarette on a log or stump. Be sure all matches, ashes, and burning tobacco are dead out before leaving the area.

• Protect water quality. Bury body waste in a shallow hole, five to eight inches deep, in the biologically active layer where bacteria and fungi will help decompose waste fairly rapidly. This is a good reason to carry a small, lightweight garden trowel. Locate a spot at least two hundred feet from campsites, trails, and existing or potential watercourses, so that rain and snow runoff will not carry pollutants to lakes and streams. Fish entrails should be burned whenever possible, and should never be thrown into water sources.

• Keep all wash water at least one hundred feet from water sources. Do not use any type of soap or detergent in or near water sources or potential watercourses. Even "biodegradable" soaps contain ingredients that can pollute water. Usually, sand or gravel can clean pots more effectively than soaps.

• A California fishing license is required by anyone over sixteen years of age who plans to fish. California fishing regulations apply in wilderness areas.

• All mechanized and motorized equipment, including motorcycles, chainsaws, and snowmobiles, are prohibited in wilderness areas. Some roadless areas not officially designated as wilderness may also have restrictions regarding the use of motorized equipment. Some state parks do allow bicycles on trails, but they are prohibited in other backcountry areas.

• Yield the right-of-way to pack and saddle stock on trails. Stand well off the trail until the animals have passed. Simple-minded pack animals are easily spooked by sudden noises and movements, so talk to the packer in a normal tone of voice to let the animals know you are there.

• Collecting plant and animal life, minerals, or other natural and historical objects is permitted for scientific study only. Special written authorization is required, and must be obtained in advance from either a park superintendent or forest supervisor. These permits are not issued for personal collections. Please do not pick wildflowers. Leave them for others to enjoy. Allow them to complete their life cycles so they can perpetuate the beauty of the area.

• Constructing rock walls, large fireplaces, fire rings, benches, tables, shelters, bough beds, rock or wood bridges, trenches, or other similar structures alters the natural character of the land and is not permitted. Make an effort to leave the least possible trace of your passing.

• Wilderness Visitor's Permits (known as Backcountry Use Permits in National Parks) are required all year for entry into some national forest and all national park wilderness areas in California. A Wilderness Visitor's Permit is free to anyone who agrees to abide by the regulations listed above and any special restrictions applying to a travel area. They are issued at the ranger station nearest the point of entry, and can be obtained in person or by mail in some wilderness areas.

However, there are certain advantages to obtaining a permit in person. Doing so often provides the only contact with Forest Service or park service personnel, who are quite knowledgeable on many aspects of the wilderness. They are more than happy to answer any questions, particularly about regulations, trail conditions, snowpack, problem bears, weather forecasts, etc.

Only one permit is required for each group traveling together, and that permit is issued for one trip only. It must be in the possession of a group member while traveling in the backcountry. If that trip crosses into adjacent wilderness areas, the permit will be honored in those areas. Remember that wilderness visitor's permits are required for both day hikes and overnight hikes in some national forest wilderness areas, while in other areas they may only be required for overnight camping. In national parks, permits are required only for overnight camping.

A permit system allows the issuing agency to obtain information on where, when, and how much use a particular area receives—valuable information which enables the agency to make important management decisions, such as whether limited use is required to preserve wilderness qualities of a particular area. Information recorded on wilderness permits may also aid in locating lost or injured hikers.

In most California wilderness areas, maximum group size is twenty-five persons. That number of people traveling and camping together inevitably has an adverse impact on the land, so some areas limit groups to fifteen or fewer people. If you plan on hiking with a large group, be sure to check with the ranger station nearest your trailhead about group size limits.

At many of the most heavily used wilderness trailheads, particularly in southern California and the High Sierra, a quota system has been implemented. This system allows the managing agency to limit the number of backpackers entering the wilderness on a daily basis. Such quota systems have become necessary to protect qualities of solitude and prevent continued degradation of campsites and trails. Quota systems allow a maximum number of people to use a given area while maintaining the qualities of wilderness that visitors are seeking. The following wilderness areas described in *The Hiker's Guide to California* have entry quotas in effect: Ansel Adams, John Muir, Cucamonga, San Gorgonio, San Jacinto. Yosemite and Sequoia-Kings Canyon national parks also employ quotas. To assure entry into these areas, consider obtaining your wilderness permit in advance.

A wilderness permit also allows the building of campfires where permitted. If you plan to build a campfire or use a backpack stove outside of wilderness areas, you must obtain a California Campfire Permit. For the Los Padres, Angeles, San Bernardino, and Cleveland national forests of southern California, however, a Special Campfire Permit is required. These permits are available at Forest Service stations in person only and require that applicants have at least a small shovel available for use at the campfire site.

To obtain a wilderness permit by mail, an application must be mailed no less than two weeks nor more than ninety days in advance of the outing. Applications must supply the following information: applicant's name and address; date of entry and exit; location of entry and exit; campsite locations, or destination of day hike, number of people in group; and method of travel such as on foot or horseback.

Permits are not available by mail for all wilderness areas. In some cases, hikers can make advance reservations for a permit by mail, but they must pick up the permit in person at the appropriate ranger station. If you have any questions regarding wilderness permits don't hesitate to contact the appropriate ranger station.

If the above list of wilderness rules and regulations seems confusing, or overwhelmingly restrictive, it shouldn't. In most cases, these regulations simply embody common sense. They represent choices between degradation or preservation of California's vanishing wildernesses.

The National Wilderness Preservation Act of September 3, 1964, defines wilderness as "an area of undeveloped federal land retaining its primeval character and influence without permanent improvements or human habitation...where the earth and its community of life are untrammeled by man ... where man is a visitor who does not remain ... and is protected and managed so as to preserve its natural condition...." The U.S. Forest Service manages wilderness areas in accordance with the Wilderness Act, striving to maintain their primitive character—by protecting native plants and animals and preserving healthy watersheds, while at the same time providing the public an opportunity to use the wilderness and benefit from the wilderness experience.

With increasingly heavy use in California's roadless areas, such wilderness qualities and experiences are becoming more problematic. The regulations applied in California's wilderness areas simply attempt to maintain those qualities that we, as backcountry visitors, seek.

In addition to the rules and regulations listed above, other simple practices can help hikers minimize their imprint upon the wilderness:

• Respect the right of other visitors to enjoy solitude. Loud voices and clanging pots destroy the peaceful qualities most visitors are searching for. Allow plenty of room between your party and other campers to assure privacy and solitude.

• Use of backpack stoves is highly recommended. In some areas, wood fires are prohibited. Never build a fire in sub-alpine or timberline areas where dead wood is scarce and lends aesthetic value to an austere landscape. It is difficult to justify a few hours of meager warmth in a timberline environment, burning wood from trees that have withstood the ravages of icy winds and deep snows for hundreds or even thousands of years. Moreover, campfires leave an indelible mark upon the landscape and should be built only in emergencies, or when dead and downed wood is in abundance and fire danger is low. If you must build a fire, choose a site with an existing fire ring—don't build a new one.

• Avoid creating new campsites. Camp on existing sites whenever possible. Unfortunately, too many existing campsites are either badly overused or are too close to water sources or trails. If you must camp on a previously unused site, choose a durable spot, such as sandy or pine needle-covered terrain. If you clear your sleeping area of rocks, twigs, or pine cones, be sure to scatter them back over your site before leaving. Never uproot or damage vegetation or perform any excavation at your campsite. Leave it as primitive as you found it.

During your travels through California's wilderness areas, you may occasionally meet a backcountry ranger. He or she will be glad to answer questions concerning the wilderness. Unfortunately, however, too much of a ranger's time is spent cleaning up after careless hikers, dismantling fire rings, and offering reminders or issuing citations to those who forget or refuse to abide by regulations. So minimize this unpleasant burden on backcountry rangers by doing your part to protect our precious wilderness areas.

HAZARDS IN THE BACKCOUNTRY

It seems that there are as many reasons for seeking wild places as there are hikers. One thing, above all, that hikers have in common is the desire for a safe and enjoyable outdoor experience.

City life takes its toll on many hikers, and a long weekend in the wilderness may be the focus of anticipation all year. But in their haste to escape the rat race, to "get away from it all," some hikers forget the potential hazards that exist in those wild areas.

The following list addresses the kinds of hazards typical in the backcountry. No matter what the situation, though, good judgment—an awareness of potential hazards and how to deal with them—is your best insurance.

• A good first-aid kit, and a working knowledge of the use of its components, is essential.

• Before venturing into the backcountry, gather as much information as possible about the area you will be visiting. Study maps, and read as much as you can about the area. Contact the ranger station nearest your hike for information about swollen streams, problem bears, snow on the route, carnivorous insects, etc. The ideal time to gather this information is when you obtain your wilderness permit.

• Before departing, leave a detailed travel plan with a responsible person, and stick to that plan religiously. If you fail to return at the designated time, that person should contact a county sheriff or district ranger in your travel area so that a search and rescue operation can be activated. If you return later than planned, be sure to notify the above-mentioned agencies so search operations can be discontinued.

• Always be prepared when entering any wild area. Carry a topographic map and check it frequently as your hike progresses so you will stay oriented. A topographic map in combination with a compass, and a working knowledge of their use, is a must.

Winter camping in the High Sierra requires knowledge of the special hazards associated with winter, and familiarity with the techniques required to survive during extreme cold. Photo by Rick Marvin.

- When traveling cross-country (which should be attempted only by experienced hikers), observe landmarks and locate them on your map as you go along. Remember that country looks quite different from opposite directions.
- Proper equipment selection is also important. Good, sturdy footwear (preferably lug-soled boots), dependable shelter, warm clothing (wool, fiber-pile, and other fabrics that retain insulation when wet are best), and plenty of food are basic items for any hiker's pack. Gear should be lightweight, with as little bulk as possible. Excellent books are available which offer help in the selection of proper outdoor gear.
- Choose a hike within the capability of the members of your group, and stay together on the trail, particularly toward nightfall.
- If a storm develops or darkness is descending, make camp as soon as possible. Never hike at night. Keep in mind that darkness comes quickly to the mountains.
- When hiking in hot, dry country, particularly the desert, always carry ample water. At least a gallon of water per person per day is required for strenuous activities in hot weather. Don't ration your water—simply drink whenever you are thirsty.
- It is never wise to hike alone. Solo hiking cross-country is especially dangerous.
- Never take unnecessary chances. Don't be afraid to turn back or end your trip if someone in your group becomes ill, if swollen streams or snow block your route, or if inclement weather sets in. The wilderness will always be there—make sure you are able to return and enjoy it.
- Know the limitations of your body, your equipment, and the members of your group. Don't exceed those limits.
- If you think you are lost, or are injured, stop traveling at once, stay calm, and decide upon a course of action. Study maps and try to locate landmarks that will help orient you. Do not continue until you know where you are. If you left a travel plan with a responsible person, and if you followed that plan, a search party will look for you and should have no trouble finding you.

In some areas, following a creek downstream will lead out of the mountains. But in larger wilderness areas, this practice may lead further into the wilderness and compound the problem.

A series of three signals, such as whistles, shouts, or light flashes, is universally recognized as a distress signal. Only contemplate starting a signal fire in emergencies, and even then make sure it can be done safely. Rescuers will be directed to you by smoke, not flames.

- Beware of fast water. Some of the most frequently encountered hazards in the backcountry are swiftly running streams or rivers. Although most large streams in California are bridged, those which are not require special precautions, especially during periods of spring snowmelt or after heavy rains. The power of a swiftly running mountain stream is as easy to underestimate as it is impressive. Take no chances when crossing swift streams. Search upstream or downstream for a crossing via logs or boulders, but remember—these can be very slippery.

If you can't find a crossing, your only choice is to ford the stream. During spring runoff, creeks will be at their lowest in the early morning hours before the sun begins melting the snowpack once again.

Before entering the water, plan exactly what you will do. Never ford a stream above a cascade or waterfall. Look for a level stretch of water, perhaps where the stream has divided into numerous channels. Choose a spot where you and/or your gear will wash onto a sand bar or shallow area in the event you lose your footing.

Try to cross at a 45-degree angle downstream. Some hikers use a pole or stout staff on their upstream side to aid in crossing swift waters. Remove your pants (bare legs create less friction) and your socks, but put your boots back on for better footing on the slippery stream bottom. Unhitch the waist strap on your pack so that you can dump it if you lose your footing.

• Allow plenty of time to let your body adjust. The majority of California hikers travel from low elevations to high country to do their hiking, and must acclimate themselves to the reduced oxygen in the atmosphere. A rapid rise to high altitudes often produces headache, loss of appetite, fatigue, nausea, shortness of breath, and insomnia in persons unaccustomed to the thin air. Rest, consumption of liquids, and "high energy" foods such as candy and dried fruit should help alleviate these symptoms. If they persist, however, descend to a lower elevation. And at any elevation, take it easy your first few days on the trail.

• Take shelter during thunderstorms. California hikers are fortunate to live in a state that enjoys such a mild climate. More often than not, they are treated to fine weather in the backcountry. But even in summer, storms develop quickly; and although they are usually of short duration, the high winds, lightning, and intense precipitation accompanying them create hazards not to be taken lightly.

Hypothermia

First and foremost, you must stay dry. A wet, tired hiker exposed to wind is in danger of developing hypothermia, an abnormal lowering of the body's internal temperature. Hypothermia, sometimes called exposure, can occur at relatively mild temperatures. Symptoms of hypothermia include shivering, slurred speech, fumbling hands, stumbling, and drowsiness. If you or members of your group develop any of these symptoms, immediate treatment is required. Hypothermia can be fatal if left untreated.

Wet clothing should be removed from a hypothermia victim immediately. Warm drinks—but not coffee or tea—should be given to warm the victim internally, and external warming, preferably by body-to-body contact, should begin as soon as possible.

To help hikers become familiar with hypothermia and its causes, symptoms, and treatment, the Forest Service offers a wealth of free literature on the subject.

Cold, unsettled weather is common in spring and fall, but summer storminess is largely characterized by afternoon and evening thundershowers. Backcountry travelers should always anticipate storms and carry a reliable tent, effective rain gear, and clothing that will maintain its insulating value when wet. Be sure to obtain extended weather forecasts before heading into wild country, and be alert to changing weather conditions.

Although most summer storms are brief, occasionally a tropical storm hits the state, usually in August or September, and dominates the weather for days on end. Still, it is better not to panic and hastily attempt to flee the wilderness. Just pitch camp and stay put—chances are excellent that it will be over by morning.

Lightning and Flash floods

Lightning is perhaps the most dangerous and frightening aspect of summer storms. Don't be caught on a ridge or mountain top, under large, solitary trees, in the open, or near open water during a lightning storm. Try to seek shelter in a low-lying area, ideally in a dense stand of small, uniformly sized trees. Stay away from anything that might attract lightning, such as metal tent poles or pack frames.

In the desert, where summer thunderstorms are common, avoid hiking in, and never make camp in, a wash or canyon bottom. It doesn't have to be raining where you are for a flash flood to occur. One can emanate from heavy rainfall several miles away.

Insects

Don't let insects bug you. They are unavoidable—but not unbeatable—in the backcountry, especially in June and July at higher elevations. The most common nuisance to hikers is the persistent mosquito. Your best line of defense is to anticipate annoying insects on any hike and carry a good insect repellent. Consider using a natural insect repellent. Products containing citronella are quite effective, and can make forays into bug-infested terrain tolerable, even enjoyable.

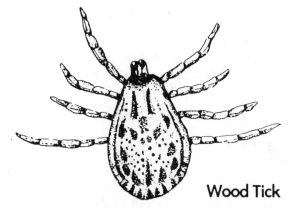

Wood Tick

Ticks are fairly common throughout wooded, brushy, and grassy areas of California. They are most active from March until early summer. All ticks are potential carriers of Rocky Mountain Spotted Fever, Colorado Tick Fever, and Tularemia (rabbit fever). The western black-legged tick, only 1/8 inch long, is responsible for transmitting Lyme Disease, a bacterial infection named for the Connecticut town where it was first recognized.These diseases are transmitted to humans and other mammals by the bite of an infected tick. Your best defense against hosting a tick is to avoid areas infested by ticks, which, of course, is not always possible or practical when hiking wild country. If you must be in an area infested with ticks, wear clothing with a snug fit around the waist, wrists, and ankles. Layers of clothing are most effective in keeping ticks from reaching the body. And since ticks don't always bite right away (they often crawl around on a potential host for several hours before deciding where to feed on a victim's blood), a strong insect repellent can also be an effective deterrent against ticks.

Examine yourself and pets frequently while in tick country. Ticks should be removed as soon as possible. It is wise to let a physician extract a tick to avoid infection and the possibility of leaving the head under the skin. But if you must remove a tick yourself, protect your hands with gloves, cloth, or a piece of paper. Tweezers work best, using a steady pulling motion, but avoid crushing the tick. The application of tincture of iodine may induce the tick to let go, as well as helping reduce infection. If the tick's head remains imbedded in the skin, a secondary infection may develop—in this case, see a physician to have it removed. Always wash your hands and apply antiseptic to the bite.

The majority of Lyme Disease infections have occurred in the coastal counties of Marin, Sonoma, Mendocino, and Humboldt, all north of San Francisco. Initial reactions include a red, circular rash at the location of the bite, and flu-like symptoms. If caught early, a variety of antibiotics usually cure the disease, but if it goes undetected and is allowed to progress, heart complications, facial paralysis, and arthritis could develop.

Symptoms of diseases transmitted by ticks generally appear in two days to two weeks after the bite and include severe headache, fever, chills, nausea, and pain in the lower back and legs. If you notice these symptoms after being bitten by a tick, see a physician immediately.

• Avoid resting or camping near rodent colonies or burrows. These locations can be infested with fleas that are potential carriers of bubonic plague.

Rattlesnakes

Never kill rattlesnakes unnecessarily. Rattlesnakes are an important segment of the ecosystem. Given a chance, a rattler sunning itself on the trail will often attempt to escape. But be wary. Rattlers won't always give warning before striking.

The most abundant California rattler, the western diamondback, delivers a painful and dangerous bite, but healthy individuals rarely succumb to its bite. Rattlers are common near water sources below 6,000 feet elevation, and sometimes range as high as 8,000 feet. Watch where you put your hands and feet in snake country, especially when stepping over logs or climbing in rocky areas, and wear good boots. The majority of snake bites occur in the lower limbs. Always carry a snake bite kit and familiarize yourself with its use.

Poison Oak

Learn to recognize and avoid poison oak. The plant is quite common in most areas of California (except the desert) below 5,000 feet elevation. The green leaves of poison oak are divided into three leaflets, which are lobed and shiny. The plant has a white or greenish-white berry and grows as a shrub or vine. The leaves turn bright red in summer and fall, dropping off the plant in winter.

Contact with any part of the plant can produce an irritating rash. Avoid touching clothes, pets, or equipment that has come in contact with poison oak. If you do come into contact with this plant, wash the area with cold water and soap as soon as possible. Also wash clothes that have contacted with the plant. An itch-relieving ointment is a wise addition to any first aid kid. Some fortunate people seem immune to poison oak, but most of us will be forced to terminate our hikes when the trail becomes overgrown with this common member of the Sumac family. Squaw bush, which does not cause a rash, is nearly identical to poison oak and the two are often confused. Nevertheless, beware of any plant you suspect might be poison oak.

Poison Oak

Bears

Take precautions against bears. Black bears inhabit most mountainous regions of California. Although rarely seen in more wild areas, they have become a problem in places where they have grown accustomed to easily attainable food. Yosemite and Sequoia- Kings Canyon national parks and surrounding areas are particularly well-known as problem-bear habitat to back-country visitors.

If you suspect there are bears in your travel area, you must keep your food supply from becoming the main course for a hungry bear. In national parks, the law requires that you store your food properly.

Keep camp clean of food scraps and keep food odors away from gear. Never leave dirty dishes laying around camp overnight. Always carry about fifty feet of cord for hanging food in a tree.

The counterbalance method of suspending food from a tree works best. Put all food, and any other items having an odor that might attract bears (such as toothpaste, soap, or trash), into two evenly-weighted stuffsacks and hang them from a sturdy tree limb at least fifteen feet above ground and ten feet from the tree trunk. Food should hang about five feet below the tree limb. Leave packs on the ground with all flaps and zippers opened so that a curious bear won't damage them while nosing around.

Keep your distance from all bears, especially bear cubs. Don't even consider recovering food from a bear—just chalk it up to experience.

Not all black bears are black, but you can be sure there are no grizzlies left in California. The last grizzly sighting in the state occurred in 1924 in Sequoia National Park.

Giardia

Assume all backcountry water is contaminated. There's nothing like drinking deeply from a clear, cold mountain stream after a long, hot day on the trail. After all, mountain water is the purest, safest water source available, right?

Most people who drink untreated backcountry water will not contract any symptoms of intestinal illness. But *Giardia lamblia*, a single-celled microscopic parasite, has been earning a lot of attention in recent years as the culprit in increasing reports of intestinal disease among backcountry users. And there are other germs, too, in California surface water which cause intestinal diseases.

All hikers should take appropriate steps to insure water is pure. Rapidly boiling water for at least five minutes is the surest way to kill *Giardia* and other water-borne microorganisms. (Since water boils at a slightly cooler temperature at high elevations, maintain the boil for at least ten minutes to be safe).

Other purification methods involve adding tincture of iodine or a saturated solution of iodine, and various water purification tablets are readily available at backpacking and sporting goods stores. Although these products are not as effective as boiling against *Giardia*, they are quite effective against most other water-borne organisms. Some filters on the market will also do a good job of purifying water. Of course the best protection is to pack water from home, but this is impractical for extended hikes. If you do use backcountry water, draw it upstream from trail crossings or from springs, which are the safest of backcountry waters, especially at their source. And if you become intestinally ill within three weeks of a backcountry visit, see a physician.

Fires

Exercise extreme caution when using any form of fire. California, with its dense blankets of chaparral and forests that are tinder dry in summer and fall, has the greatest fire danger of any place on earth. You are responsible for keeping your fire under control at all times and will be held accountable for the costs of fighting any fire and for any damage resulting from your carelessness. Those costs are enormous, not to mention the destruction to vegetation, wildlife habitat, and human life and property.

California typically has long, hot, very dry summers, at which time the fire danger is acute. Open fires are prohibited in many areas during this period. And certain national forest areas of California, primarily low elevation areas with an abundance of brush, are closed to entry during the fire season, usually from about July 1 until the first substantial fall rains. Other areas may also be closed periodically due to high or extreme fire danger. Fire restrictions and periods of closure vary on a yearly basis, so check with the appropriate agency in advance of your trip.

If you plan on building a campfire, or if you use a backpack stove, you must obtain a campfire permit (see Rules and Regulations section). If you must have a campfire, it is of the utmost importance tht you keep it small, build it on bare mineral soil, never leave it unattended, and drown it—don't bury it—before you leave, making sure it is cold and completely extinquished.

• Drive carefully in the mountains. Driving to trailheads often involves negotiating rough, dirt-surfaced mountain roads, and people unfamiliar with mountain driving must use caution and common sense. When driving to any trailhead via long, winding, and often narrow dirt roads, stay on your side of the road, and watch for cattle, logging trucks, and other vehicles. Mishaps can be avoided by driving with care and attention.

Ten Essentials

• Always carry the "ten essentials." Following is a list of items every hiker should carry into the backcountry to insure safety and survival: (1) a topographic map of the area and a compass (a compass, however, is useless unless you familiarize yourself with its use in tandem with a topographic map); (2) water and means of purification (at least one gallon per person per day in hot weather; (3) good footwear and extra clothing; (4) signal mirror (5) dark glasses and sunburn preventative; (6) pocket knife; (7) waterproof matches and fire starter; (8) first aid kid; (9) tent, tarp, or something that can be rigged for emergency shelter; and (10) food. Above all, don't forget your common sense—the bottom line is safety in the backcountry.

For an in-depth look at backcountry hazards, their causes, and how to deal with them, many hikers take courses in first aid and/or outdoor survival. All hikers should at least read one of numerous excellent books on these subjects.

Hiking with children

With the birth of a child, some new parents might think their hiking and backpacking days are over, at least until Junior is old enough to walk several miles and carry a pack. But parents who forego hiking trips during a child's formative years are not only missing out on some of the most rewarding and memorable experiences to be enjoyed as a family, but the kids will also miss a tremendous learning experience in which they will gain confidence and a growing awareness of the world around them.

Kids can enjoy the backcountry as much as their parents, but they see the world from a different perspective. It's the little things adults barely notice that are so special to children: Bugs scampering across the trail, spiderwebs dripping with morning dew, lizards doing push-ups on a trailside boulder, splashing rocks into a lake, watching sticks run the rapids of a mountain stream, exploring animal tracks on sand dunes—these are but a few of the natural wonders kids will enjoy while hiking backcountry trails.

To make the trip fun for the kids, let the young ones set the pace. Until they get older and are able to keep up with their parents, forget about that thirty mile trek to your favorite backcountry campsite. Instead, plan a destination that is only a mile or two from the trailhead. Kids tire quickly and become easily sidetracked, so don't be surprised if you don't make it to your destination. Plan alternative campsites enroute to your final camp.

Helping children to enjoy the hike and to learn about what they see, always point out special things along the trail. Help them to anticipate what is around the next bend—perhaps a waterfall, or a pond filled with wriggling tadpoles. Make the hike fun, help kids to stay interested, and they will keep going.

Careful planning which stresses safety will help make your outing an enjoyable one. Young skin is very sensitive to the sun, so always carry a strong sunscreen and apply it to your kids before and during your hike. A good bug repellant, preferably a natural product, should be a standard part of the first-aid kit. Also, consider a product that helps take the itch and sting out of bug bites. A hat helps keep the sun out of sensitive young eyes. And rain gear is also an important consideration. Kids seem to have less tolerance to cold than adults, so ample clothing is important. If your camp will be next to a lake or large stream, consider bringing a life vest for your child.

Parents with young children must, of course, carry plenty of diapers, and be sure to pack them out when they leave. Some children can get wet at night, so extra sleeping clothes are a must. A waterproof pad between the child and the sleeping bag should keep the bag dry, an important consideration if you stay out more than one night.

Allow older children able to walk a mile or two to carry their own packs, too. Some kids will want to bring favorite toys or books along. These special things they can carry themselves, thus learning at an early age the advantages of packing light.

Kids may become bored more easily once you arrive in camp, so a little extra effort may be required to keep them occupied. Imaginative games and special foods they don't see at home can make the camping trip a new and fun experience for kids and parents alike.

Set up a tent at home and consider spending a night or two in it so your child can grow accustomed to your backcountry shelter. Some kids will be frightened by dark nights, so you might bring along a small flashlight to use as a nightlight. Kids seem to prefer rectangular sleeping bags that allow freedom of movement. And a cap for those cool nights will help keep the young ones warm.

Weight conscious parents of very young children can find an alternative to baby food in jars. There are lightweight and inexpensive dry baby foods available, and all you do is add water.

Children learn from their parents by example. Hiking and camping trips are excellent opportunities to teach young ones to tread lightly and minimize their imprint upon the environment.

Thus, important considerations to keep in mind when hiking with the kids are careful planning, stressing safety, and making the trip fun and interesting. There may be extra hassles involved with family hiking trips, but the dividends are immeasureable. Parents will gain a rejuvenated perspective of nature, seen through their child's eyes, that will reward them each time they venture out on the trail.

All or part of the following hikes are suitable for family day hikes or backpacks. Carefully read each description and prepare for any hazards that may be present. After the number and name of each hike, you will find suggestions for destinations.

Hike No. 2: Borrego Palm Canyon; falls and first palm grove. **Hike No. 5:** Palm Springs Aerial Tramway to San Jacinto Peak; Round Valley area. **Hike No. 12:** Fish Creek Aspen Grove. **Hike No. 16:** Champion Lodgepole Pine. **Hike No. 20:** Icehouse Canyon to Cucamonga Peak; Cedar Glen area. **Hike No. 32:** Kelso Dunes. **Hike No. 34:** Golden Canyon to Zabriskie Point; Golden Canyon. **Hike No. 35:** Mosaic Canyon. **Hike No. 39:** Big Falls Canyon; Lower and/or upper falls. **Hike No. 40:** Pfeiffer Falls, Valley View Loop; Pfeiffer Falls. **Hike No. 45:** Mt. Wittenberg; Sky Campground. **Hike No. 50:** Jackass Peak; Albanita Meadows area. **Hike No. 51:** Blackrock Gap to Kern Peak; Casa Vieja Meadow area. **Hike No. 53:** Cottonwood Loop; Horseshoe Meadow/Cottonwood Creek area. **Hike No. 55:** Rowell Meadow Trailhead to Williams and Comanche Meadows; Rowell Meadow environs. **Hike No. 66:** Rock Creek to Upper Morgan Lake; Little Lakes Valley. **Hike No. 68:** Coldwater Campground to Tully Lake; Mammoth Creek lakes. **Hike No. 75:** Green Creek to Summit Lake; Green Lake. **Hike No. 78:** Blue Canyon; first mile or so of the canyon. **Hike No. 86:** Lakes Basin; day use only. **Hike No. 87:** Hay Meadow to Long Lake; easy access to Caribou Wilderness lakes. **Hike No. 90:** Butte Lake to Snag Lake Loop; south end of Butte Lake. **Hike No. 97:** Elk Prairie to Fern Canyon and Gold Bluffs Beach via the James Irvine Trail; Fern Canyon via Davison Road and Gold Bluffs Beach. **Hike No. 99:** Shacklford Creek to Summit Lake; first 2.5 miles offer pleasant streamside camping.

HIKE 1 *ELEPHANT TREES AREA*

General description: An easy 1.4-mile loop (or 3.2-mile round trip) day hike in Anza-Borrego Desert State Park at the foot of the Vallecito Mountains, where a fascinating array of desert plants and magnificent, austere scenery awaits visitors.

Elevation gain and loss: 100 to 220 feet.

Trailhead elevation: 230 feet.

High point: 330 to 450 feet.

Maps: Harper Canyon and Borrego Mountain SE 7.5-minute USGS quads (trail and road to trailhead not shown on quads).

Season: Mid-October through mid-May.

Finding the trailhead: From Ocotillo Wells on State Highway 78, 40 miles west of Brawley or seventy-eight miles east of Escondido, turn south onto the signed Split Mountain Road. Follow this paved road south along the western edge of Lower Borrego Valley and, soon after passing a park ranger station, turn right (west) where a small sign indicates the Elephant Trees Area, just before entering Imperial County. This turnoff is about 5.7 miles south of State Highway 78.

Follow this dirt road, rough and rocky in places, for .8 mile to the turn-around at the signed trailhead.

The hike: Many people view California's deserts as a vast wasteland, an area to drive through as quickly as possible on the way to somewhere else. California's deserts are vast indeed, but to those who have grown to love them they are anything but wastelands.

True wilderness challenges can be found here. You can hike for days across desert plains or penetrate the depths of a remote mountain range, and you may well be the only human for many miles. To trek through unknown country is the finest of wilderness experiences, one common among early explorers and immigrants but rare today.

The desert hikes described in this guide are your introduction to the offerings of California's magnificent deserts. They are remote, vast, alluring. Take these short hikes, and if you find that the desert is for you, its varied landscapes will provide a lifetime of opportunity to accept the challenge of true wilderness, to awaken the pioneering spirit that slumbers within us all.

This area is at its best in winter and spring, when many plants are displaying brilliantly colorful flowers, providing a dramatic contrast to the stark desert landscape.

Carry plenty of water for this dry desert hike.

At the trailhead, be sure to pick up the Elephant Trees Discovery Trail pamphlet. This pamphlet, keyed to numbered posts along the loop trail, describes flora and natural features representative of this area and should greatly enhance your enjoyment and understanding.

From the trailhead, proceed westward up a major alluvial fan just north of a range of low hills. Alluvial fans, common near the base of many California mountain ranges, are composed of alluvium, unconsolidated sand, gravel, rocks, and boulders deposited at the base of the mountains by running water. Here, this debris has washed out of the Vallecito Mountains to the west during frequent torrential summer thunderstorms. Because there is so little vegetation in this region, and because of the low water-holding capacity of the soil, rain simply washes off the mountains and hillsides. Where the velocity of these flash floods begins to decrease in flatter terrain below the mountains, run-off waters begin to deposit sand, gravel, and rocks carried from higher elevations. An alluvial fan is thus formed.

Among the fascinating variety of plant life encountered are ocotillo, barrel cactus, catclaw, creosote bush (the most wildely distributed plant in the desert Southwest), chuparosa, cholla, cheesebush, bur-sage, and the highly unusual elephant tree. Virtually every shrub and cactus in this area displays very colorful flowers after periods of substantial rainfall, especially in late winter and spring

Your trail sometimes crosses dry stream courses that meander across the alluvial fan. During flash floods, most common during summer thunder-storms, enormous quantities of water rush out of the Vallecito Mountains on the way to the Salton Sea. This water chooses paths of least resistance and, depending on its velocity and volume, will follow one or more of these numerous stream courses or create new channels through the unconsolidated alluvium.

At signpost No. 10, you reach the first elephant tree on the hike. This plant, extremely rare in the U.S., is found only from the southern Santa Rosa

HIKE 1 ELEPHANT TREES AREA

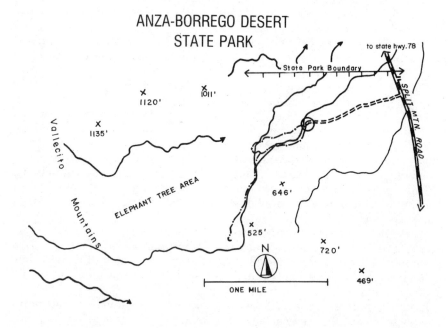

ANZA-BORREGO DESERT
STATE PARK

Mountains southward through California's Sonoran Desert, and in southwest Arizona. However, it is quite common in northwestern Mexico up to 2,500 feet elevation.

This "tree" is a fascinating addition to a typical collection of desert flora. It can reach sixteen feet in height, but specimens taller than ten feet are unlikely to be found in this area. The elephant tree, *Bursera microphylla,* is quite susceptible to frost damage. Young plants are killed by cold weather. Thus, the occurrence of these trees here indicates that frosts rarely develop in the area.

This aromatic shrub (or tree) has a widely spreading crown; thick, sharply tapered, crooked branches; small, pinnately compound, aromatic dull green leaves (microphylla means "small leaved"); papery whitish or greenish bark; small white flowers that bloom in early summer; and red to bluish berries. The stout trunk and branches vaguely suggest the legs and trunk of an elephant, hence the name. (A little imagination is required here.)

From the vicinity of signpost No. 10, more-experienced hikers wishing to extend the hike and see more elephant trees are urged to leave the nature trail here and proceed southwestward up one of the dry stream courses meandering across the alluvial fan. The "trail" is sometimes marginal, but the hiking is largely cross-country. Following any one of the dry stream courses, hike toward the massive, stark mountains on the western horizon, just north of a range of low hills. Within a mile, you should run into a short section of trail that passes a very fine elephant tree. The trail apparently ends a short distance to the south at a sign describing elephant trees.

Adventurous and experienced hikers and backpackers (with a large supply of water) are urged to continue westward up the alluvial fan (labeled "Elephant Trees Area" on the quad) where many more specimens are found. From this area, you can follow the dry stream course toward a canyon that penetrates westward into the heart of the Vallecito Mountains. Backpackers with adequate water will find a hike up this canyon to be exhilarating and rewarding, pure desert experience.

From the end of your one-mile side trip, return to the nature trail and resume hiking it, first west, then northeast. The path is occasionally lost in a dry streambed—just watch for the numbered signposts to help guide you. Soon, the trail leaves the streambed and loops back to the trailhead.

The elephant tree is a rare find in southeastern California's deserts, but specimens such as this one can be seen near the Mexican border in Anza-Borrego Desert State Park.

HIKE 2 *BORREGO PALM CANYON*

General description: A moderately easy three-mile round trip day hike in Anza-Borrego Desert State Park, part of it cross-country, into a deep, palm-dotted canyon in the San Ysidro Mountains.

Elevation gain and loss: 770 feet.

Trailhead elevation: 830 feet.

High point: 1,600 feet.

Maps: Borrego Palm Canyon 7.5-minute USGS quad.

Season: Mid-October through May.

Finding the trailhead: From San Diego County Road S-22, 1.5 miles west of Christmas Circle in downtown Borrego Springs, turn west onto Palm Canyon Road. (Borrego Springs is twenty-eight miles west of the junction of S-22 and State Highway 86 in Salton City, and sixty-five miles east of the Interstate 15-State Highway 79 junction at Rancho California.)

Turn right, after driving .1 mile on Palm Canyon Road, where a sign points to campgrounds. The road straight ahead leads .3 mile to the state park visitor center, where instructive displays and slide shows help to acquaint visitors with the wonders of the desert.

Proceeding north and then west on Palm Canyon Road, follow signs pointing toward the hiking trail. After 1.8 miles, park in the large parking area at the road's end.

The hike: Encompassing more than 600,000 acres, Anza-Borrego Desert State Park is the largest state park in the nation. Much of its land is wilderness, ranging from remote mountain ranges to low hills and desert plains.

The unusual California fan palm, found only in a few canyons and moist areas along the western and northern edge of the Colorado Desert in California, is well represented in two separate groves in Borrego Palm Canyon.

Experienced and adventurous hikers are urged to explore the rugged forks of the canyon beyond the second palm grove. The Middle Fork leads into the Los Coyotes Indian Reservation, where permission is required for entry. Hikers aren't likely to find campsites in these narrow canyons, which are visited chiefly by day hikers.

Carry plenty of water for this hike—water from the creek is not potable. The trail leads northwest from the trailhead parking area, where a sign indicates the Palm Canyon Trail. At the trailhead, pick up a pamphlet describing the natural history of the canyon. Your trail ascends an alluvial fan northwestward toward the mouth of Borrego Palm Canyon. Enroute you pass specimens of beavertail cactus, cholla, indigo bush, catclaw, mesquite, aromatic desert-lavender, creosote bush, brittlebush, ocotillo, chuparosa, and a few desert-willows near the creek. The pamphlet discusses these plants in detail.

The San Ysidro Mountains (also referred to as the Anza Upland) soar skyward to the west, north, and south. In the northwest, the noble crag of 3,960-foot Indianhead Peak pierces the desert sky more than 3,000 feet overhead. To the east, the Borrego Valley sprawls toward the abrupt west face of the Santa Rosa Mountains. Much of that desert range already is now preserved as wilderness.

You soon hop south across a small creek and meet an alternate trail leading back to the trailhead via the south side of the creek. From here, the first grove

24

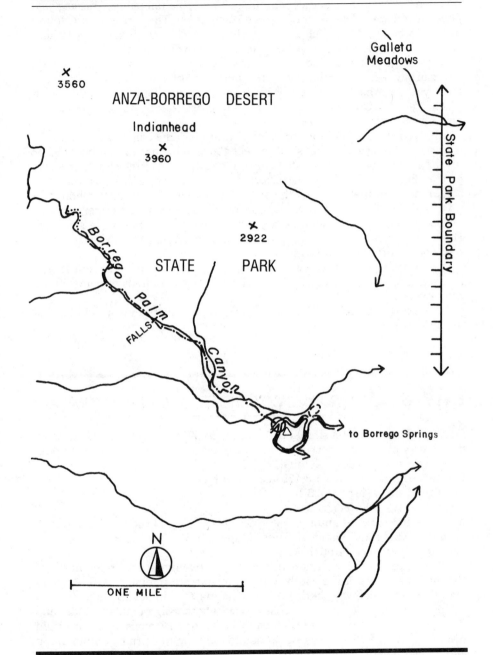

of palms is visible, crowding the canyon bottom a short distance ahead.

Upon entering the lower palm grove, the trail re-crosses the creek to its north side just below a small cascade, then proceeds northwest through a quarter-mile-long grove of fascinating palm trees. California fan palms, *Washingtonia filifera,* were named in honor of George Washington. They are generally found in groves below 3,500 feet, in moist alkaline soil near streams, seeps, and springs. They are the only palms native to the western U.S.

Leaving the palms behind, the trail reaches a point below a cascade where you can proceed no farther along the north bank of the creek. From here, then, you cross back to the south bank and pick up a faint trail leading west up the canyon. Only hikers experienced in cross-country travel should hike beyond the first palm grove.

After passing the last isolated palm, continue up the canyon. Indianhead's ever-present crag looms thousands of feet above to the north. Climbing higher up the rocky, sparsely vegetated canyon, you have over-the-shoulder views of the Borrego Valley, often distorted by shimmering heat waves. The sometimes faint path crosses the small creek several times. After hiking .5 mile beyond the first palm grove, you reach the second, or upper, grove.

This grove is sparse in comparison to the lower grove, covering less ground. However, it is more isolated and sees much less hiking traffic. Thus, the area has a more primitive feel to it.

From here, the trail becomes more difficult to follow upstream and should be used only by experienced hikers, who will find hundreds of palms in the next two miles.

After exploring this fascinating canyon, you eventually must double-back to the trailhead.

HIKE 3 *ARROYO SECO CREEK TO AGUA TIBIA MOUNTAIN*

General description: A strenuous 15.2-mile round-trip day hike (or backpack, if you carry plenty of water) in the Agua Tibia Wilderness to a pine-clad mountain range in San Diego County.
Elevation gain and loss: 3,175 feet, -100 feet.
Trailhead elevation: 1,625 feet.
High point: 4,700 feet.
Maps: Vail Lake 7.5-minute USGS quad (lower six miles of trail not shown on quad), Cleveland National Forest Map.
Season: November through May.
Finding the trailhead: From Interstate 15, twenty- seven miles north of Escondido and five miles south of the Interstate 15-Interstate 215 junction, take the State Highway 79 South exit where a sign indicates Indio.

Upon exiting the freeway, turn left (east) where a sign points to Indio and Warner Springs. Follow State Highway 79 east for 10.7 miles, then turn right (south) where a Forest Service sign points to Dripping Springs Campground and Ranger Station. Follow this paved road south, reaching the Ranger Station and parking area after 150 feet.

The hike: Agua Tibia Mountain, the western end of a long hogback ridge known as the Palomar Range or Agua Tibia Range, supports cool forests of Coulter pine on its upper slopes and offers relief to hikers who slog for miles up the mountain's hot, brush-choked lower slopes.

The Agua Tibia Range is one of many San Diego and Riverside County mountain masses belonging to California's Peninsular Ranges province. Fundamentally, these are southern California's coast ranges. They extend southward from the Los Angeles Basin for the entire length of Baja California.

Coulter pine (or big-cone pine), a conifer indigenous to California and northern Baja California, forms extensive forests along the upper reaches of the Agua Tibia Range and other relatively high ranges in San Diego County. It inhabits dry rocky slopes between 3,000 and 7,000 feet in elevation, growing in pure stands or mixing with other conifers and oaks. With needles in bundles of three, it resembles the ponderosa and Jeffrey pines. However, its distinguishing characteristic is its large cones. Reaching 10-14 inches in length and weighing as much as five pounds, its heavy, clawed cones are the largest of the American pine cones.

During the hot, dry summer of 1989, the Vail Lake Fire consumed 15,600 acres of chaparral in the Agua Tibia region, including nearly 7,000 acres in the Agua Tibia Wilderness. Most of the unusually large shrubs along the Dripping Springs Trail—shrubs that had escaped conflagration for more than 100 years—were destroyed by that exceedingly hot fire. Fortunately, the cool forests of pine and oak atop the crest of Agua Tibia Mountain were, for the most part, spared from destruction.

Many hikers might hesitate to hike in a burned over area, but the benefits of fire—an important part of the chaparral ecosytem—are readily observed along much of this hike. Where dense thickets of old, stagnant shrubs once grew, the young, tender shoots of sprouting shrubs and grasses are providing a new food source for animals. Another advantage of the fire are the unobstructed vistas—on a clear day—that accompany one throughout the length of the hike.

A wilderness permit is required here. The Dripping Springs Ranger Station is open only on a seasonal basis, and the crew is often in the field. Therefore, you should obtain your permit from the District Ranger Station in Ramona.

There is no water available in the wilderness, so be sure to carry an adequate supply for this long hike.

From the hiker's parking area, follow the paved road south through the campground for .5 mile to the trailhead. You immediately hop across the boulder-strewn bed of seasonal Arroyo Seco Creek, shaded by California sycamore, interior live oak, and Fremont cottonwood. Leaving that creekbed, you begin a southwestward ascent along an Arroyo Seco Creek tributary, entering the Agua Tibia Wilderness within a quarter-mile of the trailhead.

Soon the route leaves that tributary canyon to surmount a low ridge emanating from Peak 3329, then begins threading its way through a dense blanket of buckwheat, red shank, chamise, scrub oak, and ceanothus.

As you gain elevation, the lower reaches of Arroyo Seco Creek come into view, and the shrub cover gradually is dominated by chamise, which displays vivid white flower clusters in May and June. Passing above the 2,000-foot contour, red shank joins the chamise to form an impenetrable barrier to off-trail travel.

HIKE 3 *ARROYO SECO CREEK TO AGUA TIBIA MOUNTAIN*

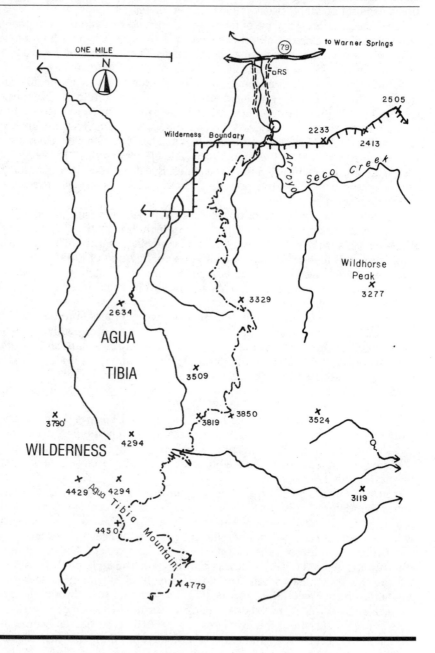

ONE MILE

N

to Warner Springs

79

RS

2505

Wilderness Boundary

2233

2413

Arroyo Seco Creek

Wildhorse
Peak
✕
3277

✕
2634

AGUA

TIBIA

✕ 3329

✕
3509

✕
3790'

✕
3850

✕
3524

✕
3819

O

WILDERNESS

✕
4294

✕
4429

✕
4294

Agua Tibia Mountain

✕
3119

✕
4450

✕ 4779

After 2.5 miles, the trail begins a southeastward course above a precipitous canyon. From here, you get your first glimpse of the conifer-clad environs of Agua Tibia Mountain, looming on the skyline ahead. The vegetation at this point consists of black sage, ceanothus, chamise, and buckwheat.

After hiking four miles from the trailhead, you pass a camping area on a ridge at 3,600 feet elevation. Once there were very large specimens of red shank and manzanita here, some reaching twenty feet in height and more than 100 years in age. Today, the blackened root crowns of these once-towering shrubs are sprouting tender branches that will eventually blanket the slopes of Agua Tibia Mountain in a vast evergreen thicket of chaparral.

The author is dwarfed by a giant manzanita bush on the north slopes of Agua Tibia Mountain. The abnormally large size of the manzanita and red shank on this slope indicates the length of time that fire—a natural and important part of the ecosystem—has been absent from this area. However, hikers may have to wait another 100 years to see magnificent shrubs such as these; a brush fire in 1989 reduced these monarchs to ashes. John Reilly photo.

Topping a 3,800-foot ridge beyond the campsites, you are confronted with an excellent view of the oak-and Coulter pine-covered northeast slope of Agua Tibia Mountain, whose shady environs beckon hikers onward.

The panoramic views that have accompanied you for several miles reach their breathtaking culmination in this area. Much of southern California is visible, from observatory-crowned Palomar Mountain in the southeast, to the Santa Rosa, San Jacinto, San Bernardino, and San Gabriel mountain ranges. Closer at hand the Agua Tibia Range plummets into the vicinity of Vail Lake, and beyond, the Temecula Valley fades into the distant southern California smog, which often reaches maximum density in the rarely-visible Riverside area.

From the ridge, a minor descent ensues, followed by a sequence of sometimes-overgrown switchbacks rising in elevation. Coulter pines begin to appear above 4,000 feet.

Above the switchbacks, the trail begins a hillside traverse, first on east-facing and then on south-facing slopes, separated from Agua Tibia Mountain by a shallow gully.

You soon enter the welcome shade of an interior live oak stand, and then reach the crest of the range and a trail sign that points left (south) to Eagle Crag, the apex of the wilderness.

The Vail Lake quad shows this ridgetop trail as a road, and indeed it is. However, it has long since been abandoned, and vegetation has encroached upon it until it is hardly recognizable as a road.

Turning left, you proceed southward, then eastward under the shade of live oak and Coulter pine, just below the ridge crest. The dominant shrubs at this point are silktassel and ceanothus. Blue penstemon decorates some sunny openings in late spring and early summer.

After walking a mile along this abandoned dirt road, you reach a saddle at 4,700 feet, shaded by Coulter pine and oak, just north of Peak 4779. At this point, the road begins a steady descent and many hikers go no farther. This saddle has been used as a campsite, and water-packing backpackers will find it a pleasant spot for an overnight stay. Day hikers will find this saddle a fine spot for a lunch break before retracing their panoramic route back to the trailhead.

HIKE 4 *HUMBER PARK TO RED TAHQUITZ*

General description: A moderately strenuous 10.4-mile semi-loop backpack in the San Jacinto Wilderness leading into one of the most well-watered mountain regions of southern California.
Elevation gain and loss: 3,100 feet.
Trailhead elevation: 6,300 feet.
High point: Red Tahquitz, 8,738 feet.
Maps: Palm Springs 15-minute USGS quad (portion of route not shown on quad), San Bernardino National Forest map, San Jacinto Wilderness map.
Season: June through mid-November.

Finding the trailhead: Proceed to Idyllwild, twenty-five miles south of Banning via State Highway 243 and twenty-two miles east of Hemet via State Highways 74 and 243. From Idyllwild, turn east onto North Circle Drive, which then becomes South Circle, then Fern Valley Road. You reach Humber Park at the road's end two miles from Idyllwild.

The hike: The high plateau of the San Jacinto Mountains, with its thick forests of pine and fir, numerous lush meadows, springs and perennial streams, and boulder-dotted landscape, closely resembles the Kern Plateau region of the southern Sierra Nevada. This area is quite popular with southern California hikers, and solitude may be hard to find on some weekends.

Climbers are attracted to the area near the trailhead by many challenging routes up Suicide Rock and Lily Rock (locally known as Tahquitz Rock). Lily Rock offers some of the most difficult rock climbing in southern California.

A wilderness permit is required and should be obtained at the Forest Service ranger station in Idyllwild. Daily entry quotas are enforced, so obtain your permit early in the day on weekends, or better yet, by mail to ensure access into this fine region.

Begin this hike at the east end of the parking area, and ascend slopes alternating between cool, shady stands of pine and fir and open, chaparral-choked slopes. During this ascent, you pass three small springs, which tend to dry up as the summer progresses. The striking, near-vertical walls of either Lily Rock or Suicide Rock are constantly in view during your climb.

After hiking 2.2 miles from the trailhead, you reach 8, 100-foot-high Saddle Junction, where trails lead in five directions. For now, take the extreme right-hand trail, the southbound Pacific Crest Trail. You will be returning via the southeast branching trail, where the sign indicates Tahquitz Valley.

Your trail leads south for 1.3 miles to the Tahquitz Peak Trail, branching west. Continuing along the Pacific Crest Trail, you reach the northeast-bound trail leading to the Little Tahquitz Valley after .6 mile. After climbing Red Tahquitz, you will return to this point and follow that trail back to Saddle Junction.

Continuing eastward, the trail soon crosses a small tributary of Tahquitz Creek. During this gentle stretch of trail, you will have occasional forest-framed views down into the Tahquitz Creek plateau, with San Jacinto Peak on the northern horizon. After hiking 1.2 miles from the previous junction, you round a minor north-trending spur ridge at the 8,400-foot contour, leave the Pacific Crest Trail, and proceed in a southerly direction on the Red Tahquitz Trail for .25 mile to the barren red rock summit of 8,738-foot Red Tahquitz. The openness of the peak affords excellent vistas. Southward lies the rugged crest of the range, known as the Desert Divide, capped by craggy summits. To the southwest one can see Lake Hemet lying at the foot of massive Thomas Mountain, adding contrast to the flat terrain of the Garner Valley. To your southeast lies the deep floor of the Coachella Valley and the Salton Sea, more than 9,000 feet below.

That deep trench, partially drowned by the Salton Sea, is known as the Salton Trough. This is the largest dry land region below sea level in the Western Hemisphere, covering more than 2,000 square miles. With a low point of 273 feet below sea level, the Salton Trough is a mere nine feet higher than Death Valley.

To the northeast are the low hills of the Little San Bernardino Mountains, the general dividing point between the Mojave and Colorado deserts. And to

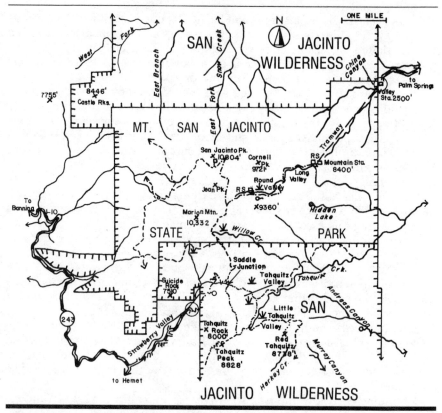

the north stand the highest peaks of the San Jacinto Mountains. Altogether, the view from Red Tahquitz affords a quite impressive and interesting view of much of southern California.

From this vantage point, you backtrack for 1.5 miles, then turn right (northeast), soon skirting the tall grass of the meadow in Little Tahquitz Valley. Campsites abound from here to Saddle Junction.

After leaving the meadow, the trail, shaded by Jeffrey pine and white fir, soon leads you to a junction with a northeast-bound trail descending along Tahquitz Creek to Caramba Camp, lying on the eastern rim of the plateau.

Turn left and pass through the lovely meadow of Tahquitz Valley. A small backcountry ranger station lies just east of the trail, where emergency services are available, provided the ranger isn't out on patrol.

As the trail jogs northwest, you get a brief glimpse of beautiful Skunk Cabbage Meadow. The meadows on this plateau are ideal locations for spotting mule deer in the early morning or evening hours. After climbing gradually through an open forest, you reach Saddle Junction and retrace your route to the trailhead.

HIKE 5

PALM SPRINGS AERIAL TRAMWAY TO SAN JACINTO PEAK

General description: A moderately strenuous 10.2-mile round trip backpack in the Mt. San Jacinto Wilderness State Park leading to one of the finest vista points in southern California.

Elevation gain and loss: 2,500 feet.

Trailhead elevation: 8,500 feet.

High point: San Jacinto Peak, 10,804 feet.

Maps: Palm Springs 15-minute USGS quad, San Bernardino National Forest map, San Jacinto Wilderness map. Also use hike No. 4 map.

Season: June through mid-November.

Finding the trailhead: From State Highway 111 just north of Palm Springs, turn west where a large sign indicates the Palm Springs Aerial Tramway. Proceed west along this steep paved road for four miles to the parking area at Valley Station.

The hike: There are two plateaus in the San Jacinto Mountains—the lower and consequently drier plateau containing the Tahquitz Creek drainage; and the higher, more sub-alpine plateau lying just east of San Jacinto Peak, which boasts two meadows over 9,000 feet in elevation. The Palm Springs Aerial Tramway provides year-round access to this higher plateau, making the ascent to San Jacinto Peak much easier than from any other point in the range.

Due to all-year access and generally good snow conditions, cross-country skiing and snowshoeing have become increasingly popular here in the past several years. Excellent skiing can be found on the upper slopes of the peak, and many visitors spend the night on top to catch the magnificent winter sunrise before enjoying superb runs back to the plateau.

A wilderness permit is required and must be obtained in advance from the State Park Headquarters in Idyllwild, either by mail or in person.

The first tram car going up from Valley Station leaves at 8:00 a.m. on weekdays and 10:00 a.m. on weekends, and the last car down from the Mountain Station leaves at 9:00 p.m. Although the round-trip tram ride costs about $12.95, it is a spectacular, exhilarating trip and well worth the price.

After the breathtaking tramway ride, you step out into Mountain Station, complete with restaurant and tourist facilities. Exit the station and switchback down into Long Valley via a paved path. At the bottom the trail jogs west, soon passing the Long Valley Ranger Station.

You now begin ascending along the course of Long Valley Creek through boulder-dotted terrain, shaded by a canopy of Jeffrey pine and white fir. After hiking 1.4 miles, avoid an eastbound trail that leads to Hidden Lake. Beyond this junction, lodgepole pines increase in frequency among the forest, becoming the dominant tree above Round Valley.

Just before reaching the west end of Round Valley, you pass a piped spring immediately south of the trail, one which offers a reliable and less-suspect source of water than Long Valley Creek. Tank up here—this is the last water before the peak.

From the spring next to the backcountry ranger cabin, you will trudge uphill in a westerly direction for .8 mile, passing through a heavy lodgepole pine forest, to the trail junction at Wellman Divide, where you turn right.

The trail contours north along the east slopes of 10,600-foot Jean Peak, where hikers enjoy a good view eastward across the heavily forested plateau. You reach a bench at the 10,000-foot level after hiking .75 mile from the previous junction.

Continuing northward, your trail crosses slopes choked with chinquapin and dotted with boulders and passes an occasional lodgepole or limber pine. The trail abruptly switchbacks just before reaching the ridge crest, and peakbaggers will be tempted to scramble the short distance northeast to the boulder-stacked summit of 10,400-foot Miller Peak.

You reach the crest of the range and a junction after hiking 1.5 miles from Wellman Divide. Turn right (north) and ascend the ridge through a sub-alpine stand of twisted limber pines, hiking .3 mile to the summit of San Jacinto Peak and passing a stone shelter near the top. The view from this peak is possibly the finest in southern California, encompassing all the major mountain ranges in this part of the state and a large slice of desert and coastal scenery. The north and east escarpments of the San Jacinto Mountains plummet more than 9,000 feet into surrounding desert valleys, rivaling the great eastern

The beauty of an austere, high mountain landscape is often enhanced by the weathered remains of an ancient tree, such as this limber pine snag in the San Jacinto Mountains. Campfires should be discouraged in these areas, however, since the only firewood available may be from such a snag.

escarpment of the Sierra Nevada, which rises as much as 10,000 feet from the floor of Owens Valley.

From the peak, hikers must retrace their route back to Mountain Station.

HIKE 6 INDIAN COVE PICNIC AREA TO RATTLESNAKE CANYON AND THE WONDERLAND OF ROCKS

General description: A rigorous, cross-country round-trip day hike of one to five miles or more leading in to one of the most fascinating landscapes in Joshua Tree National Park.
Trailhead elevation: 3,100 feet.
Maps: Twentynine Palms 15-minute USGS quad, Joshua Tree National Park visitors map.
Season: October through mid-May (avoid holiday weekends).
Finding the trailhead: From Yucca Valley, follow State Highway 62 east for fourteen miles to the signed Indian Cove Road. Proceed south on this paved road, passing the ranger station after a mile. Turn left two miles past the ranger station where a sign reads: "Bulletin board—50 feet." Continue another 1.3 miles to the picnic area at the end of the road and park.

The hike: The Wonderland of Rocks is exactly what the name implies. To many climbers and boulder scramblers, it is paradise. The Wonderland covers approximately ten square miles, from Barker Dam in the south to Indian Cove in the north. It is a region of highly eroded boulders and rock formations composed of quartz monzonite. The area supports little vegetation, and much of what does grow here often grows right out of solid rock. This region is much more arid than the western part of the Park, and the vegetation reflects the drier, harsher conditions.

This trip is for more experienced hikers who are well acquainted with cross-country boulder scrambling. There is no true destination other than the Wonderland itself. Having trekked a short distance into Rattlesnake Canyon, hikers are free to explore the boulders and rock formations in any direction.

Hikers are urged, however, to go at least as far as the waterfall area, a half-mile up the canyon. At that point a small creek falls over solid rock, forming many lovely pools between cascades. Cool rest spots abound where jumbled boulders create small, cave-like rooms.

Be sure to carry an adequate supply of water.

From the picnic area, walk east into the dry streambed of Rattlesnake Canyon, through creosote bush, Mojave yucca, and Mormon tea. From the streambed, turn right (south) and boulder-hop your way up the canyon, veering to the right where a small tributary canyon branches left.

Small frogs inhabit the moist areas of the streambed. Once you reach the base of the falls, you can ascend either side of the creek, but it requires some Class 2 scrambling. There is usually water in this area, except during extended dry periods. Above the falls, the canyon is more open.

The relatively smooth slopes of the Queen Mountains, rising east of Rattlesnake Canyon, provide an interesting contrast with the fantastic, often

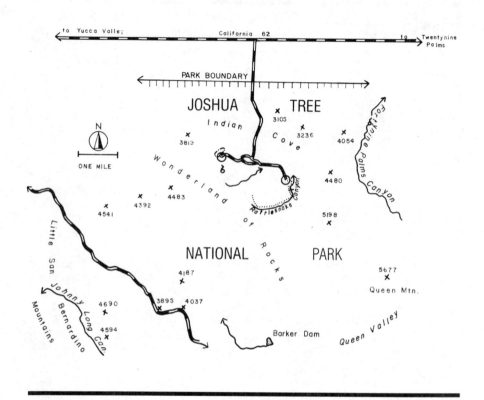

grotesque formations found in the Wonderland of Rocks. The dominant shrubs here are spiny catclaw, desert almond, and jojoba. A few pinyon pines are found here and there, growing out of solid rock.

When you tire of scrambling, climbing, or just enjoying the unbelievable scenery, carefully make your way down Rattlesnake Canyon to the trailhead.

HIKE 7 *INDIAN COVE NATURE TRAIL*

General description: A very easy .75-mile loop like in the Joshua Tree National Park, introducing hikers to wonders of the desert.
Elevation gain and loss: 50 feet.
Trailhead elevation: 3,400 feet.
Maps: Twentynine Palms 15-minute USGS quad (trail not shown on quad), Joshua Tree National Park visitors map. Also use hike No. 6 map.
Season: October through mid-May.
Finding the trailhead: From the Indian Cove turnoff on State Highway 62, 14 miles east of Yucca Valley, drive three miles south on Indian Cove Road to a sign that reads: "Bulletin Board—50 feet." Turn right and proceed .8 mile through the campground to the loop at the end of the road. The trail begins at the cluster of sings at the west end of the loop.

The hike: There are a number of nature trails in Joshua Tree National Park. They are generally short, most a mile or less. These trails have interpretive signs placed at intervals to help hikers become familiar with the flora, fauna, and natural features of the diverse landscapes found in the Park. This particular trail takes you through an interesting collection of plants typical of the Creosote Bush Scrub plant community, such as creosote bush, Mojave yucca, and pencil cholla. These plants are commonly found on the desert floor and in the foothills of desert ranges in southern California, where precipitation rarely exceeds eight inches annually.

From the end of the road, walk west along the trail, which soon drops into a shallow wash where it all but disappears. Proceed north down the wash, keeping an eye out for the interpretive signs which lead the way. You soon climb out of the wash and loop back to the trailhead, presumably more familiar now with representative species of this plant community and more appreciative of the desert.

HIKE 8 *BLACK ROCK CAMPGROUND TO PEAK 5195*

General description: A six-mile round-trip day hike (or overnighter), in the Joshua Tree National Park leading to a mountain peak in the Mojave Desert.
Elevation gain and loss: 1,195 feet.
Trailhead elevation: 4,000 feet.
High point: Peak 5195.
Maps: Yucca Valley South 7.4-minute USGS quad (trail not shown on quad), Joshua Tree National Park visitors map.
Season: Late September through mid-May.
Finding the trailhead: From State Highway 62 in Yucca Valley, turn south onto Joshua Lane, and follow signs indicating Black Rock Campground. After driving five miles through residential areas of Yucca Valley, you reach the ranger station at the campground, where you park.

HIKE 8 *BLACK ROCK CAMPGROUND TO PEAK 5195*

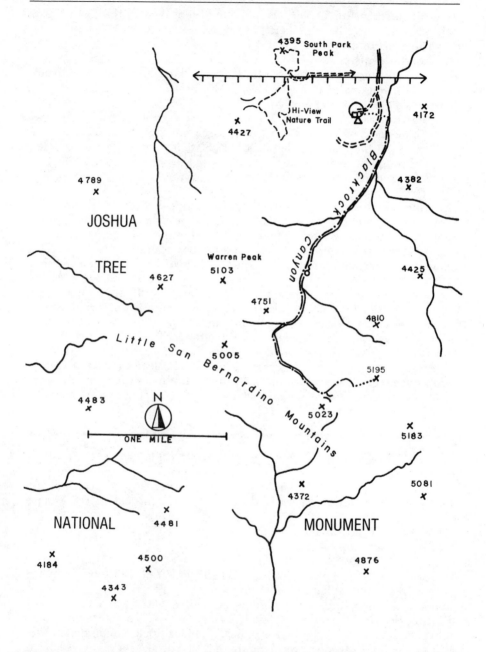

4395 South Park Peak

Hi-View Nature Trail

✗ 4172

✗ 4427

Blackrock Canyon

✗ 4789

JOSHUA

✗ 4382

TREE

Warren Peak
5103 ✗

✗ 4627

✗ 4425

✗ 4751

✗ 4810

5195

Little San Bernardino

✗ 5005

Mountains

5023

✗ 4483

N

✗ 5183

ONE MILE

✗ 4372

5081 ✗

NATIONAL

✗ 4481

MONUMENT

✗ 4184

4500 ✗

✗ 4876

4343 ✗

The hike: The hike up Black Rock Canyon to the crest of the Little San Bernardino Mountains is an excellent introduction to high desert hiking. This trip makes a fine mid-winter leg-stretcher, and hikers are rewarded with far-flung vistas from Peak 5195. Be sure to pack an adequate supply of water.

This trip can be made as an overnighter if you are willing to carry water. Hikers can follow the crest of the Little San Bernardino Mountains for days and see few, if any, other hikers. Backpackers are required to check in at the ranger station.

Always avoid this and any other desert hike during periods of thunderstorm activity—floods and lightning are real and dangerous possibilities.

Bighorn sheep inhabit the remote reaches of this range, and the wary hiker here in the northwestern corner of the Park might be fortunate enough to spot one. Mule deer also frequent this area.

The backcountry of the Joshua Tree National Park offers challenges and a true wilderness experience for those willing to accept the desert on its own terms.

Last-minute information is available at the ranger station. From there, hike due east through the campground for .25 mile to the dry streambed of Black Rock Canyon. The dry, sandy streambed serves as a trail.

Proceed westward up the wide alluvial canyon mouth, passing many Joshua trees, some California juniper, and Mojave yucca, which can be easily confused with a small Joshua tree—Mojave yucca, however, is generally smaller, and its leaves have fibrous, stringy margins. You will also encounter an incredible variety of plantlife typical of the Joshua Tree Woodland plant community: clumps of bunchgrass, boxthorn, cholla, some desert-willow, Mormon tea, rabbitbrush, and desert almond.

After hiking 1.5 miles, you pass sometimes-dry Black Rock Spring, a small, stagnant waterhole frequented by swarms of hornets. At intervals along the way, four-inch-by-four-inch posts with arrows point in the direction of the trail, which as a result is almost impossible to lose.

Beyond the spring, the canyon narrows and vegetation begins to show signs of more moisture and higher elevation. You are now accompanied by desert scrub oak, pinyon pine, juniper, beavertail cactus, bitterbrush, Mojave yucca, and some birch-leaf mountain mahogany—plants representative of the Pinyon-Juniper Woodland vegetation zone.

You top a ridge, the crest of the Little San Bernardino Mountains, after hiking 2.75 miles from the trailhead, and the trail promptly disappears. Turn left (northeast) and hike cross-country along the ridge for .25 mile to the stack of weathered rocks that marks the summit of Peak 5195.

The vistas are truly panoramic here, unlike any others obtained from more popular viewpoints in southern California. To the southwest the Coachella Valley sprawls into the haze of the distant Salton Sea. The San Jacinto Mountains can be seen soaring 10,000 feet high at the western margin of that broad valley, and with the Santa Rosa Mountains to the south they form a virtually impenetrable barrier to westward travel. To the west lies the deep gash of San Gorgonio Pass, with majestic San Gorgonio Mountain rising 10,000 feet above to the north. The entire eastern end of the San Bernardino Mountains dominates the northwestern horizon, and the Mojave Desert to the north lies vast and flat at your feet. In the southeast, the highly eroded hills of the Little San Bernardino Mountains dissolve into the haze of the desert.

There are a few stunted pinyons and junipers around the peak, and some rabbitbrush, Mormon tea, desert scrub oak, and a few Joshua trees. The sparse vegetation reflects the drier conditions that prevail here on the crest, and ground cover is much less dense than in the sheltered upper reaches of Black Rock Canyon.

From the peak, return the way you came.

HIKE 9   EAST BRANCH MILLARD CANYON TO KITCHING PEAK

General description: A moderately strenuous 9.4-mile round-trip day hike in the San Gorgonio Wilderness to an excellent viewpoint on the edge of the wildest mountain country in southern California.

Elevation gain and loss: 2,558 feet, -160 feet.

Trailhead elevation: 4,200 feet.

High point: Kitching Peak, 6,598 feet.

Maps: Cabazon, San Gorgonio Mtn., Catclaw Flat, and Whitewater 7.5-minute USGS quads, San Bernardino National Forest map.

Finding the trailhead: From Interstate 10 about 4.5 miles east of Banning, take the Fields Road exit. Follow this paved road north, through the Morongo Indian Reservation for 1.3 miles, then turn right onto Morongo Road; the sign points to Millard Canyon. After .5 mile, bear left onto Forest Road 2S05. Bear right after another .3 mile. The road turns to dirt .2 mile beyond. Your northbound road soon crosses Millard Canyon Creek, about 1.2 miles from the end of the pavement, and continues a northbound course east of the creek. After driving 2.3 miles from the creek crossing, turn right at a well-marked junction where the sign points to Kitching Creek Trail 2EO9. Stay left when, after another .6 mile, Forest Road 2S03 joins your road on the right. Your road ends after another 1.1 miles, just beyond a creek crossing. Park before crossing the creek.

The hike: Kitching Peak stands like a great throne overlooking the San Gorgonio Pass country. From its summit, massive San Gorgonio Mountain looms bold in the northwest, and San Jacinto Peak, its majestic northeast escarpment soaring 10,000 feet above the floor of Coachella Valley, seems close enough to touch. Although Kitching Peak lies at the drier southeast end of the San Bernardino Mountains, it stands high enough to capture adequate moisture from Pacific storms funneling through San Gorgonio Pass. On the upper slopes of the peak, cool stands of white fir offer welcome shade to hikers as well as to the variety of wildlife that inhabits the area.

Kitching Peak lies in a region that could be considered the wildest and most remote mountain wilderness within southern California—the headwaters of the Whitewater River. In this mostly trailless region of the San Bernardino Mountains, hikers can find solitude and a wilderness experience unavailable anywhere else in southern California's mountains. Here, in the remote southeastern corner of the San Gorgonio Wilderness, bighorn sheep, mule deer, mountain lion, and black bear thrive. In fact, unusually large black bears inhabit the area, some weighing in excess of 500 pounds.

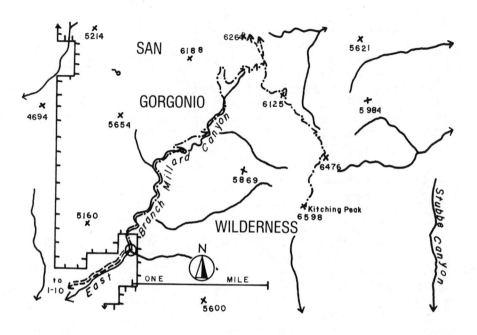

Black bears are not native to southern California. They were introduced in the San Bernardino and San Gabriel mountains from the southern Sierra Nevada in the 1930s.

Be sure to carry adequate water for this hike, and obtain the required wilderness permit from Mill Creek Ranger Station (See Hike 13). Take the unmarked trail north from the turnaround at the end of the road, under the shade of a large big-cone Douglas-fir and canyon live oaks.

You travel northeast during the first two miles of your hike while ascending the East Branch Millard Canyon, crossing and re-crossing the small creek under the cool shade of canyon live oak, incense-cedar, and big-cone Douglas-fir. Then climb up and out of the East Branch and trade the shady forest for chaparral-clad slopes as you negotiate the final switchbacks to surmount a north-south ridge dividing waters flowing west into Millard Canyon from those flowing east into the Whitewater River.

Turn right (south) on this 6,000-foot-high ridge where the sign indicates that Kitching Peak is two miles ahead. Your sometimes-brushy trail heads south on or near the ridgetop, leading through live oak and chaparral. As you gain elevation, white fir and a few sugar pines begin to contribute their welcome shade. Just before reaching the summit, the trail fades out in an overgrown patch of deerbrush. You simply bushwhack through the last several yards to reach the summit of Kitching Peak. To your southeast, the Coachella Valley sprawls into the haze of the distant Salton Sea. Of special interest is the magnificent upthrust of land that rises immediately south of the exceedingly deep nadir of San Gorgonio Pass, the mighty northeast escarpment of the San Jacinto Mountains. Imagine the immense forces within the earth that shoved that great block of the earth's crust more than 10,000 feet above the surrounding countryside.

The panorama also includes the Little San Bernardino Mountains to the east, seen across the huge dry wash of the Whitewater River. To your north and northwest lies the wild landscape of the upper Whitewater River drainage, with a backdrop of 10,000-and 11,000-foot peaks. And to your west lies the eastern extension of the San Bernardino Valley.

After absorbing this extensive vista, hikers can return to the trailhead or turn right at the above-mentioned ridgetop junction for a rewarding jaunt down into the Whitewater River country.

HIKE 10 *CHAMPION JOSHUA TREE*

General description: An easy two-mile round-trip day hike, in the San Bernardino National Forest on the "desert side" of the San Bernardino Mountains.
Elevation gain and loss: 50 feet.
Trailhead elevation: 6,040 feet.
Maps: Rattlesnake Canyon 7.5-minute USGS quad (route not shown on quad), San Bernardino National Forest map.
Season: Late September through mid-June.
Finding the trailhead: From State Highway 18, eleven miles south of its junction with State Highway 247 in Lucerne Valley and 6.7 miles northeast of its junction with State Highway 38 at the east end of Big Bear Lake, turn southeast onto signed Forest Road 3N03, directly under a prominent boulder-covered hill. A sign a short distance up this road reads: "Pioneertown 25." Follow this fair dirt road southeast, avoiding several signed spur roads. The road crosses usually-flowing Arrastre Creek five miles from the highway, just beyond Smart's Ranch. A quarter-mile beyond that crossing is a hard-to-spot junction with an eastbound set of jeep tracks—park here.

The hike: The Joshua tree is one of many unusual plants found in California's desert regions. A member of the Agave family, this unique tree is unmistakable with its stiff, narrow, foot-long dagger-like leaves and its dense flower clusters, from greenish- white to cream in color, which appear in April or May. The Joshua tree grows across a wide area, from the Mojave Desert north to the southern Owens Valley, and east through southern Nevada to southwestern Utah and western Arizona.

Growing at an elevation of 6,000 feet, the Joshua trees in Arrastre Canyon are near their altitudinal limit. Due to deep, well-drained soils and moderate precipitation here, the Joshua trees in this canyon grow to greater dimensions than those anywhere else.

This short hike, on jeep tracks all the way, passes some of the largest Joshua trees in existence, and ends at the impressive Champion Joshua Tree. The variety of plantlife and the open feeling of the pinyon pine forest combine to make this a thoroughly pleasing, leisurely stroll.

Hikers with energy to burn might consider a cross-country scramble east from the Champion to the Granite Peak ridge, which commands a wide view of the eastern end of the San Bernardino Mountains and the Mojave Desert. Granite Peak, 7,512 feet tall, is a 1.5-mile jaunt northward along this ridge, and offers a satisfying diversion and a fitting complement to the largest Joshua tree anywhere.

Your route leads east from Forest Road 3N03, following the jeep tracks through an open forest of pinyon pine, a few scattered Joshua trees, sagebrush, rabbitbrush, some juniper, and bitterbrush. Your destination lies at the foot of Granite Peak ridge, which can be seen on the eastern skyline.

As you approach the east side of wide Arrastre Canyon, large Joshua trees begin to appear, quickly dominating the forest. After a mile, just before the jeep tracks fade out, you reach the Champion Joshua Tree. Its huge, rounded, multi-branched mass obviously outclasses all others in the area, and offers a good deal of shade on a hot day. Hikers who are concerned about four-wheel drive access to the Champion may want to voice that concern to the Forest Service. This tree deserves protection. After enjoying the 32-foot tall, 15-foot diameter giant, retrace your route to the trailhead.

The Joshua trees in Arrastre Canyon, on the north slope of the San Bernardino Mountains, are the largest Joshua trees anywhere. Pictured here is the Champion Joshua Tree, an unbelivable 32 feet in height and 15 feet in diameter.

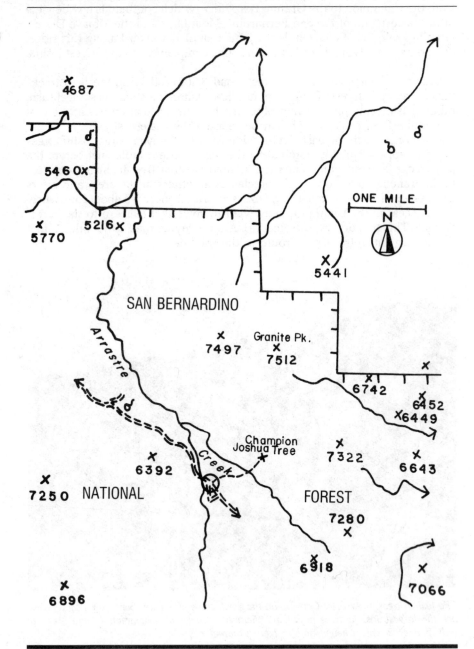

HIKE 11 *SUGARLOAF MOUNTAIN*

General description: A moderate 6.5-mile round-trip day hike (or overnighter if you pack water), part of it cross-country in the San Bernardino National Forest, to a mountain with sub-alpine environment north of the San Gorgonio Wilderness.

Elevation gain and loss: 1,372 feet, -135 feet.

Trailhead elevation: 8,715 feet.

High point: Sugarloaf Mountain, 9,952 feet.

Maps: Moonridge 7.5-minute USGS quad, San Bernardino National Forest map.

Season: Early June through early November.

Finding the trailhead: From State Highway 38, 3.5 miles southeast of Big Bear City, turn west onto signed Forest Road 2N93. You pass the signed Sugarloaf Trail after 1.3 miles—hikers not wishing to negotiate the final segment of this fairly rough dirt road can begin hiking here. Otherwise, continue driving Forest Road 2N93, the Wildhorse Road, to its summit, about 5.75 miles from the highway. Park on the west side of the road where a gate blocks a northwest-branching dirt road. This parking area lies .25 mile north of a cattle guard on 2N93.

HIKE 11 *SUGARLOAF MOUNTAIN*

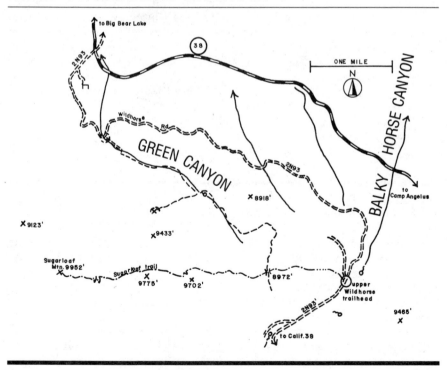

The trailhead can be reached from the south by driving thirty-four miles east from Redlands via State Highway 38 to the south end of Forest Road 2N93. This junction is hard to locate—it lies two miles east of the signed turnoff to Heart Bar State Park. Follow 2N93 north for six miles to the above-mentioned trailhead.

The hike: Hikers who are looking for solitude in sub-alpine surroundings, but are tired of encountering the hordes of hikers in the San Gorgonio Wilderness, will find that Sugarloaf Mountain is just what they have been searching for. The lodgepole- and limber pine-crowned summit provides a comprehensive view of the entire eastern end of the San Bernardino Mountains, a view unrivaled from any other point in the range.

This is the shortest way to reach the mountain, and requires a little route finding at the start. The hike begins at a virtually unknown trailhead (the highest in the range) and avoids the conventional, longer routes starting at lower elevations.

Be sure to carry plenty of water for this dry hike.

From your car, hike west up the faint jeep trail, straight up the slope at a right angle to the closed road. Follow this jeep trail to the main ridge, where it fades out near a yellow iron post with the inscription: "BN17." Follow this ridge west, cross-country, through an open forest of Jeffrey pine, large western juniper, and mountain mahogany for .25 mile, until you meet another set of jeep tracks. Follow these tracks west along the ridgetop, and after hiking .8 mile from the trailhead, just after passing through a barbed wire stock gate, you reach a trail junction. The northbound trail descends Green Canyon to the previously mentioned trailhead on Forest Road 2N93. The southbound trail descends Wildhorse Canyon to State Highway 38.

Head west on the signed Sugarloaf Trail. As you climb above 9,400 feet, lodgepole and limber pine become the dominant forest trees. The trail soon climbs up and around Peak 9775, descends to a saddle, then makes a final ascent to the summit of Sugarloaf Mountain, sometimes passing through dense stands of lodgepole pine.

Views from the mountain are excellent, especially southward to the San Gorgonio Wilderness, rising above the deep canyon of the Santa Ana River.

From the summit, hikers will carefully retrace their route back to the trailhead.

HIKE 12 *FISH CREEK ASPEN GROVE*

General description: An easy .8-mile round-trip day hike on the outskirts of the San Gorgonio Wilderness, in the San Bernardino National Forest.
Elevation gain and loss: -200 feet.
Trailhead elevation: 7,410 feet.
Maps: Moonridge 7.5-minute USGS quad, San Bernardino National Forest map.
Season: Late May through mid-November.
Finding the trailhead: From State Highway 38, thirty- two miles east of Redlands and 14.5 miles south of Big Bear City, turn south onto Forest Road

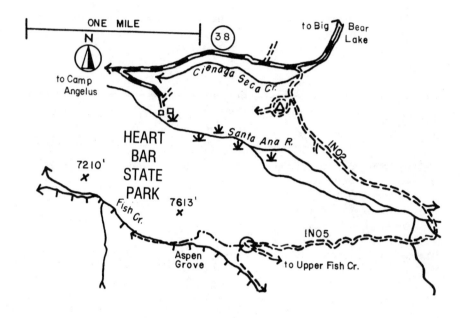

1N02, where a sign reads: "Heart Bar Campground , Coon Creek 6, Fish Creek 8." Follow this dirt road southeast for 1.25 miles to a junction with Forest Road 1N05, where you turn right. Follow this road for 1.5 miles to the signed Aspen Grove Trailhead.

The hike: The San Bernardino Mountains have by far the most diverse plantlife in southern California, and perhaps in the entire state. The fascinating collection of plants in this range includes almost everything from desert and coastal to alpine species. These mountains boast the largest known Joshua tree and lodgepole pine. They also support some rare species found nowhere else in southern California. In Holcomb Creek, for example, near long-abandoned beaver dams, lies an isolated stand of narrowleaf cottonwood, a Rocky Mountain species. And quaking aspen are found in two separate groves—one stand is located in upper Arrastre Creek, not far from the Champion Joshua tree; the other is found along the lower reaches of Fish Creek, on the northern boundary of the San Gorgonio Wilderness.

This short stroll leads you to the aspens of Fish Creek, where the laughing stream and the shimmering leaves of aspens create a most peaceful and unique southern California setting. This walk is especially attractive after the first frosts of autumn, when the aspens wear a dramatic display of fall color, unequaled in all of southern California's mountains. A wilderness permit is required and can be obtained at Mill Creek Ranger Station (see Hike 13).

Two trails begin at the trailhead. The left fork ascends to the headwaters of Fish Creek; the right fork descends to the aspen grove.

Begin your descent into Fish Creek via the right fork, across manzanita covered ground shaded by Jeffrey pines and white firs. After .4 mile of descent, you enter the aspen grove growing along Fish Creek—a small grove, but pleasant nonetheless.

From the aspens, backtrack to the trailhead.

HIKE 13 *SOUTH FORK TRAILHEAD TO SAN GORGONIO MOUNTAIN*

General description: A moderately strenuous 22.5-mile semi-loop backpack in the San Gorgonio Wilderness, touring the most scenic mountain wilderness in southern California.

Elevation gain and loss: 4.599 feet.

Trailhead elevation: 6,900 feet.

High point: San Gorgonio Mountain, 11,499 feet.

Maps: Moonridge and San Gorgonio Mtn. 7.5-minute USGS quads, San Bernardino National Forest map, San Gorgonio Wilderness map.

Season: Late June through mid-October.

Finding the trailhead: From Interstate 10 in Redlands, turn north onto State Highway 38 and follow signs pointing to Barton Flats. You reach the Mill Creek Ranger Station after driving nine miles from Interstate 10. If you did not obtain your required wilderness permit by mail, you can obtain it here. Keep in mind, however, that daily entry quotas are in effect.

Continue following State Highway 38 to the Jenks Lake Road (twenty-five miles from Interstate 10), and then turn right and follow this good paved road, ignoring the left turn to Jenks Lake, and the closed Poopout Hill Road on your right. After 2.5 miles you reach the large hiker's parking area at the South Fork Trailhead.

The hike: Glacial cirques, virgin forests, windswept alpine ridges, two subalpine lakes, a lush meadow, and panoramic vistas make this one of the finest and most memorable hikes in southern California.

From the trailhead, the initial 2.25 miles of the hike leads you past brushy Horse Meadows, across the closed Poopout Hill Road, and into the San Gorgonio Wilderness. Beyond the road you climb a moderately steep draw, top out on a 7,800-foot saddle, and shortly thereafter the old trail from Poopout Hill joins your trail on the left. Presently you begin a gently ascent toward South Fork Meadows, passing through a cool forest of pine and fir.

After 3.5 miles of hiking, avoid an eastbound trail leading to Grinnell Ridge Camp. Instead, climb moderately for .25 mile along the South Fork Santa Ana River to a junction in South Fork Meadows. You will be returning via the left fork where the sign indicates Dry Lake.

HIKE 13 SOUTH FORK TRAILHEAD TO SAN GORGONIO MOUNTAIN

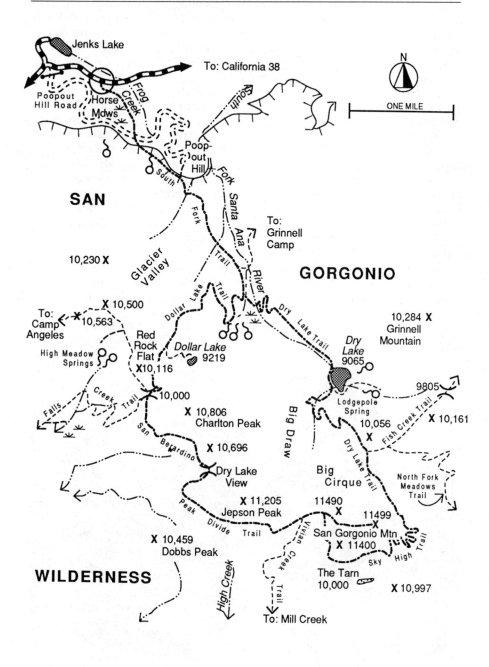

Jenks Lake

To: California 38

N

ONE MILE

Poopout Hill Road

Horse Mdws

Frog Creek

Poop-out Hill

South Fork

South Fork Santa Ana River

SAN

To: Grinnell Camp

GORGONIO

10,230 X

Glacier Valley

Dollar Lake Trail

X 10,500

X 10,563

To: Camp Angeles

Red Rock Flat

Dollar Lake 9219

10,284 X
Grinnell Mountain

High Meadow Springs

X 10,116

Dry Lake Trail

Dry Lake 9065

9805

Falls

Creek Trail

10,000

X 10,806
Charlton Peak

Lodgepole Spring

Fish Creek Trail

X 10,161

San Bernardino

X 10,696

Big Draw

10,056 X

Dry Lake View

Big Cirque

Dry Lake Trail

North Fork Meadows Trail

Peak Divide Trail

X 11,205
Jepson Peak

11490 X

11499 X

San Gorgonio Mtn

X 10,459
Dobbs Peak

Vivian Creek Trail

X 11,400

Sky High Trail

WILDERNESS

High Creek

The Tarn 10,000

X 10,997

To: Mill Creek

49

Turning right, you quickly climb out of the lush oasis of South Fork Meadows, leaving ferns, grasses, and abundant water behind. The trail switchbacks through pine and fir forest, crosses an open, brushy slope choked with manzanita and chinquapin, and meets the left-branching Dollar Lake Trail about 1.9 miles from the meadows. Dollar Lake has been so heavily used in previous years that the Forest Service has closed the lake to camping. It is recovering nicely and makes a pleasant spot for a lunch break. The lake is about .6 mile off the main trail, and if you need water, there is a good spring about 200 feet above the south end of the lake. This is your last easily accessible water for more than ten miles.

Bearing right at the Dollar Lake Trail junction, you ascend .9 mile to 10,000-foot-high Dollar Lake Saddle and reach a four- way trail junction. The westbound trail traverses the crest of San Bernardino Mountain, passing High Meadow Springs after .9 mile. The southbound trail descends past Plummer Meadows to Mill Creek Canyon. But you turn left (east), and cross the south and west slopes of Charlton and Little Charlton peaks, reaching Dry Lake View Trail Camp (no water) after 1.3 miles. The trail then rounds the west ridge of Jepson Peak, where the limber pine forest becomes stunted and ground-hugging. Unobstructed vistas begin opening to the west and south.

The most turbulent weather in southern California occurs along this high ridge—battered trees offer the most vivid evidence of violent, unrestrained winds and blowing and drifting snow.

After following the contours of Jepson Peak's southern slopes, using a worn granite tread, you reach a saddle at the 11,050-foot level from which you can see Dry Lake Basin, and in wet years the "semi-permanent" snowfields that cling to the north slopes of this high ridge.

The trail soon rounds Point 11,171 and meets the trail coming up from Vivian Creek on the right. After another .2 mile, you meet the right-branching Sky

Prostrate limber pines high in the San Gorgonio Wilderness provide stark evidence of the severe weather here in this highest region of southern California. Photo by Rick Marvin

High Trail, your route of return. But for now, continue straight ahead (east) and hike .5 mile to the highest point in southern California, crossing barren alpine fell fields.

Due to the broad, nearly flat nature of San Gorgonio Mountain, you must traverse the rim of the summit plateau for views in all directions. The view from the summit is impressive, encompassing the eastern end of the San Gorgonio Wilderness and extending north to Big Bear Lake and beyond. The hazy coastal valleys to the southwest, with their sprawling urban areas and millions of people, evoke an especially keen sense of appreciation for the San Gorgonio Wilderness and its offer of escape (even if temporary) from the fast-paced, hectic lifestyle that characterizes living in southern California.

From the summit, backtrack .5 mile to the Sky High Trail, and turn left (south), traversing the west then south slopes of San Gorgonio Mountain. After less than a mile, amid thickening timber, you get a glimpse of the dry lakebed of The Tarn, 400 feet downhill to the south. If you're lucky, you might even spot a bighorn sheep in this area—they are fairly common in the rugged, trailless headwaters of the Whitewater River.

Beyond The Tarn, you begin switchbacking down east-facing slopes, passing the twisted wreckage of an airplane enroute.

About 4.5 miles from the summit of San Gorgonio Mountain, you reach another major trail junction at 9,936-foot-high Mine Shaft Saddle. The east-bound trail leads to Fish Creek, and another trail branches right from that trail after .25 mile, descending to North Fork Meadows, one of the least-used trails in the wilderness.

Turn left, and begin a 2-mile descent to moraine-dammed Dry Lake. The descent is shaded by lodgepole pnes, with clums of chinquapin comprising the understory.

About .5 mile before reaching Dry Lake, which is dry only during years of scant precipitation, you begin crossing the eastern edge of a moraine which was created when the large (by southern California standards) glaciers occupying the north slopes of Jepson Peak and San Gorgonio Mountain began to recede, slowly dumping their load of debris quarried from the upper slopes of the two peaks.

After reaching the west shore of Dry Lake—the largest lake in the wilderness and 9,065 feet above sea level—bear left and avoid the eastbound trail leading .4 mile to Lodgepole Spring and its adjacent campsites. Your route hugs the west shore of the lake, crosses its outlet, and follows this creek downstream.

You soon begin swithbacking into South Fork Meadows, emerging from lodgepole pines into a stand of Jeffrey pine and white fir. After the trail levels, hop across Dry Lake's outlet creek, then cross the infant South Fork Santa Ana River before reaching the South Fork Meadows Trail junction. From here, turn right and retrace your route to the trailhead.

HIKE 14 *JOHN'S MEADOW, ANDERSON PEAK*

General description:A rigorous 19.3-mile loop backpack in the San Bernardino National Forest, touring the western San Gorgonio Wilderness.

Elevation gain and loss: 4,455 feet.

Trailhead elevation: 6,760 feet.

High Point: Anderson Peak, 10,864 feet.

Maps: Forest Falls and Big Bear Lake 7.5 minute USGS quads (route from trailhead to San Bernadino Peak Divide Trail not shown on quad), San Bernadino National Forest Map, San Gorgonio Wilderness Map.

Season: Mid-June through October.

Finding the trailhead: From Redlands, drive east on State Highway 38 for twenty-five miles to the Jenks Lake Road, just east of the Ponderosa and Whispering Pines trailheads. Follow the Jenks Lake Road east for .3 mile, then turn right (south) where a sign indicates the parking area. Follow this rough dirt road for .5 mile to its end at the trailhead.

The San Bernardino Valley, typically obscured by smog and haze, shows its hilly detail in this view form the 10,864-foot-high summit of Anderson Peak in the San Gorgonio Wilderness.

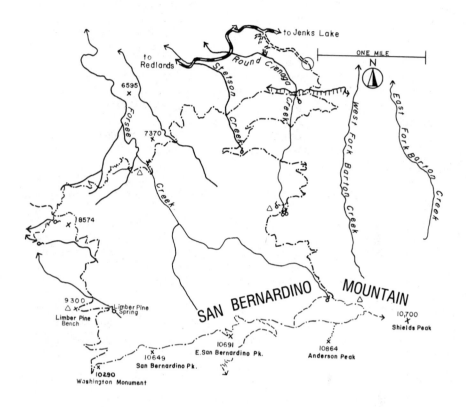

The hike: This excellent loop trip explores the western end of the San Gorgonio Wilderness, and includes an ascent of the highest peak west of Dollar Lake Saddle. The unmaintained trail leading past Johns Meadow to the San Bernadino Peak Divide offers a refreshing change of pace from more popular, sometimes crowded San Gorgonio Wilderness trails. A wilderness permit is required.

From the parking area, walk south for .4 mile, then turn right (you will be returning via the left fork). Your trail traverses north-facing slopes in a westerly direction, under a canopy of white fir, incense-cedar, and Jeffrey and ponderosa pine. During this gentle traverse, you obtain occasional forest- framed views northward to Sugarloaf Mountain and the Big Bear- Santa Ana River Divide.

After 2.25 miles, you pass through a low saddle and descend to ford Forsee Creek, then proceed westward through a forest of Jeffrey pine and white fir, soon passing the Johns Meadow campsites where the trail becomes faint.

Continuing west, cross a meadow-lined creek, turn right, and make your way through a grassy area in a northwesterly direction above the creek. Avoid the left-branching path that climbs steeply immediately after crossing the creek.

The trail presently switchbacks up the north slopes of the San Bernardino Peak Divide through a forest of pine and fir, crossing a few small creeks and willow-choked gullies en route.

Upon intersecting the San Bernardino Peak Divide Trail after hiking 5.2 pleasant miles from the trailhead, turn left (east). As you rise above the 8,600-foot level, lodgepole pine begins dominating the forest. You reach the excellent campsites on Limber Pine Bench after 1.7 miles, and .3 mile beyond that you pass reliable Limber Pine Spring.

Continuing to ascend, you pass just below the Washington Monument, about .75 mile west of San Bernardino Peak. The site of the monument offers a more sweeping panorama than the peak itself. This monument was erected in 1852 as an initial base line triangulation point, and subsequent land surveys for southern California were based on calculations obtained from this initial point.

The trail continues east, passing just north of San Bernardino Peak and San Bernardino East Peak, both easy climbs from the trail.

About 3.7 miles from Limber Pine Spring, you meet the Momyer Creek Trail—climbing 5,300 feet out of Mill Creek Canyon in six miles—on your right.

You next meet a northeast-bound trail descending .5 mile to Trail Fork Springs, a reliable and very cold piped spring 10,400 feet above sea level. Bear right, continuing east for .4 mile, then turn right (south) and ascend the steep north slopes of Anderson Peak via a faint trail for .25 mile to the 10,864-foot summit, which is surrounded by granitic boulders and stunted lodgepole pines.

Vistas are excellent from here, especially eastward to the high peaks of the San Gorgonio Wilderness.

From the summit, backtrack to the San Bernardino Peak Divide Trail, turn right, and hike east for .3 mile to a trail junction in Anderson Flat. Then turn left (northwest) and descend .4 mile to Trail Fork Springs, continuing to descend along the headwaters of Forsee Creek and past Jackstraw Springs, elevation 9,300 feet, and its associated campsites after another 2.3 miles.

Below 8,600 feet, Jeffrey and sugar pine and white fir become the dominant forest trees. You intersect the Johns Meadow Trail about 4.1 miles below Jackstraw Springs, and backtrack the final .4 mile to the trailhead.

HIKE 15 *PONDEROSA AND WHISPERING PINES NATURE TRAILS*

General description: Two very easy .75-mile loop hikes through a peaceful San Bernardino Mountain forest.
Elevation gain and loss: Ponderosa Trail, 165 feet, - 165 feet; Whispering Pines Trail, 150 feet.
High point: Ponderosa Trail, 6,450 feet; Whispering Pines Trail, 6,550 feet.
Trailhead elevation: 6,400 feet.
Maps: Big Bear Lake 7.5-minute USGS quad (trails not shown on quad), San Bernardino National Forest map.
Season: May through November.

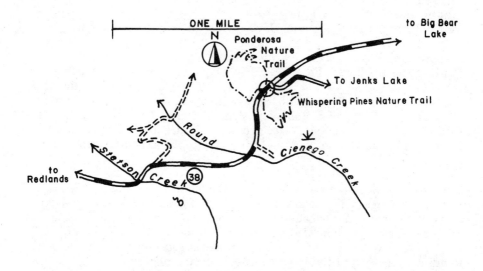

Finding the trailhead: The trailheads are on either side of State Highway 38, about fifty yards west of the western end of the Jenks Lake Road, about twenty-five miles east of Redlands and 23.5 miles south of the highway's junction with State Highway 18 at the eastern end of Big Bear Lake. Park in the turnouts on either side of the highway.

The hike: These nature trails are well suited for a leisurely stroll through the mountains and are especially beneficial for families with small children or anyone desiring a relaxing walk through a cool mountain forest. Small signs describe the workings of nature in this pleasant transition forest, allowing newcomers to the mountains to better appreciate this fine country. Moreover, these short walks should whet the appetites of novice hikers for longer excursions into one of southern California's finest hiking areas, the nearby San Gorgonio Wilderness. The Whispering Pines Trail, south of the highway, has interpretive signs that are also in braille, allowing sightless persons to enjoy this refreshing mountain world.

Both trails travel through open forests of ponderosa, Jeffrey, and sugar pine, white fir, canyon live oak, and black oak.

The Ponderosa Trail proceeds north from the highway, crests a low hill, switchbacks down to a small flat, then ascends gentle slopes back to the highway.

The Whispering Pines Trail gently climbs south from the highway, tops out on a hill, then loops back to the trailhead.

HIKE 16 *CHAMPION LODGEPOLE PINE*

General description. A very easy .6-mile round-trip stroll in the San Bernardino National Forest, featuring the world's largest known lodgepole pine.
Elevation loss and gain: -90 feet.
Trailhead elevation: 7,680 feet.
Maps: Big Bear Lake 7.5-minute USGS quad, San Bernardino National Forest map.
Season: Mid-May through mid-November.
Finding the trailhead: From State Highway 18 on the south shore of Big Bear Lake, two miles west of Big Bear Lake Village, turn south onto the Mill Creek Road, (Forest Road 2N10). Stay on this road for 4.8 miles (the pavement ends after 1.1 miles), following signs indicating Champion Lodgepole Pine at numerous junctions. After driving 4.8 miles, turn right (west) onto Forest Road 2Nll, and proceed west for a mile to the signed Lodgepole Pine Trail.

The hike: Between the Santa Ana River Canyon in the south and Big Bear Lake in the north rises a well-watered, thickly forested plateau reminiscent of the Tahquitz Creek plateau in the San Jacinto Mountains. Lush meadows and several small, willow-clad streams enrich this interesting plateau.

A leisurely downhill walk leads hikers to the largest known lodgepole pine, standing at the end of the largest meadow on the plateau.

Lodgepole pines, easily identified by needles in bundles of two and by their scaly, light-orange to light-brown bark, are usually found on dry, well-drained slopes above the 8,500-foot level in southern California's mountains, but are occasionally found invading wet meadows at lower elevations. The lodgepole pines on this plateau are among the finest specimens anywhere.

From the trailhead, your route leads past a trail sign and picnic table, then descends north through a forest of Jeffrey pine and white fir along a small, grassy-banked creek. The surrounding boulder-dotted slopes are interrupted at times by clumps of chinquapin and mountain whitethorn.

The trail soon levels off near a meadow, where lodgepole pines contribute to the forest, and quickly reaches a junction with a westbound trail leading to Siberia Creek. Turn right (north) and within 50 feet you skirt the edge of a large, forest-rimmed meadow and immediately afterwards reach the fenced-in champion. This impressive tree stands 110 feet high and has a circumference of twenty feet.

After enjoying this peaceful locale, retrace your route to the trailhead.

HIKE 17 *DELAMAR MOUNTAIN*

General description: A 1.2-mile, round-trip day hike in the San Bernardino National Forest, partially cross-country, leading to a forested viewpoint north of Big Bear Lake.
Elevation gain and loss: 648 feet.

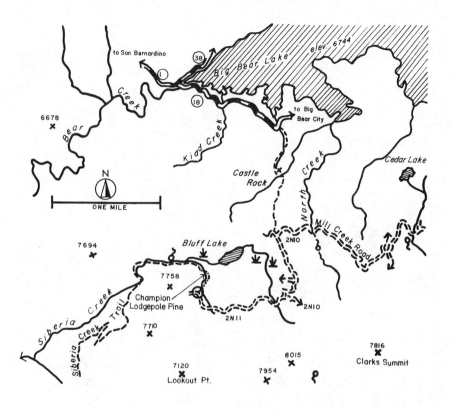

Trailhead elevation: 7,750 feet.
High point: Delamar Mountain, 8,398 feet.
Maps: Fawnskin 7.5-minute USGS quad (route not shown on quad), San Bernardino National Forest map.
Season: Late May through mid-November.
Finding the trailhead: From Fawnskin on the north shore of Big Bear Lake, turn northwest onto Rim of the World Drive (Forest Road 3N14), where a sign indicates Holcomb Valley. Follow this road for 1.8 miles (the pavement ends after .4 mile), avoiding several signed spur roads, to northbound Forest Road 3N12 where a sign indicates that Holcomb Valley is six miles ahead. Follow Forest Road 3N12 northeast, passing several signed spur roads, for 1.7 miles to the trailhead. Park on the north side of the road, just east of the junction with northbound Forest Road 3N94, and across the road from a Pacific Crest Trail (PCT) marker and a sign that reads: "Horse and Foot Traffic Only."

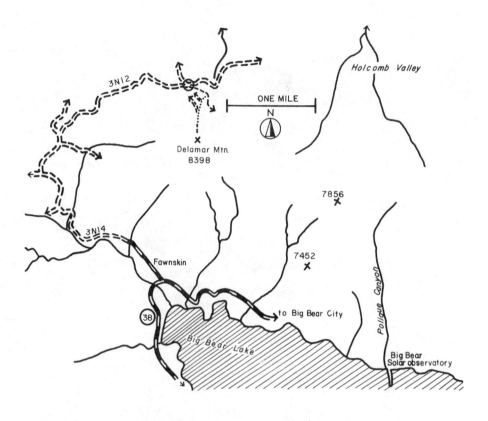

The hike: This seldom-visited yet easily accessible mountain, mantled by a pine and fir forest, provides views of Big Bear Lake and the San Gorgonio Wilderness, and offers a refreshing (if brief) escape from civilization.

From your car, walk southeast across the road to the "Horse and Foot Traffic Only" sign and proceed eastward along the Pacific Crest Trail. After walking 150 yards along the PCT through an open forest of Jeffrey pine and white fir, leave the PCT where it makes a southeastward bend, then climb steeply up the small ridge in a southerly direction. After climbing for about 50 yards, cross an old bulldozer trail, created years ago when this forest was selectively cut.

About 100 yards above that track, you encounter another bulldozer trail. Follow it in a southerly direction on or near the ridgeline. This route dwindles to trail width as you gain elevation.

Upon reaching the small, rounded summit area, the trail disappears completely, and you must make your way a short distance south through a patch of mountain whitethorn to a rock pile which forms the high point of Delamar Mountain. Here in a cool conifer forest, you have good views south across Big Bear Lake to the San Gorgonio Wilderness on the southeastern skyline. Views are also good to the north across the green spread of Holcomb Valley.

After enjoying this pleasant mountain, carefully retrace your route back to the trailhead.

HIKE 18 *CLEGHORN PASS TO CAJON MOUNTAIN*

General description: A moderately easy eight-mile round-trip day hike to the finest viewpoint in the western San Bernardino National Forest.
Elevation gain and loss: 765 feet.
Trailhead elevation: 4,545 feet.
High point: Cajon Mountain, 5,310 feet.
Maps: Cajon 7.5-minute USGS quad, San Bernardino National Forest map.
Season: October through May (avoid the area during periods of substantial snow).
Finding the trailhead: From State Highway 138 above the western end of Lake Silverwood, eleven miles east of Interstate 15 and eleven miles northeast of Crestline Junction on State Highway 18, take the Cleghorn Road exit and drive west up the canyon. The pavement ends after a mile and becomes a rough dirt road for the remaining 3.2 miles to Cleghorn Pass. Park in the large clearing at the pass. If the gate at the pass is open, proceed south on the good dirt road for 2.3 miles to the westbound Cajon Mountain Road. This will eliminate 4.6 miles of hiking and 455 feet of elevation gain.
The hike: This leisurely day hike, on fire road all the way, provides an unparalleled view of Cajon Canyon and the San Andreas Rift Zone, through which Interstate 15 passes.

The area may be closed periodically due to fire danger. Conditions vary each year, so be sure to consult the Forest Service to find out if the area is open to travel. Carry plenty of water.

From Cleghorn Pass, the road traverses north and east-facing slopes staying close to the ridgeline. You pass through areas of chaparral broken intermitently by grassy slopes. Among the trees along this stretch are black oak, whose yellowing leaves offer virtually the only fall color in southern California's mountains. You will also notice both big-cone Douglas-fir and incense-cedar, which is typically found in canyon bottoms.

After strolling 2.3 miles, you reach the westbound Cajon Mountain Road, where a sign incorrectly indicates that Cajon Lookout is four miles ahead. Turn right (west), passing the always-locked gate, and begin traversing north-facing slopes covered with canyon live oak, big-cone Douglas-fir, incense-cedar, and some California bay.

After 1.7 miles, you reach the summit of Cajon Mountain, capped with a lookout tower and microwave tower. Your attention may well be diverted immediately from these works of man, however, since the vistas are spectacular, rivaling those obtained from an airplane.

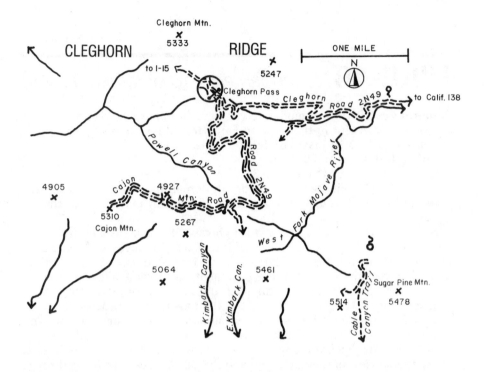

The high eastern peaks of the San Gabriel Mountains skyrocket above the deep cleft of Cajon Canyon. Also visible are portions of the San Bernadino Valley to the south, and the western peaks of the San Bernadino Mountains. From the peak, retrace your route to your car.

HIKE 19 *MT. BALDY ROAD TO CASCADE CANYON*

General description: A fairly rugged two-mile round-trip day hike in the Angeles National Forest, featuring two beautiful waterfalls. (The hike to to the upper falls should be attempted by experienced hikers only.)
Elevation gain and loss 300 feet, -450 feet.
Trailhead elevation: 3,850 feet.
Maps: Mt. Baldy 7.5-minute USGS quad, Angeles National Forest map (most of the route is not shown on the quad).

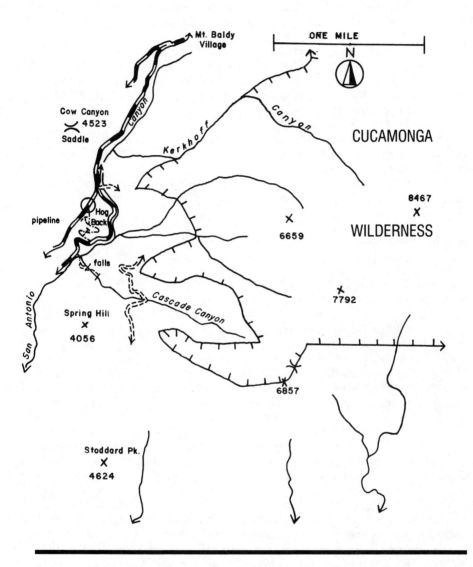

Season: November through May (avoid this hike during periods of high water, when fording San Antonio Creek may be difficult and dangerous).

Finding the trailhead: From Claremont, follow either Padua or Mills avenues north. These roads join near the foothills and become Mt. Baldy Road. Follow Mt. Baldy Road to the trailhead at the top of Hog Back grade.

Alternately, from Interstate 10 in Ontario, follow either Mountain or Euclid avenues north through Upland. These roads also join near the foothills and continue on past the lower San Antonio Forest Service Station to intersect Mt. Baldy Road coming up from Claremont. Turn right onto Mt. Baldy Road and proceed north to the trailhead.

The trailhead is on the right (east) side of Mt. Baldy Road almost at the top of Hog Back (the long steep grade above the tunnels) and just before the road begins to descend toward Mt. Baldy Village. Park on the right hand (east) side of the road in a large turnout, 1.25 miles south of Mt. Baldy Village.

The hike: Of all the precipitous tributary canyons descending into the depths of the middle reaches of San Antonio Canyon, Cascade Canyon is, perhaps, the most scenic. This aptly-named canyon contains numerous cascades and waterfalls over which a small creek plunges in rapid succession during its hurried descent into San Antonio Canyon.

The upper reaches of this rugged chasm are home to numerous Nelson bighorn sheep, and hikers who ascend into the upper canyon may see a few of these rare creatures scampering effortlessly among the cliffs of loose rock that characterize the area.

This hike, through chaparral and shady streamside vegetation, takes hikers into the lower reaches of the canyon where two beautiful waterfalls plunge over rock precipices.

Carry plenty of water; the potability of Cascade Canyon's creek is questionable.

From the parking area, proceed south down a wide bulldozer track. After a short distance, and where the track switchbacks in a southwesterly direction, leave the track and hike south on a faint trail toward two telephone poles. You soon meet a wide path and turn left (east).

This wide path switchbacks down into San Antonio Canyon along the south slopes of Hog Back, amid chaparral consisting of holly- leaf cherry, buckwheat, toyon, birch-leaf mountain mahogany, canyon live oak, and manzanita.

After negotiating one switchback, you cross over a pipeline that descends Hog Back's steep, boulder-strewn south slopes. In 1892, a tunnel was bored through Hog Back Mountain and a power house was built at its foot. Water was transported through this tunnel from San Antonio Creek above Hog Back and fell 412 feet via a flume to the power house. The installation transmitted high voltage current (10, 000 volts) as far away as Pomona and San Bernardino.

Your descent continues beyond the water pipeline, quickly entering the shade of California bay and canyon live oak. You soon intersect the old Mt. Baldy Road, which was abandoned after portions of the road were washed away during floods in the 1960s. Turn right and proceed downhill.

Just after a steep switchback, a well-worn trail branches left (east) from the road. Turn left onto this trail, and after about 40 feet bear right toward the concrete gauging station along San Antonio Creek.

From the gauging station, hop across San Antonio Creek and enter the white alder-shaded mouth of Cascade Canyon. Ascend eastward up the canyon along the small, reliable creek on a sometimes-faint, sometimes-cross-country path and beneath the shade of white alder, California bay, and big-leaf maple.

After hiking a quarter mile from the gauging station, you round a bend in the creek and are suddenly confronted by near- vertical rock walls forming a natural amphitheater. Cascade Canyon's creek plunges over this precipice, forming the first, or lower, falls. This falls is especially impressive when the creek is at its fullest, usually in late winter or early spring. Red columbine decorates the spray-watered wall next to the fall, and California sycamore shades overheated hikers.

Hikers wishing to ascend the canyon to the second, or upper, falls should first descend back toward the mouth of the canyon. But this route should be attempted only by hikers experienced in route finding and dangerous cross-country hiking. One misstep on parts of this route could easily be your last, so extreme caution is mandatory.

Just upstream from the alder stand at Cascade Canyon's mouth, follow a faint trail south for a very short distance to a campsite perched above the south bank of the creek. From here you will notice a cable coming from the gauging station to a point just above the campsite. Walk southeast up the slope under the cable, then follow a shallow gully or draw that parallels the course of the creek. Poison oak is common here.

Where this gully fades out, just before reaching the rim of the amphitheater above the lower falls turn right and strain your way up slippery north-facing slopes covered with canyon live oaks and big-cone Douglas-firs.

The rest after a long day's hike to a highly scenic campsite more than compensates for the exertion required to get there. Photo by Rick Marvin.

Big-cone Douglas-fir (or big-cone spruce) is closely related to the Douglas-fir, but its range is limited to southern California. It occurs in much drier areas than its close relative, being well-adapted to more arid conditions, and is found on north-facing slopes and in canyons between 2,000 and 6,000 feet.

As you approach a fairly flat section of a very minor east- west ridge, you will meet an eastbound game trail about fifteen feet below the crest of that ridge. Turn left (east) onto this narrow and often faint path. Views are excellent from here into upper San Antonio Canyon, and include Mt. San Antonio, the apex of the San Gabriel Mountains.

This route traverses very steep north-facing slopes, passing slippery gullies and crossing bands of rotten rock. Soon it passes above the cliffs surrounding the lower falls, then descends to the creek above those falls. From here you can see the upper falls seventy-five yards upstream.

A short walk up the creek soon brings you to this spectacular waterfall. The pleasant locale is shaded by white alder and big- leaf maple, and is decorated by wildflowers in spring and early summer. Parallel grooves worn into the rock by the plunging lower half of this falls effectively illustrates the erosive action of water.

After enjoying this highly scenic canyon, carefully retrace your route back to Mt. Baldy Road.

HIKE 20 *ICEHOUSE CANYON TO CUCAMONGA PEAK*

General description: A moderately strenuous fourteen-mile round-trip day hike or overnighter leading into the heart of the Cucamonga Wilderness.
Elevation gain and loss: 3,959 feet, -100 feet.
Trailhead elevation: 5,000 feet.
High point: Cucamonga Peak, 8,859 feet.
Maps: Mt. Baldy, Telegraph Peak, and Cucamonga Peak 7.5-minute USGS quads (Cedar Canyon Trail or Chapman Trail not shown on quads), Angeles National Forest map.
Season: Late May through mid-November.
Finding the trailhead: Proceed to Mt. Baldy Village in San Antonio Canyon, about eleven miles north of Interstate 10 in Ontario via Euclid or Mountain Avenues, both of which join the Mt. Baldy Road in the foothills. Mt. Baldy Village is also 10 miles north of Claremont via Padua or Mills Avenues, which also join the Mt. Baldy Road. From the village, continue up the Mt. Baldy Road for 1.5 miles and turn right, proceeding .1 mile to the large parking area at the roadend.

The hike: The San Gabriel Mountains belong to California's Transverse Ranges province. These ranges extend east-west across the framework of California's predominantly northwest-southeast- trending mountains and valleys. The Transverse Ranges province is approximately 300 miles long, stretching from the Eagle and Pinto mountains in the east to Point Arguello near Santa Barbara in the west. Typically, the highest terrain lies near the eastern terminus of each of the ranges constituting this province.

Cucamonga Peak stands high on the eastern end of the San Gabriel Mountains, soaring out of the deep gash of the San Andreas Rift Zone. This flat-topped "volcano-shaped" mountain is an easily recognizable landmark, familiar to many southern Californians. It is one of the most remote mountains in the range. The shortest route to its lofty summit involves a minimum of 6 miles of hiking and thousands of feet of elevation gain. But hikers who complete this strenuous trip are rewarded with sweeping vistas of a large portion of southern California.

The sub-alpine forest of weather-beaten lodgepole pine on this flat, sandy summit offers a cool respite from oppressive summertime heat in the valleys below. Hikers relaxing on the summit often see a variety of raptorial birds, due to the strong thermals that often sweep the slopes of the peak.

This fine hike, in addition to featuring remote sub-alpine mountain terrain, also surveys an environment both devastated and left intact by wildfire and graphically illustrates how vegetation recovers from such destruction. The destructive Thunder Mountain Fire of November 1980 raged through portions of upper San Antonio Canyon and its tributaries. Strong Santa Ana winds that accompanied the blaze caused it to jump from one area to another, leaving a patchwork of unburned vegetation between charred scars. Cedar Flat (also known as Cedar Glen) and the summit of Cucamonga Peak, for example, were unscathed and remain in primitive condition. But in other areas, such as the lower reaches of Icehouse and Cedar canyons, the vegetation was almost

HIKE 20 *ICEHOUSE CANYON TO CUCAMONGA PEAK*

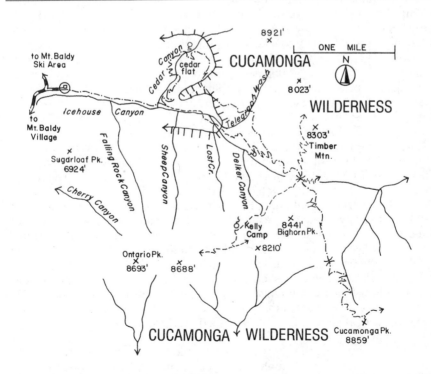

completely destroyed. Most areas of the landscape, however, are rapidly recovering.

Usually taken as a day hike, this trip can be extended by an overnight stay in Cedar Flat or Kelly Camp, both of which have water.

A wilderness permit is required, and can be obtained at the Mt. Baldy Ranger Station, open on weekends only, or at the Lytle Creek or Glendora ranger stations during the week.

From the parking area walk 100 yards east along a paved lane, to the trailhead. Enroute you will pass a large concrete foundation, all that remains of the old Icehouse Lodge, which was consumed by a fire in 1988. A sign here shows a map of the area. You proceed up the canyon on the steadily ascending, sometimes- rocky trail, passing the devastated remains of several cabins. The route leads through a forest of partially burned big-cone Douglas-fir, canyon live oak, incense-cedar, and white alder, passing several wildflower-cloaked springs.

You reach a junction after hiking a mile from the trailhead. The Icehouse Canyon Trail continues straight ahead, rejoining your route about .75 mile below Icehouse Saddle. That trail offers a shorter but somewhat more strenuous route to Icehouse Saddle, and is better suited for the return trip.

Now, however, turn left onto the Chapman Trail, where a sign indicates that Cedar Springs is 1.25 miles and that Cedar Glen is 1.5 miles ahead. This trail climbs up out of Icehouse Canyon and begins ascending the lower reaches of Cedar Canyon, home of a major Icehouse tributary. You occasionally cross Cedar Canyon's intermittently flowing stream and, after hiking 1.25 miles through a partially burned forest, you reach reliable Cedar Springs, the last source of water on the trail. You reach 6,400- foot Cedar Glen after another .25 mile, shaded by a cool stand of Jeffrey pine and white fir, but curiously there is no cedar. This spot is an excellent choice for an overnight stay but is heavily used on many weekends throughout the year.

Beyond Cedar Glen, the trail rounds a spur ridge emanating from Telegraph Peak, enters the small (13,000 acres) but beautiful Cucamonga Wilderness, and begins a protracted traverse through stands of pine and fir and across open talus slopes, with ever-more-frequent views back down Icehouse Canyon to the mountains beyond. To the south, directly across Icehouse Canyon, rises the densely forested north slope of Ontario Peak.

After hiking 1.75 miles from Cedar Glen, the Icehouse Canyon Trail joins your route on the right, and you then climb the final .75 mile through a park-like forest to 7,600-foot Icehouse Saddle, and major trail junction. The north-bound trail leads to Baldy Notch and the Mt. Baldy Ski Area via Timber Mountain, Telegraph Peak, and Thunder Mountain. The southwest-bound trail leads to Kelly Camp a mile away, the last campsite with water, and on to Ontario Peak. You take the southeast-bound trail where a sign indicates Cucamonga Peak. An eastbound trail descending to the Middle Fork Lytle Creek quickly departs to your left as you begin traversing the eastern slopes of Bighorn Peak. The trail soon passes a few abandoned mine shafts and after a mile reaches Cucamonga Saddle. From here the trail climbs 1,200 feet in a single mile to the summit of Cucamonga Peak through a thick north slope forest of pine and fir. Above 8,600 feet, the forest is dominated by lodgepole pine.

Eventually reaching the short path leading to the summit, you turn right– the main trail (rarely used) continues east and ends at a trailhead at the head of the South Fork Lytle Creek. This trailhead is the former site of the largest living conifer in southern California, a 7-foot, 8-inch diameter sugar pine dedicated to Joe Elliot, early supervisor of the San Bernardino National Forest.

After turning right, ascend the final sandy slopes to scale the 8,859-foot summit of Cucamonga Peak, where a magnificent vista unfolds. Massive 11,499-foot San Gorgonio Mountain, the highest point in southern California, dominates the eastern horizon 30 miles distant. At your feet lies the San Bernardino Valley, 7,500 feet below and 4 miles away.

Keep a sharp eye out on the precipitous slopes south and east of the peak, you may be lucky enough to spot one of the many Nelson bighorn sheep that inhabit the most rugged and remote reaches of the range. This endangered species is protected by law.

After taking in the absorbing vista, hikers double back to the trailhead.

Spring in the high country offers a challenging wilderness experience for prepared hikers.
Photo by Rick Marvin

HIKE 21 *MT. SAN ANTONIO*

General description: A strenuous 8.5-mile round-trip day hike (or overnighter if you pack water) to the highest mountain in the San Gabriel Mountains, in the Sheep Mountain Wilderness.

Elevation gain and loss: 3,189 feet, -1,435 feet.

Trailhead elevation: 8,310 feet.

High point: Mt. San Antonio, 10,064 feet.

Maps: Mt. San Antonio 7.5-minute USGS quad, Angeles National Forest map.

Season: June through mid-November.

Finding the trailhead: Drive to Blue Ridge Summit on the Angeles Crest Highway (State Highway 2), about two miles west of Big Pines and fifty-three miles east of La Canada. Turn east onto the unsigned Blue Ridge Road (dirt) from the east side of the large Inspiration Point parking area, and after driving six miles bear left where a right-branching road begins a descent toward Prairie Fork. Continue east for 1.75 miles to the trailhead and the small parking area on the south side of the road, just before the road begins descending to the east.

Southern California's three major mountain ranges are visible from this vantagepoint near Mt. San Antonio. In the foreground are the San Gabriel Mountains and the Mt. Baldy Ski Area, and in the distance—barely visible beyond southern California's infamous smog— are the San Bernardino Mountains on the left and the San Jacinto Mountains on the right.

The hike: From the loftiest summit in the San Gabriel Mountains, hikers are rewarded with a vast sweep of coastal, desert, and mountain scenery encompassing a great portion of southern California.

Hikers completing this strenuous up-and-down trek on a steep, unmaintained trail will fully understand what John Muir meant when he called the San Gabriel Mountains "more rigidly inaccessible than any other I ever attempted to penetrate."

This is prime bighorn sheep habitat, and the wary hiker is likely to see one or more of these agile, majestic creatures.

Be sure to carry plenty of water.

From the trailhead, you immediately descend to a saddle at 8,200 feet above sea level, then climb a ridge up and over Point 8555 on a narrow path resembling a game trail. A difficult stretch of uphill trail awaits after you have descended to another saddle. From this point, scramble up a sharp-edged ridge; precipitous rocky slopes fall abruptly more than 1,000 feet on either side. This is the most difficult and dangerous segment of the hike and should be attempted only by experienced hikers.

Beyond that loose and slippery pitch, the trail becomes much easier to follow, soon climbing 9,648-foot Pine Mountain through a cool forest of lodgepole pine, where scattered clumps of chinquapin comprise the only ground cover.

From Pine Mountain, the trail drops steeply to an open, brushy saddle at an elevation of 9,151 feet. A short distance above that saddle, you pass a rarely-used south-branching trail descending into Fish Fork. You, however, begin a moderate ridgetop ascent through sub-alpine forest to 9,575-foot Dawson Peak.

The trail descends steeply once again to a saddle at 8,800 feet above sea level, passing a few Jeffrey pines enroute. From here the trail climbs more than 1,200 feet upon the north ridge of Mt. San Antonio. Footing is often bad on this very steep section of trail, but hikers are rewarded with a sense of accomplishment as they labor up the last few feet to the open summit of Mt. San Antonio, the only peak in the San Gabriel Mountains rising above 10,000 feet.

The summit stands just above timberline; the stunted and weather-beaten lodgepole pines a short distance downslope attest to the severe winds and deep snow drifts that are prevalent here for half the year.

The entire San Gabriel Mountains are visible, as are the other major mountain ranges of southern California. On a very clear day (which unfortunately is quite rare in southern California), one can see the Sierra Nevada as far north as the Mt. Langley area, far to the northwest. Telescope Peak, towering above Death Valley, can be seen in the north, and far to the northeast rises Charleston Peak near Las Vegas. The vast, seemingly barren landscape of the Mojave Desert sprawls northward from the foot of the San Gabriel Mountains; and the urban areas of southern California, like the Pacific Ocean, are visible to the south and west. Such an all-encompassing vista is worthy of the highest summit in the range.

After absorbing the magnificent panorama, carefully reverse your strenuous up-and-down route to the trailhead.

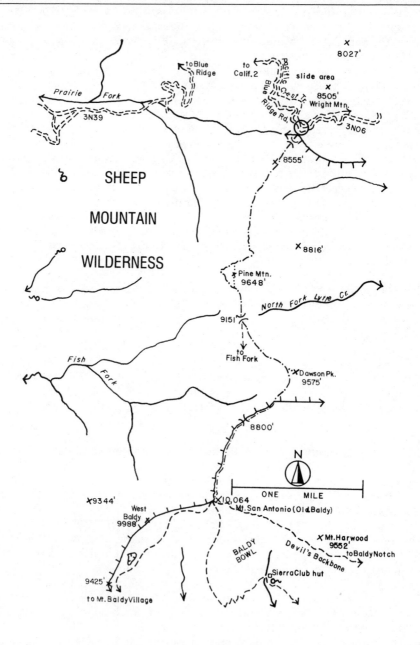

HIKE 22 *DAWSON SADDLE TO MT. BADEN-POWELL*

General description: A moderate 8.2-mile round-trip day hike (or overnighter if you pack water) in the Sheep Mountain Wilderness to a view-filled, wind-swept, sub-alpine summit in the San Gabriel Mountains.

Limber pines are commonly found in high-altitude areas of southern California's mountains growing in tandem with lodgepole pines. Their distingushing feature, however, are needles in bundles of five, compared with needles in bundles of two on lodgepole pines. Fine specimens of limber pines such as this one can be seen along the Pacific Crest Trail near Mt. Baden-Powell in the San Gabriel Mountains.

Elevation gain and loss: 1,856 feet, -360 feet.
Trailhead elevation: 7,903 feet.
High point: Mt. Baden-Powell, 9,399 feet.
Maps: Crystal Lake 7.5-minute USGS quad (route from trailhead to Pacific Crest Trail not shown on quad), Angeles National Forest map.
Season: Late May through mid-November.
Finding the trailhead: Drive to Dawson Saddle, the high point of the Angeles Crest Highway (State Highway 2), 47 miles east of La Canada and ten miles west of Big Pines. The trail begins 150 yards east of Dawson Saddle, across the highway south of a large turnout.

The hike: At 7,903 feet, Dawson Saddle provides the second-highest trailhead in the San Gabriel Mountains, permitting easy access to the high country. A trail was constructed in the early 1980s that bypasses the old path going over 9,138-foot Throop Peak. This new trail joins the Pacific Crest Trail on the crest of the range and makes the ascent to Mt. Baden-Powell much easier and yet less popular than the traditional route starting at Vincent Gap.

No water is available along this hike.

HIKE 22 *DAWSON SADDLE TO MT. BADEN-POWELL*

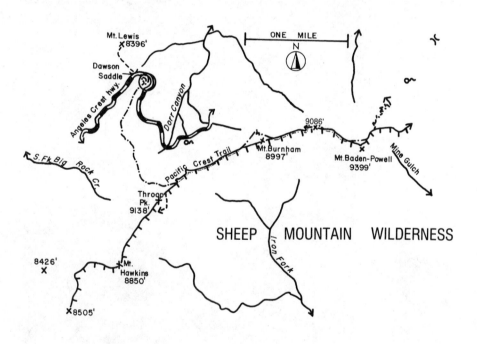

After locating the beginning of the trail, you ascend two switchbacks while rounding the point directly above Dawson Saddle. The trail then proceeds in a southerly direction, on or near the ridgeline, in a forest of Jeffrey, sugar, and lodgepole pine and white fir. At times, you will see traces of the old path leading up to Throop Peak.

After traversing the north slope of Throop Peak, and 1.6 miles from the trailhead, you intersect the Pacific Crest Trail at an elevation of about 8,850 feet. Turn left (east), descending along the ridge crest, then climb up and around 8,997-foot Mt. Burnham, entering a lodgepole and limber pine forest. Then descend once again, round the north slopes of Hill 9086, and soon thereafter you meet the Mt. Baden-Powell Trail. Turn right (south) and ascend the final sub-alpine slopes for .1 mile to the summit, passing some wind-tortured limber pines, distinguished by needles in bundles of five. Some of these trees are believed to be as much as 2,000 years old.

On the summit is a small concrete monument erected by the Boy Scouts in honor of their founder, Lord Baden-Powell. Views are excellent and far-ranging, rivaling those from Mt. San Antonio.

From the summit, retrace your steps to Dawson Saddle, or, if you have a car waiting, you can descend the Mt. Baden-Powell Trail four miles to Vincent Gap Trailhead, five miles east of Dawson Saddle on the Angeles Crest Highway.

HIKE 23 *SMITH MOUNTAIN*

General description: A moderate 6.8-mile round-trip day hike in the Angeles Naitonal Forest's San Gabriel Wilderness, traversing chaparral-clad slopes and ending at a panoramic viewpoint in the heart of the San Gabriel Mountains.
Elevation gain and loss: 1,811 feet.
Trailhead elevation: 3,300 feet.
High point: Smith Mountain, 5,111 feet.
Maps: Crystal Lake 7.5-minute USGS quad, Angeles National Forest map, San Gabriel Wilderness map.
Season: Mid-October through late May.
Finding the trailhead: From Interstate 210 in Azusa, turn north onto State Highway 39 (Azusa Avenue); the sign indicates National Forest Recreation Areas. Drive north through Azusa and into the foothills along the San Gabriel River. After driving 14.5 miles from Interstate 210, bear left where the East Fork Road crosses the river via a bridge.

You reach the signed Bear Creek Trailhead 6.2 miles from the East Fork Road. Park in the large turnout on the west side of State Highway 39, across the road from the Valley of the Moon Penny Pines Plantation.

The hike: The San Gabriel Wilderness encompasses more than 36,000 acres of extremely rugged terrain, ranging from chaparral-choked canyons and ridges to rich conifer forests in the high country. Only a few trails penetrate its margins; the interior remains a vast, wild region where black bear, mule deer, and mountain lion make their home.

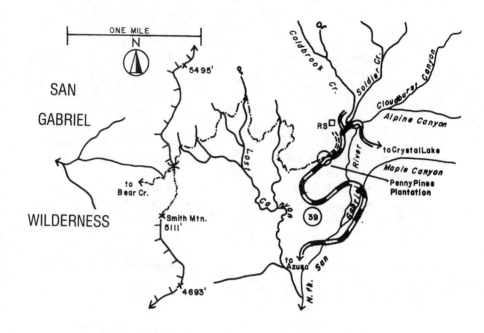

Since the area lies so close to the millions who live in the Los Angeles Basin, it is remarkable that a true wilderness experience can be found and enjoyed here in the heart of the San Gabriel Mountains.

Smith Mountain is the southernmost 5,000-foot peak on a long south-trending ridge separating the North Fork San Gabriel River from Bear Creek and the San Gabriel Wilderness.

From its open summit, a large portion of the San Gabriel Mountains and the rugged depths of the San Gabriel Wilderness meet your gaze.

Carry plenty of water for this dry hike.

Information and fire permits (for backpackers) can be obtained Friday through Sunday at the San Gabriel Entrance Station, located at the mouth of San Gabriel Canyon, or at Glendora Ranger Station during the week.

Your trail begins at the northwest end of the large parking area. It traverses east-facing slopes, proceeding in a southerly direction high above the highway. You soon cross a low ridge and enter the Lost Canyon drainage.

Among the vegetation along the first three miles of trail are buckwheat, chamise, white sage, yucca, scrub oak, ceanothus, yerba santa, birch-leaf mountain mahogany, silktassel, and holly-leaf cherry.

The trail bends in and and out of several draws that funnel runoff into Lost Canyon. These gullies are shaded by canyon live oak, California bay, willow, California sycamore, and big-leaf maple—attesting to the availability of moisture in these usually dry watercourses and to the cooler microclimate that prevaiils here.

You reach 4,300-foot Smith Mountain Saddle after hiking 2.8 miles from the trailhead. The ridge to the north and south delineates the eastern boundary of the San Gabriel Wilderness.

The Bear Creek Trail descends westward from here into the depths of Bear Creek Canyon. But you turn left (south) and begin climbing the steep north ridge of Smith Mountain. Your trail, a use path ascending an overgrown firebreak, climbs steeply for 800 feet through scrub oak and manzanita.

Big-cone Douglas-firs soon appear on sheltered northwest- facing slopes just west of the ridge. Scrambling over or around a few granitic outcrops adds excitement to this often steep climb. Views continue to expand as you gain elevation.

After hiking .6 mile from the Bear Creek Trail, you find yourself standing atop the open summit of Smith Mountain, with an unobstructed view in all directions.

The summit itself is crowned by a small boulder, and the surrounding vegetation consists primarily of manzanita, silktassel, scrub oak, buckwheat and chamise. Blue penstemon decorates the peak in the spring.

The Tecolote Fire in 1985 consumed 3,000 acres in the San Gabriel Wilderness but fortunately stopped short of the summit of Smith Mountain.

On your return trip, simply amble back down the trail to the highway.

HIKE 24 SOUTH FORK BIG ROCK CREEK TO THE DEVILS CHAIR

General description: A moderate 5.5-mile round-trip day hike or overnighter in the Angeles National Forest, leading into the intriguing rock formations of the Devils Punchbowl at the northern foot of the San Gabriel Mountains.
Elevation gain and loss: 850 feet, -400 feet.
Trailhead elevation: 4,600 feet.
High point: Devils Chair, 5,050 feet.
Maps: Valyermo 7.5-minute USGS quad, Angeles National Forest map.
Season: Mid-September through May.
Finding the trailhead: There are several ways to reach the trailhead, all of them originating from State Highway 138. Probably the best and most straightforward route is 165th Street East, also known as Bobs Gap Road, which turns south from State Highway 138 about 4.5 miles east of Pearblossom and twenty-six miles west of Interstate 15. Follow this road south across the desert and over a low range of hills into a farming area along the San Andreas Rift Zone. After driving 7.5 miles south of State Highway 138, turn left (east) and proceed eastward for .3 mile, then turn right (south) and follow the paved road along Big Rock Creek, passing the Sycamore Flat Campground; after 2.5 more miles turn right (south) once again onto the dirt road leading to South Fork Campground. After one mile turn right into the hiker's parking area, just below the campground.

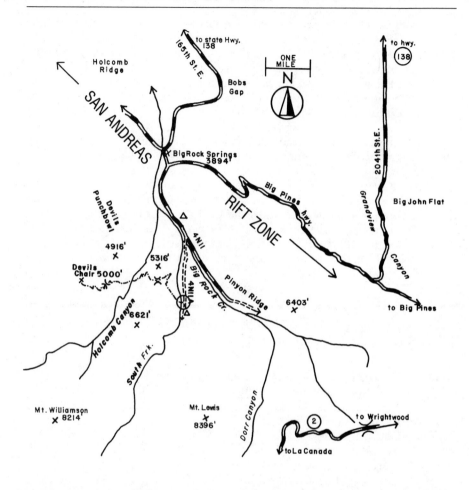

The hike: The Devils Punchbowl is another of California's numerous striking rock formations. Lying at the northern foot of the San Gabriel Mountains along the San Andreas Rift Zone, this unusual, highly eroded sandstone-conglomerate-shale formation is especially interesting. The trail leads hikers to its best viewpoint, the Devils Chair, where the entire hellish landscape of the Punchbowl spreads out to your north, with the barrens of the Mojave Desert fading into the distance beyond.

This hike can be taken as an overnighter; there are good campsites in Holcomb Canyon next to the creek.

Carry an adequate supply of water.

From the parking area, you immediately boulder-hop your way across the South Fork Big Rock Creek and find the obvious trail on the west side. Runoff in this canyon can be substantial during the spring snowmelt period; therefore, caution is advised when crossing this creek.

From the west side of the creek, the trail switchbacks up to the low gap visible on the western skyline, through scrub oak, manzanita, mountain mahogany, and some pinyon pine.

From the gap you have good views east and west along the north slopes of the San Gabriel Mountains, and a portion of the Devils Punchbowl is visible to the west across Holcomb Canyon.

The trail presently descends 400 feet into the depths of Holcomb Canyon via chaparral-covered slopes. The perennial stream flowing through this canyon is shaded by large oaks and big-cone Douglas-firs, under which pleasant camp-sites can be located.

You then hop across this creek (which also runs high in spring) and begin a steep 480-foot ascent up the west wall of the canyon. Above this ascent, the trail heads west through a pinyon pine forest, where you will be rewarded with good views across the highly eroded hills and canyons of the Devils Punchbowl.

The trail hugs the rim of the formation, then turns north for a short descent to the rock point of the Devils Chair. Hand rails help steady faint-hearted hikers, for the near-vertical slopes of slippery, rotten rock drop precipitously away on all sides.

The Devils Punchbowl lies along the great San Andreas Fault. One may notice the similarity between the Devils Punchbowl and the Mormon Rocks, which lie just west of Interstate 15 along State Highway 138, about twenty miles east of the Punchbowl. At one time these formations may have been a single formation, but horizontal movement along the fault has displaced them. The west side of the San Andreas Fault is slowly moving northward, while the east side slips southward.

After enjoying this unusual area, backtrack to the trailhead.

HIKE 25 *TWIN PEAKS*

General description: A strenuous 9.6-mile round-trip day hike or overnighter leading into the high country of the San Gabriel Wilderness.
Elevation gain and loss: 2,161 feet, -1,200 feet.
Trailhead elevation: 6,800 feet.
High point: East Twin Peak, 7,761 feet.
Maps: Waterman Mtn. 7.5-minute USGS quad (trail from Waterman Mountain to Twin Peaks not shown on quad), Angeles National Forest map, San Gabriel Wilderness map.
Season: Late May through November.
Finding the trailhead: The trailhead is in the Buckhorn Flat area, about one mile east of Cloudburst Summit on the Angeles Crest Highway (State Highway 2), thirty-three miles east of La Canada or twenty-two miles west of Big Pines. Park in the turnout on the east side of the highway directly above the Buckhorn Forest Service Guard Station.

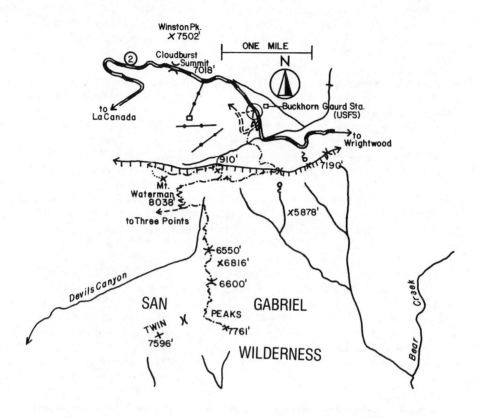

The hike: This strenuous trip tours the San Gabriel Wilderness high country, passing through park-like forests and traversing boulder-dotted slopes. This is bighorn sheep country, and the quiet and observant hiker may spot one or more of these magnificent animals scampering among the granitic boulders, cliffs, and outcrops that characterize this wild and rugged corner of the San Gabriels.

Carry an adequate supply of water for this dry hike.

From your car, cross the highway and locate the trailhead where a large sign indicates the Mt. Waterman Trail. Turn left (south) onto this well-graded trail; avoid a jeep trail climbing directly up the slope to the west.

Proceeding south along the Mt. Waterman trail, you cross a closed dirt road after .25 mile and resume hiking the trail across the road. Soon, you hop across a small creek and climb to the crest of the range through an open pine and fir forest. At the crest, there is a rope tow and a ski run a few yards east of the trail. Here you turn right (west) and climb moderately along or near the ridge, meeting the Mt. Waterman Summit Trail after hiking 1.75 miles from the trailhead. A .75-mile (one way) side trip can take you from here to the boulder-stacked summit of Waterman Mountain, which, at 8,038 feet above sea level, is the high point of the San Gabriel Wilderness. The north slope of the mountain is the location of a small ski area.

From this junction, begin your long descent to Twin Peaks Saddle. Twin Peaks loom boldly in the south across the deep gash of the saddle. After negotiating several switchbacks, you reach another junction, three miles from the trailhead. Straight ahead (west) is Three Points and the Angeles Crest Highway, five miles away. You turn left here, where the sign reads: "Twin Peaks Saddle 1, No Trail Beyond Saddle."

The trail presently contours in an easterly direction, soon crossing a small creek, the headwaters of Devils Canyon, offering a year-round source of water. You continue descending, finally reaching 6,550-foot-high Twin Peaks Saddle.

Contrary to the sign at the last junction, there is a trail beyond the saddle. The route contours in a southerly direction across smooth, openly forested slopes to another saddle, this one slightly higher than the last. From here, it's a 1,200-foot climb up the north slope of Twin Peaks via a very steep unmaintained path. The cool forest of Jeffrey and sugar pine and white fir provides adequate shade during this strenuous climb. The switchbacks on this trail make a weak attempt to ease the grade. At last, you reach the summit ridge and walk southeastward to the 7,761-foot-high summit of east Twin Peak.

On this boulder-littered peak, you obtain inspiring views into the San Gabriel Wilderness with its deep, brush-choked canyons and rugged topography. Most of the San Gabriel Mountains are visible to the east and west, and the sprawling metropolitan areas of the Los Angeles Basin lie at your feet more than 7,000 feet below.

From here you retrace your route to the trailhead.

HIKE 26 *SIERRA PELONA*

General description: A moderate 4.4-mile round-trip day hike in the Angeles National Forest to a windswept ridge offering far-reaching vistas from the San Gabriel Mountains to the southern Sierra Nevada.
Elevation gain and loss: 1,350 feet.
Trailhead elevation: 3,200 feet.
High point: 4,550 feet.
Maps: Sleepy Valley 7.5-minute USGS quad, Angeles National Forest map.
Season: Mid-October through May.
Finding the trailhead: From the junction of the Spunky Canyon Road and the Bouquet Canyon Road at the upper (east) end of Bouquet Reservoir, eighteen miles southeast of Saugus, proceed east on the Bouquet Canyon Road for 2.1 miles. The trailhead is marked with a small Pacific Crest Trail sign, and lies just east of an "ICY" road sign, on the south side of the road.

The trailhead can also be reached from State Highway 14 in Palmdale by following Los Angeles County Road N2 west for about 8.2 miles, then turning south onto Bouquet Canyon Road and driving 4.2 miles to the trailhead.

The hike: The Sierra Pelona is one of several long hogback ridges lying between the San Gabriel Mountains to the southeast and Interstate 5 to the west.

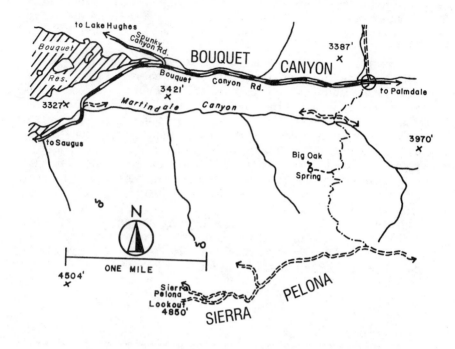

This hike follows the north slopes of the central Sierra Pelona massif, ascending to the crest through chaparral and scattered oaks. The outstanding feature of Sierra Pelona is the superb, 360-degree panorama obtained from the summit ridge.

The hike is usually open all year, but can be uncomfortable during the heat of summer. Strong Santa Ana winds also buffet this exposed mountain occasionally, especially in autumn.

Be sure to carry plenty of water.

From the Pacific Crest Trail marker, your trail leads southwest through chaparral consisting of birch-leaf mountain mahogany, scrub oak, chamise, buckwheat, and an occasional canyon live oak. As you gain elevation you also gain vistas of Bouquet Canyon, Bouquet Reservoir, and the surrounding mountains.

After hiking .4 mile, you crest a minor east-west ridge and intersect Forest Road 6N06. Beyond the road, your trail descends slightly to cross Martindale Canyon's dry streambed, then resumes climbing north-facing slopes.

After hiking .6 mile from Forest Road 6N06, you meet a short lateral trail in a live oak stand, leading west to Big Oak Spring, a possible campsite and the site of what was formerly the world's largest canyon live oak. Unfortunately, that tree was destroyed by a brush fire.

Your trail continues southward, ascending grassy slopes decorated in spring by lupine, western wallflower, and some mariposa tulip. After another 1.2 miles of moderate ascent, you reach the crest of Sierra Pelona and a junction with Forest Road 6N07, where sweeping vistas are revealed. A short jaunt east, or especially west, reveals the best panoramas.

To reach Peak 4,850, the former site of the Sierra Pelona fire lookout tower, hike 1.6 mile west along Forest Road 6N07, staying left at two junctions, gaining 300 feet of elevation enroute. The finest vistas on the mountain are obtained from the lookout. Wind gusts as high as 100 miles per hour have been recorded here.

After reveling in the superb panorama, you will reluctantly descend to the trailhead.

HIKE 27 *MT. PINOS TO GROUSE MOUNTAIN*

General description: A moderate 6.4-mile, view-filled, round- trip day hike (or backpack if you carry water) in the Los Padres National Forest, along a high, conifer-clad mountain range south of the San Joaquin Valley.
Elevation gain and loss: 700 feet, -850 feet.
Trailhead elevation: 8,800 feet.
High point: Mt. Pinos Trailhead, 8,800 feet.
Maps: Sawmill Mountain 7.5-minute USGS quad (trail not shown on quad), Los Padres National Forest map.
Season: Late May through mid-November.
Finding the trailhead: From Interstate 5, three miles north of Gorman and forty-one miles south of Bakersfield, take the Frazier Park exit and follow the main paved road, the Frazier Park-Cuddy Valley Road, west. Avoid a south-bound road to Lockwood Valley after driving eight miles west from Interstate 5. After driving 11.7 miles from Interstate 5, bear left where the sign indicates Mt. Pinos; the Mill Potrero Road branches right and leads northwest to State Highway 166.

Your paved road now begins a steady climb to Mt. Pinos, passing two Forest Service campgrounds enroute. After another 8.2 miles, at the large parking area for the Chula Vista walk-in campground, you turn left onto the very rough road leading to Mt. Pinos. After driving 1.8 miles, you reach the trailhead and parking area at the Condor Observation Site, just beyond a right- branching spur road leading to the summit microwave tower. Low-powered and low-clearance vehicles may have a difficult time negotiating this very rough 1.8 miles of dirt road.

The hike: Mt. Pinos, the high point of a major east-west ridge that lies about fifteen to twenty miles west of Tejon Pass, lies in a region where the South Coast Ranges, the Transverse Ranges, and the Tehachapi Mountains coalesce. Geologically, the Mt. Pinos area is part of the South Coast Ranges. It appears, however, due to its east-west alignment, to be associated with the Transverse Ranges.

The entire region is mantled in a thick conifer forest and laced with numerous trails and streams. Several trail camps throughout the Mt. Pinos Ranger District beckon overnight campers.

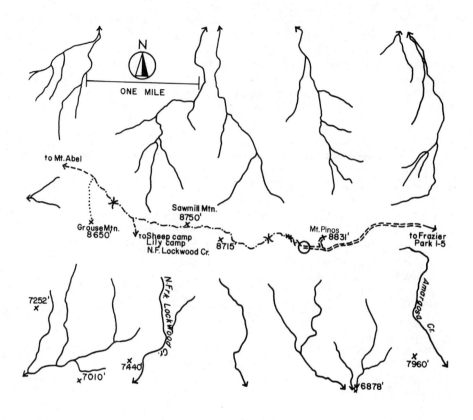

This ridgetop hike traverses the Mt. Pinos high country and ends with an easy cross-country jaunt to a seldom-visited mountain covered by a thick Jeffrey pine forest. Grouse Mountain's central location on this high ridge offers an isolated destination for city-weary hikers. Few people ascend the gentle forested slopes of this mountain. It offers an easy opportunity to enjoy nature's solitude and is a satisfying leg-stretcher.

Backpackers willing to carry water will find ample opportunity for camping along most of this route.

Be sure to carry plenty of water.

From the parking area, your hike begins at the Mt. Pinos Trail sign. The trail starts out as a paved path, passing several gnarled and twisted Jeffrey and limber pines. You soon branch left onto the trail proper; the paved path continues a short distance to a bench-furnished viewpoint.

You are accompanied by panoramic vistas as you switchback down the west slope of Mt. Pinos. These vistas include the southern Sierra Nevada and the alpine peaks of the Great Western Divide to the north, lying beyond the patchwork of farmlands in the southern San Joaquin Valley. To the southeast, south, and southwest lies the forested terrain of the western Transverse Ranges, beckoning hikers to explore their intriguing landscape.

The west slope of Mt. Pinos is sub-alpine in character, and switchbacking your way down the mountain you pass many stunted limber pines. The trail is decorated in spring and early summer with western wallflower and Indian paintbrush.

You soon enter a stand of white fir and Jeffrey pine, and presently the trail bottoms out at an 8,350-foot saddle. You then begin a moderate ascent up the east ridge of Sawmill Mountain in a forest dominated by Jeffrey pine.

The trail eventually levels off on the summit plateau of Sawmill Mountain. A short walk north to the 8,750-foot-high point, clad in stunted Jeffrey and limber pines, reveals sweeping views of the San Joaquin Valley and the southern Sierra Nevada.

The trail next descends west to join with a southbound trail leading past two trail camps to the North Fork Lockwood Creek. Backpackers will want to turn left here. But most hikers will stay right, descending to a saddle 8,350 feet above sea level. The trail then rises once again along the forested northeast slopes of Grouse Mountain. This mountain is not labeled on the quad; it is the mountain between Sawmill Mountain and Cerro Noroeste (also known as Mt. Abel).

At a point almost due north of Grouse Mountain, where the trail begins a slight descent, leave the trail and head southwest until you reach the flat summit ridge of the mountain. (Use of the topographic quadrangle for this portion of the hike is highly recommended). Upon reaching the summit ridge, turn south and walk along the undulating ridgetop through a pleasant, park-like forest. In a little less than one-half mile, you reach the south summit and high point of Grouse Mountain at 8,650 feet, marked by a small rock cairn. Views are somewhat limited because of the Jeffrey pine forest, but the peaceful nature of this isolated mountain easily makes up for the lack of vistas.

Eventually, hikers will backtrack to the trailhead.

HIKE 28 *PEAK 7416, PINE MOUNTAIN*

General description: A moderate, 6.8-mile round-trip day hike (or backpack if you carry water) in the Los Padres National Forest through a cool pine and fir forest in the western Transverse Ranges.
Elevation gain and loss: 1,041 feet, -600 feet.
Trailhead elevation: 6,975 feet
High point: Peak 7416.
Maps: Reyes Peak, Lion Canyon, and San Guillermo 7.5- minute USGS quads, Los Padres National Forest map.
Season: Late May through mid-November.
Finding the trailhead: From State Highway 33, about twenty-five miles south of its junction with State Highway 166 (which is seven miles east of New Cuyama) and forty-seven miles north of Ventura, turn east where a sign indicates the Pine Mountain Recreation Area. Follow this narrow oiled road

eastward. The oiled surface ends after about six miles and you continue east on dirt road for one more mile to the dead end and traiihead. There are primitive campgrounds available on Pine Mountain for car campers, but no water is attainable.

The hike: West of the San Gabriel Mountains and Interstate 5, the Transverse Ranges rise to impressive heights before fading into the lower ranges at the extreme western terminus of the province near Point Arguello.

From Pine Mountain in the south, to Frazier Mountain in the east, to the Mt. Pinos massif in the north, this high, well- watered region, covered by many square miles of conifer forest, sees much fewer visitors than other thickly forested high-country areas of southern California.

This hike along Pine Mountain ends at Peak 7416, the easternmost 7,000-foot-high peak on this high ridge. However, backpackers may want to descend north into Beartrap Creek, or take advantage of several trail camps along Piedra Blanca Creek to the east of Pine Mountain. Campsites in those canyons are shaded by ponderosa and Jeffrey pine, juniper, and pinyon pine. Water is usually available.

Those who arrange a car shuttle can hike out to Sespe Creek at the southern foot of Pine Mountain, a point-to-point hike of about 12.5 miles.

Carry water for this dry, ridgeline hike.

Backpackers who carry an adequate supply of water will find almost unlimited campsite possibilities in the open, park-like forest that characterizes the entire hike.

Where the road is blocked to further access for vehicles, you hike eastward along the south slopes of Peak 7109 via the retired road. After hiking less than .2 mile, you leave the road where it bends southeast and pick up an eastbound trail just beyond the berm on the east side of the road.

These sandstone cliffs on the south slopes of Pine Mountain in the Los Padres National Forest, reminiscent of Utah's canyon country, are an unusual sight in California's backcountry.

The trail begins traversing north-facing slopes, soon passing under Reyes Peak, which, at an elevation of 7,510 feet, is the highest point on Pine Mountain .

The old Reyes Peak quadrangle shows the north slopes of Pine Mountain barren of vegetation. However, as you will immediately notice, these north slopes are cloaked in a thick pine and fir forest.

Your undulating trail, shaded the entire distance by Jeffrey, ponderosa, and sugar pine and white fir, stays on or just north of the ridgecrest. On your eastward course you often have good views northwest into the Cuyama Valley, north to the highly eroded sandstone hills surrounding the upper Cuyama River, and beyond to the Mt. Pinos massif. You also obtain occasional conifer-framed views eastward to the thickly forested terrain of the western Transverse Ranges province.

When your trail touches the crest at occasional ridgetop saddles or gaps, your gaze reaches southward to the chaparral- choked hillsides that plunge deep into Sespe Creek.

HIKE 28 *PEAK 7416, PINE MOUNTAIN*

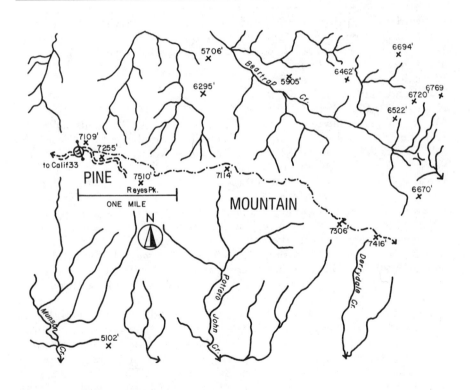

After rounding the north slopes of Peak 7114, about 1.75 miles from the trailhead, you have views into the headwaters bowl of Potrero John Creek. Here, under Peak 7306, lie broken sandstone cliffs, reminiscent of Utah's canyon country.

On the more open stretches of trail, you cross grassy slopes decorated by currant, yellow lupine, western wallflower, and snowplant in the early spring.

A short distance beyond an inverted orange triangle attached to a metal post, reading "NH36," you round a minor, boulder-covered, north-trending ridge, descend slightly to a small saddle, and then negotiate a few switchbacks. Just beyond, where the trail and ridge begin steadily descending to the east, you leave the trail and scramble a short distance south to the boulder-heaped summit of Peak 7416. Views are somewhat limited due to the thick Jeffrey pine forest.

From this peak, either retrace your route to the trailhead or, if equipped for an overnight stay, descend via trail into Piedra Blanca Creek where good, conifer-shaded campsites await.

HIKE 29 *LANFAIR VALLEY TO FORT PIUTE*

General description: A moderate 4.7 mile loop day hike to the only perennial stream in the east Mojave Desert, lying within the Mojave National Preserve. A portion of the hike retraces the steps of westbound pioneers along the old Mojave Road.
Elevation gain and loss: 800 feet.
Trailhead elevation: 3,450 feet.
High point: Piute Hill, 3,600 feet.
Maps: Lanfair Valley and Homer Mtn. 15-minute USGS quads: or Signal Hill and Homer Mtn. 7.5-minute metric USGS quads, or BLM New York Mts. Desert Access Guide, Map 9, and Needles, Map 13.
Season: October through April.
Finding the trailhead: Follow Interstate 40 for 108 miles east from Barstow or thirty four miles west from Needles to the Goffs exit. Leave the freeway here and proceed twelve miles northeast to Goffs, your last source of gas and other services. Turn left (northwest) at Goffs onto Lanfair Road, paved for the first ten miles, graded dirt thereafter. About sixteen miles from Goffs, the signed Cedar Canyon Road branches left, and 100 yards beyond turn right onto an eastbound dirt road indicated by a small "PT&T" sign pointing east. Follow this fairly narrow graded dirt road, avoiding several lesser used roads branching right and left. After 5.6 miles bear left where a sign indicates the Rattlesnake Mine and a right-forking road. Ahead, your undulating road becomes narrower and rougher, simply a service road accessing a buried telephone cable. About 3.4 miles from the Rattlesnake Mine junction, the road crosses a sandy wash that may present an obstacle to vehicles with low clearance. As the road approaches the foot of the low Piute Range 9.5 miles from Lanfair Road, turn left onto a poor dirt road just before reaching a cattle guard. This road has a high center in places but is passable to carefully driven passenger cars. Proceeding north, you'll pass the Mojave Road (the return leg of the loop) and a corral, and after 1.3 miles reach the trailhead, a large turnout on the east side of the road overlooking Piute Gorge.

The hike: Insights into natural history, from folding and faulting exposed in a rugged canyon to streamside, or riparian vegetation (unique in the eastern Mojave Desert), to trailside petroglyphs along the Old Government (or Mojave) Wagon Road, are primary attractions of this fine day hike.

Portions of this unique hike trace part of the Mojave Road. This route, established along old Indian trails, was a major travelway for settlers and mail carriers during the latter half of the 19th century between Prescott, Arizona and Los Angeles. The route evolved into a wagon road, and its course took advantage of the few water sources scattered throughout the Mojave Desert. Since this route passed through Indian lands, there were, inevitably, conflicts between travelers and the native population. As a consequence, a series of five redoubts, or temporary forts, were constructed between Fort Whipple near Prescott, Arizona and Camp Cady near Daggett, California.

"Fort Pah-Ute" was one such redoubt, located on a sun-baked hillside near the perennial waters of Piute Creek. This was the first stop for westbound travelers beyond the crossing of the Colorado River. This fort was occupied by as many as eighteen enlisted men between the fall of 1867 and the spring of 1868. They escorted travelers as they passed through Indian lands. By 1883, as the more southerly route of the Southern Pacific Railroad was completed, the Mojave Road fell into disuse.

A hiker ponders the meaning of trailside petroglyphs in Piute Canyon, part of the BLM's East Mojave Naitonal Scenic Area.

Today, a 130-mile segment of this historic route can be traced across the eastern Mojave Desert, and much of its course is popular with four-wheel-drive enthusiasts. But since much of this hike passes through a wilderness area closed to motor vehicles, hikers can follow the route at a wagon's pace, contemplating the hardships those hardy 19th century pioneers faced daily on their long westward journeys.

This trip is a fine choice for a winter or spring day hike when many hiking areas remain buried in snow. Campsites are scarce, but those who nevertheless choose to stay overnight should remember to camp at least 300 feet from water sources and that no camping is allowed in the fort ruins. Carry an ample water supply, and don't drink from Piute Spring unless you purify the water.

Before beginning your hike, pause to enjoy the view before plunging into the canyon below. The broad expanse of Lanfair Valley stretches westward toward the unusual mesa of Table Mountain, and northwest to the pinnacle-capped crest of the New York Mountains. To the north and south is the low volcanic ridge of the Piute Range, and below you Piute Gorge cuts northward into a scenic badlands landscape.

The trail descends eastward at first, upon the resistant band of conglomerate that forms the rim of the gorge, quickly reaching a saddle littered with black volcanic boulders and decorated with creosote bush and bunchgrass.

The trail then jogs north, descending steeply into the dry wash of Piute Gorge, where hikers turn right, following the wash downstream. Almost at once you pass an obvious fault zone on the canyon wall, at a contact zone between volcanic breccia and grey volcanic rocks, where the strata dips downward toward the west.

Spring wildflowers that add color to the rugged, rocky canyon include Indian paintbrush, and the yellow blossoms of hymenoxis.

The canyon is quite narrow as you follow a serpentine course through the Piute Range. Broken cliffs and pinnacles of red and grey rock rise as much as 300 feet above, the strata sliced, offset, and contorted by numerous minor faults and folds. A particulary noticeable S-shaped fold offers insights into the dynamic geologic processes that have created and continue to shape the landscape of the Mojave Desert.

The hiking is easy along the gravel and slickrock bed of the wash. Mojave yucca, beavertail and barrel cactus dot the broken slopes above.

As the canyon bends southeast, it suddenly becomes choked with tamarisk, willows, and desert-willows. Also present are the tall, yellow flower stalks of prince's plume. A little bushwhacking lies ahead, and one mile from the trailhead you reach Piute Spring, where a vigorous flow of water issues from the canyon floor. Shaded by tall willows, the spring is a veritable oasis surrounded by parched desert.

To continue, hikers must forge their way through dense streamside vegetation along the trickling stream for .3 mile. Beyond this obstacle, the canyon opens up considerably where a southwest-trending canyon joins on the right. Hikers returning from the fort ruins should take the trail that leads south from this point to quickly join the Mojave Road.

Presently, hikers should cross the creek and follow the eastbound trail traversing the slope north of the wash, thus avoiding the thick vegetation that chokes the canyon bottom. Mojave yuccas, barrel cactus, cholla, and a variety of flowering shrubs clothe this sun-drenched south-facing slope.

Soon, the fort ruins come into view to the east. Piute Valley, framed by the

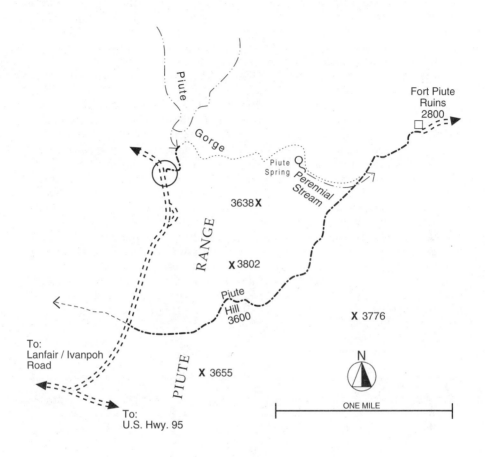

slopes of Piute Canyon, stretches away beyond, while the Dead Mountains and hazy desert ranges in Arizona reach t o the horizon.

About 1.7 miles from the trailhead, a row of volcanic boulders just south of the trail feature some fine petroglyphs, and further on, more carved boulders lie next to the trail. Soon thereafter the trail joins the end of the rough dirt road climbing up from Piute Valley, 1.8 miles from the trailhead. Two ruins of low rock walls are all that remain after more than 100 years to remind us of the short-lived redoubt of Fort Piute. The lower and larger rock wall of the corral lies just above the roadend to the north. Above it lies the blockhouse, its walls built of native stone and slightly better preserved than the corral. With a little imagination one can visualize the lonely life soldiers led at this remote desert outpost. It is not surprising that the desertion rate was high. Not only was there the bleak, parched desert stretching away for over 100 miles in all directions, but the lure of nearby goldfields must have been adequate inducement for many to abandon Army life.

From the fort, return .5 mile to the aforementioned canyon fork, and turn left (south) quickly joining the Mojave Road. Almost at once, wagon wheel ruts are visible where the road crosses a stretch of red rock. Proceeding southwest up the canyon, a boulder just south of the road features another fine petroglyph. Be sure not to disturb or deface any Indian artifacts you may encounter, leave them for others to appreciate.

Ahead the route altenates between the wash and open slopes, but eventually abandons the wash and begins the steep climb over Piute Hill. The road is eroded and overgrown in places with creosote bush, but otherwise it has changed little since its heyday. Hiking the road allows hikers to contemplate the arduous journey of early settlers across the empty desert.

Views are somewhat limited by nearby slopes and ridges as you ascend, but you'll notice an increase in Mojave yucca on adjacent slopes. One mile from the fork of the canyon and 800 feet above the fort, the road tops out on the Piute Range at a saddle known as Piute Hill. From here broad vistas meet your gaze to the south, west, and north. The Mojave Road can be traced westward as it stretches away into the valley below.

From the hill the road winds steeply down the west slope amid abundant cholla and Mojave yucca. Hikers have the option of pro proceeding northwest, cross-country, for one mile to the trailhead where cars are visible below, or following the Mojave Road for .5 mile to the edge of the valley, crossing a fenceline enroute. From the juncture of the Mojave Road and the trailhead access road, hikers turn right and stroll .9 mile to the trailhead, in spring enjoying the lavender blooms of beavertail cactus and the yellow flowers of hymenoxis along the way.

HIKE 30 *KEYSTONE CANYON TO NEW YORK PEAK*

General description: A strenuous 4.5 mile day hike, part cross-country, to a remote mountain peak in the Mojave National Preserve, featuring distant panoramas, the opportunity for challenging rock climbing, and a rare stand of white fir trees.

Elevation gain and loss: 2,082 feet.

Trailhead elevation: 5,450 feet.

High point: New York Two Peak, 7,532 feet.

Maps: Ivanpah 15-minute USGS quad; or Ivanpah 7.5-minute USGS metric quad; or BLM New York Mts. Desert Access Guide, Map 9.

Season: Mid-April through mid-December (summers are hot but tolerable atop the peak).

Finding the trailhead: From Interstate 15, thirty seven miles northeast of Baker and fifty four miles southwest of Las Vegas, Nevada, take the Nipton Road exit, also signed for Searchlight. This paved road leads southeast for 3.6 miles to its juncture with Ivanpah Road, signed for Cima. Turn right and proceed south here, avoiding the right-forking Morning Star Mine Road after another 3.3 miles. Your road proceeds southeast toward the massive New York Mountains, eventually crossing the railroad tracks and jogging east. The pavement ends after another 8.6 miles, and the graded dirt road presently climbs over a low ridge. Bear right 4.7 miles from the pavement where the Hart Mine Road branches left. A one-lane dirt road forks right (southwest) 1.2 miles farther, where the Ivanpah Road begins a southeastward bend. Turning right onto this unsigned road, avoid a left-forking road almost at once, staying right on the wider road. Bear right again after .6 mile and reach a left-forking mining road 2.4 miles from the Ivanpah Road, just before dipping into the wash of Keystone Canyon. Another spur of the mining road forks left just past the wash, and since the main canyon road ahead is narrow with little parking space, and passable only to high clearance vehicles, most hikers should consider turning left here, proceeding the short distance to a wide parking area.

The hike: The scramble to New York Peak is not only a rewarding hike to vast panoramas on a mountain "island" in a desert "sea," it is also a trip into the past, where relict plant species survive from a time when the east Mojave enjoyed a cooler and wetter climate.

Surrounded by vast lowlands, desert ranges such as the New Yorks rise high enough to capture substantial moisture from passing Pacific storms, and in summer, as tropical moisture invades the region from Mexico, and rises on updrafts created by the mountain masses, thunderstorms are generated. Although the climate of the Mojave Desert has become considerably drier since the last Ice Age (approximately 10,000 years ago), the moisture those ranges are able to milk from passing storms is enough to nurture plant species that have long since retreated to more favorable climes, such as in the high ranges of southern California, for instance.

Silktassel and yerba santa, shrubs common on the damp coastal slopes in southern California, thrive in the higher elevations of the New York Mountains. But most unusual is the presence of a small stand of Rocky Mountain white fir near the crest of the range. This is a tree common in the montane forests in the southern Rocky Mountains, and a related species occurs in the coastal mountains from southern California northward to Oregon. It is found primarily above 6,000 feet where average annual precipitation may be double that which falls on the New Yorks. In the Mojave Desert, this tree is found only in the highest ranges: the Kingston, Providence, New York, and Clark Mountains which hosts the largest stand of 1,000 trees.

This hike should be undertaken only by hikers experienced in cross-country travel, route finding, and boulder scrambling. Experienced hikers can find a number of routes to the crest of the range, from where the summit is but a short scramble away. A variation of the described route goes by way of Keystone Spring, climbs a brushy draw southward to an east-trending limestone ridge, and follows that ridge west to the crest and on to the peak.

Whichever route you choose, carry a topo map and an ample water supply. The hike is most suitable as a day hike as there are few possible campsites enroute.

From the aforementioned parking area, proceed up the rough road into Keystone Canyon. Vegetation here is abundant and diverse, including one-leaved pinyon, Utah juniper, silktassel, turbinella oak, yerba santa, prince's plume, sagebrush, squawbush, Apache plume, cliffrose, and Mojave sage.

As the canyon turns south, imposing granite pinnacles crowning the New Yorks form a rugged backdrop to the wooded canyon. After .6 mile avoid

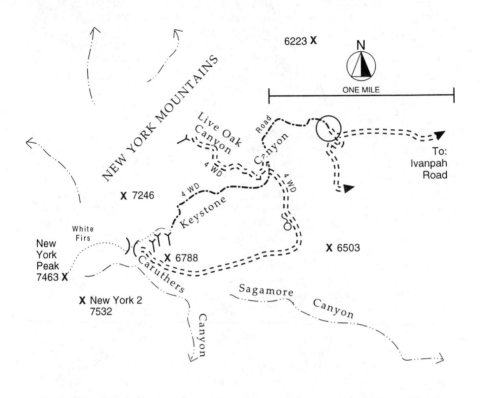

an old mining road that forks right, leading south, then west into Live Oak Canyon. One-tenth mile beyond is another junction. The left fork ascends a tributary canyon, ending after .25 mile at Keystone Spring, where another possible route to the peak begins.

But you should bear right, climbing higher into Keystone Canyon, which becomes increasingly wooded, presently including ceanothus, serviceberry, Mojave yucca, snowberry, and prickly pear in addition to previously cited flora. This old road becomes steep and severely eroded as it climbs to an abandoned small-scale copper mine and ends 1.5 miles from the trailhead. Old ore car tracks extend outward from the mine shaft, and the colorful copper ores of azurite (blue) and malachite (green) litter the ground nearby. Be sure not to drink the water seeping from this (or any other) mine shaft.

Ahead lies a strenuous, brushy scramble leading to the ridge above on the southwestern skyline. This area lies at the contact zone of the limestone that dominates the terrain to the east and the granite that is prevalent to the west. Two steep, southwest-trending gullies rise toward that ridge from the mine, and hikers can follow either to reach their objective.

The left-hand gully, cut into limestone, has remnants of an old mining trail, and passes two more mine shafts but is a rough scramble on loose rock with much bushwacking. The advantage of following the right hand gully is that it climbs through granite, offering more stable footing, but is equally brushy.

Ascending either gully, hikers will enjoy a neck-streching view of a prominent granite pinnacle looming boldly on the crest above. The climb ends after .2 mile, 500 feet above the mine, on a narrow saddle with a shallow prospect pit and more colorful copper ore. To gain the crest of the range, you leave the limestone ridge, climbing steep slopes westward among granite boulders, gaining another 500 feet in .25 mile. The footing is good, making this climb less strenuous than the last.

Turbinella oak dominates the understory here, while in spring cryptantha adds a touch of fleeting color. Juniper persists, but two-needle pinyon has supplanted its one-leaved cousin. Botanists consider this tree to also be a relict species in California, found only in the New Yorks and the Little San Bernardino Mountains in the California desert.

Finally, hikers attain the crest of the range just south of the towering granite pinnacle. From here follow the crest southwest, scrambling over and around the boulders that dot the ridge. You'll likely be entertained by flocks of colorful violet-green swallows as they swoop and soar among the crags.

When the crest begins to trend more toward the south, begin looking for a shady north-facing slope on your right. Upon this slope you'll see a few of the thirty white firs that grow among the thick forest of pinyons.

Ahead looms New York Peak, 7,463 feet, and to its left lies New York 2, 7,532 feet. Hikers not inclined to scale those crags may want to terminate their hike here along the crest. To reach either summit, continue along the rugged ridge. Class 3 and 4 routes are required to attain both peaks. More challenging routes on these peaks and nearby crags should appeal to any rockclimber.

While vistas from the summits are unsurpassed in all the Mojave Desert, those enjoyed from the crest are also far-reaching and panoramic. The broad Ivanpah Valley lies almost at your feet to the north, stretching past Ivanpah Dry Lake into Nevada. On the northern horizon are the Spring Mountains and lofty Charleston Peak. Far to the northeast and over 100 miles distant the Virgin Mountains form the horizon near the Utah border. Eastward beyond the invisible Colorado River trench rise the desert mountains of western Arizona. Southeastward, ranks of low mountains march into the distant haze of the Colorado Desert. Toward the southwest, the San Jacinto, San Bernardino, and San Gabriel Mountains form the horizon 125 miles distant, seen over a sea of arid desert ranges. Cima Dome and Teutonia Peak lie closer at hand to the west, and in the northwest rises the prominent bulk of Clark Mountain, and further still are Telescope Peak and the Panamint Mountains.

Hikers must eventually leave this rugged and remote range, carefully retracing their route to the trailhead.

HIKE 31 CIMA ROAD TO TEUTONIA PEAK

General description: An easy half-day hike, three miles round-trip in the Mojave National Preserve, leading to a rockbound vista point in the Mojave Desert, high on the flanks of Cima Dome.

Elevation gain and loss: 720 feet.

Trailhead elevation: 5,035 feet.

High point: Teutonia Peak, 5,755 feet.

Maps: Mescal Range 15-minute USGS quad (trail not shown on quad); or BLM New York Mts. Desert Access Guide, map 9.

Finding the trailhead: From Interstate 15, 23.5 miles northeast of Baker, take the Cima exit and bear south onto the Cima Road, quickly entering the East Mojave National Scenic Area. This paved road climbs steadily southeastward up the Shadow Valley toward the broad hogback of Cima Dome, reaching the trailhead parking area on the right hand (west) side of the road after 11.2 miles. If you reach a group of boulders on your left with a large white cross on them, you've gone .1 mile too far.

HIKE 31 CIMA ROAD TO TEUTONIA PEAK

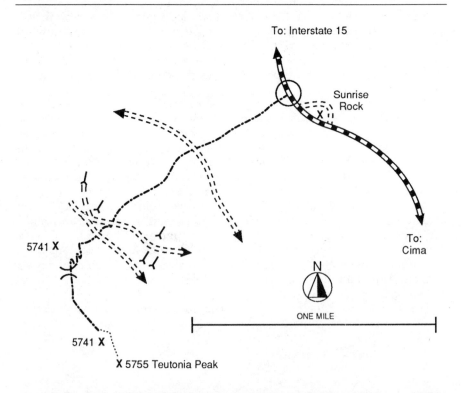

The hike: This very scenic hike passes through perhaps the most luxuriant Joshua Tree forest in the California desert, enroute to the craggy prominence of Teutonia Peak, the high point of unique Cima Dome. Hikers will be delighted by the abundance of flowering shrubs and wildflowers and enjoy expansive vistas of much of the east Mojave Desert.

Cima Dome is now protected as Wilderness in the Mojave National Preserve, making the area a fine choice for a short desert backpack.

With so many volcanic landforms in the California desert, Cima Dome may at first glance appear to be just another volcanic cone, but it isn't. Encompassing seventy-five square miles, Cima Dome is an ancient mountain range in the advanced stages of old age. Erosion of this range has completely enshrouded it in its own detritus, forming a remarkably symmetrical, broad sloping alluvial surface known to geologists as a pediment. Teutonia Peak and a few residual crags forming a northwest-trending ridge along the eastern margin of the dome are all that remain to remind us that a prominent mountain range once stood here.

Carry an ample water supply for this hike, and if you enjoy desert wildflowers, a good wildflower book will aid in identification of the diverse flora.

Approaching Teutonia Peak in the eastern Mojave Desert, a hiker contemplates the rewards of scrambling over trailside boulders to revel in the endless desert vistas that await.

From the trailhead proceed southwest along an old jeep road (closed to vehicles). Rising gently at first, you pass among scattered granite boulders and a forest of picturesque Joshua Trees. Among the abundant trailside flora you'll find Mojave sage, Mojave yucca, Indian paintbrush, Mormon tea, bladder sage, blackbrush, cholla, rockcress, cliffrose, spiny menodora, and boxthorn. After .5 mile you reach a fenceline at .5 mile and climb over it via a tall stile. Ignore the jeep road that follows the fence to the left and right. From here the boulder-stacked summit of the peak looms 500 feet above toward the southwest.

Proceed along the jeep trail for another .5 mile, where you will reach another jeep route forking right and left. Turn right, following the old road toward a fenced-off mine shaft. After about 500 yards, the trail turns left (southwest) off the road, soon reaching another fence and a jeep trail. Another site allows an easy crossing of the fence.

The trail leads you to the foot of the dome, where at 5,200 feet, you notice an increase in Utah junipers among the previously cited flora. Now you negotiate several switchbacks to attain the summit ridge at 5,400 feet. The trail climbs southeastward along or near the ridge, ending at about 5,700 feet just short of the tall crags of the north peak. The actual summit lies a short distant south, and a class 3 to 4 scramble is necessary to attain either summit.

Hikers not inclined to scale steep rock will nevertheless enjoy expansive vistas from the open ridge. Toward the southwest lies Cima Dome and beyond are the San Jacinto and San Bernadino mountains. Northwestward, Shadow Valley stretches toward the distant Kingston Range. To the north, Clark Mountain rises abruptly and to the east are the Ivanpah Mountains. To the southeast loom the New York Mountains. Toward the south notable landmarks include the Providence Mountains, the Kelso Dunes and the Granite Mountains.

After soaking up the tremendous panorama, simply retrace your steps to the trailhead.

HIKE 32 *KELSO DUNES*

General description: A unique half-day desert hike, three miles round-trip in the Mojave National Preserve, to the tallest sand dunes in the California desert.
Elevation gain and loss: 524 feet.
Trailhead elevation: 2,590 feet.
High Point: 3,114 feet.
Maps: Flynn 15-minute USGS quad; or BLM Providence Mts. Desert Access Guide, Map 12.
Season: October through April.
Finding the trailhead: From the Baker exit off Interstate 15, sixty-three miles northeast of Barstow, and ninety-one miles southwest of Las Vegas, turn right (east) onto signed Kelbaker Road. Another sign here indicates Kelso is thirty-five miles ahead and warns that no services are available for seventy-six miles, so be sure to have a full tank of gas and plenty of water. The Kelbaker Road, narrow but paved, eventually reaches the historic Kelso Depot after thirty-four miles, built in 1924. Ignore the Kelso-Cima Road, which forks left just before you

cross the Union Pacific Railroad tracks. Ahead the Kelbaker Road climbs a steady grade, passing the juncture with the unmaintained paved road leading southeast to the Vulcan Mine, an important source of iron ore during World War II. A sign indicating Kelso Dunes-3 is reached 7.6 miles from Kelso, and just north of the substation. Turn right (southwest) here onto the wide but rough dirt road and proceed 2.8 miles to a sign on the north (right hand) side of the road indicating parking. Hikers can park here or in another turnout just ahead.

From Interstate 40, fifty two miles west of Needles and seventy eight miles east of Barstow, hikers can take the Amboy-Kelso exit and follow the Kelbaker Road northeast for fourteen miles to the trailhead turnoff just beyond the power substation.

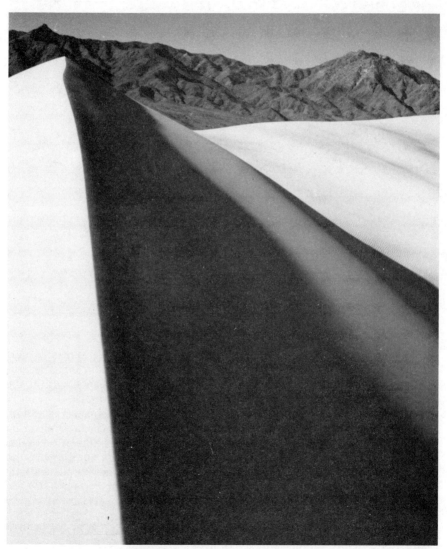

The Kelso Dunes, tallest of California's dune systems, contrast sweeping, wind-rippled slopes, brilliant white in the midday sun, with a backdrop of somber-hued desert mountain ranges.

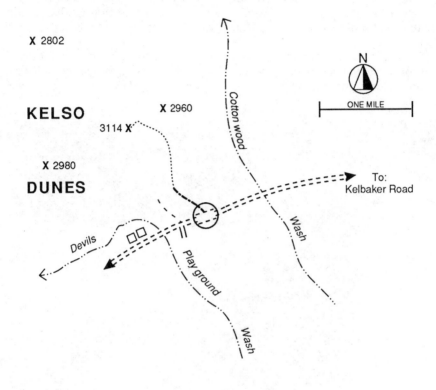

The hike: To many people, sand dunes represent the essential desert landscape. But dune systems are few and widely scattered in California's deserts, most of which are administered by the National Park Service within the California Desert Conservation District, a 25-million-acre expanse.

Surprisingly the vast, sandy expanse of the Kelso Dunes hosts vegetation, including many species growing solely in sandy environments. Colorful spring wildflowers and far-ranging vistas are major attractions of a hike in the Kelso Dunes, but their most interesting attribute is the booming, or rumbling sound the sand makes as hikers create miniature sand avalanches while walking along the narrow crest of the dunes.

To protect this fragile environment, the National Park Service has wisely chosen to bar access to off-road vehicles, including mountain bikes.

Even on a cool day, the sand reflects much light and heat, so carry plenty of water for this short but memorable jaunt.

Beginning from either parking area, well-worn trails lead northwest to the foot of the dunes. Once hikers reach the dunes they can wander at will, enjoying the unique experience of hiking on sand hills.

For far-ranging vistas, the 3,114-foot high point of the dunes beckons. Avoid the direct route up the steep slip face. Instead climb above the dunes' foothills to the skyline ridge just east of the high point, then follow the narrow sandy crest to the top.

This high point is a fine vantage point from which to appreciate the vast emptiness of the Mojave Desert. In the distant southwest horizon lies the San Gorgonio Wilderness, while closer are the barren Bristol Mountains. Stretching west to east are more dunes and far to the northwest lies Soda Dry Lake, the sump for the Mojave River. In the northeast rise the broad slopes of Cima Dome and farther still the high point in the Mojave Desert, Clark Mountain. Eastward lies the immense wall of the Providence Mountains.

From the high point of the dunes, either retrace your route or glissade down the steep sandy slopes to the trailhead.

HIKE 33 *COFFIN PEAK*

General description: An easy 2.5-mile round-trip half-day hike in Death Valley National Park, recommended for hikers with route-finding experience, to a mile high summit in the Black Mountains near Dante's View.

Elevation gain and loss: +553 feet, -220 feet.

Trailhead elevation: 5,200 feet.

High point: Coffin Peak, 5,503 feet.

Maps: Funeral Peak 15-minute USGS quad, or Death Valley National Park and Vicinity USGS quad.

Season: March through May, and October through early December.

Finding the trailhead: From the junction of State Highway 190 and Badwater Road just south of Furnace Creek Visitor Center in Death Valley, proceed eastward via State Highway 190 past the Furnace Creek Inn, following Furnace Creek Wash southeastward. After 3.5 miles the short spur road to Zabriskie Point (see Hike 34) forks right, but you continue on the highway to the signed junction with the road to Dante's View, 10.8 miles from Badwater Road. Turning right here you follow a canyon east of the Black Mountains, ignoring a left-forking road leading to Ryan and the Butte Mine enroute. Beyond the junction with the Greenwater Road (dirt) leading to Shoshone, your road climbs a broad alluvial surface, ascending steadily into the Black Mountains. 12.7 miles from State Highway 190 a sign indicates: no trailers beyond this point. Turn left (south) here and park in the wide turnout, featuring pit toilets and a picnic table. Dante's View lies .6 mile up the road, where incomparable vistas of Death Valley and the surrounding countryside have made that viewpoint famous.

The hike: Any experienced hiker driving to the magnificent viewpoint of Dante's View is urged to take the easy cross-country jaunt to Coffin Peak where equally unforgettable vistas can be enjoyed in solitude from this fine vantage point atop the Black Mountains. Not particularly notable for wildflowers, some desert trumpet and Indian paintbrush adorn this seldom-trod route.

This hike may entice some hikers to return for extended treks in the Black Mountains. Water sources are virtually nonexistent, and it is necessary to cache water along the crestline route. A southbound trek along the Black Mountains' crest offers endless panoramas, a true desert wilderness experience and access to old mine ruins, including the mining boom camp of Furnace. The Greenwater Road offers easy access to hikers establishing water caches.

The hike begins at the picnic site perched atop the crest of the range. Proceed over a minor hill, paralleling the Dante's View Road just north of east. A few creosote bushes persist here in the upper limits of their range, but vegetation on the hike is dominated by members of the Shadscale Scrub plant community. At this point Mormon tea, shadscale, and spiny menodora—typical rigid, spiny desert shrubs—dominate the arid upper reaches of the range along with abundant grasses.

HIKE 33   *COFFIN PEAK*

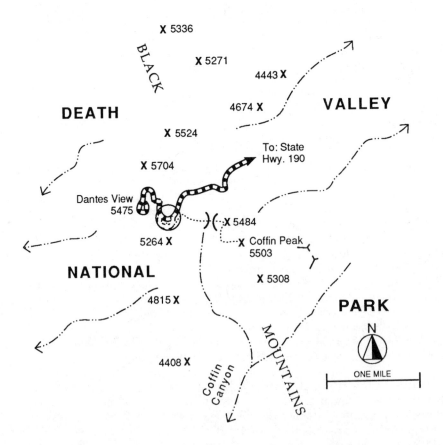

Soon the ridgecrest jogs southeast, and you presently climb the first major rocky hill, noting the debut of horsebrush and boxthorn among the previously cited shrubs. Topping out on this 5,360-foot hill, proceed east along the broad crest amid desert varnished boulders, enjoying views into Death Valley and the Panamint Mountains on one side and the prominent peaks of the southern Funeral Mountains on the other. Once over the next hill your route descends fifty feet northeastward to a saddle along the narrow crest, only to climb once again to Hill 5484, not so rocky as the last hill.

Past this broad summit the crestline route jogs south then east while hikers enjoy increasingly expansive views. The conical summit to the southeast is Coffin Peak, today's goal. Upon bending eastward a faint path can be utilized to avoid the rockiest section of the ridge as it drops to another saddle. A final ascent gaining 150 feet brings you to the commanding viewpoint of Coffin Peak.

The vista includes the dark peaks of the Black Mountains marching off toward the south and southeast, beckoning the adventurous to explore their seldom-visited environs. The broad expanse of the Greenwater Valley, clad in a perpetually green blanket of creosote bush, spreads out below to the east, and rising beyond are the eroded slopes of its namesake range. To the northeast, the prominent, colorfully layered southeastern peaks of the Funeral Mountains, featuring aptly named Pyramid Peak, foreground the distant Amargosa Desert. Charleston Peak and the lofty Spring Mountains rise to form the eastern skyline seventy miles away in Nevada. Toward the southeast, prominent desert mountains include the Nopah and Kingston ranges.

South slopes drop abruptly from the peak into the gaping maw of Coffin Canyon, its broad wash disappearing below into a narrow gorge flanked by the contorted red and black strata of the Copper Canyon conglomerate, a rock formation approximately 10 million years old. Beyond those colorful foothills Mormon Point juts out into the valley floor to the south, and at the southern end of the valley are the Owlshead Mountains.

The broad alluvial fans draping the foot of the Panamint Mountains to the west are some of the most extensive such fans in the Park. Those mountains, tilted eastward along an active fault zone, boast the greatest precipitation in the monument. That moisture has washed a great deal of debris that has eroded from the mountains, and subsequently deposited it at the eastern foot of the range as floodwaters lose velocity and dump first boulders, then gravel, and finally sand that, over time forms the fans.

Death Valley is also being tilted toward the east and is actively sinking in relation to the surrounding ranges. This tilting has pushed the salt pan, or playa, toward the foot of Black Mountains. The small fans at the foot of this range can be in part attributed to the relative youth of this fault block range, thus the fans have not had as much time to develop as those in the Panamints have.

The great relief of the eastern wall of the Panamints, rising 11,331 feet in fifteen lateral miles, is exceeded in only three other locations in North America. But the relief of the nearby Inyo Mountains and Sierra Nevada rivals that of the Panamints, with each range rising over 10,000 feet above their neighboring valleys. This is representative of the Great Basin landscape, where actively rising ranges abut actively sinking basins and valleys.

The sinking block of Death Valley, termed a graben by geologists, is presently the sump for the Amargosa River drainage, which arises northwest of Las Vegas in southwestern Nevada. In the past when the climate was wetter, 600-foot deep Lake Manly occupied Death Valley, fed not only by the waters of the Amargosa, but from the Owens and Mojave rivers as well.

Closer at hand, shadscale and grasses clothe the summit, while a few formidable barrel cactuses, and some boxthorn grow nearby.

On the northwestern skyline, Dante's View and its usual crowds of sightseers is in view but seemingly a world away.

After enjoying this isolated yet easily accessible locale, hikers usually backtrack to the trailhead.

HIKE 34 *GOLDEN CANYON TO ZABRISKIE POINT*

General description: A moderate three mile point-to-point (or six mile round trip) day hike in the Death Valley National Monument, touring the starkly beautiful badlands landscape that central Death Valley is famous for.

Elevation gain and loss: +980 feet, -100 feet.

Trailhead elevation: 160 feet below sea level.

High point: Zabriskie Point, 710 feet.

Maps: Furnace Creek 15-minute USGS quad.

Season: November through April.

Finding the trailhead: From the Furnace Creek Visitor Center on State Highway 190 in Death Valley, follow the highway south then east for 1.2 miles to a paved southbound road signed for Badwater. Proceed south on this road for two miles to a sign indicating Golden Canyon, where hikers turn left, reaching the parking area within 100 yards.

Hikers approaching the monument from the south should take the Baker exit off of Interstate 15 and follow State Highway 127 north for fifty-six miles to the small town of Shoshone. Two miles north of town turn left (west) onto State Highway 178. Follow this road for 68.8 miles to the Golden Canyon trailhead.

The hike: This spectacular low elevation hike tours the finest badlands scenery in the Park and makes a fine winter jaunt when many hiking areas are buried in snow. But beyond incredible scenery, the badlands of Golden Canyon offer insights into one of the more recent episodes of geologic history in the Park, a region that is rich in fully-exposed rock strata representing millions of years of earth history.

The initial 1.1 miles of the hike along the wash in Golden Canyon is a self-guiding nature trail. The trail guide available at the trailhead is keyed to numbered posts in the canyon, describing features along the way.

This canyon bottom segment is an easy jaunt for most any hiker, but the badlands can intensify the searing desert heat and should be avoided from mid-spring through mid-autumn. The segment from the canyon to Zabriskie Point is more demanding, with moderate climbing and no shade. Even during the cooler months, hikers should wear a hat and carry plenty of water.

Your trip to Zabriskie Point begins at the mouth of Golden Canyon, where bright red rocks quickly give way to dark brown conglomerate and layers of green mudstone. Remnants of the old oiled road that once enabled visitors

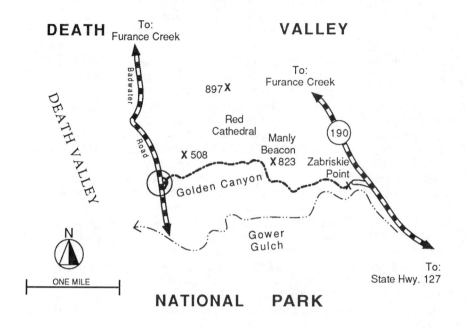

to drive through the canyon persist only along the initial .1 mile, the remainder having been washing away by infrequent but often torrential flash floods.

In fact, the likelihood of being rained on in the canyon is remote, considering the weather station at Furnace Creek records an average of only 1.65 inches of moisture annually. Moreover, entire years have passed without any significant moisture, giving Death Valley the distinction of being one of the driest regions in North America.

Shortly, yellow siltstones and mudstones dominate in the canyon. These soft rocks and those at the canyon's mouth are part of the Furnace Creek Formation, deposited in desert lake beds three to eight million years ago. These sediments contain evaporites, or salt deposits, which are formed as saline water evaporated. Borax is one of the evaporites present in these sediments, and the 20-mule team wagons that hauled borax out of the valley are a famous part of the region's history.

The canyon remains quite narrow throughout its length, wedged between broken cliffs and badlands slopes. It is seemingly lifeless, save for the buzzing of a few insects and ravens soaring and croaking among the hills and cliffs.

As you proceed, the fluted cliffs of Red Cathedral, at the head of the canyon, loom even closer. Sighting a striking yellow pinnacle rising skyward to the east (Manly Beacon) you soon reach a post indicating the hiking trail, 1.1 miles from the trailhead. At this point, hikers can either return to the trailhead, continue up the canyon for .6 mile to the foot of Red Cathedral, or turn right onto the trail bound for Zabriskie Point.

Hikers turning right follow the trail into the heart of the badlands via a narrow gully. Ignore the numerous use trails climbing nearby slopes. Soon the trail climbs steeply to a sidehill ascent beneath the face of Manly Beacon, topping out on a 480-foot saddle. Superb views, framed by the badlands of Golden Canyon, extend westward to the mesquite-fringed salt pan of Death Valley and to the Panamint Mountains beyond. The upthrust strata flanking Golden Canyon are seen in raw detail—truly a landscape standing on edge. Southward, the colorful Black Mountains rise abruptly above the extensive badlands, which stretch eastward toward your goal, Zabriskie Point.

Amid a confusion of use trails, an arrow sign in the gully below to the south indicates the correct route. Descending at first, the trail then undulates through the badlands to a wash feeding Gower Gulch. This area is fun to explore (on a cool day) and hikers reaching Gower Gulch may notice evidence that the canyon is occasionally swept by an unusually large amount of runoff for a canyon with such a small drainage area. The reason is the Park Service has diverted Furnace Creek Wash into the gulch just south of Zabriskie Point to protect the developments at Furnace Creek from destructive flash floods.

Arrow signs help guide hikers over hills and across gullies to the trail's terminus at Zabriskie Point, 50 yards west of the parking area. From the point, the eroded badlands are seen in their entirety, foregrounding distant view of Death Valley and the immense bulk of the Panamint Mountains.

Hikers who haven't arranged a car shuttle to Zabriskie Point much retrace the route to the Golden Canyon trailhead.

Hikers camping in the desert must take special precautions to insure their safety in one of California's harshest, most unforgiving environments. Photo by Rick Marvin.

HIKE 35 *MOSAIC CANYON*

General description: A moderately easy round trip day hike of 3.5 miles or more in Death Valley National Park, following a narrow, highly scenic canyon on the north slopes of Tucki Mountain, just south of Stovepipe Wells in Death Valley.

Elevation gain and loss: 1,050 feet.

Trailhead elevation: 950 feet.

High point: 2,000 feet.

Maps: Stovepipe Wells 15-minute USGS quad, or Death Valley National Park and Vicinity, USGS quad.

Season: October through April.

Finding the trailhead: From Stovepipe Wells Village on State Highway 190, 69 miles east of Olancha and U.S. Highway 395, and twenty-two miles northwest of Furnace Creek, proceed west along the highway to the Mosaic Canyon sign and turn south. This dirt road is passable to passenger cars, but it is quite rough as it steadily ascends a broad, creosote bush-clad alluvial fan for 2.3 miles to the trailhead at the mouth of the canyon.

The hike: Canyons in the Park offer endless opportunities for both day hiking and for venturing deep into mountain ranges on extended backpacks. Erosion in the often narrow canyons has exposed the rock strata in intricate detail, particularly in Mosaic Canyon, one of the most easily accessible canyons in Death Valley.

This canyon is a moderately popular day hiking area, owing to its proximity to the Stovepipe Wells tourist complex and its easy access. There is no trail in Mosaic Canyon; hikers simply follow the wash as far as their desire and ability will allow.

Keep an eye out for sidewinders, the only poisonous snake in the Park. Although they aren't as common here as in other canyons, be alert when scrambling over and around dry falls in the upper reaches of the canyon. If rain or thunderstorms threaten then flash floods are a possibility and the hike should be aborted. As always, carry plenty of water on any desert hike.

From the trailhead, quickly drop into the canyon and follow the gravel bed of the wash upstream. Tucki Mountain's broken cliffs soar nearly a mile above. The wash quickly leads hikers into a narrow chasm where beautiful stream-polished marble and mosaic breccia are well-exposed. Much of the breccia (a formation composed of angular rock fragments recemented into stone) contains stream-polished marble set in a mosaic pattern.

After .3 mile the canyon jogs east and widens a bit. Notice the stratified (layered) nature of the marble here. It is rock formed by the metamorphism of limestone and dolomite (sedimentary rocks). Local faulting has tilted the layers upward toward the west.

All through the canyon the soaring, broken cliffs of Tucki Mountain, virtually devoid of vegetation, are reminiscent of a landscape on the surface of the moon.

Along this eastbound stretch, a use trail shortcuts the wash, where desertholly and desert trumpet make a fleeting appearance. But soon the canyon turns toward the south, becoming quite narrow once again. At one point

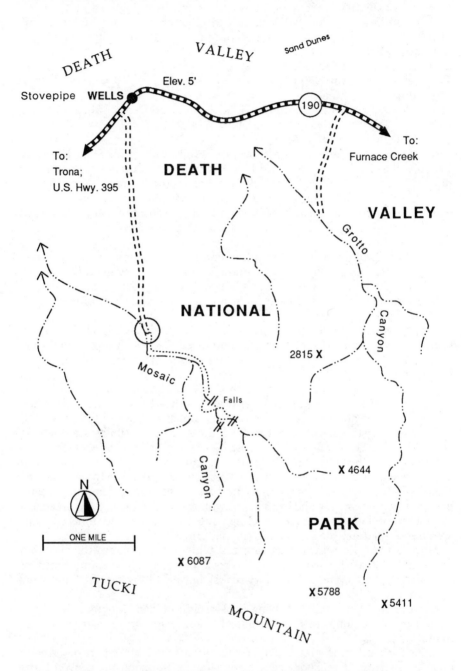

DEATH VALLEY Sand Dunes

Stovepipe **WELLS** Elev. 5'

190

To:
Trona;
U.S. Hwy. 395

To:
Furnace Creek

DEATH

Grotto

VALLEY

NATIONAL

Mosaic

2815 X

Canyon

Falls

N

Canyon

X 4644

ONE MILE

PARK

X 6087

X 5788

X 5411

TUCKI

MOUNTAIN

numerous boulders composed of breccia are wedged into the narrow gorge, forcing brief detours. The wash becomes even more narrow up ahead, and several low slickrock dry falls must be climbed. Some hikers may wish to terminate their hike here.

Along this narrow stint hikers will enjoy excellent exposures of mosaic breccia, while gray marble dominates the wash up ahead. After 1.25 miles hikers encounter an impassable eighteen-foot dry fall, but it is easily bypassed via a use trail climbing the right hand slope about fifty yards downstream.

Many deep canyons offer easy access into the rugged mountains that surround Death Valley. Here hikers enjoy a leisurely stroll in Mosaic Canyon, a popular day hike near Stovepipe Wells.

There may be cairns indicating the route, which climbs above a ledge of marble amid creosote bush and Mormon tea.

At 1.5 miles Mosaic Canyon forks abruptly southward, but is quickly blocked by a 12-foot dry fall (passable via a Class 3 ledge). Above it becomes increasingly rugged. The larger canyon forking eastward soon requires a scramble over a four-foot dry fall, and 150 yards beyond a high dry fall further impedes progress. Although passable via a Class 4 climb, average hikers will probably want terminate their excursion here, pausing to soak up the barren yet majestic beauty of this desert canyon before backtracking to the trailhead.

HIKE 36 *WILDROSE CANYON TO WILDROSE PEAK*

General description: A moderate 8.4-mile round-trip day hike or overnighter to a lofty Panamint Mountains summit in Death Valley National Monument, from which hikers can see the highest and lowest points of land in the conterminus U.S.

Elevation gain and loss: 2,294 feet, -100 feet.

Trailhead elevation: 6,870 feet.

High point: Wildrose Peak, 9,064 feet.

Maps: Emigrant Canyon and Telescope Peak 15-minute USGS quads, or Death Valley Park and Vicinity USGS quad (trail not shown on quads).

Season: Mid-April through November.

Finding the trailhead: Proceed to the Wildrose Ranger Station in Wildrose Canyon, located in the western reaches of the Park. To get there, follow State Highway 178 east from Ridgecrest, then north past Trona and into the Panamint Valley. After driving 52.6 miles, bear right onto the paved road signed for Wildrose. You'll reach the junction with the northbound Emigrant Canyon Road after another 8.8 miles. Alternately, from State Highway 190 eight miles southwest of Stovepipe Wells Village in Death Valley, follow the southbound Emigrant Canyon Road through the Panamints for 20.6 miles to the aforementioned junction. A sign at the junction indicates that Wildrose Campground (open all year, with water and thirty campsites at 4,100 feet) is .25 mile, and the Charcoal Kilns are six miles east (up the canyon).

Proceeding generally eastward from that junction, you soon pass the campground and ranger station, following the narrow paved road as it climbs into the broad valley of Wildrose Canyon. The pavement ends after five miles, and the wide but rough dirt road leads another two miles to a wide turnout opposite the charcoal kilns. Park here.

The hike: Of the few established trails that exist in the vast reaches of the Park, most are very short nature trails that barely scratch the surface of the Death Valley hiking experience. Death Valley hiking is desert hiking and caching water is a necessity for extended treks. By contrast, the two moderately long maintained trails to Telescope and Wildrose peaks offer a mountain hiking experience.

The lofty Panamint Mountains stand high enough to bear the distinction of being the wettest area in the Park. This island of high country hosts vast stands of pinyon-juniper woodland, and atop 11,049-foot Telescope Peak, a forest of bristlecone pine.

Aside from the sweeping vistas enjoyed from Wildrose Peak, the most notable features of this hike are the ten charcoal kilns at the trailhead. Constructed in 1876, the kilns supplied charcoal from the pinyon-juniper forests of Wildrose Canyon to the Modoc Mine in the Argus Range, twenty miles distant across the Panamint Valley. The charcoal was necessary to process lead and silver ore. A pamphlet available at the trailhead describes the history of the kilns in detail.

This hike begins at the kilns, climbs through woodlands among which are scattered stumps dating back to the mining days, to the crest of the Panamints and ultimately to Wildrose Peak where an awe-inspiring panorama of desert and mountains unfolds. The popular trail to Telescope Peak, beginning a rough two miles up the road from the Charcoal Kilns, often remains closed by snow until mid to late May in most years. But the trail to Wildrose Peak, even though it climbs above 9,000 feet, opens up much earlier due to its southern exposure, and the vistas enjoyed from its summit rival those obtained from nearby Telescope. Even during summer when Death Valley is sizzling in 120-plus degree heat, Wildrose Peak remains relatively cool and is a pleasant jaunt until the snow flies.

Be sure to carry an adequate water supply. Flies and gnats can be bother-some during the summer. Hikers intending to stay overnight should bear in mind that camping is permitted no closer than five miles from a maintained campground and one mile from maintained roads. Since Thorndike Camp is

These beehive-shaped charcoal kilns, located at the Wildrose Peak trailhead, offer hikers a glimpse into the colorful history of the region before they begin their climb to the magnificent viewpoint in the Panamint Mountains.

only one mile above the trailhead (eight campsites, no water) backpackers must hike at least as far as the peak before establishing a campsite. A backcountry camping map is available at the visitor center at Furnace Creek to assist hikers in planning backpacking trips in the Park.

The trail begins just northwest of the kilns, indicated by a small sign. An easy traverse ensues, passing above Wildrose Canyon amid a woodland of Utah juniper and singleleaf pinyon, where sagebrush and Mormon tea form a scattered understory. From the start, views are magnificent. Westward lies the rugged High Sierra, from Mt. Whitney southward beyond solitary Olancha Peak, framed by the broad foreground valley of Wildrose Canyon. That formidable alpine barrier, capped by giant granite crags and perpetually white with snow is especially attractive on a hot summer day. Beyond the trough of the Panamint Valley to the west lies the Argus Range, former site of the Modoc and other rich mines, which blocks the remainder of the southern Sierra from view.

Notice that numerous trailside junipers are host to the parasitic plant juniper mistletoe, which may eventually kill some of these gnarled high desert trees.

Proceeding into a shallow wooded canyon, the trail, apparently an old road, descends slightly to reach the canyon bottom where, after .9 mile, it joins with another old road (closed) southwestbound down the canyon. Bearing right the grade becomes mode rate as you ascend northeastward.

Scattered stumps upslope to the south may be remnants of the trees cut during the heyday of the charcoal kilns, still well-preserved in the dry climate of the Panamints.

After 1.2 miles the trail passes a USGS water level recording device, and a pause here reveals a fine view southward to the north slopes of lofty Rogers Peak, named for a member of the ill-fated party of settlers who became stranded in Death Valley in 1850. That peak's slopes, scarred by a road serving a transmitting facility, hosts snowfields that last through May in most years.

Beyond, cliffrose makes it debut among the understory, and in May penstemon decorates trailside slopes. The route soon narrows to a trail and rises steeply under the partial shade of the thick pinyon-juniper woodland. Presently, old man prickly pear, bearing an armor of formidable spines, and buckwheat further diversify the understory.

After 1.8 miles the trail attains the crest of the Panamints at a 7,750-foot saddle then begins a traverse upon the east-facing slopes where hikers capture vignettes of the vast white playa on Death Valley's floor, lying 8,000 feet below. The Spring Mountains in southwestern Nevada, crowned by 11,918-foot Charleston Peak, forms the distant eastern horizon when not obscured by late spring and summer heat haze.

At first the trail gives away a little elevation, but it soon begins climbing once again upon crunchy metamorphic rocks, where the woodland briefly thins out, presently dominated by compact, conical pinyons, offering even better views into the valley and the desert ranges beyond.

The grade soon eases as you regain the crest at 8,000 feet where your destination, the broad dome of Wildrose Peak, looms closely ahead. The trail now climbs upon wooded south-facing slopes where the views of Rogers Peak and forested Telescope Peak are enjoyed. Dropping slightly into a wide saddle, hikers gear up for the final 900-foot ascent.

The trail then climbs steeply on or just north of the crest where a few switchbacks help to ease the grade. Prickly pear, sagebrush, buckwheat, lupine,

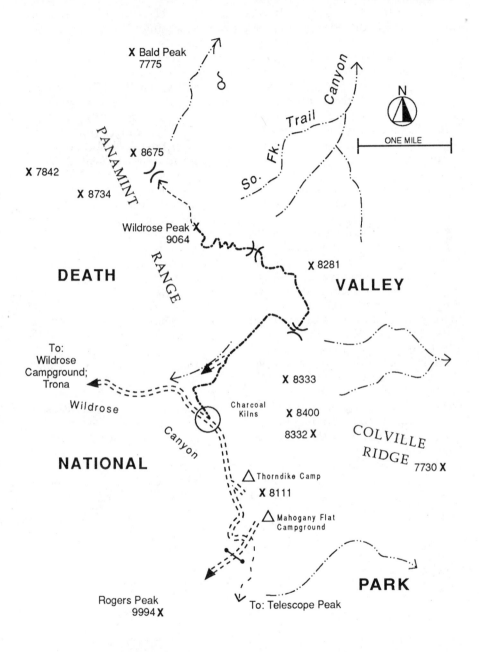

X Bald Peak
7775

Canyon

Trail

So. Fk.

N

ONE MILE

X 8675

X 7842

X 8734

PANAMINT

Wildrose Peak **X**
9064

X 8281

DEATH

RANGE

VALLEY

To:
Wildrose
Campground;
Trona

X 8333

Wildrose

Charcoal
Kilns

X 8400

8332 **X**

Canyon

COLVILLE
RIDGE 7730 **X**

NATIONAL

△ Thorndike Camp

X 8111

△ Mahogany Flat
Campground

PARK

Rogers Peak
9994 **X**

To: Telescope Peak

and some penstemon grow on the rocky slopes amid scattered pinyons. Hikers may notice that the junipers, preferring lower and drier elevations, are absent at this point.

Soon the trail begins switchbacking in earnest, elevating hikers beyond the last wind-flattened pinyons and onto a false summit. Proceeding gently along the open, rocky crest, you reach the peak after another .2 mile.

From the small but flat summit area where sagebrush, Mormon tea, and prickly pear thrive, an unobstructed 360-degree panorama unfolds; more than ample reward for your efforts. Nearly the full length of Death Valley spreads out at your feet, stretching ninety miles from northwest to southeast. Beyond it rises the barren Amargosa Range, separated by fault zones into three distinct sub-ranges. Beyond it are other desert ranges, the Nopah, Resting Spring, Kingston Spring, and others fading into the distant heat haze of the California and Nevada desert. The tree-clad oasis of Furnace Creek stands out on the searing flats of Death Valley below to the northeast.

Directly below to the northeast exceedingly steep slopes, briefly clad in pinyon-juniper woodland, fall away into the South Fork of Trail Canyon, where a few old mine buildings reflect the desert sun nearly 5,000 feet below. Beyond Trail Canyon, the layered east slopes of the Panamints are seen dipping steeply toward the east, indicating that portion of this fault-laced range is being downdropped along its eastern side. Just west of those layered slopes, the dirt road ending at Aguerreberry Point is visible. Hikers who so desire can continue beyond the peak, following the crest of the range to that road, preferably with a car shuttle. Northwest the Panamints merge with the massive Cottonwood Mountains, plunging over 1.5 vertical miles into Death Valley. Further still are the White Mountains, crowned by 14,246-foot White Mountain Peak.

Barely a silver of the Panamint Valley is visible to the west, above which rises the Argus Range and Inyo Mountains. But on the western horizon is perhaps the most inspiring vista of all, the jagged summits of the Sierra Nevada, stretching from the Palisades in the northwest to Owens Peak in the southwest, and including the incomparable heights of Mt. Whitney.

Far to the south past the eroded ranges of the Mojave Desert are the San Gabriel Mountains.

Much can be said of the rewards of camping near Wildrose Peak, where hikers enjoy vast panoramas in the changing light of day, not to mention the glorious sunrises over the desert ranges and sunsets over the Sierra. From the peak simply retrace your steps to the trailhead.

HIKE 37 *HELL'S GATE TO DEATH VALLEY BUTTES*

General description: A moderate four-mile round-trip, cross-country day hike in Death Valley National Park, for experienced hikers, to a panoramic vista point along the eastern edge of Death Valley.

Elevation gain and loss: 1,132 feet, -375 feet.

Trailhead elevation: 2,260 feet.

High point: 3,017 feet.

Maps: Chloride Cliff and Stovepipe Wells 15-minute quads, or Death Valley National Park and Vicinity USGS quad

Season: October through April.

Finding the trailhead: This hike begins at Hell's Gate, a road junction and rest stop partway between Death Valley and Beatty, Nevada. To get there, follow State Highway 190 east from Stovepipe Wells for 8.7 miles to the junction with the northbound road to Scotty's Castle, and turn left (northwest), proceeding .7 mile to another junction. A sign here indicates Beatty, and hikers should turn right (northeast), following the paved road through Mud Canyon's badlands hills for 6.5 miles to the large parking area and road junction at Hell's Gate, where picnic tables and Death Valley information are available.

From the east, Nevada Hwy. 374 leaves U.S. 95 in Beatty, leading 19 miles to the trailhead via Daylight Pass.

From the Furnace Creek Visitor Center, follow State Hwy. 190 northwest for 11 miles to the Beatty cutoff, turn right, reaching the trailhead after 10 miles.

The hike: Hikers with a desire to gain broad vistas of Death Valley must usually commit themselves to one or more days of trailless desert walking to reach the distant peaks of the surrounding mountains. But the short scramble to Death Valley Buttes, three prominent hills at the foot of the Grapevine Mountains, should appeal to hikers without the time or energy required for such demanding treks. For a modicum of effort, this short hike provides the feeling of accomplishment gained by forging your own route across a trailless desert ridge, where the sweeping panoramas of central Death Valley and the tall mountains nearby are ample reward.

The buttes are eroded remnants of the Grapevine Mountains, buried by detritus derived from that range as a result of erosion.

In a region as arid as Death Valley (Furnace Creek averages a scant 1.65 inches of moisture annually) little vegetation exists to control erosion, and over time fans of alluvium coalesce to form a continuous apron of debris at the foot of mountains, known to geologists as bahadas. As the mountains continue to erode, lower ridges are eventually buried in alluvium, until only isolated hills rise above this "sea" of sand, gravel, and boulders. In this phase of development, the alluvial surface is termed a pediment. Death Valley Buttes are surrounded by such a pediment, a vast sloping surface that stretches for miles along the foot of the Grapevine and Funeral mountains. Other examples of a pediment and remnant mountains can be seen west of Ubehebe Crater on the flanks of the Last Chance Range.

The route to the buttes is straightforward and easy to follow, but the narrow rocky ridge that must be climbed is recommended only for experienced hikers. The hike can be taken as a round trip, or done as a loop. The area can be quite cool in winter and very hot at times during spring and fall.

Hikers are likely to become dehydrated in the dry desert air, even on such a short hike as this, so carry plenty of water.

From Hell's Gate, proceed cross-country toward the buttes in a south-westerly direction. Quite soon you are likely to encounter remnants of the old phone line the connected the mining boom towns of Rhyolite (near Beatty, Nevada) and Skidoo, high in the Panamint Mountains to the southwest, around the turn of the century.

A .6 mile jaunt across the cobble-strewn pediment allows hikers to become familiar with shrubs typcial of the creosote bush scrub plant community, the most ubiquitous assemblage of shrubs in the California desert below 5,000 feet. Perpetually green creosote bush dominates and is especially attractive when covered with yellow blooms in early spring. Also common are bursage, desertholly saltbush, and beavertail cactus, which brightens the landscape with its delicate rose-colored springtime blooms.

Rising toward the buttes, the desert trumpet with its unusual bulbous stems, makes an interesting addition to the scattered groundcover.

A profusion of tiny yellow flowers decorates the creosote bush—California's most ubiquitous desert shrub—each year with the onset of Spring.

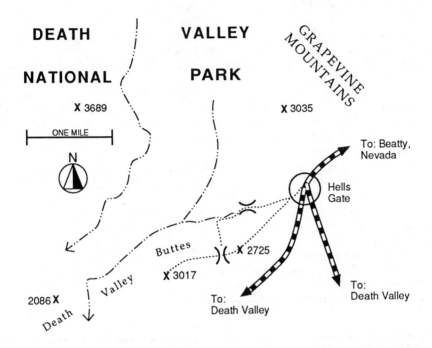

Soon, hikers should leave the gentle terrain and scramble southward to the prominent ridgeline emanating from the easternmost butte. Upon attaining the crest, follow it westward over a few minor summits. The loose and broken rock makes for poor footing.

You may notice that creosote bush has presently been left behind, but desertholly saltbush persists on the dry and rocky ridge. This plant prefers dry, alkaline slopes and washes, and is quite common below 3,000 feet in the Death Valley region. Brittlebush decorates the slopes of the buttes with its large yellow blooms in early spring.

Approaching the easternmost butte, a semblance of a climber's trail helps to avoid more rugged sections of the narrow crest, and soon you reach the 2,725-foot summit, one mile from Hell's Gate. Vistas are breathtaking, surveying a vast sweep of desert and mountain scenery. The apex of the buttes, Peak 3017, blocks much of the westward view, but in other directions there are no obstructions.

From here hikers have the option of backtracking to the trailhead or continuing on to the next, and highest, summit. To proceed, carefully descend the steep ridge west to a saddle at 2,450 feet. Ahead the narrow ridge ascends 500 feet in .6 mile to Peak 3017.

You will be rewarded for your efforts as you gaze out upon the immense landscape of Death Valley. From the northwest to northeast, the Grapevine Mountains reach skyward, exceeding 6,000 feet. This range receives so little precipitation that not even a single juniper can be seen in the highest reaches. The prominent, colorful peak to the north-northeast is Corkscrew Peak, about 6,000 feet. This mountain would make a fine destination for a strenuous day hike or overnighter. The route is plainly visible from this vantage point, following the broad alluvial fan northward from Hell's Gate.

The equally barren Funeral Mountains stretch far into the southeastern distance. The extensive playa on the valley floor, glistening white with salt and alkali reaches southeastward toward Badwater, which at -282 feet, is the lowest point on the continent. The impossibly high barrier of the Panamint Mountains rises above the valley in stark relief. The high point of the range, 11,049-foot Telescope Peak, will be sparkling with residual spring snow while the valley may be baking in 100-degree heat.

The road leading to the valley from Hell's Gate points westward toward massive Tucki Mountain, and north of there lie the sprawling sand dunes of Mesquite Flat. The Cottonwood Mountains form the western horizon, an immense, barren wall rising over 8,000 feet from the valley floor.

Hikers at this point can either return the same way to the trailhead, or consider leaving the crest at the above-mentioned 2,450-foot saddle. From there a possible route descends north to the valley below the buttes and then leads eastward north of the buttes and back to the trailhead. Enroute, hikers who keep their eyes peeled may find several sleeping circles, presumably used by native peoples during their hunting-gathering-trading forays through the valley.

HIKE 38 *THE RACETRACK TO UBEHEBE PEAK*

General description: A moderate four-mile round-trip day hike to a remote desert peak in the northwest corner of Death Valley National Park.
Elevation gain and loss: 2,168 feet; -200 feet.
Trailhead elevation: 3,710 feet.
High point: Ubehebe Peak, 5,678 feet.
Maps: Ubehebe Peak 15-minute USGS quad (trail not shown on quad), or Death Valley Park and Vicinity USGS quad.
Season: October through May (expect occasional light snow during winter).
Finding the trailhead: Follow State Highway 190 to Furnace Creek on the floor of Death Valley, 120 miles from Baker, 110 miles from Ridgecrest, and ninety miles from Olancha and Lone Pine. The visitor center and Death Valley Museum are located here, where books, maps, and information are available. Proceed northwest along the paved highway, following signs that indicate Scotty's Castle and Ubehebe Crater. Forty-eight miles from Furnace Creek is the Grapevine Entrance Station, where an entry fee is collected. Proceed .1 mile beyond, turning left where a sign indicates Ubehebe Crater. The right-forking road leads to Scotty's Castle and eventually joins U.S. Hwy. 95 in Nevada after twenty-eight miles. Your paved road heads northwest across upper Death Valley. Avoid the signed dirt road leading to Big Pine (75 miles) after 2.7 miles. After another 2.8 miles, turn right onto a dirt road signed for

Racetrack. On your return, the loop road will take you to the rim of immense Ubehebe Crater, 500 feet deep and nearly .5 mile across. Trails lead into the crater, and another climbs .5 mile above to Little Hebe Crater. Both are worthwhile excursions if you have the time and energy. Presently the road climbs 2,500 feet in eleven miles upon a broad alluvial surface between the Cottonwood and Last Chance ranges. The road typically has a rough washboard surface and occasional deep gravel. Passenger cars occasionally make the trip, but a high clearance vehicle is recommended. After the road tops out on a Joshua tree-clad saddle, it descends gradually for eight miles to Teakettle Junction, where you bear right. After another 5.7 miles you reach a turnout on the right (west) side of the road opposite an interpretive sign on the edge of the Racetrack playa. The hike begins here.

The hike: Ubehebe Peak, rising to a modest 5,678 feet at the southern end of the remote Last Chance Range, is an obscure summit that probably escapes the notice of many visitors traveling to this isolated corner of the monument, most of whom make the long, rough journey to contemplate the mysterious trails left behind by the sliding rocks of the Racetrack.

At 3,700 feet, the Racetrack is one of the highest elevation dry lakes in the Park. Its shimmering white surface is highlighted at its northern end by the Grandstand, a cluster of gray boulders buried deeply in lake bed sediments. But despite the interpretive sign opposite the Grandstand, this is not the best spot on the playa to see evidence of the "racing" rocks. After climbing Ubehebe Peak, drive two miles to the southern end of the playa and walk eastward toward the foot of prominent Peak 4560. Rocks eroded from this steep mountain, including some large boulders, have left many noticeable tracks on the playa surface. The phenomena is not fully understood, but apparently the rocks move when the lake bed is slickened by abundant rainfall and swept by strong winds of 70 m.p.h. or more.

Hikers on the summit of Ubehebe Peak are treated to an aerial-like view of the Racetrack and panoramic vistas ranging from lofty Sierra Nevada peaks to sunken desert flats. Spring wildflowers and shrubs from two distinct life zones are well represented along the old mining trail that climbs to the crest of the range. To attain the summit of Ubehebe Peak, a brief Class 2 to 3 scramble is necessary, but hikers who choose to forego the scramble will still enjoy broad vistas from the open crest. This is a typically dry desert hike, so be sure to carry an ample water supply.

The trail begins west of the parking area. Faint at first, it soon becomes obvious as its rock-lined course leads west, climbing gently up the alluvial fan at the foot of Ubehebe Peak, the prominent knob rising nearly 2,000 feet above and less than one mile distant. The fan is clothed in creosote bush, and the intriguing desert trumpet briefly decorates trailside slopes before the trail jogs northwest.

Presently the trail climbs steadily beneath the broken desert-varnished cliffs of imposing Peak 5519. Broken rock along the trail attests to the natural gray color of the rocks in this portion of the Last Chance Range.

Above the fan, endless switchbacks ensue, climbing the rocky slope on a moderately steep grade. Creosote bush dominates here, but buckwheat, bunchgrass, and the showy yellow spring blooms of Death Valley goldeneye are also common.

Finally you negotiate two final switchbacks while passing through a band of limestone where colorful malachite, a blue-green copper ore, is exposed in a shallow prospect pit. After hiking 1.5 miles you surmount the crest of the Last Chance Range at 4,950 feet, where you can pause and enjoy well-earned panoramas of deserts and distant mountains. Peaks to the north are inviting and easily climbed, but the best views are those captured from Ubehebe Peak, only .5 mile south.

From the saddle, the trail is less well-defined as it climbs steadily very near the crest of the range. As you gain elevation, creosote bush is left behind, and

Hikers enroute to remote Ubehebe Peak will enjoy crag-framed views of The Racetrack playa, home of the mysterious sliding rocks.

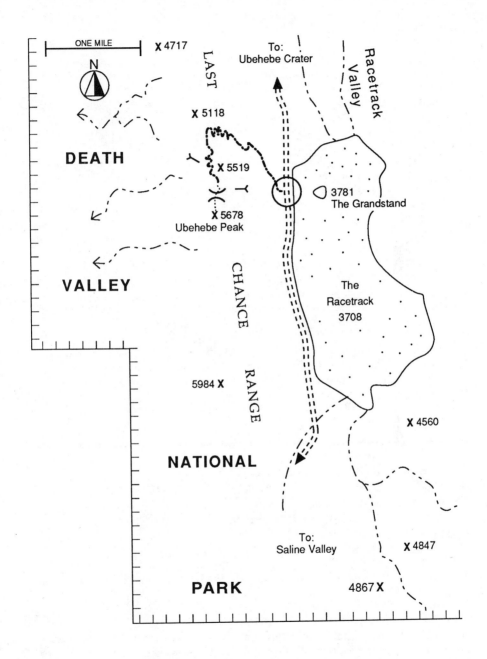

presently the vegetation is dominated by horsebrush and boxthorn. The latter is a rigid spiny shrub with small, succulent gray-green leaves. Its spine-tipped branches are an adaptation typical of succulent (and some non-succulent) desert plants to protect their moist foliage from thirsty wildlife. These two shrubs are indicators of the Shadscale Scrub plant community of the northern Mojave Desert, generally found between 3,000 and 6,000 feet elevation.

The trail switchbacks a few times above another prospect pit, its blue-green copper ore contrasting with the surrounding desert varnish-stained slopes and the dull green shrubs. The trail soon climbs to a rocky shoulder just short of peak 5,519, a short easy scramble to your left. Here the trail fades into obscurity, and hereafter hikers must choose their own route. The logical course follows a short scrambling traverse to a rocky knoll atop the crest. Eastward, broken cliffs plummet nearly 2,000 feet into the broad expanse of The Racetrack.

The knob of Ubehebe Peak lies a short distance south along the crest. But to reach it, you must first carefully follow this narrow rocky ridge as it descends 200 feet into a saddle, then negotiate the class 2-3 ridge, quickly gaining 470 feet. The small summit area, composed of quartz-poor granite rock, offers an unobstructed and particularly striking eagle's eye panorama. The Last Chance Range is a sub-range of the more extensive Panamint Range, and its steep flanks, typical of Great Basin ranges, rises steeply and abruptly on either side to a narrow crest. The deep trough of Saline Valley lies 4,500 feet below to the west, and beyond it soars the 10,000-foot eastern wall of the Inyo Mountains, punctuated by a crest of lofty, pointed summits. This range is one of only four California mountain ranges boasting over 10,000 feet of vertical relief. Still farther west are a few snowy peaks of the Sierra.

Eastward, beyond the Racetrack and its namesake valley, the colorfully banded, barren wall of the Cottonwood Mountains rears abruptly skyward to a crest of 7,000 to 8,000-foot desert peaks. The view southeastward includes the extensive wooded plateau of 7,454-foot Hunter Mountain. From this peak, simply return to your car.

HIKE 39 *BIG FALLS CANYON*

General description: An easy 2.5-mile round-trip day hike in the Santa Lucia Wilderness to a beautiful cascading creek in the South Coast Ranges.
Elevation gain and loss: 280 feet.
Trailhead elevation: 800 feet.
High point: 1,080 feet.
Maps: Lopez Mountain 7.5-minute USGS quad, Los Padres National Forest map.
Season: Mid-October through May.
Finding the trailhead: From U.S. 101 in Arroyo Grande, fifteen miles south of San Luis Obispo and fifteen miles north of Santa Maria, take the Lopez Lake exit and go east on State Highway 227, following signs pointing to Lopez Lake. After driving .9 mile from U.S. 101, turn right and leave State Highway 227 where a sign points to Lopez Lake. Your paved road eventually crosses Lopez Lake's dam and follows above its southern shoreline. Just before entering

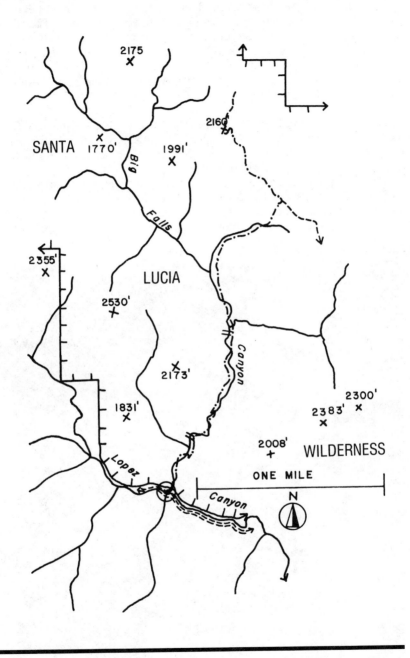

SANTA 1770'
2175'
2160'
1991'
2355'
LUCIA
2530'
2173'
1831'
2300'
2383'
2008'
WILDERNESS
Lopez
ONE MILE
Canyon
N
Big Falls
Canyon

the Lopez Lake Recreation Area, turn right onto Hi Mtn. Road, 10.3 miles from State Highway 227. Turn left onto Upper Lopez Canyon Road after another .8 mile. The Hi Mtn. Road continues straight ahead, reaching Arroyo Grande Station (Forest Service) after 1.1 miles.

Proceed north, then west on the Upper Lopez Canyon Road, bearing right after another 6.3 miles where a sign points to Lopez Canyon. The pavement ends .1 mile beyond, and you proceed up the canyon, crossing and re-crossing shallow Lopez Canyon Creek fifteen times. This section of road may be impassable after hard rains.

You reach the signed trailhead after driving 3.6 miles from the end of the pavement. Parking is somewhat limited here.

The hike: The Santa Lucia Wilderness lies near the southern end of the Santa Lucia Range east of San Luis Obispo. Few trails penetrate into this small but rugged wild area. Due to the dense chaparral that blankets the hillsides, off-trail travel is generally impossible.

The trail up Big Falls Canyon penetrates a major westward- flowing tributary of Lopez Canyon, and ascends to the crest of the range. The many, large, deep pools in this canyon host a healthy population of small trout, although fishing is poor. Newts are also commonly seen in portions of the creek.

Poison oak causes a severe rash—learning to recognize and avoid this plant can prevent an enjoyable hike from becoming a miserable one.

Portions of this route are sometimes overgrown with poison oak, so hikers should exercise reasonable caution to avoid any irritation. The Forest Service periodically clears the poison oak from the trail, so hikers might consider following the trail beyond the upper falls and climbing to the crest of the range where good views of the surrounding countryside unfold.

From the trailhead, follow the path downstream a short distance, boulderhop across Lopez Canyon creek, turn northeast, and enter lower Big Falls Canyon and the Santa Lucia Wilderness. Soon, after crossing to the south bank of Big Falls Canyon Creek, you pass an information sign and re-cross to the north bank. Your trail, shaded by live oak and California sycamore, is frequently lined with poison oak.

As you ascend northeasterly along the bottom of shady Big Falls Canyon, you pass several deep, lovely pools—excellent swimming holes.

You soon climb up and around the impressive lower falls, passing several trails leading to the falls themselves. At this point, the fragrant California bay begins to contribute shade to the already well-shaded canyon. Deep pools near the lower falls are excellent for cooling off after completing the hike.

You then ascend past the upper falls, where the creek tends to dry up in dry years, or in mid-summer during years of normal precipitation. Soon, the trail, decked with thickets of poison oak, climbs beyond this point to Hi Mountain Ridge, the crest of the range in another 1.2 miles. Hikers with ample time and energy might choose to loop back to Lopez Canyon via the southbound trail along that ridge and the trail descending into Little Falls Canyon.

From this point, most hikers will backtrack to the trailhead.

HIKE 40 *PFEIFFER FALLS/VALLEY VIEW LOOP*

General description: An easy 1.7-mile semi-loop hike in Pfeiffer-Big Sur State Park to a beautiful waterfall and an excellent viewpoint, leading through towering Coast Redwoods.
Elevation gain and loss: 500 feet.
Trailhead elevation: 310 feet.
High point: Valley View, 800 feet.
Maps: Big Sur 7.5-minute USGS quad (part of trail not shown on quad), Los Padres National Forest map.
Season: All year.
Finding the trailhead: From State Highway 1, two miles south of Big Sur and 112 miles north of San Luis Obispo, turn southeast and enter Pfeiffer-Big Sur State Park. A three dollar day-use fee is collected at the entrance booth. Turn left at the stop sign just beyond the entrance booth, and very soon bear right where a sign on the left-hand road indicates "lodging." One-tenth mile beyond, adequate parking is available, just before reaching an "Authorized Vehicles Only" sign.

The hike: Pfeiffer-Big Sur State Park encompasses a small region of the lower Big Sur River about five miles upstream from where it empties into the Pacific Ocean.

The park protects some of the southernmost Coast Redwoods in California.

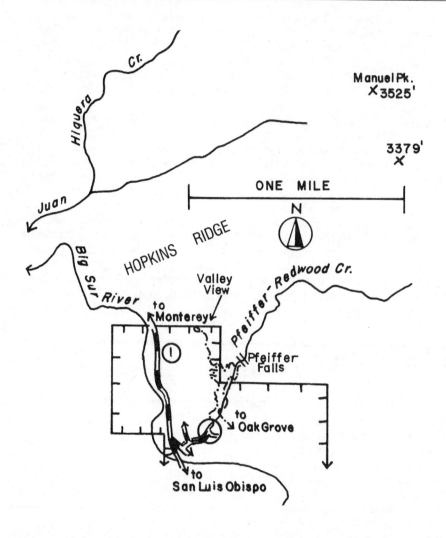

This leisurely stroll is well-suited for families with children or anyone else in the Big Sur area wishing a break from highway driving and a chance to stretch their legs.

Carry plenty of water.

From the parking area, walk northeastward across the road to locate the sign indicating Pfeiffer Falls, Valley View, and Oak Grove. Proceeding northeast along Pfeiffer-Redwood Creek, you very soon pass a northwest-bound trail on your left descending from Valley View. You will return via that trail.

Staying right at that junction where the sign points to Pfeiffer Falls and Oak Grove, continue your course along the small creek and beneath the shade of Coast Redwood, tanbark-oak, California sycamore, and California bay. Redwood sorrel is the dominant ground cover here.

A short climb over a redwood stairway brings you to a junction with the southeast-bound Oak Grove Trail, where you bear left.

In another .4 mile, after passing the upper end of the left- branching Valley View Trail, cross the creek and ascend a series of redwood stairs, soon reaching the base of the thirty-five-foot-high precipice over which Pfeiffer-Redwood Creek plunges.

From this pleasant locale, descend the redwood stairway and turn right onto the Valley View Trail. This trail quickly climbs out of the redwoods and enters a tanbark-oak forest. As you continue to gain elevation, coast live oak begin to dominate the scheme of the forest.

At the point where your trail begins to descend, turn right (northwest) where the sign points to Valley View. The trail climbs northwest along a small ridge shaded by coast live oaks. This stretch of trail has poison oak, and ends at a loop in an oak grove. Views from this point easily justify the effort.

Thickly forested Pfeiffer Ridge blocks your view immediately to the west, but to the northwest the Pacific coast is visible where Point Sur's surf-battered knob juts into the ocean. Directly below to the west lies the narrow valley draining the Big Sur River, a major drainage on the west slope of the Santa Lucia Range.

From this viewpoint, you return to the previously mentioned junction and turn right, descending back toward Pfeiffer-Redwood Creek. Nearing the canyon bottom, you re-enter a Coast Redwood and tanbark-oak forest, cross the creek via a wooden bridge, and retrace your steps the short distance to your car.

HIKE 41 *MT. CARMEL*

General description: A strenuous 9.8-mile round-trip day hike in the Ventana Wilderness leading to a dramatic vista in the Santa Lucia Range.

Elevation gain and loss: 2,767 feet, -400 feet.

Trailhead elevation: 2,050 feet.

High point: Mt. Carmel, 4,417 feet.

Maps: Big Sur and Mt. Carmel 7.5-minute USGS quads, Los Padres National Forest map, Ventana Wilderness map.

Season: October through May.

Finding the trailhead: From State Highway 1, 11.5 miles south of Carmel and fourteen miles north of Big Sur, turn east onto Palo Colorado Road. Follow this paved but sometimes steep and narrow road for 7.4 miles to the trailhead and campground at Bottchers Gap.

The hike: This moderately strenuous hike takes you to the northwestern sentinel of the Ventana Wilderness, 4,417-foot-high Mt. Carmel, where magnificent views of the Pacific Ocean and the rugged Ventana Wilderness await.

Poison oak is plentiful, but water is scarce.

Your trail proceeds northeast from the hiker's parking area, where a sign designates the route as the Skinner Ridge Trail and lists various backcountry destinations.

You soon begin a .4-mile northward traverse on chaparral-covered, west-facing slopes. You occasionally have ocean views to the west, and over-the-shoulder views of the massive cone of 3,709-foot-high Pico Blanco soaring majestically into the sky to your south.

Your route soon approaches upper Mill Creek, well-shaded by live oak and madrone. For the next 1.8 miles, the trail ascends in a northeasterly direction, sometimes near the creek and sometimes along chaparral-, oak-, and madrone-covered slopes, to the crest of Skinner Ridge, where you enter the Ventana Wilderness. This section of trail is intermittently lined with poison oak at times.

A shady northward jaunt along this live oak- and madrone-clad ridge brings you to a junction at a saddle 3,200 feet above sea level. The left-hand trail descends northwest to Apple Tree and Turner Creek trail camps.

Continuing northward from the saddle, your route wastes no time gaining elevation, but the expansive views of the Pacific Ocean to your west and the rugged interior of the Ventana Wilderness to your east help to make the steep ascent pass quickly.

After climbing 900 feet in one mile, you finally reach the open ridge just west of Devils Peak's black oak-covered summit.

You soon reach a sign reading Palo Colorado, pointing back the way you came. Here you leave the Skinner Ridge Trail and proceed northward just west of the high point of Devils Peak on a faint trail. The Skinner Ridge Trail continues eastward into the Ventana Wilderness.

You soon leave the shade behind, just north of Devils Peak, and proceed north along the sometimes-brushy ridgeline trail, and after .8 mile reach the small stack of boulders crowning Mt. Carmel's summit.

Ventana Double Cone and the rugged interior of the Ventana Wilderness dominate the scenery from the slopes of Mt. Carmel near the central California coast.

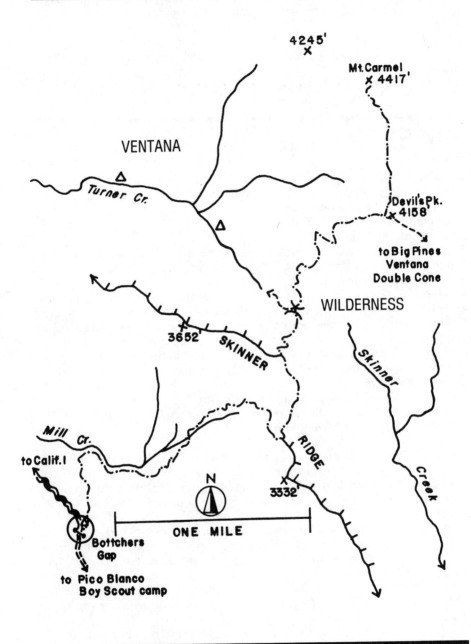

4245'
X

Mt. Carmel
X 4417'

VENTANA

Turner Cr.

Devil's Pk.
X 4156

to Big Pines
Ventana
Double Cone

WILDERNESS

3652 SKINNER

Skinner

Mill Cr.

to Calif. 1

RIDGE

Creek

N

3332

ONE MILE

Bottchers
Gap

to Pico Blanco
Boy Scout camp

From here a magnificent, all-encompassing vista unfolds. To the northwest sprawls Monterey Bay. To your west, the Santa Lucia Range plummets more than 4,000 feet in just 5.5 miles into the Pacific Ocean. To your east and southeast stands the rugged interior of the Ventana Wilderness, beckoning adventurous hikers with its network of trails, lovely creeks, and backcountry isolation.

From the peak, return the way you came. Backpackers will want to continue east on the Skinner Ridge Trail, where several trail camps and remote mountain scenery await.

HIKE 42 *PINE VALLEY*

General description: A moderately strenuous, 12.9- mile semi-loop backpack in the largest wilderness area—Ventana Wilderness—in the South Coast Ranges.
Elevation gain and loss: 3,660 feet.
Trailhead elevation: 4,350 feet.
High point: 4,750 feet.
Maps: Chews Ridge and Ventana Cones 7.5-minute USGS quads, Los Padres National Forest map, or Ventana Wilderness map (topographic).
Season: October through May.
Finding the trailhead: From U.S. 101 in Greenfield, fifty-nine miles north of Paso Robles and thirty-nine miles south of Salinas, turn west onto Monterey County Road G-16. Proceed west on this paved road, following signs pointing to Carmel Valley. After driving west from Greenfield for 29.3 miles, turn south onto signed Tassajara Road. Bear left after 1.3 miles at the junction with westbound Cachagua Road. The pavement ends after another 1.6 miles. You reach the trailhead after another 7.5 miles, just beyond the turnoff to China Campground. Parking is limited to several cars.

The Tassajara Road can also be reached by following County Road G-16 east from Carmel for about twenty-three miles.

The hike: The Santa Lucia Range, part of the South Coast Ranges of California, rises abruptly eastward from the Pacific Coast to a region of 4,000- and 5,000-foot-high peaks and ridges. The heart of this extremely rugged, often brush-choked range is protected within the boundaries of the Ventana Wilderness.

Over 200 miles of trails criss-cross this interesting area, offering easy access into its remote and scenic interior. The area is especially enjoyable when more typical high-elevation wilderness areas are rendered inaccessible by deep winter snowpack.

A great portion of the vegetation in the Ventana Wilderness was consumed by the Marble Cone Fire of August 1977. Chaparral is the primary vegetation in the wilderness, and is adapted to periodic fires which are, in fact, beneficial to this vegetation. Fires help to germinate seeds that can only be released from their hard coverings by very high temperatures. Fire also helps eliminate dead and diseased vegetation, and adds beneficial nutrients to the soil upon which renewed growth can flourish.

Summers can be hot in the Ventana Wilderness, and snow sometimes dusts the higher peaks and ridges in winter. Nevertheless, with careful planning, the area can be enjoyed throughout the year.

Pine Valley has the only source of water on the hike. However the numerous springs in the area are seasonal, so be sure to carry an adequate water supply.

A campfire permit is required for all fires. In some years, fire conditions can be severe enough that all fires, including backpack stoves, may be prohibited during August and September. Thus, hikers should check with the ranger station in King City prior to embarking on their trip.

Your hike begins on the west side of the Tassajara Road where the signed Pine Ridge Trail heads west. The trail soon enters a "ghost" forest of pine and oak, destroyed by the Marble Cone Fire. As is so often the case in chaparral plant communities, that rapidly spreading blaze destroyed existing plants but did not kill their root systems. Thus, the increasingly dense growth you see today is a result of "crown-sprouting," an adaptation many plants in this community have developed to re-establish themselves immediately after a fire.

Hikers often find the regrowth in the wilderness to be quite vigorous. Thus, on this hike you will soon be thrashing through sometimes-dense chaparral. In spring, you are also likely to be host to a tick or two during the first 3.5 miles of hiking along Pine Ridge.

During this undulating 3.5 miles of trail to Church Creek Divide, you pass through sections of burned forest alternating with open, grassy hillsides that offer sweeping views into the rugged interior of the Ventana Wilderness.

As you begin the final switchbacking descent to Church Creek Divide, ponderosa pine, black oak, and madrone begin to mix with the mostly Coulter pine and tanbark-oak forest.

Upon reaching 3,651-foot-high Church Creek Divide, you are confronted with a four-way junction. The northwest-bound Carmel River Trail descends

The tall pines and lush meadows of Pine Valley in the Ventana Wilderness offer a refreshing change-of-pace form the brush-covered hillsides in the Santa Lucia Range.

into Pine Valley, forming the return leg of your loop. To the left, the southwest-bound trail descends to a trailhead on the Tassajara Road near Tassajara Hot Springs.

You continue west on the Pine Ridge Trail, indicated by a sign pointing to Big Sur Station and State Highway 1.

Proceeding westward, you pass through cool stands of black and live oak, ponderosa and Coulter pine, and madrone. The understory consists primarily of a species of ceanothus. Ceanothus (more commonly known as California lilac) is a common shrub in California's mountains, ranging from foothill areas to montane forests. Its bright panicles of flowers, usually blue or white, add fragrance to the warming spring air.

The forest along the initial stretch of Pine Ridge Trail west of Church Creek Divide was largely untouched by the Marble Cone Fire, and so remains a pleasant, shady walk.

After walking .4 mile, you pass above the possible camping area labeled Divide Camp on the quad, situated below the trail in a fern- and grass-covered opening. A seasonal stream provides water for campers using this seldom-occupied site.

As you near the next trail junction, you pass back into a "ghost" forest. This fairly open hillside provides westward views to the rugged summits of 4,727-foot-high Ventana Cone and 4,853-foot-high Ventana Double Cone.

At a point 2.2 miles west of Church Creek Divide, you reach a hard-to-spot junction with a northwest-bound trail. A sign indicating this junction lies just above the trail in overgrown brush. You turn right here, leaving the Pine Ridge Trail, and begin descending through a recovering stand of oak under stark ponderosa pine snags. During this descent, you can glimpse the meadowy expanse of the Pine Valley floor below and to the north. This sometimes faint trail descends for one-half mile to another junction. Hikers should stay alert during this descent. The trail is overgrown and can be easily lost.

At this trail junction, the sign points southwest to Bear Basin, but that faint trail becomes impossible to follow within one-half mile. You continue straight ahead—the sign points to Pine Valley.

This segment of trail is much easier to follow than the previous one-half mile, and steadily descends for 1.3 miles to the floor of lush Pine Valley. Upon reaching the valley, you first pass through Pine Valley Camp, then hop across the Carmel River. Pine Valley Camp is a superb location for an overnight stay. There are two picnic tables and fireplaces here, and a cold piped spring. The camp is shaded by tall ponderosa pines, and lush ferns and grasses complete the setting.

A .75 mile jaunt downstream from the camp leads to impressive Pine Falls, offering a winning diversion for overnight campers.

After crossing the willow- and alder-clad Carmel River the trail approaches a fenceline and a gate. The Carmel River Trail heads northwest through the gate, very soon passing a cabin on private property. But you turn right, and follow the trail southeast, paralleling the fenceline.

The north side of this aptly-named valley is bounded by some intriguing rock outcrops, providing a backdrop that contrasts with the mellow character of the valley. Pine Valley was fortunately spared the destructive fury of the Marble Cone Fire. Thus, its environs provide a vivid change-of-pace from the surrounding scorched hillsides.

HIKE 42 *PINE VALLEY*

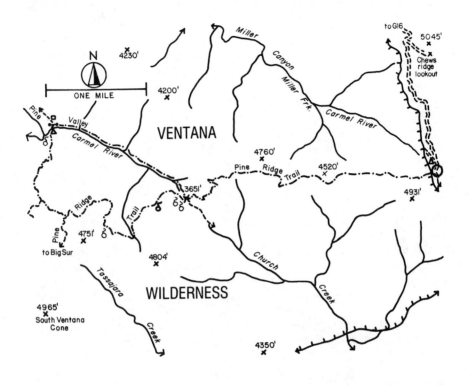

Your trail generally follows the course of the Carmel River as you leave the ferns, grasses, and pine forest. Presently, you hop across two small tributary creeks, then step across the infant Carmel River four times. After hiking 1.8 miles from Pine Valley Camp, you reach Church Creek Divide, turn left, and retrace your steps for 3.5 miles to the trailhead.

HIKE 43 *PINNACLES NATIONAL MONUMENT*

General description: A moderate 4.4-mile loop day hike, touring the striking, eroded remnants of an ancient volcano in the South Coast Ranges.
Elevation gain and loss: 1,450 feet.
Trailhead elevation: 1,270 feet.
High point: 2,600 feet.
Maps: North Chalone Peak 7.5-minute USGS quad, Pinnacles National Monument map.
Season: October through May.
Finding the trailhead: From State Highway 25, thirty-two miles south of Hollister and thirty-five miles north of the State Highway 25-198 junction (which is thirty-seven miles west of Coalinga), turn west onto State Highway 146 where a sign points to Pinnacles National Monument. Follow this paved road south, then west, for 3.7 miles. Then turn left where a sign indicates the visitor center and picnic area. After another 1.2 miles, park directly opposite the visitor center. A three-dollar day-use fee is charged for parking within the National Monument and allows entry for seven consecutive days.

The hike: The Pinnacle Rocks, remnants of an ancient volcano, are the highlight of this moderately easy hike in the Gabilan Range. The region is semi-arid, receiving the bulk of its annual precipitation during the cool winter months. Long, hot, dry summers are the rule here, as in most of California. The vegetation, which is adapted to California's Mediterranean-type climate, consists primarily of chaparral. Digger pines, a California endemic, clothe the upper slopes in stands almost thick enough to be called forests .

The aptly named Pinnacle Rocks, remnants of an ancient volcano, are continually visible to hikers along the High Peaks Trail in central California's Pinnacles National Monument.

Views are panoramic along the ridgetop segment of the hike, where hikers are surrounded by strange fingers and crags composed of volcanic breccia. Be sure to carry water and watch for rattlesnakes.

From the parking area opposite the visitor center, some very impressive cliffs and crags are seen on the northwestern skyline, crags you will soon be scrambling over and around. From this point, walk southwest up the road for about 150 feet to the signed Bear Gulch Trail. Follow the trail through the picnic area to a large sign displaying a map of the area. The trail then begins ascending Bear Gulch through vegetation consisting of California buckeye, toyon, coast live oak, and blue oak.

Boulders and cliffs soon make an appearance across the canyon to your north, and as they begin to enclose the canyon bottom in shade, poison oak and monkey flower join the understory.

Soon reaching the first of many trail junctions, you bear right where the sign points to the high peaks. (You will stay right at all trail junctions along this hike.)

Presently, the High Peaks Trail descends slightly to cross almost-always-dry Bear Gulch, passing a stack of moss-encrusted boulders under a shady canopy of coast live oak before negotiating a few gentle switchbacks.

Digger pines and volcanic boulders begin to increase in numbers as you ascend, until both are quite numerous atop Pinnacle Rocks ridge.

Avoiding all left-branching trails, the High Peaks Trail continues its steady yet gentle ascent toward the Pinnacle Rocks. The dry, sunny slopes this trail traverses are dominated by chamise, and include specimens of manzanita and buckbrush (a ceanothus species).

As the trail nears the jagged crags that comprise Scout Peak, it begins a series of switchbacks across chaparral-covered slopes. Scant shade is cast by the sparse stand of digger pines that cling to this rocky slope.

The trail, wedged between Scout Peak and a group of impressive, finger-like rocks, surmounts the crest of Pinnacle Rocks ridge about 1.75 miles from the trailhead. The spectacular crags of The Fingers can be seen about one half mile west.

Turning north at the ridgetop junction, you continue your hike along the High Peaks Trail. Vistas are grand along this pinnacle-ridden stretch of trail.

Turkey vultures are quite common along this ridge, and are frequently seen soaring among the crags.

In the west across the broad Salinas River Valley rises the Santa Lucia Range, capped by mile-high peaks. To the north and south your view is filled by the rounded, grass- and chaparral- covered slopes of the Gabilan Range. The Pinnacles are a part of the Gabilan Range, but provide a stark contrast to the typical rounded topography of the range.

The trail bypasses some of the most rugged crags, but where no bypass is possible, it ascends these rugged rocks directly, via steep steps cut into solid rock, with handrails provided for safety.

You frequently glimpse lookout-topped North Chalone Peak in the south. At an elevation of 3,304 feet, it is the highest point in the National Monument.

As you near the end of this exhilarating section of trail, you will notice across Chalone Creek Canyon to the north, the dramatic pinnacle-crowned dome of the Balconies.

Leaving the bulk of the pinnacle formations behind, your trail descends past the last left-branching trail. Your route, presently the Condor Gulch Trail,

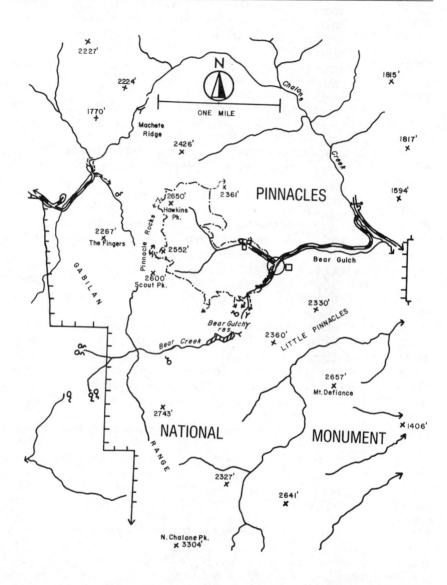

begins descending moderately southeastward, offering good views of the south walls of Hawkins Peak. The slopes are clothed in chamiso, the abundant digger pines doing little to shade hikers on this sun-drenched mountainside.

You soon contour above a spur road and some outlying National Monument buildings, and then descend a short distance to complete the loop at the trailhead.

HIKE 44 BIG BASIN REDWOODS STATE PARK

General description: A moderate six-mile loop day hike through a Coast Redwood forest in the Santa Cruz Mountains.
Elevation gain and loss: 1,320 feet.
Trailhead elevation: 1,000 feet.
High point: 1,350 feet.
Maps: Big Basin and Franklin Point 7.5-minute USGS quads (trail not shown on quads), Big Basin Redwoods State Park map No. 2.
Season: All year.
Finding the trailhead: The trailhead lies directly west of the Big Basin Redwoods State Park Headquarters on the west side of State Highway 236. To reach Big Basin, head north from Santa Cruz for thirteen miles via State Highway 9, then turn left and follow State Highway 236 to Big Basin.

Big Basin can also be reached by following Interstate 280 south from San Francisco for about twenty miles. Then turn south onto State Highway 35 and proceed south for about twenty-five miles. You then turn west onto State Highway 9, and after six miles turn west again onto State Highway 236 and proceed eight miles to Big Basin.

Directly across the highway from Park Headquarters, proceed through the entrance station, paying the three dollar day-use fee, and park in the large hikers' parking area on the left.

Coast redwoods, among the earth's tallest trees, dominate the forest in Big Basin Redwoods State Park along the central California coast. Once widespread over much of the northern hemisphere, the range of the Coast Redwood—because of gradual changes in climate over several million years—is presently restricted to the coasts of central and northern California and southwestern Oregon.

The hike: This trip takes hikers through California's first Redwood State Park. The trail leads through magnificent Coast Redwood forests while traversing the often-steep terrain of the Santa Cruz Mountains. Although fairly rigorous, the hike is suitable for most hikers.

Several backcountry trail camps in the State Park offer visitors a rare opportunity to camp among impressive Coast Redwoods. If you plan on camping in the backcountry, check with the visitor center in Big Basin for details. Be sure to carry an adequate supply of water.

Begin this hike at a large sign indicating the Redwood Trail, and proceed west. Very soon you meet a southbound trail leading to Blooms Creek Campground and a northbound trail leading to the Campfire Center. Proceed straight ahead to the Skyline-to-the-Sea Trail.

You soon reach a junction near a rest room—the Redwood Trail branches left here. Go straight ahead, shortly crossing Opal Creek via a wooden bridge where you intersect the Skyline-to-the- Sea Trail. The northbound segment of this trail forms the return leg of your loop.

Turn left and begin hiking southward under massive Coast Redwoods and tanbark-oaks. After .2 mile, turn right where the sign points to Berry Creek Falls.

You now begin a one-half mile ascent, dwarfed by the gigantic Coast Redwoods and Douglas-firs. At the top of this climb, you reach a five-way ridgetop junction. The forest at this point consists of Douglas-fir and tanbark-oak. This change in forest type reflects the drier, warmer conditions that prevail on this ridge, conditions that are unsuitable for the development of a Coast Redwood forest.

Proceed northwest from this junction, staying on the Skyline- to-the-Sea Trail. Your trail contours across west-facing slopes, thickly forested once again with large Coast Redwoods, as it descends toward Kelly Creek.

You reach another junction within a quarter mile. This right- branching trail leads up to the Sunset Trail (the return leg of your loop), but you stay left and continue descending into the depths of Kelly Creek. Hikers without the time or energy required for this six-mile hike may elect to utilize the short connector trail to loop back to the trailhead via the Sunset Trail, forming a 2.1-mile loop.

After another .6 mile you reach a junction in Kelly Creek Canyon. You can take either fork; they both rejoin within one- half mile.

As you descend farther into this shady canyon, sword fern, redwood sorrel, and trillium increase their abundance in the evergreen huckleberry-dominated understory.

About 1.6 miles below the five-way ridgetop junction, you meet the northbound Timms Creek Trail, marked by a four-inch- square wooden post. Although all trail junctions in the state park are well-marked, these small posts can be easy to miss for a hiker striding along, fully absorbed in the quiet beauty of the area.

Upon leaving the Skyline-to-the-Sea Trail, turn right onto the Timms Creek Trail, immediately crossing Kelly Creek on a redwood log. Your trail begins a gentle ascent along the shady environs of West Waddell Creek. This trail is noticeably much less used than the Skyline-to-the-Sea Trail.

After a pleasant upstream jaunt, negotiate a few switchbacks and you will reach the Sunset Trail, .9 mile from Kelly Creek. Turning right onto this trail, you begin a gentle contouring descent, and after one-quarter mile, you cross

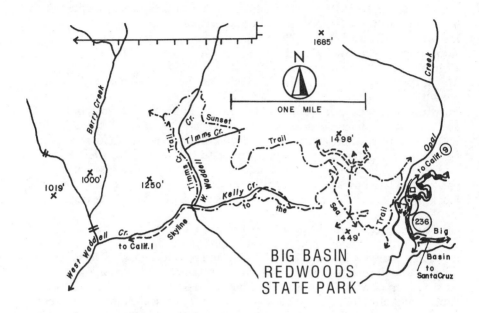

West Waddell Creek via a wooden bridge. Small trout can be seen in the pool just above the bridge.

The trail presently begins a gentle, generally southeastward ascent. Douglas-firs are found dominating drier, mostly south- facing slopes and ridgetop sites, while the Coast Redwoods favor lower, moister, more shady environments .

After hiking 1.6 miles from the crossing of West Waddell Creek, you pass a right-branching connector trail, and .2 mile beyond you reach a junction with the Middle Ridge Fire Road. You cross the road and descend eastward; the sign indicates that Park Headquarters is .9 mile ahead.

You quickly pass the northbound Ridge Fire Trail after .1 mlle, and within the next half-mile you intersect the Skyline-to- the-Sea Trail just above a picnic area along Opal Creek. You now turn right (south) and walk .2 mile to a sign indicating Jay Trail Camps and Park Headquarters. Here you turn left (east) and retrace your steps to the trailhead.

HIKE 45 *MT. WITTENBERG*

General description: A moderate 4.7-mile loop day hike to a windswept coastal peak, in Point Reyes Naitonal Seashore, featuring colorful wildflowers (in spring), Douglas-fir forests, and ocean vistas.

Elevation gain and loss: 1,365 feet.

Trailhead elevation: 105 feet.

High point: Mt. Wittenberg, 1,470 feet.

Maps: Point Reyes 15-minute USGS quad, Point Reyes National Seashore map.

Season: All year.

Finding the trailhead: From State Highway 1 in the small hamlet of Olema, about thirty-six miles north of San Francisco and twenty miles west of San Rafael, turn west where a large sign indicates the Point Reyes National Seashore Headquarters. After one-half mile from State Highway 1, turn left where a sign points to the Visitor Center. You reach the trailhead after another .3 mile. Park in the large parking lot opposite the visitor center where a locked gate blocks the road to further travel. This trailhead is .8 mile from State Highway 1.

The hike: Point Reyes National Seashore is a land of contrasts. There are densely forested ridges, grassy coastal slopes, surf-battered beaches, rocky headlands plunging into the Pacific Ocean, and several lagoons. This hike leads hikers through forests of Douglas-fir and across lush, green meadows. Views from the top of Mt. Wittenberg, the high point of the National Seashore, are superb, and offer a bird's-eye view of the varied landscapes that characterize the region. A vivid display of wildflowers greets those who come in spring. Blacktail deer are very abundant and are likely to be seen in large herds.

Carry an adequate supply of water.

There are several backpacker's camps located throughout the area. If you plan on backcountry camping, check with the visitor center for details. The weather in the area is highly variable. During winter the area is swept by strong Pacific storms, and during the summer a cold fog often enshrouds the coastal slopes. Thus, careful planning is necessary to thoroughly enjoy this hike.

It is believed that in 1579 Francis Drake, an English explorer, beached his vessel, the Golden Hinde, in the protected enclosure of the bay that now bears his name.

In 1603 Spanish explorer Don Sebastian Vizcaino bestowed the name La Punta de los Reyes after anchoring in Drakes Bay to wait out a storm.

From the trailhead parking area, head south past the locked gate, avoiding the signed Earthquake Trail that immediately branches left. Stroll .2 mile south on the closed road. Then turn right onto the signed Sky Trail. A moderate ascent brings you into a shady forest of tanbark-oak and towering Douglas-firs. The lush understory is dominated by ferns. Once the trail levels off, fragrant California bay joins the forest.

After you negotiate a few switchbacks, your trail breaks into the open in beautiful green meadow surrounded by dense Douglas- fir forest. From this point, Inverness Ridge forms the western skyline, crowned by the grassy summit of your goal, Mt. Wittenberg.

The trail continues climbing through a series of lovely meadows, then rises moderately and re-enters Douglas-fir shade.

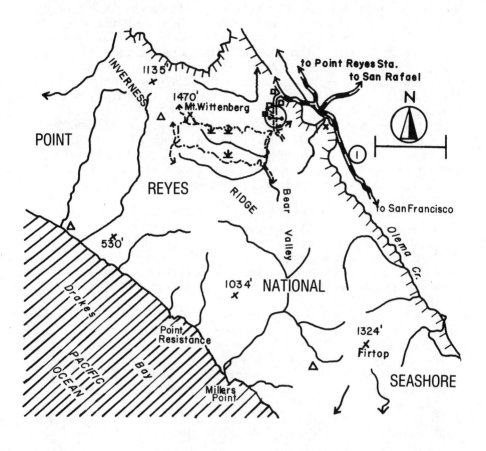

Pausing to catch your breath, you have tree-framed views to the east of the grassy, oak-dotted hills rising beyond the San Andreas Rift Zone. Continuing a moderate, sometimes switchbacking ascent, you soon reach an unmarked junction with a northwest- bound path. The Sky Trail continues west. Turning right here, you ascend grassy slopes dotted with occasional Douglas-firs, and soon surmount the grassy, wildflower-carpeted summit region of 1,470-foot-high Mt. Wittenberg. Stunted Douglas-firs cling to the more sheltered north slope of the peak, but are unable to prosper on the summit itself.

Mountain peaks, such as that of Mt. Wittenberg, lying in immediate proximity to the northern California coast seem remarkably sub-alpine. Winds of more than seventy-five miles per hour are frequently recorded between January and May each year at Pt. Reyes. The effect of these winds is reflected in the stunted Douglas-firs atop Inverness Ridge.

In spring, a profusion of ferns, grasses, blue lupine, California poppy, and tidy tips carpet this peak and the higher elevations of Inverness Ridge.

The magnificent vista that unfolds from atop Mt. Wittenberg offers a superb panorama of the surrounding area. Specifically, your view includes wind and surf-battered Pt. Reyes Beach in the northwest, and to the west the rocky headland of Pt. Reyes juts into the Pacific Ocean; closer at hand is Drakes Bay and the shallow lagoons of Drakes Estero and Estero de Limantour, the Pacific Ocean dominates the view from west to south; to the southeast, heavily forested Inverness Ridge fills your gaze and beyond lies Mt. Tamalpais and some of San Francisco's skyscrapers; and, to the east-southeast is the forested valley of the San Andreas Rift Zone, beyond which rise pastoral, grassy hills dotted with stands of oak. While relaxing on the peak you are likely to observe a variety of raptors as they soar on the strong winds that frequently buffet Inverness Ridge.

Blacktail deer are especially abundant, and because they are protected here, they are more easily observed than in areas where they are hunted. From the summit, avoid a faint northwest-bound path and descend southward, soon picking up a steep trail that descends to a wide, grassy saddle where you rejoin the Sky Trail. Just before reaching the destination and mileage sign at the saddle, avoid another northwest-bound trail.

Proceed west on the Sky Trail. A sign indicates that the Meadow Trail, the return leg of your loop, is .4 mile ahead.

Begin descending the wide trail west, then south, around a grassy, above-timberline hill, passing a few stunted Douglas-firs enroute. As you proceed, you may glimpse the grassy clearing of Sky Campground in the northwest. Camping in the National Seashore is restricted to backcountry campsites such as the Sky Campground.

You reach a signed, four-way junction after .4 mile, turn left (east) onto the Meadow Trail, and re-enter Douglas-fir forest. Backpackers will want to turn right (northwest) here, hiking one-half mile to Sky Campground.

After hiking one-half mile east on the Meadow Trail, you break into the open and proceed through a quarter-mile-long ridgetop meadow, then re-enter a forest of Douglas-fir, California bay, and tanbark-oak. The descent soon becomes moderate as you approach Bear Valley.

You presently cross a small creek on a wooden bridge, then turn left and stroll down the closed road for .8 mile to complete the hike at the trailhead.

HIKE 46 SUMMIT SPRINGS TRAILHEAD TO SNOW MOUNTAIN

General description: A moderate eight-mile round-trip day hike or backpack in the Snow Mountain Wilderness to a sub-alpine peak in the North Coast Ranges.
Elevation gain and loss: 1,966 feet, -150 feet.
Trailhead elevation: 5,240 feet.
High point: Snow Mountain East, 7,056 feet.
Maps: Crockett Peak, Potato Hill, Fouts Springs, St. John Mtn. 7.5-minute USGS quads, Mendocino National Forest map.
Season: Late May through mid-October.
Finding the trailhead: From Interstate 5 in the Sacramento Valley, seventy

miles south of Red Bluff and sixty- three miles north of Sacramento, turn west onto State Highway 20. After 8.6 miles, turn right onto Leesville Road at a hard-to-spot junction where a sign reads "Stonyford 30." Follow this sometimes-rough and narrow paved county road through peaceful, rolling grass and blue oak-covered hills. After 13.3 miles, bear right where a sign indicates that Lodoga is nine miles ahead. The left fork leads south to State Highway 20. Your north-bound road brings you to a junction at Lodoga after another 8.9 miles. Bear left, proceeding toward Stonyford and avoiding several signed spur roads enroute. After seven miles, you pass the Stonyford Ranger Station on your right (where wilderness permits can be obtained); one-half mile beyond, turn left onto Market Street in downtown Stonyford.

Hikers driving from the north via Interstate 5 can take the Maxwell exit (also signed for Stonyford), located sixty-two miles south of Red Bluff. Follow the paved county road through the town of Sites, climb over Grapevine Pass, and descend to Lodoga, 23.5 miles from I-5, and follow the aforementioned directions to reach Stonyford.

After .2 mile, turn left again onto Fouts Springs Road (Forest Road M 10/18NOl). A sign here indicates Fouts Springs and Letts Lake. You follow this paved road into the mountains via the Stony Creek drainage, avoiding several signed spur roads. After 8.1 miles, bear left where the Fouts Springs Ranch Road turns right. A sign here indicates that Letts Lake is nine miles ahead and the town of Upper Lake forty-two miles ahead.

Your paved road soon leaves the floor of South Fork Stony Creek and begins a mountainside traverse, alternating with short stretches of dirt surface. You pass a left-branching road to Sanborn Cabin after another 4.3 miles, and 1.6 miles beyond that junction, bear right where the Letts Lake Road branches left. Your road, now a good dirt road, crosses forested slopes and reaches a junction with the southbound road leading to Goat Mountain Lookout, 5.1 miles from the previous junction. Turn right here where the sign points to Summit Springs and Bear Creek Station. After 2.1 more miles, you turn right onto Forest Road 24N02, leaving Forest Road M10/18NOl. A sign here points to Summit Springs. Very soon you bear right again where a sign indicates Blue Slide Ridge. After 1.7 miles from Forest Road M10/18NOl, you reach a four-way junction at the Lake-Colusa county line. Take the northbound road where the sign points to Summit Springs and the Summit Springs Trail. You climb steeply on this good, dirt, ridgetop road for 1.8 miles to the trailhead at the end of the road, avoiding two right-branching roads along the way. This trailhead is 24.7 miles from Stonyford.

The trailhead can also be reached from the town of Upper Lake, which lies above the north end of Clear Lake. From State Highway 20 in Upper Lake, turn north where a sign indicates the ranger station is one mile ahead and Lake Pillsbury is thirty-one miles ahead. After reaching the ranger station, and obtaining your wilderness permit, follow paved northbound County Road 301 for 15.5 miles, then turn right onto dirt Forest Road M 10/18NOl. The sign here indicates Bear Creek and Snow Mountain. Following this road into the mountains, you pass occasional signs pointing to Bear Creek Station. At one point the road crosses wide and shallow Bear Creek. When Forest Road M10/18NOl branches south, you stay left, soon passing Bear Creek Station, and very soon thereafter turn right onto Forest Road 17N16, 7.3 miles from County Road 301. Follow this road for 5.5 miles to the above-mentioned four-way junction at the Lake-Colusa county line, and drive 1.8 miles to the trailhead. The trailhead is thirty-one miles from Upper Lake.

The hike: The North Coast Ranges head north from the San Francisco Bay area into northwestern California, where they merge with the Klamath Mountains. They are made up of numerous mountain ranges aligned in a northwest-southeast pattern.

Remote Snow Mountain lies near the southern end of the Mendocino Range, one of the longest mountain crests in the North Coast Ranges complex. Its 7000-foot-high summit stands at timberline, bearing the brunt of furious Pacific storms and capturing great quantities of moisture. By contrast, the general timberline in the Sierra Nevada to the east lies well above 9,000 feet.

Be sure to carry water, since most of the springs and streams in the area are seasonal. Backpackers should have no trouble locating campsites on this hike. Cedar Camp, two miles from the trailhead, and the bowls just east of Snow Mountain offer good possible campsites.

A wilderness permit is required to enter the Snow Mountain Wilderness.

From the trailhead shaded by ponderosa and sugar pine, white fir, and black oak, your wide, steep trail ascends northeastward, disguised as an old set of jeep tracks. The trail very soon leaves the forest and climbs to an open hillside sparsely vegetated with grasses and lupines. From here, views instantly expand to include the Sacramento Valley in the east, and the uninterrupted, mountainous terrain of the North Coast Ranges in the west.

You soon leave the jeep tracks, branching right onto the trail, and begin traversing oak- and manzanita-covered slopes, accompanied by a 360-degree panorama. In the northwest looms the high Snow Mountain West. In the south are the forested summits of the Mendocino Range, dominated by the lookout-tower-capped summit of 6,121-foot-high Goat Mountain, the southern sentinel of the range.

You presently begin a traverse of west-facing, oak-clad slopes that are occassionally interrupted by a few white firs and ponderosa pines. When you reach a minor west-trending ridge, the trail enters a white fir stand and turns east. A moderate ascent along this ridge follows, soon reaching the crest of the range amid a stand of weather-tortured Jeffrey pines, their branches pointing in the direction the prevailing wind blows. Next the trail jogs north and traverses west-facing slopes just below the crest in a Jeffrey pine and white fir forest.

Soon you level off on the flat crest and enter a cool red fir stand, then reach a junction with an eastbound trail leading to Fouts Camp. You bear left here and proceed north on the faint trail. Watch for blazes if you lose the route.

After a minor descent, the trail approaches a small, but beautiful, green meadow surrounded by red firs that are reflected in a vernal pool at the lower end of the meadow. Here is another trail junction. The left-branching trail, according to the sign, leads northwest to Milk Ranch and could be used to loop back via the basin just west of Snow Mountain.

But for now, you turn right; the sign indicates that Snow Mountain is two miles ahead. A sign at the meadow's edge calls the area Cedar Camp, although there are no cedars here. Your trail crosses the meadow and heads north, soon crossing over the crest of the range and traversing northeast-facing slopes above the head of the Trout Creek drainage.

You then top out on a 6,600-foot-high saddle and pass into the Dark Hollow Creek drainage, a tributary of the Middle Fork Stony Creek.

In an open, forested bowl, accompanied by a ground-hugging understory of manzanita and ceanothus, your route passes a right-branching (northbound) trail leading to the Bonnie View trailhead (no public access) four miles away. You bear left here. The trail proceeds on the level through a northeast-facing bowl, passing a few grassy-banked, seasonal streams enroute. Your northbound trail soon crosses a minor spur ridge, bends northwest, then passes an impressive double-trunked western juniper before entering another small bowl. These bowls appear to have originated as a result of glaciation.

From this bowl you can see your destination, Snow Mountain East, thrusting its tan-colored flanks into the sky. You soon reach a small creek and climb to a tiny meadow at its source. From here you get a glimpse of the Sacramento Valley in the east.

The red fir forest becomes sparse as you ascend this increasingly rocky basin. Corn lilies grow in profusion in the wetter meadows in this bowl. The trail soon bends southwest while ascending a few small grassy benches, and quickly surmounts the crest of the range where there is a four-way junction.

A typical High Sierra trail leads hikers through alpine terrain, with jagged, snowy summits constantly visible in all directions. Photo by John Rihs

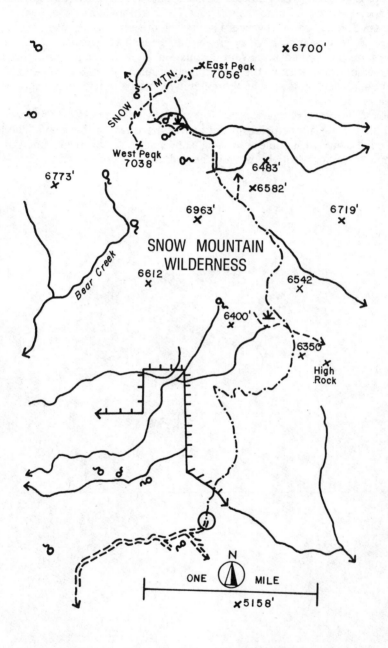

The trail straight ahead (northwest) descends into a north-facing bowl, crosses the ridge just south of 6,684-foot-high Signal Peak, then descends to Milk Ranch. As mentioned previously, adventurous hikers may want to utilize that trail to loop back to Cedar Camp.

The left-branching (southbound) trail climbs 190 feet in one- half mile to the open summit of Snow Mountain West. You turn right, ascending the faint trail for one-half mile to the 7,056- foot-high summit of Snow Mountain East. The view from the summit, an all-encompassing 360-degree panorama, is superb. From your vantage point high atop the Mendocino Range, you can gaze north-westward to the Yolla Bolly Mountains near the northern tip of the range. Those mountains and the Snow Mountain area provide the only true subalpine environment in all of California's Coast Ranges.

Your view from the southeast to the northwest is strictly of mountains, taking in a large portion of the North Coast Ranges.

In the north-northeast rises the snowy cone of Mt. Shasta, THE landmark of northern California. And in the northeast rises an almost-equally impressive mountain, Lassen Peak.

In the immediate eastern foreground, the Mendocino Range plummets into the often-smoggy Sacramento Valley. And beyond rises the forested western slope of the Sierra Nevada.

The Sutter Buttes add contrast to the exceedingly flat terrain of the Sacramento Valley in the southeast.

From Snow Mountain East, return to the four-way trail junction, and either climb up to Snow Mountain West for more excellent vistas, or backtrack to the trailhead.

HIKE 47 WALKER PASS TO MORRIS PEAK

General description: A moderate 8.8-mile round-trip, partially cross-country day hike (or overnighter if you carry plenty of water) to a view-filled summit on the southern Sierra Nevada crest.
Elevation gain and loss: 1,965 feet.
Trailhead elevation: 5,250 feet.
High point: Morris Peak, 7,215 feet.
Maps: Walker Pass 7.5-minute USGS quad (trail not shown on quad).
Season: April through November.
Finding the trailhead: The trailhead lies on the north side of State Highway 178 at Walker Pass, across the road from the historical marker. Walker Pass is about 8.7 miles west of Freeman Junction on State Highway 14, and seventy-four miles east of Bakersfield via State Highway 178.

The hike: The crest of the extreme southern Sierra Nevada contrasts markedly with the heavily forested Greenhorn Mountains and the Western Divide to the west. Those high ridges capture the bulk of moisture from Pacific storms. Thus, the Sierra crest south of Olancha Peak is quite arid. Only sparse forests exist on the highest slopes of this segment of the Sierra Nevada crest, consisting primarily of pinyon pine. These drab, sometimes monotonous forests do have

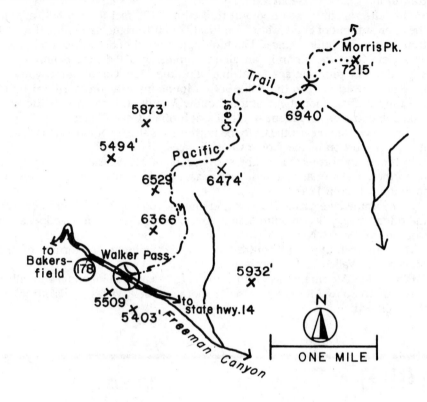

their advantages, nevertheless. In autumn, for example, many people make a point of visiting a pinyon pine stand to harvest their delicious nuts.

When hikers are barred from deeply snow-packed High Sierra trails in winter, they can view that same High Sierra from a fairly comfortable vantage point atop Morris Peak, because its ramparts are rarely visited by deep snow.

Carry an ample water supply; none is available along this ridgeline trek.

The trail leads northeast from the pass, rising moderately at first before leveling off on a gentle grade. Soon passing above scattered clumps of Joshua trees, you obtain excellent eastward views down Freeman Canyon to Indian Wells Valley and beyond to the El Paso Mountains.

Your steadily ascending trail jogs northward after you encounter rabbitbrush on the open slopes, and good views are obtained to the south across the gap of Walker Pass to the pinyon-forested Scodie Mountains, the southernmost extension of the Sierra Nevada.

You pass numerous side-hill cattle trails at one point, attesting to the Bureau of Land Management' s policy of leasing public lands to individuals for grazing purposes.

You eventually pass a Pacific Crest Trail (PCT) marker and a "No Motor-cycles" sign, and soon enter the realm of pinyon pines. Here you begin a series of switchbacks ascending east-facing slopes, then resume a northbound traverse, quickly crossing to the west side of the Sierra Nevada crest. After hiking 2.1 miles from Walker Pass, you reach a pinyon-shaded campsite situated on a saddle just west of Peak 6474.

Beyond the campsite, good views are available northwest to High Sierra peaks, with the fascinating Dome Land country in the foreground. These vistas are especially exciting when the southern Sierra is under its annual blanket of snow.

After hiking 1.75 miles from the campsite, you reach a Sierra crest saddle just north of conical Peak 6940. At this point, leave the Pacific Crest Trail and ascend the steep, boulder- and pinyon pine-covered Sierra Nevada crest to the northeast. You soon level off on a false peak, then continue east on the level before rising steeply once again. You then climb over a few minor hills and find yourself standing atop the 7,215-foot-high summit of Morris Peak, where a superb vista unfolds.

Peak baggers may wish to follow the PCT north toward Owens Peak and the Spanish Needles. The BLM has developed several springs along the route, allowing for an extended stay in this rugged portion of the Sierra crest. Otherwise, hikers should retrace their steps back to the trailhead.

HIKE 48 *BIG MEADOW TO THE DOMELAND*

General description: A rigorous, 21.4-mile loop backpack on the southern Kern Plateau, in the Domeland Wilderness.
Elevation gain and loss: 4,750 feet, -4,750 feet.
Trailhead elevation: 7,840 feet.
High point: 9,580 feet.
Maps: Kernville 15-minute USGS quad (neither the road to trailhead, nor the trail from .4 mile beyond trailhead to Machine Creek, shown on quad), Sequoia National Forest map.
Season: Late May through October.
Finding the trailhead: From Kernville, proceed north along the Kern River Road for about nineteen miles, then turn right (east) onto the Sherman Pass Road. Do not take the left- forking road which immediately crosses the Kern River and ascends into the Western Divide country.

After driving about 5.7 miles from the river, turn right (south) where a sign indicates Big Meadow. Follow this dirt road as it ascends southeastward, avoiding numerous signed spur roads. After driving 9.8 miles from the Sherman Pass Road, you reach a junction. The right-hand (southeast) fork, Forest Road 22S01, leads southward along the western margin of Big Meadow, as indicated by the sign. You take the left-hand fork, Forest Road 23S07, rising steeply at first, for .7 mile to the north end of Big Meadow, then turn left (north) where a sign indicates the Main Summit Trail. Follow this spur road for about 100 yards to its end and park.

The hike: Occupying the southern end of the Kern Plateau are the awe-inspiring domes, spires, and crags of the Domeland Wilderness, rising out of a dark green conifer forest. This trip encompasses a great variety of Domeland scenery, including sub- alpine forests of foxtail pine, picturesque meadows, and some of the most intriguing rock formations in the entire wilderness.

Campsites in the thickly forested terrain of the Domeland Wilderness abound. Water becomes increasingly scarce, though, as the summer wears on. Cattle can be seen grazing in Manter Meadow and in the forks of Trout Creek, usually from about July through September; water purification is a must during that period.

A wilderness permit is required, and can be obtained at the ranger station in Kernville.

From the trailhead, walk northward along the course of small Salmon Creek under the shade of Jeffrey and lodgepole pines and white firs. After .4 mile, the Main Summit Trail continues straight ahead, while your trail branches right.

Ascending along an intermittent tributary of Salmon Creek, you soon pass a small sloping meadow, then splash through the runoff of a cold, reliable spring, the least-suspect source of water on the entire hike.

After leaving the lodgepole pines and red firs behind, you ascend the final steep slopes to a pass which is 9,580 feet above sea level and shaded by the southernmost stand of foxtail pines in California. Foxtail pines grow in timberline forests in the southern Sierra Nevada, from here northward to near the southeastern boundary of Kings Canyon National Park. They can also be found in isolated stands in the Klamath Mountains of northwestern California. This tree is readily identifiable by its needles in bundles of five, arranged densely around the ends of the branches. With a little imagination, these branches can be seen to resemble a fox's tail. This pine is nearly identical to the bristlecone pine of the Great Basin and the southern Rockies, the primary difference being that the scales on the cones of bristlecone pines have an obvious, slender, incurved prickle, or bristle; the foxtail pine has a minute, unnoticeable prickle on its cone scales.

From the pass, your trail descends into the upper reaches of Little Trout Creek, which you hop across just below a lodgepole pine-encircled meadow.

A brief traverse then leads you to a steep northeast-trending ridge, where you are treated to red fir-framed vistas, including the Great Western Divide in the northwest, and the Sierra crest as far north as 12,123-foot-high Olancha Peak in the northeast.

Your trail descends steeply along this ridge, then levels off along the often-dry course of Snow Creek. The open Jeffrey pine forest in this area reflects a decrease in precipitation compared to the high ridge you crossed earlier.

You soon step across Little Trout Creek once again, and meet a westbound trail ascending Machine Creek; cross this creek and proceed downstream.

The trail soon crosses Trout Creek (where the fishing is fair), then, with brushy slopes closing in, climbs steeply over a low hill, descending briefly to reach a closed jeep road. You stroll eastward along this road for .7 mile, where the Dark Canyon Trail branches north.

The green expanse of Woodpecker Meadow lies a short distance south of your jeep road, seemingly out-of-place in this arid, brushy region. From this point you get your first glimpse of the majestic Domeland country, lying on the southeastern horizon.

The typical high-elevation campsite in the Sierra Nevada offers little protection from the weather. Photo by Rick Marvin.

Beyond the Dark Canyon Trail, you continue eastward, passing a piped spring and crossing Dark Canyon's creek. About .4 mile beyond the Dark Canyon Trail another jeep road branches north, and soon thereafter you turn right (south) at a signed junction, leaving the jeep road.

Your trail presently heads south through dense brush, enters a stand of Jeffrey pine after .75 mile, then descends to the rockbound course of Trout Creek, which you immediately ford. The trail climbs steeply through brushy terrain above the south bank of the creek, then continues southward along slopes covered with buckthorn, mountain mahogany, oak, and manzanita. The spectacular vertical rock formations the trail is approaching will excite even the most seasoned hiker. You soon cross a small creek, re- enter forest cover, then climb 500 feet to another small creek flowing over solid rock in the shadow of impressive, near-vertical rock walls.

The trail crosses the creek and begins a steep ascent in the shade of Jeffrey pines and white firs to a saddle at an elevation of 8,000 feet. From this saddle, a highly recommended side trip to Dome 8300 (about .3 mile northeast) begins. A short cross- country jaunt northeast along the ridge leads you to the open, rocky summit area of this dome, where all the Domeland and much of the southern Sierra is visible. This is, perhaps, the finest viewpoint in the entire wilderness. Many peaks on the Kern Plateau meet your gaze, including much of the alpine crest of the Great Western Divide and the Sierra Nevada crest as far north as Mt. Whitney. To your south lies the Domeland plateau, where granitic rock formations of virtually every description soar above the thickly forested landscape.

From the saddle, hike southward through park-like forest to another saddle, then descend past a northeast-branching trail leading across the Domeland plateau to the east.

Continuing your southward course, you parallel a small creek for one-half mile. Striking rock formations rise directly above the creek to your east, and walls and crags dot the slopes of the high ridge to the west.

After leaving the creek behind, you cross over a low ridge, then stroll through open, Jeffrey pine-covered ground, soon crossing another small creek, usually dry by September. The trail then crosses a low, boulder-stacked ridge and descends to a junction with a southbound trail that skirts the eastern margin of Manter Meadow, one of the most scenic camping areas in the wilderness. Hikers who choose to camp near the meadow will find adequate sites below its outlet creek. A small spring that feeds Manter Creek just below the meadow offers relatively safe drinking water, but for safety's sake, this source should be purified, as should any water obtained in the wilderness. And hikers should be especially careful to purify water from Manter Creek, for it drains the summertime home of a large herd of cattle which graze in the wilderness as part of the Forest Service's multiple-use land management policy.

Turning right at that trail junction, you proceed southwest, occasionally managing glimpses of the large meadow through openings in the forest. You soon step across a muddy gully below a grassy opening, and then parallel a fenceline, shortly passing an old cabin on your left.

The trail now heads westward along a Manter Creek tributary, and you begin the final ascent of the hike through a shady pine and fir forest. You exit the Domeland Wilderness after surmounting another saddle, this one at 8,300 feet above sea level, then descend westward along an old bulldozer track created when the forest in this area was selectively cut. About .8 mile from the saddle

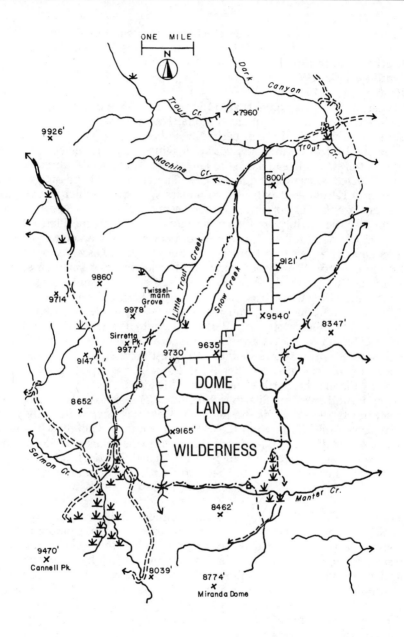

you emerge onto the dirt road just east of Big Meadow, turn right (north) and follow this road for .8 mile to your car at the Main Summit Trailhead.

HIKE 49
WEST MEADOW TO STONY MEADOW, RINCON TRAIL

General description: A moderate 14.6-mile point-to-point backpack along the western edge of Kern Plateau, in the Sequoia National Forest.

Elevation gain and loss: 1,400 feet, -5,450 feet.

Trailhead elevation: 8,720 feet.

High point: 8,790 feet.

Maps: Hockett Peak and Kernville 15-minute USGS quads (Kern Plateau roads not shown on quads), Sequoia National Forest map.

Season: Early June through early November.

Finding the trailhead: A network of logging roads has been constructed on the central Kern Plateau since the late 1950s. These roads are not shown on the outdated topographic quadrangles. Therefore, while passing the ranger station in Kernville, it will be two dollars well spent which is used to buy a Sequoia National Forest map, more a necessity than a luxury once you encounter the terribly confusing network of roads on the Plateau.

From Kernville, follow the Kern River Road north for about nineteen miles, then turn right; the left fork crosses the Kern River and ascends to the Western Divide country. Your paved road climbs steadily eastward, crossing over Sherman Pass (at an elevation of 9,200 feet) after 14.4 miles, then proceeds on an undulating northeast course across the Kern Plateau. After driving 5.6 miles from Sherman Pass, you reach a junction at the north end of small, narrow Paloma Meadows. Turn left (north) onto dirt Forest Road 22S41, soon passing Bonita Meadows and traveling across thickly forested terrain. Bear right after 3.4 miles where southbound Forest Road 22S41A branches left. You reach the roadend after another 1.1 miles, where adequate parking space is available along the north edge of West Meadow.

The turnoff from the Sherman Pass Road (Forest Road 22S05) can also be reached from U.S. 395 via the Kennedy Meadows Road. After driving about thirty-seven miles west from U.S. 395, turn south at Blackrock Junction and follow Forest Road 22S05 south for 10.7 miles to the Paloma Meadows junction.

Be sure to leave another vehicle at the signed Rincon Trailhead, 2.8 miles east of the Kern River on the Sherman Pass Road. If you don't, hitchhiking back to West Meadow will be difficult at best.

The hike: This backpack trip, downhill almost all the way, surveys a variety of Kern Plateau scenery on trails seldom used by man. Combining isolated camping experiences in deep forest with wide panoramas obtained while traversing open hillsides, this easy and memorable hike allows newcomers to the Kern Plateau to gain appreciation for a fine land that sees few visitors.

Wildlife is plentiful, and water is usually close at hand, except along the Rincon Trail, where you pass several small but unreliable creeks.

Hikers may want to avoid the area between June and late August, when grazing cattle are present.

Begin this hike by walking west from the trailhead on good trail through a lodgepole pine forest. You soon cross over a low ridge and descend to long, narrow Corral Meadow, reaching a junction after .8 mile. You turn right and begin descending along the grassy banks of the small creek.

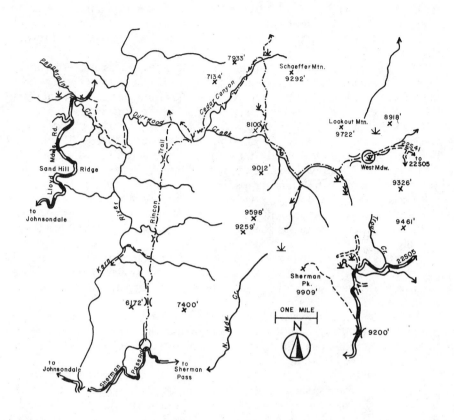

About 1.2 miles from Corral Meadow, a signed trail branches left (south), heading for Sherman Peak. Bearing right, you continue descending along Durrwood Creek through dense lodgepole pines and small meadows, and after another 1.2 miles you reach the sagebrush-clad clearing labeled "Schaeffer Meadow" on the quad.

Here your trail leaves Durrwood Creek and passes through a low gap to the north, shaded by a Jeffrey and sugar pine and white fir forest. You cross two more saddles along your northbound course, and 1.6 miles from Durrwood Creek reach the small grassy clearing of Stony Meadow. An icy creek slices through the meadow, emanating from the steep west slopes of 9,292-foot-high Schaeffer Mountain, whose near-vertical cliffs provide an exciting 800-foot-tall backdrop to the meadow.

Proceed through the meadow to a mauled trail sign. Straight ahead, a faint, unmaintained trail leads over the ridge into Rattlesnake Creek. You turn left, and begin a protracted descent into Cedar Canyon. Part way down the canyon, incense-cedar increases its frequency among other forest trees, joining a ground cover of gooseberry, currant, and the fragrant kit-kit-dizze.

You leave the conifer forest at an elevation of 6,400 feet, cross Cedar Canyon's creek, and continue descending along the north side of the creek. Beyond this ford, you have good eastward views into the extremely rugged middle reaches of Durrwood Creek. The route quickly becomes hemmed in by chaparral, including mountain mahogany, ceanothus, fremontia, live oak, and Brewers oak.

During this descent, you have superb views down to and across Kern Canyon to Slate Mountain, The Needles, and the Western Divide. As you begin a series of switchbacks down into Durrwood Creek, the alpine peaks of the southern Great Western Divide briefly meet your gaze in the northwest.

Turn left after hiking 3.7 miles from Stony Meadow; the main trail descends westward above Durrwood Creek. Your trail, however, drops .1 mile to a boulder-hop ford of Durrwood Creek, much larger here than where you left it in Schaeffer Meadow. The creek is shaded by Jeffrey and ponderosa pines and white alders. A few fair campsites can be found near this ford.

Proceed over a low, brushy ridge on a southwesterly course, intersecting the north-south Rincon Trail after 1.1 miles. You will be following the course of the Kern Canyon Fault on the southbound Rincon Trail from here to the end of the hike.

Along this route, you cross over five low saddles and four intermittent creeks, sometimes in chaparral and sometimes in a forest of ponderosa pine, incense-cedar, and Brewers oak, which puts forth a golden display with the onset of autumn.

The final saddle involves a steep, sustained ascent of 750 feet. Before beginning this ascent, avoid a westbound trail down to the Kern River. Just before topping that saddle, you will be treated to unobstructed views northward up Kern Canyon to the Great Western Divide.

Upon reaching the saddle 5,540 feet above sea level, you will have an excellent southward view along the Kern Canyon Fault, which cuts the deep V-notch in the ridge across Brush Creek. From here you glide down the moderately steep trail to the Rincon Trailhead.

HIKE 50 *JACKASS PEAK*

General description: A 2.4-mile round-trip in the Sequoia National Forest, partially cross-country (class 2) day hike for experienced hikers, leading to an excellent viewpoint on the central Kern Plateau.
Elevation gain and loss: 645 feet.
Trailhead elevation: 8,600 feet.
High point: Jackass Peak, 9,245 feet.
Maps: Monache Mtn. 15-minute USGS quad (road to trailhead and part of trail not shown on quad), Sequoia National Forest map.
Season: Late June through October.
Finding the trailhead: Drive to the Blackrock Ranger Station on the Kern Plateau (described in Kern Peak hike, No. 51), thirty-seven miles west of U.S.

395 and fifty miles north of Kernville. From the ranger station, drive north on paved Forest Road 21S03 for 3.8 miles, then turn right (northeast) onto Forest Road 20S37 where a semi-permanent sign indicates the Monache Jeep Road. Follow this dirt road for 3.6 miles, then bear right where the Monache Jeep Road departs to the left (north). Stay left after another 1.3 miles at the junction with southbound Forest Road 20Sll. Continue another .8 mile to the trailhead at the end of the road.

The hike: The Kern Plateau offers hikers exceptional backcountry experiences in both designated and non-designated wilderness. The wide swath of plateau country visible from Jackass Peak's easily attainable summit will entice hikers to partake in additional investigation of this fascinating and seldom-visited region of the Sierra Nevada. Carry plenty of water.

From the trailhead, hike southeast on the old abandoned logging trail for .3 mile through a forest of Jeffrey pine and red fir to the juncture with the Albanita Trail, and turn left (east). This trail is rarely used by anything other than deer and an occasional trailbike, although you probably won't encounter the latter because they are barred from entering the South Sierra Wilderness, the boundary of which lies less than one mile ahead.

After hiking another .2 mile, you reach a saddle on a ridge 8,800 feet above sea level. From this point you get your first glimpse of Jackass Peak's granite crag. You leave the trail here, hiking cross-country in a northeasterly direction. You pass through another small saddle just west of the peak and work your way around to the northeast side, where you can scramble more easily up rock to the summit.

The two outstanding features of the Kern Plateau make themselves apparent to the north from your rocky viewpoint: Monache Meadows, the largest meadow in the Sierra Nevada; and Olancha Peak, which at an elevation of 12,123 feet is the highest point on the Kern Plateau. Also visible is the Sierra crest as far north as the Mt. Langley-Mount Whitney region, with the Great Western Divide's sawtooth ridge lining the western horizon.

From the peak, carefully retrace your route back to the trailhead; or, if you feel unsatisfied after the short class 2 jaunt to Jackass Peak, the hike can be extended into a backpack of two to three days. Several peaceful meadows dot the conifer- clad landscape east of the peak. These grasslands are seldom visited, and the trails to them are often faint or nonexistent, but the going is easy and the camping is pleasant. A wilderness permit is required to enter the South Sierra Wilderness, and can be obtained at the Blackrock Ranger Station.

At the point where you leave the trail to scramble up Jackass Peak, continue walking east on the trail, entering the South Sierra Wilderness upon cresting a low ridge and meeting a southbound trail on your left.

Continuing east through thick conifers, you very soon avoid a left-branching trail and drop down into the bowl containing spreading Albanita Meadows. The trail here is often faint; simply follow the main trunk of the meadow eastward toward the craggy Finger Rock massif on the eastern skyline.

You will soon pass fenced-in Aqua Bonita Spring along the southern margin of this lodgepole pine-encircled spread. This is your best source of water in the area, but wise hikers will purify it nonetheless.

About .25 mile east of the spring, a faint tread branches south, leads over a low ridge, and drops into the upper reaches of infrequently visited Hooker

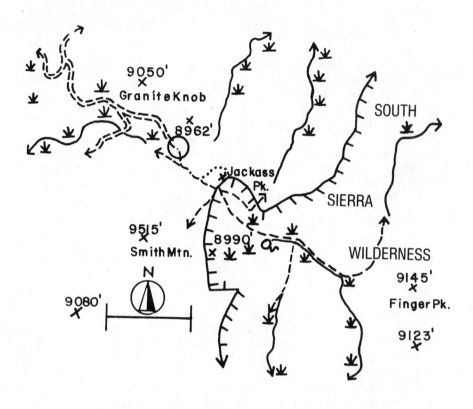

Meadow. Boasting one of the finest aspen stands on the Kern Plateau, this remote locale is especially impressive after the first frosts of autumn have turned the aspens' shimmering leaves into a brilliant show of yellows and oranges.

The small stream draining Hooker Meadow tends to dry up in its upper reaches as the summer wears on, so a downstream jaunt will probably be necessary to obtain water.

Back at the trail junction in Albanita Meadows, you may elect to continue eastward, following the north side of the small stream draining Albanita Meadows and forming the headwaters of Lost Creek.

Where the meadow-bordered creek bends south, a trail branches left and briefly heads east into the forest. This rarely used path soon jogs north and crests a low ridge, entering a well- drained forest of pine and fir. After a brief and gentle descent, you reach the upper end of long and narrow Lost Meadows. You soon capture an inspiring view of Olancha Peak in the north, with a green expanse of meadow in the foreground and framed by nearby lodgepole pines.

Campsites are plentiful, but the creek draining the meadow tends to dry up as the season progresses. It may be wise to pack water the short distance from Aqua Bonita Spring after mid-July.

From the trailhead, Aqua Bonita Spring is a hike of about 1.75 miles. Hooker Meadow lies about .75 mile south of Albanita Meadows, and Lost Meadows lies about 1.5 miles northeast of Albanita Meadows. Elevation gain in this area is almost nonexistent, making a hike in this part of the South Sierra Wilderness an ideal choice for novice hikers or families with children.

HIKE 51 *BLACKROCK GAP TO KERN PEAK*

General description: A moderately strenuous 26.6-mile round-trip backpack in the Golden Trout Wilderness, leading into the heart of Kern Plateau.
Elevation gain and loss: 3,920 feet, -1,350 feet.
Trailhead elevation: 8,940 feet.
High point: Kern Peak, 11,510 feet.
Maps: Hockett Peak and Kern Peak 15-minute USGS quads (trail from Blackrock Gap to Casa Vieja Meadows, trail from Redrock Meadows to Toowa Range, and road to trailhead not shown on quads), Sequoia National Forest map.
Season: Late June through mid-October
Finding the trailhead: Fron Kernville, drive about nineteen miles up the Kern River Road then turn right (east) onto the Sherman Pass Road, Forest Road 22S05. This road quickly climbs eastward out of Kern River Canyon and begins a steady ascent through the Brush Creek drainage. After 3.1 miles, you pass a gate that is usually closed between late November and late May. The road surmounts Sherman Pass 14.4 miles from the river, and you continue east, then north, avoiding numerous signed spur roads. After driving 17.2 miles beyond Sherman Pass, you reach a four-way junction. The east-branching road, Forest Road 21S02, leads to Kennedy Meadows and U.S. 395. You continue straight ahead (north), your paved road now bearing the number 21S03. You quickly pass the seasonal Blackrock Ranger Station and continue north for 8.1 miles, avoiding several signed spur roads, to the trailhead at the roadend, 59.2 miles from Kernville.

Or from U.S. 395, about nine miles north of its junction with State Highway 14 and fifty-six miles south of Lone Pine, turn west where a large sign indicates Kennedy Meadows is twenty-five miles ahead. Follow this steadily climbing road up to the crest of the Sierra Nevada. The last 2.5 miles of road east of the crest are unpaved. Pavement resumes at the crest and you follow this good road, avoiding several signed spur roads, for twenty- five miles to a junction. Turn left; the northbound road ends in three miles at the Kennedy Meadows Campground. You immediately pass the Kennedy Meadows General Store, then cross the South Fork Kern River via a bridge. The road leads west for twelve miles to Blackrock Junction, where you turn right (north), and drive 8.1 miles to the trailhead.

The hike: This pleasant backpack through red fir and lodgepole pine forest, occasionally interrupted by verdant, wildflower- filled meadows, leads hikers to the best viewpoint on the Kern Plateau, the remote alpine summit of Kern Peak. In addition to being one of the most isolated and seldom-visited mountains on the Kern Plateau, Kern Peak offers superb, awe-inspiring vistas encompassing hundreds of square miles of lonely, relatively unknown wilderness —undoubtedly one of the finest wilderness viewpoints in California.

But hikers won't be beating a path to its summit—mainly because few hikers even know about the area, and secondly because getting to the trailhead involves driving many miles of confusing (but paved) logging roads, dodging logging trucks along the way.

Solitude-seekers should be more than satisfied after leaving the last vestiges of hikers behind at Redrock Meadows and ascending the slopes of the Toowa Range with no more company than mule deer, black bear, and Clark's nutcrackers.

Hikers uncomfortable without the guidance of a trail should avoid the final two miles to the peak, which require some moderate route-finding.

Campsites abound on the thickly forested terrain of the central Kern Plateau, and water is plentiful. Cattle will be found grazing some of the meadows along this hike, usually from early July through September, so water purification is a must during that period.

Fishing for pan-sized golden trout is fair in Ninemile Creek and in Long Canyon Creek.

Since the first road on the Kern Plateau opened the area to logging in the late 1950s, a good portion of the plateau has been penetrated with roads. One advantage of this construction is the resulting easy access to the best of the Kern Plateau, that portion which is protected as the Golden Trout Wilderness.

This is good hiking country, where walking is easy and the scenery is pleasant and sometimes spectacular. Signs of overuse are minimal—the area isn't as popular with hikers as are regions of the High Sierra, but it certainly is no less attractive.

A wilderness permit is required, and can be obtained at the Kernville or Blackrock ranger stations.

From the road's end, walk north past a corral for .2 mile to Blackrock Gap, where you enter the Golden Trout Wilderness. The route then descends along a tributary of Ninemile Creek for 1.7 miles under the shade of towering red firs to a junction with an eastbound trail. Continuing north, your trail skirts the western margin of sloping Casa Vieja Meadows, soon passing a southwest-branching trail immediately before bypassing a Snow Survey cabin on your left.

A short distance beyond the cabin, you emerge from lodgepole pine forest to ford Ninemile Creek at the lower end of Casa Vieja Meadows. Immediately beyond the ford you meet a westbound trail leading to Jordan Hot Springs, a small enclave of civilization that is the destination of the majority of hikers in this region.

Resuming your northerly course, you quickly pass a closed eastbound jeep trail that leads past the seasonal ranger station visible .1 mile east. Soon leaving the grasslands of the meadows behind, your trail passes over a low gap, descends to a ford of Lost Trout Creek, then traverses lodgepole pine-shaded slopes to the grassy banks of Long Canyon Creek, about three miles from Casa Vieja Meadows.

After fording this noisy stream, a short uphill stretch brings you to another junction. The eastbound trail continues ascending Long Canyon, but you turn left (west), climb over a low hill, and enter Beer Keg Meadow where the trail

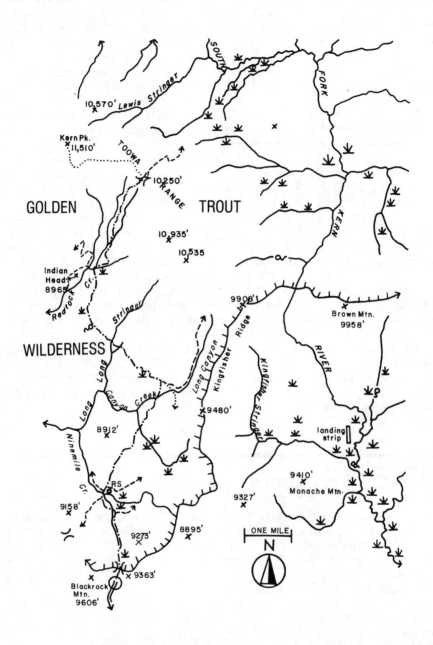

becomes faint. Continuing your northwestward course, you soon cross two branches of Long Stringer, where open, grassy environs offer good views southwestward to the heavily forested hill of 9,121-foot-high Manzanita Knob. About one-half mile beyond the last ford of Long Stringer, you pass unusual River Spring. Here a large stream emerges from between two small boulders just below the trail. This is the purest source of water encountered on this hike, and shouldn't be contaminated by any cattle that might be in the area.

Beyond the spring, you pass through a small meadow, then traverse slopes shaded by lodgepole pine and red fir. Before beginning a short descent into Redrock Meadows, you will glimpse the copper-colored crag of Indian Head, its 500-foot-tall face rising precipitously above Redrock Creek.

Upon entering the first of Redrock Meadow's grassy clearings, bear right where a westbound trail departs to your left. Your sometimes-faint trail ascends the easternmost fork of Redrock Creek, curves in a northwesterly direction through dense lodgepole pine forest, crosses another small creek, and begins the steep ascent to the crest of the Toowa Range in red fir shade.

You leave the trail at the crest of the Toowa Range, 10,250 feet above sea level, a major east-west ridge dividing the waters of the Kern River from its South Fork. Your route, now cross- country, leads westward along the crest of this ridge through a thick forest of lodgepole and foxtail pine. After walking one mile along the gentle crest, you are confronted with the steep east slopes of Kern Peak, rising abruptly out of a small cirque. Staying just north of the crest, you jog southwestward, and a short but steep scramble up to the low point on the cirque's headwall brings you to the summit ridge. You ascend this ridge through a sparse forest of foxtail pine, the expanding vistas luring you onward to the barren summitt of Kern Peak, where a breathtaking view of the Kern River drainage is revealed.

Little remains of the long-abandoned fire lookout tower that once capped this peak.

Topographic quads may be helpful in identifying distant landmarks.

From the peak, carefully retrace your cross-country route back to the trail, then backtrack to the trailhead.

HIKE 52 JORDAN PEAK

General description: An easy 1.5- or four-mile round-trip day hike to a subalpine peak and far-flung vistas of the southern Sierra Nevada, in the Sequoia National Forest.
Elevation gain and loss: 715 or 915 feet.
Trailhead elevation: 8,200 or 8,400 feet.
High point: Jordan Peak, 9,115 feet.
Maps: Camp Nelson 15-minute USGS quad (most roads and trails not shown on this outdated map), Sequoia National Forest map.
Season: Mid-June through October.
Finding the trailhead: There are two ways to locate the beginning of this remote hike: (1) eleven miles from Porterville via tortuously twisting and turning State Highway 190; or (2) from Kernville via the Kern River Road and the Western Divide Highway.

(1) Follow State Highway 190 east from Porterville for about forty miles to a junction with northbound Forest Road 21S50. This junction is marked by a sign pointing north to Golden Trout Wilderness Packtrains 7.5 miles ahead. There is also a highway sign at this point indicating Johnsondale, California Hot Springs, and Kernville, with mileage listings to these points.

Turn left (north) here. The pavement ends after 4.5 miles, and here you turn left where a sign points to Clicks Creek Trailhead. Continuing northwest on Forest Road 21S50, bear right 1.2 miles from the end of the pavement where a sign points to Clicks Creek Trailhead, Jordan Peak Lookout, and Summit Trailhead. After driving another 1.7 miles, turn left where a sign points to Jordan Peak Lookout. This westbound road is closed annually from November 1 through June 1. If you intend to take this hike at a leisurely pace, park here; if you are in a hurry, drive west for 1.2 miles to the signed trailhead.

(2) From Kernville, drive north up the Kern River on locally signed Sierra Way. After driving about nineteen miles along the Kern River, bear left where the unsigned Sherman Pass Road branches right, then cross the river via a two-lane bridge. After driving four miles from the river, avoid a left-branching road leading to the abandoned lumber mill town of Johnsondale, and .6 mile further avoid a right-branching road leading to Camp Whitsett and beyond. Turn left where the sign points left to the Western Divide Highway. Avoid a left-branching road to Thompson Camp after eight miles from the river, where a sign indicates California Hot Springs. After driving 11.2 miles from the Kern River, turn right onto the Western Divide Highway; a sign here points to State Highway 190, Ponderosa, and Camp Nelson. Follow this good paved road north, avoiding several signed spur roads. At a point about 15.2 miles from the previous junction, and 26.5 miles from the Kern River, make a sharp right turn onto Forest Road 21S50, just beyond a sign listing mileages to Camp Nelson, Springville, and Porterville. From here follow description (1) to reach the trailhead.

The hike: The sweeping vistas available from the summit of Jordan Peak easily justify the long mountain drive to the trailhead. Hikers planning a trek along the Clicks Creek or Summit trails (wilderness permit required for either) are urged to take this easy warm-up hike for a grand survey of much of the terrain they will soon be hiking through.

As you will see while atop Jordan Peak, the southern Sierra Nevada was largely unglaciated. The landscape that meets your gaze, especially the Kern Plateau to the east, clearly illustrates the rounded, plateau-like character of the region that existed millions of years ago, before the Sierra Nevada batholith began uplifting to its present height. Many high, alpine peaks in the Sierra also escaped glaciation, standing high above the rivers of ice. So they, too, are remnants of the broad, gentle surfaces that characterized the region in ancient times.

After completing the easy jaunt to Jordan Peak, hikers may decide to descend the Clicks Creek Trail to the Little Kern River (wilderness permit required, contact the Sequoia National Forest Supervisor in Porterville or the Kernville Ranger Station). This well-marked trail heads northeast from Log Cabin Meadow, about 1.2 miles south of the Jordan Peak turnoff on Forest Road 21S50. The trail descends for six miles through conifer forest, following Clicks Creek most of the way, to good campsites along the Little Kern River where fishing can be good for Little Kern golden trout.

HIKE 52 *JORDAN PEAK*

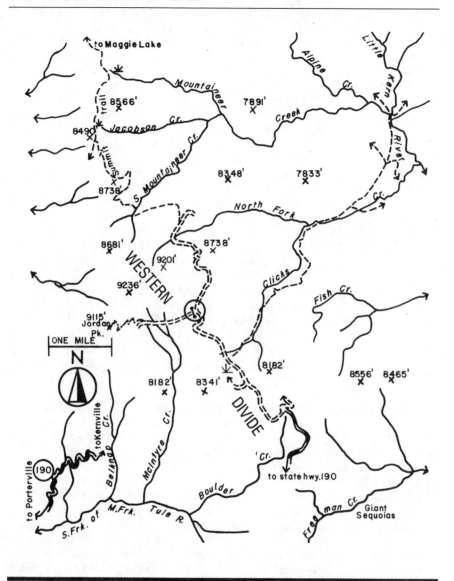

From the gate on Sequoia National Forest Road 20S71, proceed west on a gentle grade through red fir forest. You occasionally pass logged-over openings, and your road passes over a few spring-fed creeklets.

After strolling 1.2 miles, you meet the signed Main Trail on your right. The road ends at a turnout, .1 mile beyond.

The trail leads southwest and soon begins switchhbacking up a selectively cut red fir-covered slope. As you near the summit, chinquapin, mountain whitethorn, and manzanita begin to invade sunny openings. A few final switchbacks suffice to bring hikers to the summit.

Silver pines (or western white pines) will be found growing on the north slope of the peak, preferring the colder microclimate that prevails there. These trees are closely related to the five-needled sugar pine, but are distinguished by smaller cones.

Upon surmounting the summit of Jordan Peak, you immediately understand why this peak was chosen as a site for a fire lookout tower—the view is truly far-reaching, and splendid as well.

To your northeast, the jagged, alpine peaks of the Great Western Divide line the horizon. To the west lies the gaping chasm of the North Fork of Middle Fork Tule River, more than 5,000 feet below. Moses Mountain, 9,331 feet high, soars westward from the depths of that canyon, and 10,042-foot-high Maggie Mountain and its 10,000-foot-high satellite summits rise to the east.

Far to the east lies the Kern Plateau, punctuated on the eastern horizon by 12,123-foot-high Olancha Peak. Kern Peak is also visible on the northeastern skyline.

The massive flanks of Slate Mountain rise steadily to your south above Camp Nelson and the South Fork of Middle Fork Tule River until they peak at 9,302 feet above sea level. On the southwest horizon, the Mt. Pinos region can be seen, and on a clear day you can gaze across the broad plain of the San Joaquin Valley to the South Coast Ranges on the western horizon.

These are truly inspiring vistas that will cause hikers to linger. The lookout is occupied during fire season, usually from June through October.

From the peak retrace your route to the trailhead.

After an easy climb to the summit of Jordan Peak, hikers quickly realize why this mountain was chosen as the site of a fire lookout tower. The view encompasses much of the heavily forested terrain of the southern Sierra as well as the sawtooth peaks of the Great Western Divide, at the southern end of the "High" Sierra.

HIKE 53 *COTTONWOOD LOOP*

General description: A moderate 23.1-mile loop backpack at the southern end of the High Sierra, in the Golden Trout Wilderness, John Muir Wilderness, and Sequoia National Park.

Elevation gain and loss: 3,250 feet, -3,400 feet.

Trailhead elevation: 9,900 feet.

High point: New Army Pass, 12,400 feet.

Maps: Olancha, and Kern Peak 15-minute USGS quads (Pacific Crest Trail, Horseshoe Meadow Road, and trailhead not shown on quads), Inyo National Forest map.

Season: July through mid-October.

Finding the trailhead: From U.S. 395 in Lone Pine, turn west onto the signed Whitney Portal Road. Follow this road westward along Lone Pine Creek and through the boulder-covered Alabama Hills for 3.5 miles to the signed Horseshoe Meadow Road, and turn left (south). Ahead you can see the switchbacks of your road ascending the great eastern escarpment of the Sierra Nevada. Follow this good paved road for about 18.5 miles to the Mulkey Pass-Trail Pass trailhead. Since there is no parking here, proceed up the road, bearing right at two junctions, reaching the upper trailhead after .8 mile, the terminus of this hike.

Cottonwood Lakes in the John Muir Wilderness are the state's only source of pure-strain golden trout eggs, which are transported to the Mt. Whitney Hatchery and then, as fingerling trout, transplanted in high mountain lakes in California. The lower four Cottonwood Lakes are closed to fishing to protect the golden trout population, but many other lakes in the basin offer good golden trout fishing. Photo by John Reilly.

The hike: Stated simply, the Sierra Nevada is a huge westward-tilting block of the earth's crust uplifted along major faults at its eastern base. The eastern escarpment is abrupt, rising as much as 10,000 feet in ten miles from the floor of the Owens Valley, and sloping gently westward into the Central Valley from a crest of high peaks. This range is California's largest and most spectacular, over 400 miles long and as much as eighty miles wide. It includes perhaps the most dramatic mountainous terrain in the nation. Combine this majestic scenery with a mild climate and easy access into its remote backcountry, and the result is perhaps the most exceptional hiking country on earth.

At the southern end of the "High" Sierra, the range's majestic alpine peaks dissolve into the rounded, gentle terrain of the heavily forested Kern Plateau. Generally less spectacular (but no less worthy of exploration), the Kern Plateau sees few hikers. The numerous large grasslands and the few alpine peaks that dot this landscape offer a refreshing change-of-pace from the mostly forest-covered terrain. The Kern Plateau is home to grazing cattle during the summer months, but these bovine semi- permanent residents are rarely more than a slight inconvenience to hikers.

This fine hike is an introduction to this transition region of the Sierra, including a crossing of a pass 12,400 feet above sea level, a 14,000-foot-high peak within easy walking distance, access to remote alpine lakes, and a timberline traverse on the Pacific Crest Trail. It offers hikers a chance to escape civilization while basking in endless horizons of wilderness, refreshing to both mind and body.

A wilderness permit is required, and can be obtained at the Mt. Whitney Ranger Station in Lone Pine. Keep in mind that daily entry quotas are in effect.

From the upper Horseshoe Meadows hiker's parking area, stroll down the pavement for .8 mile to the Mulkey Pass-Trail Pass trailhead, and turn right. You then head south through a sandy foxtail and lodgepole pine forest, and you soon break into the open at the eastern end of Horseshoe Meadow, entering the Golden Trout Wilderness just before hopping across the two small creeks draining that spread. The sandy margins of this and other Kern Plateau grasslands are a result of excessive overgrazing by sheep and cattle during the late nineteenth century. These meadows have not since recovered.

As you proceed southwestward along the sandy trail, you will capture superb views of the peaks encircling the Cottonwood Creek drainage. The flat-topped mountain in the northwest is 14,027- foot-high Mt. Langley, the southernmost 14,000-footer in the Sierra. The barren upper slopes of conical Trail Peak, rising out of the heavy timber to your southwest, were once the site of a proposed ski area. Trail Peak and environs are now protected within the boundaries of the Golden Trout Wilderness.

The low, forested ridge that wanders eastward from Trail Peak is the unimpressive Sierra Nevada crest, which begins its steady climb to the spectacular alpine peaks of the High Sierra north of Trail Peak's alpine crown.

After strolling .9 mile from the trailhead, the Mulkey Pass Trail diverges from your route, and you bear right and ascend the densely forested north slopes of the Sierra crest for 1.3 miles to an elevation of 10,500 feet and Trail Pass, where there is a four-way junction.

Straight ahead (south), a trail descends into Mulkey Meadows. Mulkey Creek was the original source of golden trout planted in Cottonwood Creek. Golden trout, the California state fish, originally existed only in a few tributaries of the upper Kern River drainage until introduced into Cottonwood Creek in the

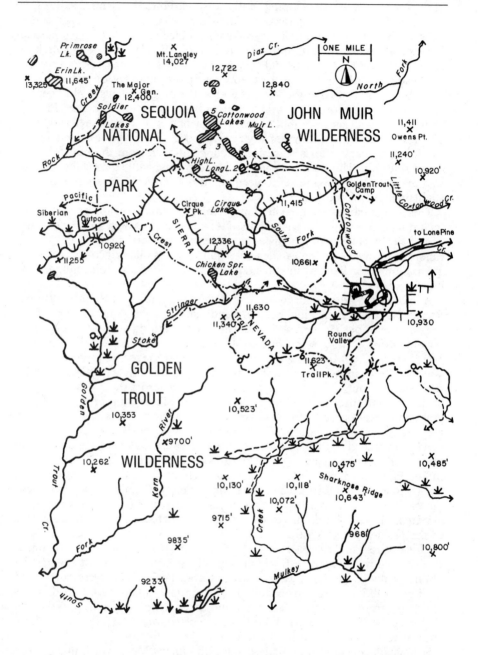

1870s. Today, Cottonwood Lakes 1, 2,3, and 4 are the state's only source of pure-strain golden trout eggs. All four of these Cottonwood Lakes are closed to fishing to protect the) golden trout population.

At Trail Pass, you turn right (west) onto the Pacific Crest Trail, and traverse north-facing slopes after a few short switchbacks. As you approach Poison Meadow and the first adequate campsites along the hike, you pass a northwest-trending spur trail offering access to a corral and possible campsites. Immediately beyond the spur trail, you splash through the waters of an icy spring cascading down from above your trail; this is the last reliable source of water until Chicken Spring Lake, more than four miles ahead.

Your route traverses foxtail pine-shaded slopes above the sagebrush margin of Poison Meadow on its westward ascent, soon surmounting the crest of the Sierra Nevada at a 10,800-foot-high saddle and beginning a view-filled three-mile traverse, first west, then north, to Cottonwood Pass.

About three-quarters of a mile beyond the saddle, you pass just below the wildflower-speckled environs of an early-season spring that is the source of the South Fork Kern River. Shortly beyond the spring you can glimpse South Fork Meadows to the southwest, as well as numerous other Kern Plateau grasslands and Kern Peak's alpine summit, to the south.

Upon reaching Cottonwood Pass, at 11,200 feet above sea level, you are confronted with another four-way junction. The eastbound trail descends to Horseshoe Meadow and your trailhead, while the westbound trail switchbacks into Big Whitney Meadow 1,400 feet below.

But you continue your northbound trek along the Pacific Crest Trail, soon crossing the often-dry outlet stream draining Chicken Spring Lake. This lake, sometimes heavily used, depends upon aerial transplants to maintain a golden trout population.

Your trail presently climbs above the lake and begins a protracted timberline traverse along the sandy southwestern slopes of the Sierra crest. The vast green, sand-rimmed expanse of Big Whitney Meadow to your southwest provides a vivid contrast with the dark-green forested hills that surround it. The extensive, snowy crags of the Great Western Divide stand boldly on the western skyline, an impressive view accompanying hikers for miles.

The trail soon contours into a small cirque, rounds a ridge, and passes a sign informing hikers that they are entering Sequoia National Park. After your trail begins descending, you capture glimpses of the jagged crest of the Kaweah Peaks Ridge between trailside foxtail pines. You can also see the flower-dotted spread of Siberian Outpost's sub-alpine meadow sloping away to the west. After hiking less than one mile from the park boundary, you part company with the Pacific Crest Trail and turn right (north). After a short hill climb, the trail begins a forested descent into the headwaters of Rock Creek. Ahead you can gaze northward to the awe-inspiring peaks encircling the upper Rock Creek drainage. A few miles to the northwest, Joe Devel Peak soars out of the heavily forested landscape, the southernmost 13,000-foot-high peak in the Sierra Nevada.

You reach a junction along a Rock Creek tributary after hiking 1.25 miles from the Pacific Crest Trail. A highly recommended side trip begins here, following the northbound trail to the Soldier Lakes, then crossing the low ridge just west of The Major General and ascending into the headwaters of Rock Creek. The Mount Whitney 15-minute USGS quad is recommended for this cross-country route. The alpine basin at the head of this drainage abounds with beautiful fish-filled lakes, and is surrounded by a host of impressive peaks rising well above the 13,000-foot level.

From the above-mentioned junction, your trail turns right (east) and ascends along a meadow-lined creek toward the massive granite hills that form the crest of the Sierra. Soon rising above timberline, the trail makes a few switchbacks and, angling toward a low gap in the crest, suddenly veers southeast and ascends the final sandy, alpine slopes to New Army Pass. The vistas from this high pass are far-reaching, extending as far eastward as Telescope Peak in the Panamint Range. To the west, much of the Great Western Divide can be seen, and to the north are the high peaks girdling upper Rock Creek.

The relatively gentle south slope of Mt. Langley, two miles to your north along the undulating crest of the Sierra Nevada, offers an easy opportunity for hikers with some cross-country experience to break the 14,000-foot barrier, and it provides superb vistas as well.

From the pass, the trail switchbacks down the steep headwall of a cirque and levels off on the floor of the basin. Stunted timber begins to appear as you pass High Lake and descend to forested Long Lake. Long Lake and South Fork Lakes sometimes offer good fishing, but have been known to freeze out fish populations during hard winters. Remember that Cottonwood Lakes 1, 2, 3, and 4 are closed to fishing, but the remainder of the lakes in the basin are open to fishing from July 1 through October 31, with a limit of five trout permitted. Only artificial flies with single barbless hooks may be used.

From Long Lake, your route descends eastward toward upper South Fork Lake, then jogs northeast to skirt the southern shore of Cottonwood Lake No. 2 Just beyond that lake you meet a northbound trail leading to the upper Cottonwood Lakes. You continue east, soon bypassing the grass-rimmed shore of Cottonwood Lake No. 1, then switchback down a foxtail pine-covered slope to meet the right-branching trail leading to South Fork and Cirque Lakes.

Continuing downstream, you meet another trail in less than one mile, immediately after hopping across Cottonwood Creek. Turn right and proceed downstream along the sometimes meadow-fringed creek. You soon re-cross to the creek's south bank, and pass the fenced-in private property of Golden Trout Camp (also known as Thacher School).

You reach a signed trail leading to Horseshoe Meadows trailhead about 1.1 mile below the last stream crossing. Turn right onto that trail, briefly skirting a long meadow. A pleasant .6 mile stroll through the forest leads to an easy crossing of grassy-banked South Fork Cottonwood Creek. Shortly thereafter, bear left onto the newer trail, traversing among foxtail and lodgepole pines for one mile to the roadend and your cars.

HIKE 54 *ALTA PEAK*

General description: A strenuous 12.6-mile round-trip day hike or backpack in Sequoia Naitonal Park leading to a superb alpine vista point on the western slope of the Sierra Nevada.

Elevation gain and loss: 3,944 feet.

Trailhead elevation: 7,260 feet.

High point: Alta Peak, 11,204 feet.

Maps: Triple Divide Peak 15-minute USGS quad, Sequoia/Kings Canyon National Park map.

Season: Late June through mid-October.

Finding the trailhead: From Visalia, follow State Highway 198 east for 53.5 miles, then turn right (east) where a large sign indicates Wolverton. This turnoff is about three miles northeast of Giant Forest. Turn east onto Wolverton Road and drive 1.5 miles to the large turnaround at the trailhead. Avoid the road branching right to the Wolverton Corrals, one quarter mile from the highway.

Or from Fresno, follow State Highway 180 east for fifty-eight miles to the junction with General's Highway at the Wye, then turn southeast and drive twenty-six miles to the trailhead.

The hike: Most alpine peaks in the Sierra Nevada involve at least some scrambling or basic rock climbing, and so are accessible only to those with the skills and conditioning required to attain their summits. But by taking advantage of an easy trail, anyone who takes this hike has the opportunity to stand upon the alpine summit of Alta Peak and enjoy an all-encompassing vista, rivaling the best viewpoints in the Sierra.

This trip surveys west slope scenery ranging from red fir forests to lichen-encrusted granite slabs atop Alta.

A wilderness permit is required for overnight camping in national parks, and should be obtained at the Lodgepole Visitor Center, about 1.5 miles north-east of the Wolverton turnoff.

The trail begins near the eastern edge of the large parking area, where a large sign identifies various backcountry destinations. After a short climb, turn right (east); the westbound trail descends to the Marble Fork Kaweah River. Your gentle ascent through red fir forest leads you on an easterly, then southeasterly course. After 1.7 miles, you meet the Lakes Trail on your left, which leads to several overused sub-alpine lakes where camping is strictly regulated.

Continue your ascent through fir forest along Wolverton Creek for .9 mile to the low saddle of Panther Gap, where your route intersects the Alta Trail coming from the Giant Forest. From this point you can see the high peaks of the Great Western Divide in the east. The fantastic jumble of spires and crags visble to the south across the deep trench of the Middle Fork Kaweah River are the Castle Rocks.

Proceeding east along the Alta Trail, accompanied by ever- expanding vistas, you begin a one-mile traverse across mostly open south-facing slopes, with Jeffrey and sugar pine for occasional shade, to a southbound path descending to the High Sierra Trail. Bear left and contour into the bowl that contains Mehrten Meadow and the first adequate campsites on the hike. The cliffs and

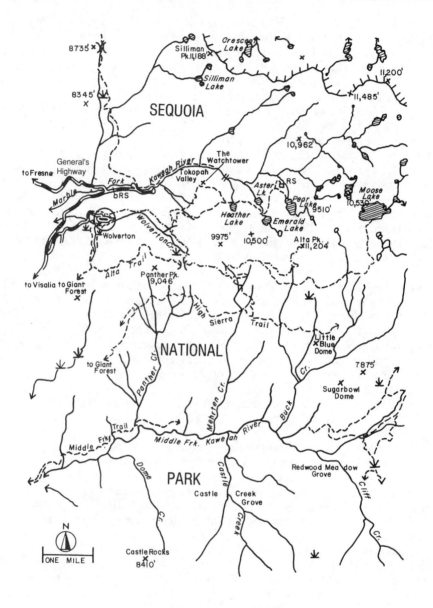

crags associated with Alta Peak and the granite dome of Tharps Rock looming above the meadow combine with the excellent views to make this a highly scenic camping area. Water is usually available in the small creek until late summer.

Near the east side of the Mehrten Meadow bowl, about 1.1 miles from the previous junction, turn left onto the Alta Peak Trail. The Alta Trail continues eastward, leading to Moose Lake and providing access to the alpine Tableland.

Your trail crosses an avalanche chute emanating from Alta Peak and climbs steep slopes under imposing Tharps Rock. Views are good across Mehrten Meadow to the western Sierra Nevada foothills and the San Joaquin Valley on clear days

As the trail emerges onto more open, rocky slopes, silver pine makes its debut and quickly dominates the forest. After crossing a small creek, you negotiate a single switchback, then climb very steep rock-and-gravel slopes, passing a few solitary, weather-tortured foxtail pines. The trail fades out just before reaching the summit, and you scramble up granite slabs to attain Alta Peak.

The view from the peak takes in a large slice of the Sierra Nevada, from the Mt. Goddard region in the north to the peaks of the Great Western Divide rising out of Mineral King valley in the south. Mount Whitney's sloping summit plateau is unmistakable on the eastern horizon. To the west lies the vast haziness of the San Joaquin Valley, with the South Coast Ranges forming the western horizon, visible only on clear days.

From the peak, retrace your route to the trailhead.

HIKE 55 ROWELL MEADOW TRAILHEAD TO WILLIAMS AND COMANCHE MEADOWS

General description: A moderate 13.8-mile loop backpack surveying pleasant meadow and forest country on the western slope of the southern Sierra Nevada, in the Jennie Lake Wilderness and Kings Canyon National Park.
Elevation gain and loss: 3,070 feet.
Trailhead elevation: 7,830 feet.
High point: Kanawyer Gap, 9,600 feet.
Maps: Giant Forest and Triple Divide Peak 15-minute USGS quads, Sequoia National Forest map, or Sequoia-Kings Canyon National Park map.
Season: July through mid-October.
Finding the trailhead: Drive to the Big Meadows turnoff from the Generals Highway—the main road leading through Sequoia National Park, connecting state highways 180 and 198. This turnoff is about sixty-three miles east of Fresno via State Highway 180 and the Generals Highway, and 72.5 miles east of Visalia via State Highway 198 and the Generals Highway.

Upon locating this turnoff, turn east and follow the paved road toward Big Meadows, indicated by signs at numerous junctions. After driving 4.75 miles from the highway, bear right where the sign indicates Kings Canyon Pack Station and the Horse Corral Meadow. After another 4.1 miles, turn right immediately before the paved road crosses Horse Corral Creek where a sign indicates Rowell Meadow Trailhead and Horse Corral Pack Station. Follow this fairly rough dirt road generally south for two miles to its end at the trailhead parking area, high above Boulder Creek canyon

Access to remote backcountry and good fishing streams awaits hikers who negotiate this fine loop through an uncrowded, meadow-dotted and forest-covered landscape.

Far-flung panoramas are the reward for the short side trip to Mitchell Peak, where the snowy battlements of jagged High Sierra summits contrast with the heavily forested terrain lying in the foreground.

Finding water is no problem on this hike.

A wilderness permit is required for overnight camping in Kings Canyon National Park and can be obtained at the Grant Grove Visitor Center located 1.5 miles north of the junction of State Highway 180 and Generals Highway. This junction is 1.5 miles east of the Big Stump entrance station.

The trail begins on the east side of the road, just north of the parking area. From here, the trail heads east through a forest of red and white fir. It soon jogs south and begins traversing rocky and forested slopes far above Boulder Creek canyon

After hiking 1.4 miles, the trail bends northeast, traversing sunny, rockbound slopes above Gannon Creek, a noisy Boulder Creek tributary.

The trail eventually approaches a small creek and begins ascending along its course, presently under a canopy of lodgepole pines. Leaving that small creek behind, your trail levels off on a meadow-floored, wildflower-brightened, lodgepole-shaded plateau, soon passing just north of the Rowell Meadow Snow Survey shelter. A wilderness ranger uses this cabin as a base camp during the summer season.

Lush Williams Meadow makes a fine destination for an overnight stay in this heavily forested region of Kings Canyon National Park.

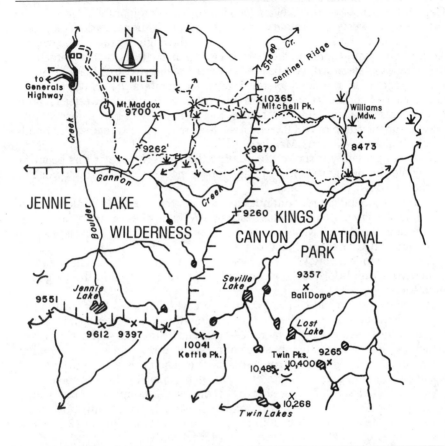

The trail continues east from the cabin, soon passing a southbound trail leading to JO Pass, Gannon Creek, and Jenny Ellis Lake.

You continue eastward through the lodgepole pine forest, passing several excellent campsites, to an easy crossing of a small creek just below a pool filled with small trout. At the trail junction on the east bank of the creek, turn left (north) toward Marvin Pass. The right-branching trail forms the return leg of your loop.

Your trail leads north through meadow-carpeted lodgepole forest, crosses a small creek, and soon enters a drier forest of red fir and lodgepole pine while ascending to Marvin Pass. At an elevation of 9,050 feet, you reach the pass and a trail junction after hiking one mile from the previous junction.

Turning right (east) here onto the Kanawyer Gap Trail, you climb moderately for .6 mile to the old Mitchell Peak Trail, branching left (north) from your trail. This unsigned junction is difficult to locate, obscured as it is by an overgrown clump of chinquapin. Hikers who appreciate seemingly endless views are urged to take the 2.25-mile round-trip hike to the 10,365-foot- high summit of Mitchell Peak.

Continuing east, you soon find yourself traveling through a meadow dominated by shoulder-high corn lilies; shortly thereafter you reach Kanawyer Gap, 9,600 feet above sea level and shaded by a predominantly lodgepole pine forest on the western boundary of Kings Canyon National Park. The jagged alpine peaks of the Great Western Divide and the High Sierra line the eastern skyline but, unfortunately, are barely visible through the heavy forest.

Descending eastward, you pass a few springs and two small creeks, while the lodgepole forest quickly blends into mixed conifers. Two miles of hiking and 1,600 feet of descent will deposit you within .25 mile of the western margin of Williams Meadow. Before reaching the meadow, you hop across a small creek at an elevation of 8,000 feet, cross three more small streams, and finally reach mile-long Williams Meadow.

The trail presently turns south, skirting the western edge of this beautiful lodgepole-rimmed grassland. An easy ford is necessary near the lower end of the meadow.

Your southbound course continues just west of this meadow- bordered creek draining Williams Meadow. The best possible campsites on the hike (except for those in the Rowell Meadow area) will be found west of the trail between Williams and Comanche Meadows.

About one mile below Williams Meadow is small, wet Comanche Meadow, which your trail briefly approaches before veering away into the lodgepole pine forest.

Just west of the meadow lies trail junction. The left-branching (eastbound) trail leads past Sugarloaf Valley to the Roaring River and beyond. Anglers will surely want to sample the sometimes-excellent fishing in the Roaring River, which can be reached after six miles of pleasant, forested, eastbound hiking.

But for this hike, you turn right at this junction and begin a steady, moderate-to-steep westward ascent. White firs soon begin replacing the lodgepole pines on these well-drained slopes, shortly becoming the dominant forest tree.

As you gain elevation, you will obtain occasional views southward to the broken granite crowning the Silliman Crest, and eastward to the 12,000- and 13,000-foot-high peaks of the Great Western Divide.

En route you cross a small, cold creek, then ascend the final one-half mile to the lodgepole pines and red firs of Pond Meadow Gap, where you re-enter lands administered by Sequoia National Forest.

A westward descent of 1.4 miles under a shady canopy of pine and fir brings you to a junction with a southeast-bound trail leading to Seville Lake and other glacial tarns nestled beneath the Silliman Crest.

Continuing straight ahead, you quite soon reach the junction with the north-bound Marvin Pass Trail; then retrace your route through Rowell Meadow and back to the trailhead.

HIKE 56 *BIG BALDY*

General description: A pleasant 4.6-mile round-trip day hiking jaunt in Kings Canyon National Park leading to a rocky viewpoint standing high above one of the most magnificent Giant Sequoia groves in the Sierra Nevada.

Elevation gain and loss: 611 feet.

Trailheadd elevation: 7,600 feet.

High point: Big Baldy, 8,211 feet.

Maps: Giant Forest 15-minutes USGS quad, Sequoia/Kings Canyon Naitonal Park map.

Season: Mid-May through mid-November.

Finding the trailhead: The trailhead, signed Big Baldy Ski Touring Trail, lies on the west side of the Generals Highway .2 mile north of the Big Meadows turnoff (see Williams Meadow hike, No. 55). Parking is available in the wide shoulder a short distance south of the trailhead.

The hike: Recreational opportunities on Big Baldy, ranging from a leisurely hike, to intermediate cross-country skiing, to class 5 rock climbing near this mountain's exfoliating granite crown, all combine to make this peak the destination of a variety of outdoor enthusiasts.

Add to these opportunities its far-ranging and widely contrasting views and you have a rewarding excursion that beckons to all.

Carry plenty of water.

The Big Baldy Ski Touring Trail heads southwest from the highway through red fir forest. Lupine, currant, chinquapin, and mountain whitehorn (a ceanothus species) are among the many understory plants decorating this seciton of trail. After beginning a moderate ascent of north-facing slopes, you can peer down into the Redwood Creek drainage where massive, towering Sequoias are easily distinguished from other conifers, even at this distance.

You soon begin a southbound course just west of Big Baldy Ridge after entering Kings Canyon National Park. Sugar and Jeffrey pines quickly make their debut to add diversity to the fir forest.

At times your trail coincides with the ski route, as attested by the yellow triangles attached to trailside trees.

Soon after completing another west-slope traverse, hikers are confronted with a view of the dome-like summit of Big Baldy about one mile south,its smooth granitic northwest face rising almost 800 near-vertical feet, and its crags should stimulate the imaginations of accomplished and would-be climbers alike.

The trail briefly enters the realm of bare rock, edging very close to the brink of a westward-plunging cliff, but soon reenters fir forest and climbs moderately to the exfoliating granite crown of Big Baldy. A benchmark on the summit indicates that this peak is two feet higher then the elevation given on the quad.

The trail continues south from Big Baldy for three-quarters of a mile to Peak 8168 and unobstructed southward views. From Big Baldy itself, views north, west, and east are superb.

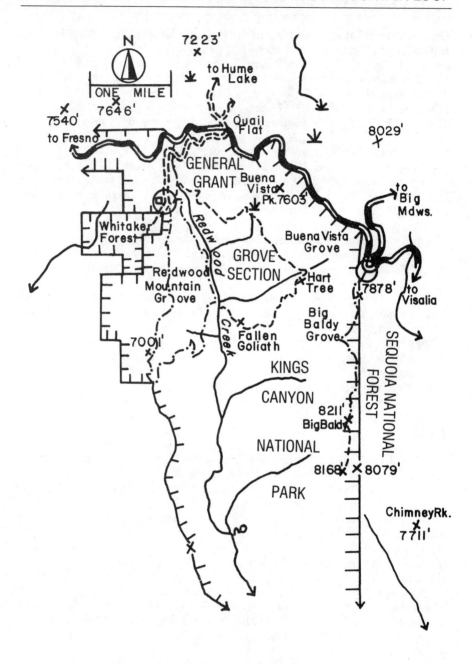

N

ONE MILE

7223'

7540'
to Fresno

7646'

to Hume Lake

Quail Flat

8029'

GENERAL GRANT

Buena Vista Pk. 7603

to Big Mdws.

Whitaker Forest

Redwood

Buena Vista Grove

Redwood Mountain Grove

GROVE SECTION

Hart Tree

7878'

to Visalia

Creek

Fallen Goliath

Big Baldy Grove

7001'

KINGS

CANYON

SEQUOIA NATIONAL FOREST

8211'
BigBaldy

NATIONAL

8168' 8079'

PARK

ChimneyRk.
7711'

To the west, huge Sequoias are silhouetted against the sky along Redwood Mountain's crest. To the southeast lies the fascinating sheer dome of Chimney Rock. Beyond, the Great Western Divide forms a sawtoothed horizon.

The many cliffs and rock faces surrounding Big Baldy Ridge will entice climbers to return with the equipment and skills necessary to scale these near-vertical environs.

Cross-country skiers will be lured back to Big Baldy in winter to experience this fascinating landscape in an entirely different setting.

A pause on the summit allows hikers time to contemplate the vastness of th Sequoia forest in the Redwoood Mountain Grove to the immediate west. This is the largest and perhaps the finest of all Giant Sequoia groves, and those wishing to see more of it will find that the bulk of the grove is accessible only by trail; only one road penetrates its fringes. (See Redwood Mountain Loop, hike No. 57.)

From Big Baldy you return to the trailhead the same way you came, only now enriched by nature's gifts of beauty and solitude.

HIKE 57 *REDWOOD MOUNTAIN LOOP*

General description: A moderate 6.25-mile loop hike or backpack in Kings Canyon National Park, leading through a magnificent forest of Giant Sequoias, well off the beaten track of most Sequoia grove hikers.

Elevation gain and loss: 1,450 feet.

Trailhead elevation: 6,200 feet.

High point: 6,950 feet.

Maps: Giant Forest 15-minute USGS quad, Sequoia/Kings Canyon National Park map.

Season: Mid-May through November.

Finding the trailhead: From Fresno, proceed east on State Highway 180 for 53 miles, to The Wye—the junction of northbound State Highway 180 and eastbound Generals Highway. Bearing right at that junction, drive east 3.5 miles to the junction of a northbound Sequoia National Forest road (signed for Hume Lake) and a southbound Kings Canyon National Park road, and turn right (south)—a sign here reads "Kings Canyon National Park." Follow this dusty and often-narrow dirt road for 1.9 miles to Redwood Saddle. Turn left here and proceed for .1 mile to the trailhead parking area, shaded by gargantuan Sequoias.

The hike: While throngs of tourists are pounding out the Sequoia trails of the Giant Forest, only a handful of hikers will be exploring the majesty and solitude of the Redwood Mountain Grove.

Like the Coast Redwood, the fossil history of the Sequoia goes back several million years, indicating that these trees were much more widespread than their present locations might suggest. In the distant past, California had a wet, mild climate and precipitation was distributed throughout the year.

Beginning in Pliocene times (5.2 million to 1.8 million years ago), California's summer seasons started becoming drier, and warmer, until now the bulk of precipitation occurs during the winter months.

These climatic changes had a major effect on the distribution of many plant species, eliminating entire species and plant communities, resulting in the evolution of species adapted to California's present-day climate.

Extensive glaciation occurred throughout much of North America during Pleistocene times (1.8 million to 10,000 years ago), as a result of a general cooling trend throughout much of the western portion of North America. Extensive glaciation in the Sierra Nevada also served to eliminate many plant species and cause the redistribution of others. The Sequoia, for example, now inhabits areas on the western slope of the Sierra Nevada that were not scoured by the action of glaciers. These giant trees are presently found in numerous groves scattered along the Sierra's western slopes. They thrive on all but the steepest well-drained slopes within the montane forests of the Sierra Transition Zone, generally between 5,000 and 7,000 feet in elevation—the zone of maximum precipitation in the Sierra.

As California's climate continues its slow but sure evolution (undetectable in a human lifetime), the Giant Sequoia and the Coast Redwood will probably, eventually, become extinct. These species are no longer widespread because they have adapted to a specialized environment, dominated by a particular climatic regime. Thus, in an evolutionary sense these species are in their "twilight years."

The wood and the bark of the Sequoia (the latter growing as much as a foot or more thick) is highly resistant to fire and attack by insects. Most fires in Sequoia forests are ground fires, burning low-lying shrubs and trees and burning off the forest litter. On this hike, you will pass through an area "prescription burned" by the National Park Service. Here you will witness how beneficial fire can be for the reproduction of Sequoias, for at one point you must bushwack through dense Sequoia saplings.

A wilderness permit is required for camping in national park backcountry, and should be obtained at the Grant Grove Visitor Center (see hike 55).

Be sure to carry an adequate supply of water.

Your hike begins on the signed Sugarbowl Trail. The left- branching Redwood Canyon-Hart Tree Trail will be the home-bound segment of your loop.

Proceeding south on the Sugarbowl Trail, you ascend gently through a forest of Giant Sequoias, white firs, and sugar pines. Quite soon you pass a sign proclaiming "Research Area/Ecology of Sequoias/Do Not Disturb." In some areas of Kings Canyon and Sequoia national parks, prescribed burns are conducted during periods of low fire danger. Thus, at certain times of the year, particular areas of these parks may be off-limits to hikers.

The trail heads south along and just east of Redwood Mountain's crest. Rarely, the towering Sequoias are located in unmixed stands, but most often they are found with white firs and sugar pines, many of which are also impressively large.

As you progress southward, your trail occasionally leads into sunny openings just east of the crest of Redwood Mountain. In these drier openings, the Sequoias are replaced by ponderosa pines, black oaks, incense-cedars, some sugar pines, and white firs. Ground cover in these areas consists of manzanita and the fragrant, lace-leaved kit-kit-dizze. You will be treated to superb views into the depths of Redwood Canyon, east to the sheer granite of Big Baldy Ridge, and southeast to the alpine peaks of the Great Western Divide.

Just south of Peak 7001, you reenter a nearly-pure stand of Sequoias and begin descending along the crest of Redwood Mountain, soon reaching a

Giant Sequoias, the largest living things on earth, offer abundant shade to hikers in the Redwood Mountain Grove of Kings Canyon National Park. These giant trees are found only in a few scattered groves on the western slope of the Sierra Nevada. Like their close relatives, the Coast Redwoods, Giant Sequoias once occupied a much greater range than their present locations might suggest. But as California's wetter, milder climate gave way millions of years ago to extensive glaciation, and then less precipitation, the result was a redistribution of plant species struggling to adapt to California's present-day climate.

destination and mileage sign. You now begin a descent into Redwood Canyon via the east slopes of Redwood Mountain. The Sequoias quickly give way to a mixed conifer forest on these dry, east-facing slopes. Big Baldy's sheer granite face dominates your eastward view, and you can briefly spy the lookout-capped dome of Buck Rock in the northeast.

As you descend, you pass a seasonal creek, and nearing the bottom of Redwood Canyon, your trail becomes overgrown at times with the regrowth that resulted after the last prescribed burn conducted here by the Park Service.

As you proceed, Giant Sequoias soon rejoin the forest, and you quickly reach a canyon-bottom trail junction, where you turn left. The Hart Tree Trail heads south, eventually looping back to Redwood Saddle. This alternative route would add 2.75 miles and 400 feet of elevation gain to the total while passing the Hart Tree, the tallest known Giant Sequoia.

Your route now ascends more or less along the course of Redwood Creek where hikers are dwarfed by the sheer bulk of the Sequoias that crowd the canyon. After hiking 1.75 miles from the previous junction, the Hart Tree Trail joins your route on the right. Bearing left here, you climb the final 150 feet in one-quarter mile to the trailhead under the protective canopy of Giant Sequoias.

HIKE 58 ONION VALLEY TO WHITNEY PORTAL

General description: A rigorous 46-mile point-to-point backpack of one week or longer for experienced hikers, featuring far-reaching vistas, vast alpine terrain, and excellent fishing amid awe-inspiring surroundings in the John Muir Wilderness, and Sequoia-Kings Canyon National Park.
Elevation gain and loss: 11,580 feet, -11,020 feet.
Trailhead elevation: 9,180 feet (Onion Valley).
High point: Mount Whitney, 14,495 feet.
Maps: Mt. Pinchot, Mount Whitney, and Lone Pine 15- minute USGS quads, Inyo National Forest map, or Sequoia-Kings Canyon..
Season: Mid July through early October.
Finding the trailhead: From U.S. 395 in Independence, turn west onto Market Street where a sign indicates Onion Valley. Follow this steadily ascending paved road for fifteen miles to the large hikers parking area at the road's end.

To find the Whitney Portal Trailhead, turn west from U.S. 395 in Lone Pine onto the signed Whitney Portal Road and proceed 13 miles to the trailhead just east of the small store.

The hike: This memorable high country trek traverses a portion of the John Muir/Pacific Crest Trail through some of the most magnificent mountain terrain in the nation. The far-ranging views from the sixteenth-highest mountain in the United States (there are fifteen higher summits in Alaska) are only some of many tremendous views hikers will obtain along this route.

Although portions of this route can be quite popular with hikers, solitude can still be found. Once over Forester Pass, a multitude of opportunities exist for satisfying side trips to some of the most remote and spectacular lake basins in the range. One could spend weeks in the upper Kern River drainage, exploring lonely lake basins, climbing peaks, fishing, or simply contemplating the beauty of this glorious land.

Plan at least one week for this hike; two weeks would be more appropriate to fully enjoy the magnificence of this alpine wilderness.

Fishing is good in many of the high lakes and most of the streams along the way.

Nights can be cool at these high elevations; overnight lows in the 20s are common at elevations of 12,000 feet and more, even in July and August.

A wilderness permit is required. It would be wise to obtain your permit in advance, since the daily quota for permits at the Onion Valley Trailhead is often filled on summer weekends.

This point-to-point trip requires either that hikers leave another vehicle at the Whitney Portal Trailhead or that they hitchhike fifty-three miles back to the Onion Valley Trailhead.

From the Onion Valley Trailhead, head west past an information sign and begin a northwest traverse across open slopes and into a red fir stand. Just before reaching the first switchback, you may notice an unmaintained right-branching trail, leading into Golden Trout Lake's basin.

Your path shortly levels off on a small bench, the first in a series of benches in this glacial east-side canyon, and then you enter the John Muir Wilderness.

The trail now climbs 500 feet among scattered lodgepole and foxtail pines to tiny Little Pothole Lake. A short, level stretch allows hikers to catch their breath before another steep ascent, this one of 400 feet, to Gilbert Lake. The sky-piercing crag of 13,632-foot-high University Peak can be seen over a low, tree- covered ridge to the southwest of Gilbert Lake.

After a stroll around the sparsely forested north shore of this overused lake, you climb briefly along Independence Creek to the outlet of Flower Lake and a junction with a southbound trail leading into the Matlock Lake basin.

Hikers who wish to camp before ascending to Kearsarge Pass might consider the Matlock Lake area, which is used comparatively little. Bench Lake, nestled in a cirque 350 feet above Matlock Lake, offers very private camping as well as good fishing.

Whitebark pines begin dominating the forest as you ascend above Flower Lake through boulder-dotted terrain. You soon level off briefly on a timberline bench which has a trickle of water— the last easily attainable water before the pass.

The route now switchbacks up a rocky slope among stunted whitebark pines, passing high above isolated Heart Lake. The trail levels off on yet another bench, sandy and sparsely vegetated with wind- and snow drift-flattened whitebarks. The trail from here to the pass is plainly visible, maintaining a gentle grade while traversing the south slopes of Mt. Gould.

Big Pothole Lake, lying in a 100-foot depression, comes into view as you make the final traverse to surmount the knife-edged Sierra Nevada crest at Kearsarge Pass, 11,823 feet above sea level. To the east, the Independence Creek drainage plunges abruptly into Owens Valley, where the town of Independence and U.S. 395 are visible. The Inyo Mountains soar skyward to the east of the valley. To the west, Bullfrog Lake lies below the reddish, glacially scoured slopes of 11,868-foot-high Mt. Bago. To the southwest lie the Kearsarge Lakes, nestled in a high basin below the broken crags of the Kearsarge Pinnacles. And far on the southwestern horizon are some of the most awe-inspiring mountain peaks in California—the Kings-Kern Divide and the jagged northern peaks of the Great Western Divide.

Entering Kings Canyon National Park, your route descends rocky slopes for about .75 mile to a junction. The right-hand trail traverses high above the basin and meets the John Muir Trail after about two miles. You turn left and descend .1 mile to a junction with the trail to popular Kearsarge Lakes, where camping is limited to one night and no wood fires are allowed.

You turn right again and descend the grassy and rocky basin under increasing timber, soon contouring above Bullfrog Lake's north shore. The superb view south across the lake's placid waters, dominated by the fluted pyramid of East Vidette, is yet another of the splendid vistas captured along this magnificent high-mountain trek. Bullfrog Lake itself, though, has been closed to camping for many years due to past overuse, and will remain so indefinitely.

After leaving Bullfrog Lake, your trail passes two small tarns, then descends to meet the John Muir-Pacific Crest Trail. This junction marks the first legal camping area on your hike since the Kearsarge Lakes, although campsites are scarce.

Glacial ice has the incredible grinding and excavating power to transform a stream-cut canyon's V-shaped profile into a broad U-shaped valley, such as Bubbs Creek Canyon along the John Muir Trail in Kings Canyon National Park.

Presently shaded by lodgepole pines, you begin a 1,000-foot descent into Bubbs Creek, crossing two small streams enroute and capturing inspiring views into upper Bubbs Creek and the U-shaped canyon of Center Basin, in the southeast. You finally emerge onto the floor of Bubbs Creek Canyon and reach a junction. You turn left and proceed up the canyon, passing the tree-covered area labeled "Vidette Meadow" on the quad. The heavy lodgepole pine forest and the large stream of Bubbs Creek make this a pleasant, sheltered camping area. Most of the campsites between here and Whitney Portal are at or above timberline.

The trail continues ascending the U-shaped valley of Bubbs Creek, flanked by the towering crest of the Sierra on the east and the jagged ridge of East Spur on the west. About 3.5 miles from the previous junction you meet—but avoid—the unmaintained Center Basin Trail on your left. That trail ascends Center Basin and crosses the Sierra crest at Junction Pass, then descends into the east-side Shepherd Creek drainage, re-crosses the crest at Shepherd Pass, then descends to the John Muir Trail in upper Tyndall Creek. This was the main route of the John Muir Trail before Forester Pass was opened in 1932. The lakes in Center Basin offer good fishing and secluded camping.

Bearing right, your trail soon crosses Center Basin's creek and ascends grassy and rocky slopes clothed in thinning timber. Passing under the precipitous west slopes of 12,760-foot-high Center Peak, you have inspiring views up the canyon to some very rugged peaks, dominated by the landmark pyramid of 13,888-foot- high Junction Peak.

After climbing past a few persistent whitebark pines and the last sheltered campsites for miles, you quickly reach the boulder-covered outlet creek of often-frozen Lake 12,248. The gap of Forester Pass can be seen above the rocky slopes southwest of the lake. The smooth northwest wall of Junction Peak soars above the southeast end of the lake, where the Kings-Kern Divide joins the Sierra crest.

From this lake, your trail makes a long switchback while ascending a north-trendingridge. Leaving the ridge and ascending alpine slopes, your route (often obscured by snow) makes several final switchbacks to surmount the Kings-Kern Divide at Forester Pass, which at an elevation of 13,200 feet is the highest pass on the John Muir-Pacific Crest Trail. Most of the Sierra Nevada crest is visible, from Junction Peak north to the Palisade Crest, in addition to a host of alpine peaks lying west of the crest in Kings Canyon National Park. To your south lie several lakes 12,000 feet or more above sea level, the Great Western Divide, and the deep trench of Kern Canyon. A sign at this cold and windy pass informs hikers that they are entering Sequoia National Park.

West of Forester Pass, the highest lake in California can be seen nestled in a high cirque on the slopes of Caltech Peak. At an elevation of more than 12,880 feet, it's not surprising that this alpine lake is almost always frozen.

Your southbound trail presently descends via numerous switchbacks dynamited into solid rock. In early summer, this stretch of trail is snow-covered and is treacherous at best.

After reaching the floor of the basin, you skirt two large lakes lying at the western foot of Diamond Mesa's alpine plateau. You then descend to ford a Tyndall Creek tributary and traverse above a small lake. The pointed crown of 14,018-foot-high Mt. Tyndall can be seen from here, rising four miles to the east on the Sierra crest.

You soon circumnavigate an isolated stand of timber, then meet a west-bound trail leading to Lake South America and the remote headwaters of the upper Kern River. Many rewarding side trips can be made via this trail, if time allows.

Continue south on the John Muir-Pacific Crest Trail, soon entering lodgepole and foxtail pine timber and reaching a junction one-half mile below the Lake South America Trail with an eastbound trail leading to Shepherd Pass.

Just over .1 mile beyond that junction, you meet yet another trail, branching southwest and descending Tyndall Creek to Kern Canyon. Bearing left, a short forested ascent brings you to two small tarns that are quite popular at times. You now begin a gentle traverse along the west slopes of Tawny Point, passing several impressive, wind-sculptured foxtail pines.

After hiking 1.5 miles from the previous junction, your trail levels off on the alpine expanse of Bighorn Plateau, where another glorious vista unfolds, surpassed only by the summit views from Mount Whitney. From this point, you obtain your first glimpse of the unmistakable sloping summit plateau of Mount Whitney, lying on the southeastern horizon.

Your trail descends to Wright Creek from the plateau via several grassy benches. A ford of Wright Creek (difficult in early summer) brings you to some good campsites shaded by lodgepole and foxtail pines on the large stream's southern banks. You then cross over a low ridge and descend to a ford of Wallace Creek (also difficult in early summer), where you meet the westbound High Sierra Trail on your right and the eastbound trail to Wallace Lake on your left.

Beyond Wallace Creek, you begin a moderate 550-foot ascent to a pass 10,964 feet above sea level. Hikers stopping to catch their breath on this steady ascent are rewarded with new inspiring vistas. The broad, sloping plateau of Mt. Barnard, rising above the head of Wallace Creek in the northeast, was once labeled a 14,000-foot-high peak before being re-surveyed by the USGS. Now, with an official elevation of 13,990 feet, it is the highest peak in California less than 14,000 feet above sea level. Its easy southwest slopes beckon peakbaggers and reward them with breathtaking panoramas.

From that foxtail pine-shaded pass, you descend to the lush, wildflower-speckled spread of Sandy Meadow. The Kaweah Peaks Ridge and aptly-named Red Spur are seen across the meadow on the western horizon, framed by trailside lodgepole and foxtail pines.

Beyond Sandy Meadow, you cross a small creek, ascend to a low, foxtail pine-covered ridge, and shortly reach a junction. The Pacific Crest Trail continues south, but you turn left onto the John Muir Trail. Soon the massive, avalanche-scarred west slope of your destination—Mount Whitney—comes into view.

The trail soon approaches the grassy banks of Whitney Creek, where Mt. Chamberlain comes into view on the southeastern skyline, rising near-vertically above the Crabtree Lakes basin. The peaks in this region have typically gentle, unglaciated summit plateaus and south-facing slopes that contrast dramatically with their precipitous north faces—which were scoured, scarred, and quarried by repeated glacial episodes.

Just after fording Whitney Creek, you meet a southwest-bound lateral leading to the Pacific Crest Trail. This trail drops into Crabtree Meadows where solitude-seeking hikers can leave it and begin hiking east on unmaintained trails into the Crabtree Lakes basin. Middle Crabtree Lake, labeled "Lake 11,312" on the quad, contains a good population of large golden trout.

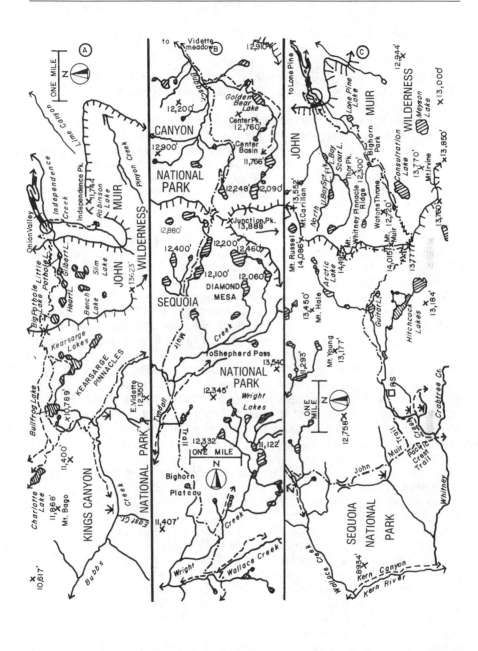

Continuing east on the John Muir Trail, you soon pass the seasonal Crabtree Ranger Station and skirt a small pond before recrossing Whitney Creek. A short, steep climb brings you to the outlet of Timberline Lake (closed to camping), where the bulk of Mount Whitney is framed by low, rocky, sparsely forested hills.

Soon leaving the last timber behind, you cross over a low rise, then descend to the inlet stream of appropriately-named Guitar Lake. Campsites around this alpine lake are terribly overused and should be avoided. The near-vertical north walls of Mt. Hitchcock are partially obscured from view by the rounded, glacially-smoothed ridge separating Guitar Lake from the lesser-used Hitchcock Lakes.

From Guitar Lake the trail ascends past a small lake—the last water until Trail Camp in Lone Pine Creek. You then ascend to the head of the basin and begin negotiating a well-designed series of switchbacks leading up the west slope of the Sierra Nevada crest. This high-elevation ascent will leave even those in top physical condition short of breath.

As you near the trail junction at the top of this climb, notice that the fragrant blue flowers of the sky pilot are the only visible forms of life at this altitude.

You finally reach the junction with the Mount Whitney Trail at an elevation of 13,480 feet, marked by a metal sign listing various destinations. The deep blue Hitchcock Lakes lie directly below you, and the fluted north face of Mt. Hitchcock, soaring 1,400 feet above the lakes, will tempt climbers to return with their gear to challenge this peak's mighty walls.

You turn left (north) onto the Mount Whitney Trail, and after a few switchbacks traverse the west slopes of 14,015-foot-high Mt. Muir, a 350-foot class 3 scramble from the trail. You proceed north along the spectacular, windswept Sierra crest, passing several windy notches in the crest and accompanied by continuously inspiring vistas.

Passing just west of Keeler Needle, an easy scramble to your east, you negotiate the final, often-snow-covered ascent to the summit plateau. A stroll of .3 mile eastward on the plateau brings you to the summit of Mount Whitney. A Park Service sign bolted to the summit slab indicates the exact elevation of the peak within inches. The summit shelter, just west of the peak, was constructed in 1909 by the Smithsonian Institution to provide shelter for astronomers.

Needless to say, the view is a vast one, probably the most spectacular vista accessible by trail in the range.

The entire Great Western Divide is visible to the west across the absurdly straight trench of Kern Canyon. To the northwest, the peaks of the western slope fade into distant, timber-covered hills beyond the jagged crest of the Kings-Kern Divide. The Sierra crest is visible as far north as the Palisades.

Kern Peak and portions of the Kern Plateau meet your gaze to the south. The town of Lone Pine lies more than 10,000 feet below to your east in the Owens Valley, which stretches from Owens Lake in the south to the vicinity of the town of Big Pine in the north. The Inyo-White Mountain chain rises abruptly east of the valley, with Telescope Peak and the Panamint Range forming the far southeastern horizon.

Reluctantly leaving the summit, retrace your route for two miles to the trail junction at an elevation of 13,480 feet, turn left, and ascend 120 feet to Trail Crest's pass 13,600 feet above sea level. The trail then descends via approximately 100 switchbacks and flattens out at the 12,000-foot level and Trail Camp, usually crowded with Mount Whitney-bound hikers.

Beyond Trail Camp, you soon pass above large Consultation Lake, cross Lone Pine Creek, and then descend briefly to another crossing of Lone Pine Creek at Trailside Meadow, a narrow strip of grassy, wildflower-speckled terrain that is closed to camping.

You soon pass above the shores of Mirror Lake (presently closed to camping because of previous overuse) and under increasing foxtail pine shade stroll through Bighorn Park, also known as Outpost Camp, usually the first stop for Whitney-bound hikers.

Avoid the lateral trail to Lone Pine Lake below the willow- choked meadow of Bighorn Park; instead, cross Lone Pine Creek one final time, and begin a steep descent.

Crossing boisterous North Fork Lone Pine Creek and passing a westbound climber's trail, you negotiate the final descent through a sparse Jeffrey pine and red fir forest to the trailhead.

Hikers who did not leave another vehicle at this trailhead will have to hitchhike back to Onion Valley. Due to the summer traffic to and from both trailheads, hitchhiking should present no major problems.

HIKE 59 COURTRIGHT RESERVOIR TO THE DINKEY LAKES

General description: A moderate 14.5-mile round-trip backpack to a lake-filled "island" of sub-alpine and alpine terrain on the western slope of the central Sierra Nevada, in the Dinkey Lakes Wilderness.
Elevation gain and loss: 1,745 feet, -970 feet.
Trailhead elevation: 8,475 feet.
High point: 9,920 feet.
Maps: Blackcap Mtn. and Huntington Lake 15-minute USGS quads (trail to Cliff Lake not shown on quad), Sierra National Forest map.
Season: July through mid-October.
Finding the trailhead: From Clovis, proceed northeast on State Highway 168 for about 40.2 miles to the community of Shaver Lake. Turn right (east) near the southern end of Shaver Lake where a sign indicates Dinkey Creek and Wishon Dam. You can obtain your wilderness permit at the Pineridge Ranger Station, .5 mile before reaching this junction. Follow this paved road generally eastward for 11.6 miles to a junction just south of Dinkey Creek.

Turn right just beyond the pack station, where the sign indicates McKinley Grove, Wishon Reservoir, and Courtright Reservoir. Follow this paved road southeast, passing through the McKinley Grove of Giant Sequoias and reaching a junction with the right-branching road to Wishon Reservoir after driving another 13.6 miles. Turn left here, following the good paved road toward Courtright Village (no services), and the Cliff Lake Trailhead, about ten miles from the previous junction.

The hike: Although separated from the true High Sierra by a low- lying forested plateau, this area stands high enough to have hosted mountain-carving

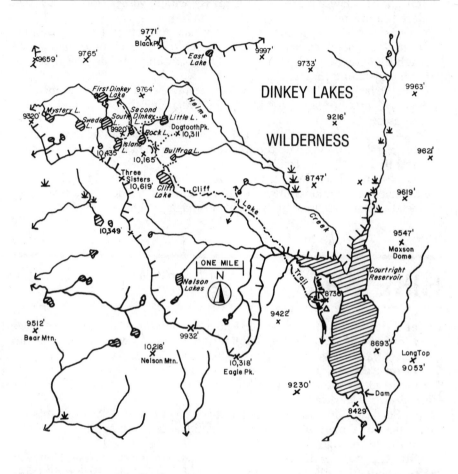

glaciers in the distant past. The results can be seen today in the form of numerous sub-alpine lakes, cirques, smoothed and polished granitic bedrock, and quarried peaks that rise well above timberline.

Not only do fishing opportunities exist in the Dinkey Lakes area, but the two prominent peaks rising above the lakes—10,619-foot-high Three Sisters and 10,311-foot-high Dogtooth Peak—can be scaled via class 2 and class 3 routes, respectively, providing expansive and complementary perspectives, encompassing a large slice of the Sierra Nevada.

There is little water available during the first five miles of this hike.

A wilderness permit is required, but advance reservations are necessary for permits from July 1 through Labor Day. Contact the Pineridge Ranger Station for more information.

From the parking area, your trail heads northwest through a red fir and lodgepole pine forest on a slightly descending grade. You will soon pass by a jeep road joining your trail on the right.

As you approach the northwest end of Courtright Reservoir, the forest becomes dominated by lodgepole pine. You soon hop across the creek draining Cliff Lake and enter the Dinkey Lakes Wilderness. This creek runs high during spring runoff, so early season hikers may be forced to wade.

Your trail presently meanders northwestward through a heavy lodgepole pine forest, reaching a four-way junction three miles from the trailhead. The northeast-bound trail is seldom used, leading to Helms Meadow and beyond, while the southwest-bound trail, equally seldom trod, leads to the Nelson Lakes and beyond.

You continue northwest on the Cliff Lake Trail, soon noting the addition of red and white fir to the previously unvaried lodgepole pine forest.

You eventually begin a switchbacking ascent along a south- facing slope clothed in silver pine and manzanita, encountering views of Courtright Reservoir and a host of granite domes that surround it. Far to the east the alpine peaks of the LeConte Divide and other High Sierra summits form a sawtoothed skyline. In the south and southwest rise Brown Peak (10,349 feet), Nelson Mountain (10,218 feet), and Eagle Peak (10,318 feet), all soaring high above their thickly forested basins.

The trail levels off above the switchbacks, and you soon find yourself walking above the northeast shore of beautiful Cliff Lake, five miles from the trailhead and 9,500 feet above sea level. Numerous possibilities for camping exist above this shore of the lake. With a backdrop of 400-foot-high cliffs and an open, boulder-dotted forest, this lake is an excellent, justifiably popular campsite.

The trail becomes faint as it passes above the lake, so watch for blazed trees. It becomes easy to follow once again as you reach a signed junction. The left-branching, descending trail leads to campsites above the upper end of Cliff Lake. Bullfrog Lake lies just over the ridge to the northeast. But you continue your northwest-bound ascent, and after .75 mile you reach a pass at an elevation of 9,920 feet.

A possible side trip, .75 mile one-way, leads northeast from this pass to the ridge immediately west of Dogtooth Peak. The peak itself is accessible only by a class 3 climb, but the ridgetop provides superb vistas for those not inclined to scale that crag. Upon attaining the ridge west of Dogtooth Peak, and amid stunted mountain hemlocks and whitebark pines, a vast sweep of Sierra Nevada terrain unfolds. Some of the better-known peaks and divides include, from northwest to southeast, Kaiser Peak; Mt. Ritter; Banner Peak; Silver Divide; Red Slate Mountain; Mt. Humphreys; Mt. Goddard; LeConte Divide; The Obelisk; Spanish Mountain; and the Western Divide country far to the southeast. In the foreground lies sprawling Courtright Reservoir and its adjacent domes, set amid a dark conifer forest. And in the west lies the Dinkey Lakes basin.

From the 9,920-foot-1level at the pass, you descend northwest into the glaciated Dinkey Lakes basin, accompanied by lodgepole pines and mountain hemlocks during your brief jaunt down to Rock Lake. Upon reaching the outlet of this lake 9,600 feet above sea level, you can either continue your trail walk to the other lakes in the basin or, if you desire solitude amid impressive surroundings, follow Rock Lake's outlet creek downstream, cross-country, for .9 mile to isolated Little Lake, set in a deep cirque at an elevation of 9,250 feet and immediately below the precipitous north wall of Dogtooth Peak ridge. This locale makes an excellent base camp for day hiking jaunts through the Dinkey Lakes basin.

The remainder of the Dinkey Lakes are accessible by trail or via short cross-country excursions.

From this fine sub-alpine lake basin, hikers eventually backtrack to the trailhead.

HIKE 60 NORTH FORK BIG PINE CREEK

General description: A moderately strenuous thirteen-mile semi-loop backpack in the John Muir Wilderness, leading into one of the most majestic east-side canyons in the Sierra Nevada.
Elevation gain and loss: 3,100 feet.
Trailhead elevation: 7,700 feet.
High point: 10,800 feet.
Maps: Big Pine and Mt. Goddard 15-minute USGS quads, Inyo National Forest map.
Season: July through mid-October.
Finding the trailhead: From U.S. 395 in Big Pine, turn west onto Crocker Street where a sign indicates Glacier Lodge. Follow this paved road into the eastern Sierra for ten miles to the signed hikers' parking area, about one-half mile below (east of) Glacier Lodge.

The hike: This scenic hike leads the hiker up a deeply glaciated canyon, passing five Big Pine Lakes, providing views of some of the highest peaks in the Sierra, and offering glimpses of the large glaciers (by Sierra standards) that still cling to their flanks.

All the lakes along this hike are fishable, and campsites and water are easy to find. The numerous side trip possibilities can extend this hike from a weekend to a week-long backpack.

For the adventurous and experienced hiker, a satisfying 19- mile loop trip is possible. From Seventh Lake at the head of the North Fork, a faint trail climbs to the prominent gap north of the lake, then descends to Thunder And Lightning Lake, merges with the unmaintained Baker Creek Trail, and intersects the North Fork Trail 1.6 miles from the trailhead.

Campfires are prohibited throughout the Big Pine Creek drainage, so be sure to carry a backpack stove.

A wilderness permit is required and can be obtained at the Upper Sage Flat Campground, two miles below the trailhead.

The trail begins at the western edge of the parking area where a sign indicates the North Fork Trail. The trail heads west over a low hill, passes just above the pack station, then climbs moderately along a south-facing slope covered with sagebrush, bitterbrush, rabbitbrush, and scattered Jeffrey pines.

Over-the-shoulder views are excellent, especially those of the U-shaped canyon of Big Pine Creek framing the Inyo Mountains on the eastern horizon. Immediately across the canyon to your south, 11,896-foot-high Kid Mountain skyrockets more than 4,000 feet directly above Glacier Lodge. In the southwest, your view includes the Middle Palisade Glacier, the Palisade Crest, and 14,040-foot-high Middle Palisade, soaring above the head of the South Fork Big Pine Creek.

After hiking less than one mile, the trail bends northwest and passes above roaring First Falls. From this point, the boulder-strewn wash of the South Fork is visible, a relatively recent feature of the landscape created by severe runoff from above-normal precipitation during the winter of 1982-83.

You reach a junction after strolling 1.6 miles from the trailhead. The righthand or northeast-branching trail climbs steeply over the ridge into Baker Creek and is seldom used. The left-branching trail descends for .3 mile to the roadend and picnic area visible directly below.

You continue straight ahead toward cascading Second Falls, and after a few short swtichbacks you enter the John Muir Wilderness. The trail quickly parallels the noisy North Fork, and lodgepole pines begin mixing into the Jeffrey pine forest.

Soon you enter the aspen-shaded Cienega Mirth area, where the brush begins to give way to grassy areas with scattered boulders and wildflowers, watered by springs emanating from the south- facing slopes to your north.

At the west end of Cienega Mirth, you pass a stone cabin and begin a steady ascent up the canyon for 1.5 miles to the next trail junction, passing through a lodgepole, whitebark, and limber pine forest. Enroute, note the contrast of vegetation on the south-facing slopes to the north with vegetation on the north-facing slopes of Mt. Alice and Peak 12,861 to the south.

The south-facing slopes are choked with mountain mahogany, and stands of timber do not replace the brush until reaching the 10,600-foot level. Above that point, a moderately thick forest of lodgepole, whitebark, and limber pine covers the slopes up to an elevation of about 12,000 feet.

By sharp contrast, the trees directly across the creek on north-facing slopes are stunted, reaching their boundaries of growth only a few hundred feet above the trail, at elevations of 9,800 to 10,000 feet. The timberline on either slope is obviously quite different, not only from each other but also from the typical elevation of timberline in this region of the High Sierra. This is an excellent example of the influence of slope aspect on vegetation types.

After reaching the above-mentioned junction, turn right; a sign here indicates Black Lake. The left-hand trail forms the homebound leg of your loop.

The trail switchbacks up the dry, south-facing slope, leading through sage-brush and curl-leaf mountain mahogany, passing a reliable spring and becoming shaded by lodgepole pine and aspen near the 10,400-foot level. You have good views across the canyon to First Lake and Second Lake during this ascent.

The trail eventually levels off, crosses the boulder-covered outlet stream of Black Lake, enters a sub-alpine forest of whitebark and lodgepole pine, and finally reaches Black Lake 10,600 feet above sea level. There are many good campsites to choose from, and the abundant trout population in the lake should keep anglers busy.

From the lake, the trail climbs over a low, forested ridge, and hikers are likely to be accompanied by the crow-like call of the Clark's nutcracker. This large, grey, black, and white member of the Jay family is commonly seen and heard in timberline forests such as this.

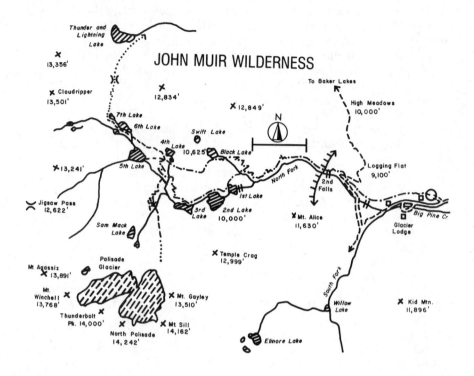

From the ridge, descend to cross the small outlet of Fourth Lake just below a small pond, soon reaching a four-way junction. The right-hand (northwest) fork leads past Fourth Lake to Sixth Lake and Seventh Lake at the head of the canyon. Straight ahead (west) the trail leads to Fifth Lake—to an elevation of 10,759 feet in one-quarter mile—undoubtedly the most beautiful lake in the Big Pine chain.

You turn left (south) and begin descending numerous switchbacks. After hiking one-half mile, you pass the signed Glacier Trail which departs on a southerly course, crosses the North Fork, ascends to Sam Mack Meadow, climbs the ridge east of the meadow, and eventually leads to a viewpoint just east of the Palisade Glacier, the largest glacier in the Sierra Nevada. Don't venture out onto the glacier unless you are experienced in glacial travel, though, and even then never do so alone.

Beyond that junction, the trail approaches the north shore of Third Lake. The western end of this lake is filling up with silt being carried down the creek from the Palisade Glacier. This active glacier has moved downslope as much as forty feet in one year. The milky-green waters of First, Second, and Third lakes attest to the immense grinding power of this slowly moving icefield.

Beyond Third Lake, the trail meanders down to massive Second Lake, reaching a glorious viewpoint above the lake's northwestern shore. Directly across the lake stands the convoluted mass of pinnacles and buttresses known as Temple Crag, just one foot short of 13,000 feet in elevation. To the west of Temple Crag are the high peaks looming above the Palisade Glacier, three of which rise higher than 14,000 feet. These majestic peaks make an unforgettable reflection in the calm waters of Second Lake.

Continuing your descent, you soon traverse above the north shore of First Lake, where the influence of drier conditions begins to show, particularly in the form of scattered mountain mahogany and an occasional Jeffrey pine.

Below the lake, you cross a small creek, reach the Black Lake Trail junction, turn right and retrace your route to the trailhead.

HIKE 61 *WHITE MOUNTAIN SAMPLER*

General description: A series of four short hikes, totaling six miles, in the Inyo National Forest, Ancient Bristlecone Pine Forest of the White Mountains. Hike No. 1 (Discovery Trail) one-mile loop hike; Hike No. 2 (Patriarch Trail), .5-mile loop hike; Hike No. 3 (Vista Trail), .5-mile loop hike; Hike No. 4 (Sheep Mountain), four miles round trip, partially cross-country.
Elevation gain and loss: Hike No. 1: 160 feet; Hike No. 2: 50 feet; Hike No. 3: 60 feet; Hike No. 4: 1,300 feet,-153 feet.
High point: Hike No. 1: 10,260 feet; Hike No. 2: 11,350 feet; Hike No. 3: 11,360 feet; Hike No. 4: 12,497 feet.
Maps: Blanco Mtn. and Mt. Barcroft 15-minute USGS quads (trails not shown on quads), Inyo National Forest map.
Season: Late June through mid-October.

The hike: Most people take only a day to drive through the Bristlecone Pine Forest in the White Mountains, and few do much hiking in the area. The White Mountains are well off the beaten track for most hikers, many of whom wonder about that high, barren-looking range on the east side of Owens Valley while enroute to the High Sierra via U.S. 395. That barren-looking range actually contains extensive sub-alpine forests of bristlecone and limber pine, perennial streams, and meadows lush enough to support limited cattle grazing. In summer, wildflowers add a touch of color to this high, barren landscape.

These four short hikes are all quite easy and can be completed in a day. Those staying the night at Grandview Campground may wish to take two days to fully enjoy this area. There is no overnight camping in the Ancient Bristlecone Pine Forest, so day hikes are the only way to go.

From U.S. 395 in Big Pine, turn east onto State Highway 168 where a large sign indicates the Ancient Bristlecone Pine Forest and tells whether the road is open. During the winter, any of a number of gates on the Bristlecone Pine road may be locked, depending on snow conditions. The gate at Sierra View definitely will be locked from late fall until spring.

Proceeding east on State Highway 168, you soon pass a sign informing travelers that no services are available for the next 109 miles, so be sure to have a full tank of gas and plenty of water.

After driving 2.3 miles, you pass a southeast-branching road leading to the Eureka and Saline valleys. The road leads through an often-narrow and spectacular canyon while ascending the western slope of the White Mountains, and suddenly emerges onto Cedar Flat on the crest of the range in a dense forest of juniper and pinyon pine.

Turn left (north) after driving thirteen miles from Big Pine, where a large sign indicates the Ancient Bristlecone Pine Forest. You soon pass an information booth and continue along this paved road just east of the crest of the range in a thick pinyon pine and juniper forest. Pinyon nut enthusiasts will want to spend time here during the fall to enjoy a harvest of these tasty nuts.

You pass the Grandview Campground 4.5 miles from the highway, and after 2.5 more miles you reach Sierra View at an elevation of 9,300 feet. A photographic stop here is a must. The Sierra Nevada from the Cottonwood Creek area near Lone Pine northward to the Mt. Dana area in Yosemite National Park can be seen to the west— undeniably one of the most majestic mountain chains in the country.

Immediately above you is the first timberline you will encounter on this trip. The pinyon pines here are stunted and ground-hugging, and they quickly fade into sagebrush slopes above. Near Patriarch Grove, you pass into absolute above- timberline terrain, where the bristlecone pines diminish into alpine fell fields.

From Sierra View, continue driving north, entering the Ancient Bristlecone Pine Forest after one mile. Soon a few limber pines appear, and where a sign indicates the 10,000-foot level, bristlecone pines begin dominating the slopes east of the road.

About ten miles from the highway, you reach the Schulman Grove at an elevation of 10,100 feet. There is a visitor center here occupying a trailer (open during summer) and a picnic area. There is also a large diplay case giving information about bristlecone pines.

Two trails begin here. The longer, more strenuous Methuselah Trail heads east, making a 4.25-mile loop while visiting some of the oldest living things on earth. Some of these bristlecone pines are more than 4,000 years old.

The shorter Discovery Trail leads north. This one-mile trail switchbacks a short distance northward on limestone slopes, passing some very impressive gnarled and twisted bristlecone pines, many of which are kept alive by a single strip of bark running along their trunks. The dead and downed trees have been weathered to the point of almost being "petrified"—the wood is like stone and has a beautiful golden appearance. There is little, if any, ground cover, and consequently this forest of ancient trees is open and offers fine vistas. Some Sierra Nevada peaks are visible westward across Reed Flat.

Where the trail reaches a band of red rock, you will have good views north along the crest of the range as far as County Line Hill and Blanco Mountain. The mostly barren landscape is broken intermittently by stands of bristlecone pine.

The bristlecones seem to favor limestone—they grow on such soils mostly east of the crest. Limestone is an unsuitable habitat for most other conifers, although some limber pine will be found growing on these sites.

Precipitation here averages approximately ten inches per year, so the area supports only a limited variety of plant life.

After enjoying the vista from the northernmost point of Discovery Trail, you switchback to the south on a lower contour, and after a mile of hiking through

Ancient bristlecone pines, among the oldest living things on earth, have been scarred and sculpted by strong winds and deep snows for thousands of years here in the Patriarch Grove of the White Mountains.

some of the most impressive, weather-tortured trees anywhere, you arrive back at the visitor center and your car.

Now that your appetites for the bristlecone pines and the White Mountains have been stimulated, drive north from the Schulman Grove. After a short distance the pavement ends, and you follow the good dirt road along or near the crest, gaining elevation and spectacular vistas along the way.

After driving thirteen miles, you reach the junction with the road to Patriarch Grove. Turn right and drive one mile to the end of the road and park at 11,300 feet above sea level, in a weather-beaten sub-alpine forest. Two trails begin here; both are short, easy, and well worth the time and effort.

First, walk west from the parking area and pick up the Patriarch Trail. This short trail makes a half-mile loop through the strange sub-alpine landscape, passing the Patriarch—not the oldest, but by far the largest bristlecone pine known on earth. This multiple-trunked giant has a circumference of thirty-six feet, eight inches.

After this short but pleasant stroll, head east across the parking area and pick up the short trail that climbs to the ridgetop 11,360 feet above sea level. From that point you can see Cottonwood Basin below to the north, where there are vivid green meadows, granite boulders and outcrops, and a good all-year stream. To the west, alpine peaks of the White Mountains crest rise above the last sparse stand of bristlecones, snow-streaked well into summer.

After returning to your car, drive one mile back to the junction with the main road. Park on the edge of the wide dirt road, being sure to stay in the roadbed to avoid crushing delicate alpine plants. Do not block the road.

Begin hiking north along the road across barren, alpine slopes, soon passing absolute timberline. After strolling 1.2 miles, you reach a high point at an elevation of 11,850 feet, where the road begins to descend.

After having completed the three short hikes back down the road, your body should have acclimatized somewhat, but the elevation here and the steepness of this cross-country hike will take its toll nevertheless.

Your destination is Sheep Mountain, about .8 mile to the southwest. You begin by laboring up smooth and very steep alpine slopes in a southwesterly direction. It would be difficult to get lost here—simply climb the steep slopes to the first summit, Peak 12,240. You then drop into a saddle through which a transmission line passes, supplying power to the University of California's Barcroft Laboratory.

From this saddle, it's 300 feet up the final alpine slopes to 12,497-foot-high Sheep Mountain, where a magnificent vista unfolds. The view north and east into Nevada is excellent, as is the southward view along the crest of the White Mountains. The great Sierra Nevada rears up majestically beyond Owens Valley, the deepest valley in the continent. To the north is Piute Mountain, Mt. Barcroft, and finally White Mountain Peak. In addition to being the highest in the range, 14,246-foot-high White Mountain Peak is the highest point in the Great Basin, as well as one of eleven peaks in California more than 14,000 feet tall.

The Great Basin is a vast region, encompassing most of Nevada and parts of Utah, Oregon, Idaho, and California. It is characterized by literally hundreds of mountain ranges aligned in a generally north-south pattern and interrupted by numerous desert valleys. These valleys are generally closed basins where the streams draining the mountain ranges end in "dry" lakes to evaporate

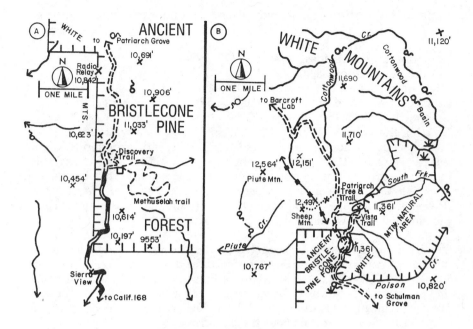

in the intense desert sun. The Great Basin has no outlet to the sea. The region contains incredible topographic relief. The crest of the Panamint Mountains, for example, plummets more than 11,000 feet into Death Valley.

Also visible from Sheep Mountain are the buildings of the Barcroft Lab lying at the 12,400-foot level on the east slopes of 13,040-foot-high Mt. Barcroft. It is a barren yet beautiful alpine landscape, accentuated in early summer by numerous snowfields.

From the Barcroft Lab, an abandoned jeep trail leads 5.3 miles to White Mountain Peak, a very worthwhile excursion.

After absorbing the superb view, carefully retrace your route back to your car.

With these four hikes, you can sample one of the most unique landscapes in California. There are many more opportunities for hiking in the White Mountains, as a quick glance at the topographic quadrangles will reveal. Much is cross-country walking. Probably the most challenging hike in the range can be made from White Mountain Peak, hiking north along the crest of the range for many miles. One could backpack in this area for a week or more, and solitude is virtually assured. Such a no-nonsense cross-contry hike, however, should be attempted by veteran hikers only. Still, all one really needs for hiking in this range is a topo map, a compass, and a sense of adventure.

This area is also moderately popular with cross-country ski enthusiasts, for this area's excellent network of roads and often superb, dry snow conditions make an expedition into the bristlecones and beyond an unforgettable winter experience.

HIKE 62 *LAKE SABRINA TO HUNGRY PACKER LAKE*

General description: A moderate 12.6 mile round trip backpack of three or more days in the John Muir Wilderness, leading to a spectacular peak-rimmed alpine lake basin in the eastern Sierra.
Elevation gain and loss: 2,140 feet.
Trailhead elevation: 8,960 feet.
High point: Hungry Packer Lake, 11,100 feet.
Maps: Mt. Goddard 15-minute USGS quad; Inyo National Forest map.
Season: July through mid-October.
Finding the trailhead: From U.S. 395 in Bishop, turn west onto Highway 168 where a sign indicates South Lake, North Lake, and Lake Sabrina. Follows this paved road up the canyon of Bishop Creek, passing an Inyo National Forest entrance station after nine miles, where wilderness permits can be obtained. Bear right after fourteen miles where the road to South Lake forks left and drive three more miles to the signed Sabrina Basin hiker's parking area at the junction with the westbound North Lake Road.

The hike: The immense glacier-carved bowl of the Middle Fork Bishop Creek, popularly known as Sabrina Basin, boasts three dozen lakes, ranging in elevation from 9,700 to 12,400 feet. Many of these lakes boast excellent fishing, and all feature a backdrop of jagged crags approaching 14,000 feet. The lower lakes are typically forest-rimmed, while the higher lakes are rockbound. Some may harbor icebergs throughout the summer.

This basin doesn't see quite as many hikers as the North and South forks of Bishop Creek, primarily because there is no trail access over the Sierra crest into Kings Canyon National Park. Moreover, wilderness permit quotas further the wilderness experience by limiting the number of hikers entering the basin each day during the peak hiking season, from July 1 through September 15.

Since there is no trail leading over the Sierra crest, Sabrina Basin is a hiking destination rather than a hiking corridor to points beyond. In addition to good fishing, hikers can spend many days exploring remote cirque basins, many of them harboring high, lonely lakes. The lofty crags of the Sierra crest offer ample challenges to seasoned mountaineers. And campsites and water in Sabrina Basin are plentiful. Be sure to carry a backpack stove since campfires are no longer allowed. Also, a wilderness permit is required and should be obtained at the entrance station in Bishop Creek.

Begin this hike by walking south on the Lake Sabrina Road. The jagged, snowy peaks of the Sierra crest, piercing the sky to the south, should divert your attention from this short section of pavement, giving you an exhilarating taste of what lies ahead. Leave the road after .6 mile, turning left at the signed trailhead.

The trail traverses mostly open slopes above the east shore of Lake Sabrina, slopes clothed in sagebrush, mountain mahogany, scattered aspen, lodgepole and limber pine, and an occasional Sierra juniper, unmistakable because of its shaggy, reddish bark.

After hiking 1.3 miles from the parking area, the eastbound trail leading to George Lake, Table Mountain, and the Tyee Lakes (see Hike 63) joins your route on the left.

Bearing right at this junction and continuing south, the trail soon crosses the outlet creek of George Lake, then shortly crosses another small creek before beginning a series of switchbacks under moderate lodgepole pine shade.

About 1.3 miles beyond the George Lake Trail, you reach beautiful Blue Lake at 10,398 feet, probably the most heavily used lake in the basin, and with good reason. The view up the canyon across the lake is outstanding. The sparsely timbered talus slopes of Thompson Ridge rise well above the 12,000-foot level east of the lake. Campsites are numerous around the irregular western shores in moderate forest cover.

The trail crosses the wide outlet of Blue Lake via a log jam and becomes faint along the west shore. Watch for ducks to lead the way when crossing bare rock stretches.

After hiking .3 mile from Blue Lake's outlet creek, you reach a junction. Straight ahead the trail ascends the canyon to Baboon Lakes. A short cross-country jaunt above those lakes lies alpine Sunset Lake and the Thompson Glaciers—a highly recommended side trip. But for now, turn right, skirt the edge of a small, stagnant pond and begin a westward course across the basin. The trail is lost across occasional bare rock, but the alert hiker should have no trouble relocating it.

After 1.2 miles of pleasant hikeing, you pass the largest of the Emerald Lakes chain, then ascend a small ridge which provides excellent vistas of the surrounding terrain. The jagged peaks along the Sierra Nevada crest seem only a stone's throw away; and, indeed, you will soon be camping in their shadow. A short descent brings you near the shore of small Dingleberry Lake, and from here on up the basin, campsites and water are easy to fine. A ford of the Middle Fork Bishop Creek is necessary a short distance above Dingleberry Lake.

You reach the junction with the trail to Midnight Lake after hiking 1.1 miles beyond the Emerald Lakes. This beautiful subalpine gem, with its backdrop of cliffs and rugged peaks, offers superb camping among stunted whitebark pines.

Turn left at this junction and ascent a low ridge surrounded by increasingly stunted whitebark pines. The trail rounds the ridge above Topsy Turvy Lake where the upper Middle Fork spreads out in all its alpine splendor. The alpine meadows, stunted whitebark pine, and breathtaking peaks make this one of the most scenic camping areas in the entire Middle Fork Bishop Creek drainage.

Continuing up the trail, you hop across the outlet of Hungry Packer Lake just above tiny Sailor Lake, then make the final ascent to the lake along this creek. You soon reach the north end of Hungry Packer Lake, 6.3 miles from the parking area, where fair campsites among stunted whitebark pines can be found. Fishing is sometimes excellent (rainbow and brook trout up to 12 inches), but veteran anglers know how temperamental fish can be in these cold, high-altitude lakes. The impressive pinnacle of 13,435-foot Mt. Haeckel, a prominent landmark that has guided you from the trailhead, soars above the upper end of the lake.

Moonlight Lake is a short cross-country walk to the east. A seldom-used route, recommended for experienced backpackers only, ascends to the source of the Middle Fork, Echo Lake, and crosses the Sierra crest at Echo Pass. This trailless route involves some class 2 scrambling on the north side; the rest of the route is mainly boulder-hopping. It is an effective means of access to the Muir Pass area of Kings Canyon National Park.

Most of the lakes in this drainage are accessible by short cross-country hikes, and hikers searching for solitude can, with a little extra effort, have many of these remote lakes to themselves.

HIKE 63 *LAKE SABRINA TO TYEE LAKES*

General description: A moderate eleven mile round trip backpack of two or more days in the John Muir Wilderness, leading to an infrequently visited lake basin, tucked under an alpine mesa in the Bishop Creek drainage of the eastern Sierra Nevada.

Elevation gain and loss: 2,640 feet; -559 feet.

Trailhead elevation: 8,960 feet.

High point: Table Mountain, 11,600 feet.

Maps: Mt. Goddard 15-minute USGS quad; Inyo National Forest map.

Season: July through September.

Finding the trailhead: Follow directions given for Hike 62.

The hike: The vast Bishop Creek drainage boasts a number of lakes that is unsurpassed in all of the eastern Sierra Nevada. About 100 lakes, ranging in size from shallow one-acre tarns to deep 300-acre lakes can be found here, and most are at, or above, timberline and backed up against jagged, snow-streaked summits. The three main forks of Bishop Creek are well known for their scenic grandeur and recreational opportunities, thus at times the area can be quite popular. Great fishing and awe-inspiring scenery in a back-country setting are primary attractions for hikers.

George Lake and the Tyee Lakes lie in remote hanging valleys on the flanks of the broad alpine mesa of Table Mountain. The matchless vista from the mountain to the peaks surrounding the headwaters of Bishop Creek is unsurpassed except, perhaps, by the view from an airplane.

This hike is an excellent alternative to popular Sabrina Basin and the South Fork Bishop Creek. The Tyee Lakes are off-the-beaten-path, receive light use, and offer good fishing.

When wilderness permit quotas are filled for the other lake basins in the drainage, particularly on busy summer weekends, consider this fine hike to Tyee Lakes. Here, quotas are only necessary on the July 4th and Labor Day holidays to preserve the wilderness experience. A wilderness permit is still required, however, and should be obtained at the entrance station in Bishop Creek. Campfires are permitted, but firewood is scarce in the timberline forests around the lakes. Hikers should forego the use of campfires to minimize their impact and carry a backpack stove instead.

From the trailhead parking area, follow Hike 62 for 1.3 miles to the George Lake junction and turn left. Presently, you begin a series of fairly steep switchbacks, enjoying increasingly good views northwestward into the North Fork Bishop Creek drainage. After one mile of climbing moderately forested slopes dotted by scattered clumps of curl-leaf mountain mahogany, you arrive in the George Lake basin. From here to the lake, the trail is sometimes faint and fades out entirely in some grassy areas. Careful scouting may be necessary to relocate the route.

If you lose the trail, simply follow the creek upstream to George Lake, two miles from the previous junction. There are numerous sandy campsites among whitebark and lodgepole pines along the northern shore. From the lake your trail switchbacks up a steep, sandy slope. Stunted whitebark pines keep you company on this ascent. The trail finally surmounts the sandy, open

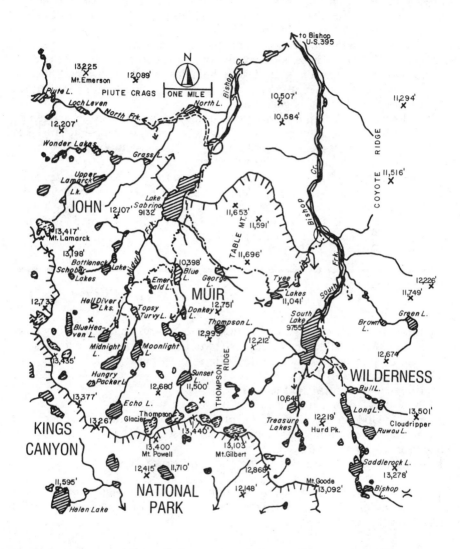

plateau of Table Mountain, where the Bishop Creek drainage unfolds below your gaze. The ground-hugging whitebark pines here attest to the severity of winters at this altitude.

From Table Mountain, the trail continues in an easterly direction and then swings southward, descending a small gully. Those inclined to camp on Table Mountain may find water in this gully in early summer, but don't depend on it.

As this trail switchbacks down the sparsely timbered slope, the hanging valley containing the Tyee Lakes comes into view. This hanging valley lies high above the South Fork Bishop Creek and was created thousands of years ago as a large glacier moved northward down the South Fork, and in the process the lower portion of the Tyee Lakes creek tributary was removed. As a result, the valley containing the lakes ends high on the wall of the broadened and deepened canyon of the South Fork.

You soon reach the north shore of the second-highest and largest of the Tyee Lakes, Lake 11,041. These lakes are fed by the runoff from a small, permanent snowfield above the upper lake, which lies in a bowl at timberline, its stunted whitebark pines offereing sheltered camping from the sometimes severe weather. Fishing is good here.

The lower lake, 1.5 miles below lake 11,041, is surrounded by lodgepole pines and aspen, the latter providing a dazzling display of fall color. The lakes in between offer pleasant camping in lodgepole and whitebark pine forest, each with its own view in a slightly different setting.

From the lakes, hikers can either return the same way to Lake Sabrina, or descend the steep, lodgepole pine-clad slope for 1.8 miles from the lower lake to the Tyee Lakes trailhead on the paved road to South Lake in Bishop Creek's South Fork Canyon. That trailhead lies on the west side of the road, five miles from the Lake Sabrina/South Lake junction.

HIKE 64 NORTH LAKE TO THE LAMARCK LAKES

General description: A rigorous seven-mile round-trip backpack (or day hike) in the John Muir Wilderness, leading to two fishable sub-alpine lakes nestled in deep cirques beaneath precipitous Sierra crest peaks.
Elevation gain and loss: 1,600 feet.
Trailhead elevation: 9,300 feet.
High point: Upper Lamarck Lake, 10,900 feet.
Maps: Mt. Goddard 15-minute USGS quad (trail beyond Grass Lake not shown on quad), Inyo National Forest map.
Season: July through early October.
Finding the trailhead: Follow directions given for Hike No. 65.

The hike: This short but fairly strenuous weekender leads hikers into a magnificent lake basin encircled by bold crags, many of which exceed 13,000 feet in elevation.

Fishing is often rewarding, and the numerous side trip possibilities (for experienced hikers) should satisfy both veteran and intermediate cross-country hikers.

Finding water and campsites is no problem.

A wilderness permit is required and should be obtained at the permit station along the road in lower Bishop Creek. Campfires are prohibited beyond Grass Lake, so be sure to carry a backpack stove.

Follow Hike No. 65 for .5 mile to the Lamarck Lakes Trail and turn left. You quickly begin switchbacking up northwest-facing slopes clothed in aspen and lodgepole pine. Midway, hikers have good views into the classic U-shaped canyon of North Fork Bishop Creek.

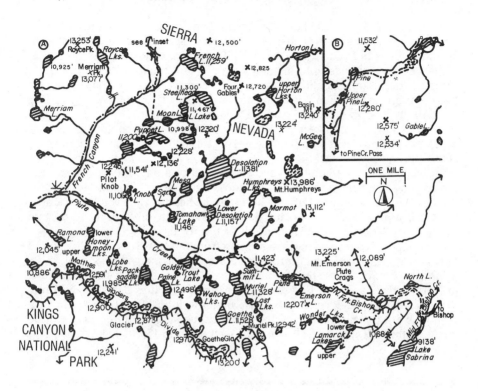

After climbing for one mile, the short lateral trail to Grass Lake departs to the left, leading to pleasant lodgepole-shaded campsites. Fishing for pan-sized trout is usually good in Grass Lake.

Turning right at that junction, however, you soon begin negotiating a series of moderately steep switchbacks. Along the way, views expand to include a host of spectacular alpine peaks in the southeast.

You eventually skirt a small tarn, then reach the deep blue oval of Lower Lamarck Lake. There are excellent campsites available here amid stunted timber. The population of large trout in this lake should keep anglers busy, and photographers will be delighted by the early morning reflections of rugged peaks in the lake's calm waters.

For cross-country enthusiasts, the Wonder Lakes dot the basin to the west, offering a remote and spectacular destination for day-hiking jaunts or remote camping.

Beyond Lower Lamarck Lake, the trail follows the outlet of Upper Lamarck Lake upstream amid thinning timber, soon reaching (at 10,900 feet above sea level) that oblong lake. Good campsites can be found above the northeast corner of the lake amid stunted but shelter-giving whitebark pines. Fishing is also productive in this deep lake.

A moderately strenuous path, worn into the headwall of the basin, leads into the Evolution Basin region of Kings Canyon National Park and begins at Upper Lamarck Lake.

From the lake, hikers can barely make out Lamarck Col on the southwestern skyline, immediately below (left of) Mt. Lamarck. The path switchbacks steeply up the headwall of the cirque behind the lake in a southwesterly direction. It then heads southeast into a small drainage and finally jogs southwest to ascend a long, sloping bench all the way to Lamarck Col. A small tarn near the top offers water when it isn't frozen. From the col, the route drops steeply for 1,300 feet to the lakes in upper Darwin Canyon.

From Lamarck Col, hikers negotiate seemingly endless boulder fields into the Darwin Canyon lakes, until rediscovering this path along the northern shore of the second lowest lake.

Below the lakes, camping is good in an area of alpine meadows, stunted timber, and glacially smoothed rock known as Darwin Bench.

From Darwin Bench, it is an easy hike into the heart of the Evolution country. With its dramatic peaks and breathtaking alpine terrain, this area displays some of the most spectacular scenery in all of California.

Enough cross-country side trips, ranging from moderate to difficult, abound in this region to keep adventurous hikers busy for many seasons.

Most hikers who cross the Sierra Nevada at Lamarck Col either loop back to North Lake via the northbound John Muir Trail, Piute Canyon, and Piute Pass, a hike of a week or more, or else hike the John Muir Trail southward, then hike out to South Lake via Bishop Pass. The latter requires a car shuttle or a hitchhike of about twelve miles to get back to North Lake.

HIKE 65 *NORTH LAKE TO PINE CREEK*

General description: A moderately strenuous twenty-four-mile, point-to-point backpack, suitable for more experienced hikers, in the John Muir Wilderness.
Elevation gain and loss: 3,820 feet, -5,700 feet.
Trailhead elevation: 9,300 feet.
High point: Piute Pass, 11,423 feet.
Maps: Mt. Abbot, Mt. Goddard, and Mt. Tom 15-minute USGS quads, Inyo or Sierra National Forest map. Also use hike No. 64 map.
Season: July through mid-October.
Finding the trailhead: From U.S. 395 in Bishop, turn west onto State Highway 168 where a sign lists mileages to South Lake, Lake Sabrina, and North Lake. Follow this paved road up Bishop Creek canyon, passing the Forest Service entrance station after nine miles, where wilderness permits can be obtained. After another five miles, avoid the left-branching road leading to South Lake, and continue straight ahead for three more miles to the signed, right-branching North Lake Road. Follow this dirt road for 1.75 miles to the signed hikers parking area just above North Lake.

To find the Pine Creek Trailhead, drive ten miles north of Bishop on U.S. 395, then turn west and proceed ten more miles up the paved Pine Creek Road to the hikers' parking area just east of the pack station.

The hike: This moderate point-to-point trail walk crosses two Sierra Nevada crest passes higher than 11,000 feet, travels through two of the most lake-filled basins in the range, and surveys vegetation ranging from Jeffrey pine forest to alpine tundra.

The scenery on this trip is so majestic that even those dedicated anglers who forget their fishing gear will find consolation in the sheer absorbing beauty of this region.

Campfires are prohibited from the trailhead to Piute Pass, but they are permitted west of the pass in the Sierra National Forest, and in the Pine Creek drainage. However, hikers employing minimum impact techniques will only build fires where firewood is in obvious abundance.

This trip requires that hikers leave another vehicle at the Pine Creek Trailhead unless they intend to hitchhike thirty-eight miles back to North Lake.

A wilderness permit is required.

From the hikers' parking area, walk back to the North Lake Road, turn right, and hike one-half mile to the trailhead at the upper end of the campground. A short distance beyond, the southbound Lamarck Trail (see Hike 64) departs to your left at a large information sign. You turn right and ascend westward through the shade of aspen, lodgepole, and limber pine. After fording the North Fork Bishop Creek twice (which may be difficult in May and June), you begin switchbacking up talus slopes below the broken red cliffs of the Piute Crags. Above that ascent, you reach Loch Leven, the first lake in this small but highly

View across upper French Canyon basin from Pine Creek Pass.

205

scenic basin. From this lake, you can see the notch of Piute Pass on the western horizon. You are surrounded by impressive alpine peaks as you ascend this canyon past several lakes and tarns, the largest being Piute Lake.

Beyond Piute Lake, you soon leave the last gnarled whitebark pines behind and ascend the final alpine slopes to Piute Pass. Your view eastward from the pass takes in the U-shaped valley containing Piute and Loch Leven lakes. Westward, your view is strictly alpine. The jagged, perpetually snowy peaks of the Glacier Divide march off to the west, forming the northern boundary of Kings Canyon National Park. Immediately to your west lies the broad expanse of alpine Humphrey's Basin, one of the largest and gentlest lake basins in the Sierra Nevada. There are more than twenty alpine lakes here, most of which offer challenging fishing opportunities. Desolation Lake, one of the largest backcountry lakes in the Sierra, offers superb (although somewhat austere) alpine camping.

North of the pass, convoluted red and brown cliffs soar to the pinnacle-topped summit of 13,986-foot-high Mt. Humphreys, the highest peak this far north in the Sierra. If you wish to partake of the magnificent vistas this peak offers, be prepared for some serious scrambling—the easiest routes are class 4, but well worth the effort.

From the pass, descend westward to round Summit Lake and continue your trail walk through the tundra-dominated landscape of Humphreys Basin. All the lakes in this basin are accessible by easy cross-country jaunts, and are so numerous that it is easy for hikers to have a lake entirely to themselves.

Your route soon passes to the north of Golden Trout Lake, at one time the most heavily used lake in the basin. That heavy use has prompted the Forest Service to restrict camping to no less than 500 feet from the lake shore.

Lodgepole pines are noted in increasing numbers as you descend along Piute Creek, offering more sheltered camping than in exposed Humphreys Basin. Fishing is good in this creek for pan-sized golden trout.

After a few short switchbacks, the trail levels off in a thick, shady lodgepole pine forest, occasionally passing small, wildflower-decorated meadows. With the pyramidal hulk of Pilot Knob looming directly above to your north, you hop across multi- branched French Canyon Creek (which can be difficult in June and early July) and soon meet the French Canyon Trail on your right, just north of the small green spread of Hutchinson Meadow.

Turn north onto this trail and begin a long, gentle ascent of French Canyon. You soon break into the open, following the edge of a narrow two-mile-long meadow. Merriam Peak stands majestically above the canyon in the north, and the broken, craggy summits of the Sierra crest lure hikers onward to the large lakes at the head of this spectacular, U-shaped canyon. Midway up this meadow, avoid a faint westbound trail that climbs to seldom-visited Merriam Lake.

At the head of the meadow, you hop across Royce Lake's outlet creek. Photographers will be tempted to ascend that creek for .5 mile to enjoy a magnificent 500-foot-high waterfall.

From the crossing, you quickly pass the last remnants of timber and continue your jaunt through open, alpine meadows. One mile below Pine Creek Pass, you meet a southbound trail providing access to several large, fishable lakes. Short cross-country jaunts in this basin lead to many infrequently visited alpine lakes.

After a short, stiff climb beyond that trail, you level off on a large grassy bench. From here a cross-country route of moderate difficulty leads to the Royce Lakes chain, well off the beaten path. These lakes offer good fishing and remote camping to those willing to forego the comforts of below-timberline camping.

Continuing northward, you skirt two small tarns and a few persistent whitebark pines, crossing the Sierra crest at Pine Creek Pass, 11,120 feet above sea level. Views are good southward to the western peaks of the Glacier Divide. The unmistakable spire of Mt. Humphreys is visible to the southeast.

A host of high peaks surrounding the Pine Creek drainage can be seen to the north, dominated by the jagged crag of 13,713- foot-high Bear Creek Spire.

You presently begin a short descent through alpine meadows and along the headwaters of Pine Creek before re-entering timber. You soon pass two small tarns with fair campsites, and continue descending under a thickening canopy of lodgepole and whitebark pines, eventually passing a signed trail leading west to Granite Park and Italy Pass. The starkly beautiful alpine lakes in Granite Park, encircled by several impressive 12,000- and 13,000- foot-high peaks, make that basin a worthy destination. The Chalfant Lakes, lying just north of Granite Park over a low ridge, provide solitude seekers with superb, rarely used campsites.

As your descent proceeds, you cross a multi-branched creek, skirt the western shore of Upper Pine Lake, then Pine Lake, both of which offer excellent views across their deep blue waters.

You soon ford the outlet creek of Pine Lake and pass the last few campsites along Pine Creek, shaded by lodgepole pines. A traverse of north-facing slopes, under the precipitous north wall of Peak 12,280, brings you to a series of short switchbacks where you lose 400 feet of elevation.

Suddenly, your trail emerges onto an access road to the Brownstone Mine. You follow this narrow dirt road as it switchbacks its way to lower Pine Creek. After hiking 1.4 miles along this road, leave it and proceed eastward on another trail. Your final descent begins immediately across the canyon from the active Pine Creek Tungsten Mill. The trail crosses several small creeks in a Jeffrey pine and red fir forest, with occasional aspen and birch adding trailside company. You eventually reach the pack station, passing a few scattered buildings, and finally reach the hikers' parking area.

HIKE 66 ROCK CREEK TO UPPER MORGAN LAKE

General description: A moderate 8.6-mile round-trip day hike or backpack in the John Muir Wilderness, leading through a lake-filled basin in the eastern Sierra Nevada.
Elevation gain and loss: 854 feet, -200 feet.
Trailhead elevation: 10,250 feet.
High point: Morgan Pass, 11,104 feet.
Maps: Mt. Abbot and Mt. Tom 15-minute USGS quads, Inyo National Forest map. Also use hike No. 67 map.
Season: July through mid-October.

Findlng the trailhead From Tom's Place on U.S. 395, twenty-four miles north of Bishop and fifteen miles south of Mammoth Junction, turn south onto Rock Creek Road where a sign indicates Rock Creek Lake. Follow this road for eleven miles to the trailhead at the end of the road. The final two miles of the road beyond Rock Creek Lake are paved but narrow, so drive with caution.

The hike: The hike to Upper Morgan Lake follows an old jeep road that once was the primary access to the Pine Creek Tungsten Mines. It makes an excellent day hike for people staying at one of the campgrounds on Rock Creek and who are interested in some backcountry fishing and a chance to stretch their legs. It can be undertaken as a backpack, but few campsites are available at Upper Morgan Lake. Lower Morgan Lake, however, boasts several spacious campsites. Little Lakes Valley, west of Morgan Pass, abounds in campsites and subalpine lakes, and families with small children will find the valley to be an excellent choice for a weekend backpack. Backpackers must remember

Hikers ascending the gentle slopes of Mt. Starr from Mono Pass will be rewarded with the rugged, magnificent scenery of the High Sierra. Mt. Humphreys, 13,986 feet above sea level, punctuates the horizon.

that campfires are prohibited from the trailhead to Morgan Pass, but are allowed at the Morgan Lakes despite the lack of abundant firewood.

A wilderness permit is required.

From the trailhead, hike south on the old jeep road, soon passing the west-branching trail to Mono Pass. The jagged, snow-streaked Sierra crest peaks loom boldly at the head of the valley, in constant view as you amble up the trail.

Beyond the Mono Pass Trail junction, your route passes four sub-alpine lakes in lodgepole and whitebark pine forest, each with good campsites and good fishing in a breathtaking, high- mountain setting.

As you near the head of the valley, you meet an eastbound trail leading to Chickenfoot Lake, one of the most popular lakes in the basin. Shortly thereafter, you pass a right-branching trail leading to Gem Lakes and the Treasure Lakes, either of which make good base camps for exploring the headwaters of Rock Creek.

Your route then makes a few short switchbacks to surmount 11,104-foot high Morgan Pass amidst a thick carpet of ground- hugging whitebark pines. Views are superb across Little Lakes Valley to the alpine peaks of the Sierra Nevada crest. To the east rise the barren peaks surrounding Pine Creek's headwaters.

From the pass, descend boulder-strewn terrain, soon traversing above the south shore of Upper Morgan Lake. Fishermen should have no trouble landing enough rainbow trout for dinner, but backpackers may have a difficult time locating a suitable campsite along the rockbound shores of the lake.

The trail continues eastward, passing Lower Morgan Lake, then leaves the John Muir Wilderness and enters an active mining area.

From Upper Morgan Lake, you double back to the trailhead.

HIKE 67 *ROCK CREEK TO PIONEER BASIN*

General description: A moderate 16.4-mile round-trip backpack into the Mono Creek headwaters, offering the challenge of a Sierra Nevada crest crossing at 12,000 feet above sea level, in the John Muir Wilderness.

Elevation gain and loss: 2,150 feet, -2,000 feet.

Trailhead elevation: 10,250 feet.

High point: Mono Pass, 12,000 feet.

Maps: Mt. Tom and Mt. Abbot 15-minute USGS quads, Inyo or Sierra National Forest maps.

Season: July through mid-October.

Finding the trailhead: Follow directions given in Upper Morgan Lake hike (No. 66).

The hike: This moderately easy trip, beginning at the highest trailhead in the Sierra Nevada, utilizes the northernmost trail crossing the Sierra crest at 12,000 feet, probably the easiest pass at that elevation in the entire range. Once over the crest, all the lake basins of upper Mono Creek are readily accessible, most of them by trail.

The six peaks of 12,000 feet or more surrounding Pioneer Basin are easily climbed via class 2 scrambles. Mt. Stanford, at an elevation of 12,851 feet,

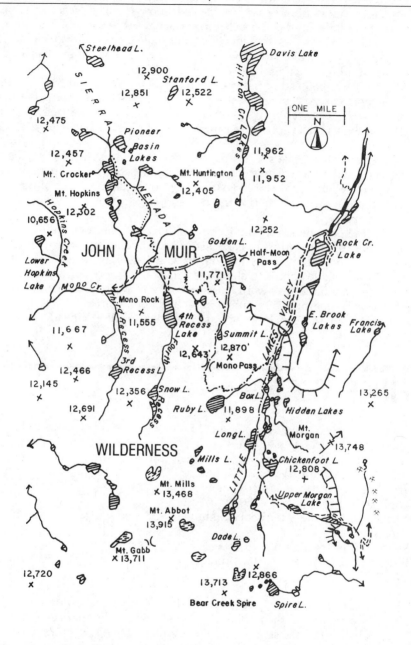

is not only the highest but perhaps the easiest to climb. Its central location above the basin offers outstanding, unobstructed views.

A wilderness permit is required. Campfires are prohibited.

The trail begins at the south end of the large parking area. The first .6 mile follows the route of the hike to Upper Morgan Lake through scattered lodgepole and whitebark pines. You then turn right at the signed junction and ascend several small benches in a southwesterly direction. After climbing for 1.3 miles, you pass the southwest-branching trail to Ruby Lake, where excellent scenic campsites can be found.

From this junction, your route switchbacks up sandy, sparsely timbered slopes. Deep, blue Ruby Lake soon comes into view, with a backdrop of impressive Sierra crest crags. You finally leave the last wind-torn whitebark pines behind, then contour into a shallow gully and labor up the last few switchbacks to the narrow sandy notch of Mono Pass. This one is 12,000 feet above sea level—there is also another Mono Pass on the Sierra crest, thirty-five miles to the northwest on the eastern boundary of Yosemite National Park. Views from the pass are good, but somewhat limited. To the north, Summit Lake occupies the sandy bench just below the pass, with flat-topped Peak 12,252 in the background. To the south, several Sierra crest peaks in the 13,000-foot range soar out of the Little Lakes Valley.

Hikers wishing for a truly panoramic view of this region of the Sierra Nevada are urged to scramble up the easy west slopes of 12,870-foot-high Mt. Starr, immediately to the east.

A descent of 1.1 miles along the sandy trail brings you to a junction with a faint route descending to Golden Lake, where the main trail bends northwest. This recommended alternative, avoiding the Trail Lakes, descends northward along the west side of the small creek, then contours above Golden Lake's rocky western shore. Good campsites can be found near the outlet of this alpine lake. The trail, more distinct below the lake, descends in a westerly direction along Golden Creek, rejoining the main trail after a total of 1.8 miles.

Those wishing to stick to the main trail will bear left 1.1 miles below Mono Pass and descend sparsely timbered slopes, pass above the small Trail Lakes and a Snow Survey cabin, then descend once again amid thickening timber to a ford of Golden Creek and the juncture with the trail descending from Golden Lake. Turn west and descend along the banks of Golden Creek, soon passing a southbound route leading to often-overcrowded Fourth Recess Lake, one of the most popular campsites in the area. Continue descending through lodgepole pine forest, then turn north (right) onto the well-worn trail leading to Pioneer Basin, just below the contour at the 10,000-foot level.

The trail climbs 400 feet in 1.2 miles to reach the lower lake in Pioneer Basin, at an elevation of 10,400 feet, which is completely surrounded by a wide, green meadow. The jagged ridge of the Mono Divide rising above the canyon of upper Mono Creek to the south adds to the scenic attraction of this fine lake. A base camp can be established here for climbing peaks, fishing, or simply relaxing in one of the most scenic and accessible backcountry lake basins in the range.

After enjoying this magnificent area, return the way you came.

HIKE 68

General description: A moderately strenuous thirty-mile round-trip backpack in the John Muir Wilderness, for experienced hikers, leading past several lakes in the majestic High Sierra.
Elevation gain and loss: 4,100 feet, -2,400 feet.
Trailhead elevation: 9,100 feet.
High point: Duck Pass, 10,800 feet.
Maps: Mt. Morrison and Mt. Abbot 15-minute USGS quads, Inyo or Sierra National Forest maps.
Season: July through mid-October.
Finding the trailhead: From Mammoth Junction on U.S. 395, about forty miles north of Bishop and twenty-six miles south of Lee Vining, turn west onto State Highway 203. Be sure to obtain your wilderness permit at the visitor center, about 3.25 miles west of U.S. 395. Although daily entry quotas are in effect from July 1 through September 15, they are rarely filled save for holiday weekends.

After driving 4.5 miles west from U.S. 395, turn left at the junction with the road to Devils Postpile and the ski area. Follow this paved road for five miles to the upper end of Lake Mary, where a sign marks the entrance to Coldwater Campground. Drive .8 mile through the campground to the large parking area at the roadend.

The hike: This week-long backpack combines a moderate climb over the Sierra Nevada crest, a view-filled traverse on the famous John Muir Trail, with an ascent to the headwaters of the Fish Creek drainage, which forms a major tributary of the Middle Fork San Joaquin River. Fishing in Tully Lake is sometimes excellent, as are all the lakes enroute and Fish Creek as well.

A wilderness permit is required.

This is bear country, so hikers must take adequate precautions to protect their food supplies.

Your dusty trail heads southward from the trailhead, climbing to a bench overlooking Arrowhead Lake, where you meet a signed trail leading down to the shores of that lake.

Continuing your southeastward course up the glaciated canyon, you pass Skelton Lake after two miles, then ascend several small benches before reaching the outlet of shallow, turquoise Barney Lake. From here, it's a 600-foot climb up to Duck Pass, the obvious low gap in the mountains to the southeast. The trail is well graded, but ascends steadily, closely following the route indicated on the quad. Sub-alpine yellow columbine is found growing here and there in sheltered nooks on this slope.

After hiking four miles from the trailhead, you surmount the crest of the Sierra Nevada at Duck Pass, 10,800 feet above sea level and shaded by scattered clumps of stunted whitebark pine. The superb vistas make this pass a worthy destination in itself. The dark pyramids of Banner Peak and Mt. Ritter are visible in the northwest, as well as a host of surrounding peaks as far north as the Mt. Dana region. You also have an excellent view back down Mammoth Creek to the unmistakable bare, rounded mass of Mammoth Mountain, capped by the summit gondola station. Massive Duck Lake, one of the largest backcountry lakes in the Sierra, lies to your southeast under the jagged peaks that enclose its basin. Smaller and more secluded Pika Lake sits on a bench above Duck Lake, offering more private camping than often-crowded Duck Lake. Bear in mind that campfires are prohibited in the Duck Lake watershed, and camping within 300 feet of the Duck Lake outlet is not allowed.

A moderate descent past Duck Lake brings you to a signed junction with the John Muir Trail, upon which you turn left and begin a sparsely forested traverse along south-facing slopes which provide some of the grandest vistas along the entire hike. The Silver Divide is the east-west ridge of alpine peaks you see to your south across the deep, U-shaped canyon of Fish Creek. You also have good views to the west down Fish Creek canyon to the peaks on the southeastern boundary of Yosemite National Park.

An early-morning reflection in Duck Lake, one of the largest backcountry lakes in the Sierra Nevada, offers a vivid example of the innumerable rewards awaiting wilderness travelers in California.

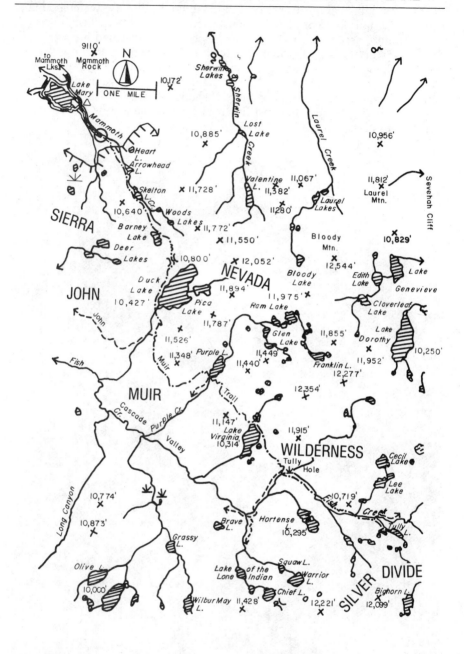

As you near Purple Lake, clumps of manzanita and chinquapin begin to appear, attesting to the dry conditions that prevail on these sun-drenched, south-facing slopes.

After hiking 2.3 miles from your juncture with the John Muir Trail, you reach the outlet of Purple Lake at an elevation of 9,900 feet. Evidence of over-use abounds at this lake—it is probably the most heavily used campsite in this region of the High Sierra. Hikers searching for solitude and peace and quiet are advised to move on.

Those who choose to stay in this basin should remember that camping and campfires are prohibited within 300 feet of the lake's outlet.

Just before crossing the lake's outlet stream, a southwest-bound trail leaves the John Muir Trail, descending along Purple Creek to the warmer, heavily forested environs of Cascade Valley.

Beyond Purple Lake, you negotiate a series of switchbacks, then pass through a narrow gap just north of the 650-foot-tall, near-vertical northeast face of Peak 11,147. Continuing your eastward course in lodgepole and whitebark pine shade, you soon ford the small creek feeding Virginia Lake, 10,314 feet above sea level and one of the most beautiful lakes in the Sierra. The view across this large lake to the alpine summits of Silver Divide is superb.

The trail presently skirts the eastern shore of the lake, passes a small tarn, then climbs to a low gap, where hikers have whitebark-framed views of the craggy peaks looming majestically at the head of Fish Creek. The impressive sight of these peaks accompanies you as you descend numerous switchbacks into the green expanse of Tully Hole.

Upon reaching Tully Hole, you follow the trail downstream for a short distance, then turn left (east) onto the Fish Creek Trail. You immediately ford Fish Creek, ascend eastward along its southern banks, and after .7 mile cross to the north banks of the creek and skirt the northern margin of the beautiful green sub- alpine meadow of Horse Heaven. This part of Fish Creek is usually infested with mosquitoes in early and mid-summer.

A series of switchbacks through lodgepole pine forest follows, avoiding the narrow gorge of Fish Creek. After this climb, the trail levels off in a sub-alpine meadow surrounded by bare, glacially smoothed granite. You soon pass the signed trail branching north to Cecil and Lee lakes.

After 1.5 miles of hiking beyond Horse Heaven, you meet the signed trail to Tully Lake and turn right. The Fish Creek Trail ascends to McGee Pass, then descends to an east-slope trailhead.

A short ascent along Tully Lake' s outlet creek brings you to the shores of this rectangular, blue-green lake. The rocky and grassy shores of the lake are occasionally interrupted by isolated stands of stunted whitebark pine. Sheltered campsites can be found on benches above the lake in these whitebark groves.

A cross-country route of moderate difficulty is possible from Red and White Lake (which is a one-mile walk east of Tully Lake and has no campsites), to massive Grinnell Lake in the Mono Creek watershed, via an 11,600-foot-high pass on the Silver Divide directly above (south of) Red and White Lake. Boulder hopping and exceedingly steep slopes make this a route for experienced backpackers only.

After enjoying this tarn-dotted basin surrounding Tully Lake, hikers eventually double back to the trailhead.

HIKE 69 *AGNEW MEADOWS TO DEVILS POSTPILE*

General description: A moderately strenuous twenty-three-mile loop backpack for experienced hikers, surveying the glorious Ritter Range, in the Ansel Adams Wilderness.
Elevation gain and loss: 4,140 feet, -4,920 feet.
Trailhead elevation: Agnew Meadows, 8,340 feet.
High point: Cecile Lake, 10,300 feet.
Maps: Devils Postpile 15-minute USGS quad, Inyo National Forest map, Ansel Adams Wilderness map.
Season: July through early October.
Finding the trailhead: There are two possible ways to reach the trailhead. The first method involves driving your own vehicle—but during the summer season you must have a vehicle containing eleven or more people or make the drive before 7:30 a.m. or after 5:30 p.m.

The second alternative, probably the more desirable method, is to park at the Mammoth Mountain Ski Area parking lot and take the Reds Meadow-Devils Postpile shuttle bus. This method minimizes traffic problems and allows flexibility in planning hikes in the area (the shuttle bus serves all the trailheads in the Devils Postpile area), in addition to reducing wear and tear on hiker's vehicles. The shuttle runs from 7:45 a.m. through 9:30 p.m. every day during the summer season, beginning operation sometime between May 31 and July 4 (depending upon snow conditions) and ending the weekend after Labor Day. The cost is about $3.50 per person for a round trip.

The Mammoth Mountain Ski Area parking lot can be reached by following State Highway 203 westward for about 7.5 miles from Mammoth Junction on U.S. 395. Mammoth Junction lies forty miles north of Bishop and twenty-six miles south of Lee Vining on U.S. 395.

The hike: This backpack trip, which takes as much as a week, samples some of the finest scenery of the majestic Ritter Range. It includes stretches of the John Muir and Pacific Crest trails, spectacular views of the dark crags of the Ritter Range, and a short cross-country scramble directly under the towering east face of the Minarets.

The popularity of portions of this route attests to its desirability as a hiking area. But crowds are no longer excessive due to daily entry quotas at all trailheads in the area, but these quotas are rarely filled except on holiday weekends.

For those who require solitude, this hike will be most enjoyable after Labor Day, when you should have this area more- or-less to yourself. But during the summer season, the short cross-country stretch between Iceberg and Minaret lakes also should provide a modicum of solitude, in addition to a challenging route.

There are black bears in the region, so backpackers should take adequate precautions to protect their food supplies.

A wilderness permit is required and can be obtained at the visitor center, about 3.25 miles west of U.S. 395 on State Highway 203.

Your trail, the permanent route of the Pacific Crest Trail, begins north of the Agnew Meadows Campground, initially switchbacking up south-facing

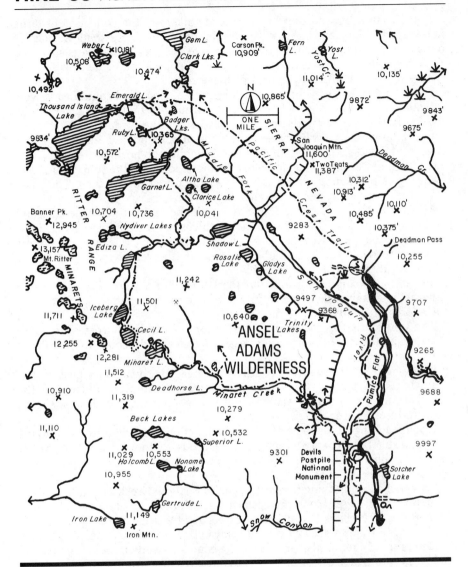

slopes clothed in red fir. Above the switchbacks, you begin a protracted westward traverse across sparsely timbered slopes while obtaining good views into the deep, U-shaped Middle Fork San Joaquin River canyon.

After hiking 2.8 miles from the trailhead, you capture a truly magnificent view southwestward across the canyon of the Middle Fork to Shadow Lake and the jagged, snowy ramparts of the Ritter Range.

Continuing your northwestward traverse, you occasionally hop across small wildflower-cloaked creeks, adding vivid contrast to these drab, otherwise dry slopes.

You pass a northwest-bound trail leading to Agnew Pass about 5.3 miles from the trailhead. Shortly thereafter, you cross Summit Lake's outlet creek, then avoid a north-branching trail also leading to Agnew Pass and a south-branching trail descending to the Middle Fork.

A short jaunt beyond that junction leads hikers to the collection of tarns known as the Badger Lakes. With no inlet or outlet, these shallow, marshy ponds are in a transitional stage between lake and meadow. Hikers spending time here will likely be amazed by the large population of harmless garter snakes around the marshy shores of these ponds.

From Badger Lakes, your mostly lodgepole pine-shaded route heads west to another junction. The right-hand fork ascends to the Clark Lakes, while the left-hand fork descends southeastward along the Middle Fork.

Continue your westward ascent along the upper Middle Fork San Joaquin River and through thinning timber, soon reaching the northeast end of large, island-dotted Thousand Island Lake and a junction with the John Muir Trail. Camping is prohibited within .25 mile of the outlet of this lake. The same restriction applies to nearby Garnet Lake.

Massive Banner Peak soars above the south end of this timberline lake, and 12,311-foot-high Mt. Davis rises to the southwest where the Ritter Range joins the crest of the Sierra Nevada. A low gap lying between these two peaks offers class 2 access into the Lake Catherine area and the very remote headwaters of the North Fork San Joaquin River.

Turning left (southeast) onto the John Muir Trail, you soon pass scenic Emerald and Ruby lakes, then climb to a rocky saddle before descending to the shores of windswept Garnet Lake.

The trail skirts the rockbound north shore of the lake, crosses its outlet stream, and turns southward after passing a trail that descends to the Middle Fork canyon.

Following a 400-foot ascent south of Garnet Lake, you top a pass 10,150 feet above sea level, where impressive views of Volcanic Ridge and the Minarets unfold. The trail then descends along a tributary of Shadow Creek, soon re-entering tree cover.

Upon reaching a lodgepole pine-shaded junction, turn right (west) onto the Ediza Lake Trail. The left-hand fork descends to the overused shores of beautiful Shadow Lake where camping and campfires are prohibited along the north and east shores.

Your trail ascends along the north bank of Shadow Creek and, after a short switchback, emerges along the eastern shores of Ediza Lake at an elevation of 9,300 feet. The backdrop of the Minarets and the imposing crags of Banner Peak and Mt. Ritter make an overnight stay in this lake basin a memorable one.

Hikers should remember that camping is not allowed on the fragile terrain along the south side of this lake. Also, campfires are prohibited between the Ediza Lake outlet and that of Minaret Lake.

Your route, presently on unmaintained trail, ascends southward along the east side of Iceberg Lake's outlet stream, soon traversing above the east shore of this highly scenic sub-alpine lake. The demanding route ahead, best hiked in late August or September due to late-melting snow, should be attempted by experienced backpackers only.

The path rises steeply for 400 feet to meet the creek draining Cecile Lake, and you scramble up the last very steep pitch to reach the boulder-littered shores of Cecile Lake (10,300 ft. and with no campsites), the highest body of water on the east slopes of the Ritter Range. Wedged between the dark wall of the Minarets and the black ramparts of Volcanic Ridge, this could easily be a scene on the moon.

There is no trail at this point, so you boulder-hop around the east shore of this alpine lake to its southern end, where two possible routes can be found descending to Minaret Lake. The first and most popular route descends a short cliff band, then follows the obvious trail down to the lake. Hikers not familiar with basic rock climbing, or those who feel uncomfortable descending exposed rock with a backpack, may elect to take the easier but slightly longer route. To find this route, proceed to the extreme southern end of the lake and climb a low, glacially smoothed hill. From here, descend into a talus-covered slope that contains a small creek draining into Minaret Lake. Descend this slope along the small creek, soon meeting the above-mentioned trail leading to the lake.

Minaret Lake, with the impressive spire of Clyde Minaret piercing the sky to the west, is an excellent choice for an overnight stay.

The trail skirts the north shore of the lake, and soon begins dropping through sparse forest along meadow-lined Minaret Creek. You shortly enter a thickening forest of lodgepole and silver pine, mountain hemlock, and some red fir. About 1.5 miles below Minaret Lake, you pass a northbound trail leading to the abandoned Minaret Mine, high on the south slopes of Volcanic Ridge. This mine operated between 1928 and 1930, and depended on dog teams coming from Old Mammoth for supplies during its two winters of operation.

Proceeding down the canyon along the long-abandoned access road to the mine, your trail soon passes a series of Minaret Creek cascades. The now-dusty, pumice-covered trail descends through heavy timber to a junction with the John Muir Trail just north of marshy Johnston Meadow. Bearing right at that junction, you soon cross to Minaret Creek's south bank, and after .5 mile, stay left where a westbound trail to Beck and Holcomb lakes joins your route.

Within one mile, you reach another junction—take the middle fork. After .25 mile, at yet another junction, bear left, quickly crossing the Middle Fork San Joaquin River via a bridge.

Once across the river, you meet a southbound trail leading the short distance to impressive Devils Postpile, a unique formation consisting of six-sided columns of basalt. The molten basaltic lava is believed to have flowed down from a vent somewhere near Mammoth Pass, filling the Middle Fork canyon from Pumice Flat south to the vicinity of Rainbow Falls to a depth of 700 feet. As the flow cooled, it fractured, forming the hexagonal columns. The top of the Postpile was scoured by the large glacier flowing down the Middle Fork, quarrying away much of this basaltic flow. Only small remnants of the flow, of which the Postpile is the most impressive, exist today.

Evidence of glaciation in the form of glacial polish can be seen by taking the short trail to the top of the Devils Postpile.

From the junction with the Devils Postpile Trail, turn left (north) and hike the final .2 mile to Devils Postpile Campground, then catch the next shuttle bus back to your car.

HIKE 70 LILLIAN LAKE LOOP

General description: A moderate 12.3-mile (or 13.4-mile partially cross-country) semiloop backpack in the Ansel Adams Wilderness, leading to several high lakes lying in the shadow of stark alpine peaks.

Elevation gain and loss: 2,600 feet.

Trailhead elevation: 7,600 feet.

High point: 9,050 feet (or Shirley Lake, 9,200 feet, if cross-country route is taken).

Maps: Merced Peak 15-minutes USGS quad (much of the trail is not shown on quad), Sierra National Forest map, Ansel Adams Wilderness map.

Season: July through mid-October.

Finding the trailhead: There are two possible ways to reach the trailhead: (1) from the town of North Fork, or (2) from Bass Lake.

(1) To reach North Fork, drive north from Fresno for 28.5 miles via State Highway 41, then turn right (east) where a sign points to O'Neals Road and North Fork. Follow this road for about seventeen miles to North Fork, then turn right where a sign points to South Fork and Mammoth Pool. Stay right just past the sawmill in South Fork where a sign points to Rock Creek and Mammoth Pool. Drive this paved road into the western Sierra, following signs indicating Mammoth Pool.

After driving 35.8 miles from South Fork, stay left where a right-branching road descends to Mammoth Pool Reservoir. A sign here points left to Minarets Station—continue driving this good paved road through a magnificent western Sierra Nevada conifer forest. You eventually pass the Minarets Work Center on your left, and you reach the end of the pavement and a three-way junction after driving 13.8 miles from the Mammoth Pool turnoff.

A sign here points left to Minarets Pack Station and Beasore Meadows. But for now, you must turn right and drive 1.8 miles to the Clover Meadow Ranger Station, where you can obtain your wilderness permit. Reservations for permits can be made over the phone or by mail, from June 28 through Labor Day, by contacting the ranger station in North Fork, but hikers must pick up their permits in person at the Clover Meadow station.

Back at the above mentioned three-way junction, turn left (west) onto Forest Road 5S07, bearing right in less than .25 mile to avoid the Pack Station turnoff. Stay left after two more miles where a right-branching road leads to the Fernandez Trailhead. About 100 yards beyond that turnoff, turn right where a sign points to Norris Creek. Follow this fairly rough, sometimes steep dirt road for about 1.9 miles to the trailhead along Norris Creek.

(2) From the north shore of Bass Lake, turn north onto Beasore Road, Forest Road 5S07, and follow signs pointing to Beasore Meadows, Clover Meadow, and Granite Creek. The pavement ends twelve miles from Bass Lake. Follow this road for 15.7 more miles to the Norris Creek turnoff, following signs along the way pointing to Clover Meadow, Granite Creek, and Fernandez Trail. Don't forget to pick up your wilderness permit at the Clover Meadow Ranger Station.

The hike: The high ridge forming the southeastern boundary of Yosemite National Park marches southwest for fourteen miles from its juncture with the Sierra Nevada crest at Rodger Peak before fading into the forest south of Madera Peak.

Dozens of alpine and sub-alpine lakes lie in glacially sculpted cirques on either side of this ridge, nestled below peaks that become progressively higher from south to north, reaching a climax at 12,978-foot-high Rodger Peak.

This ridge stands tall, collecting considerable moisture from Pacific storms. Notice that timberline is lower here than points east.

Forming a loop near the southern terminus of this alpine ridge, this trip of at least two days visits several sub-alpine lakes, wanders through magnificent forests, and occasionally rewards hikers with expansive vistas of splendid mountain scenery.

The short off-trail stretch from Stanford Lakes to Shirley Lake and then down to Lillian Lake should appeal to seasoned hikers.

On this trip, hikers will be rewarded with spectacular scenery, good fishing, and abundant campsites. Locating water is no problem once you reach Vandeburg Lake.

A wilderness permit is required.

From the parking area, you immediately descend to and hop across Norris Creek. Then turn left onto the Norris Trail. A short westward jaunt along Norris Creek under a canopy of red fir and lodgepole pine brings you to the Jackass Lakes Trail junction. Turn right here; the sign indicates the Norris Trail, and points to Fernandez Pass and Lillian Lake.

Your trail now climbs moderately steeply, then levels off under red fir shade before rising once again to meet a trail on your right descending southeast to Fernandez Trailhead and Clover Meadow.

An abundance of sub-alpine, glaciated terrain can be found at relatively low elevations in the western Ansel Adams Wilderness. Here at the 9,200-foot level, for example, Shirley Lake mirrors a landscape scraped bare by ice.

Bearing left at that junction, you soon crest an east-west ridge. Here, on the boundary of the Ansel Adams Wilderness, you meet the return leg of your loop on your right.

From this point, one can see the peaks of the Silver Divide soaring above Fish Creek in the east, and in the northeast, the dark, sawtoothed crags of the Ritter Range gnaw at the sky. In the northwest, several alpine peaks at the head of the Granite Creek drainage lure hikers onward toward their glaciated environs.

Turning left onto the trail signed for Lillian Lake at this ridgetop junction, your nearly level trail proceeds west through a forest of red fir, lodgepole pine, and a smattering of silver pine. Enroute, you pass below a lovely meadow that may contain grazing cattle in summer; cross two small creeks draining that meadow; immediately cross another small, cold creek; and begin ascending through increasingly rocky terrain. Soon you pass another soggy meadow and enter a shallow, rocky basin.

Now the trail climbs over a low, rockbound ridge, then descends to a boulder crossing of Vandeburg Lake's outlet creek under a canopy of mountain hemlock, lodgepole and silver pine, and red fir. The trail avoids the shores of that lake, instead staying well within the forest, so you won't see much of Vandeburg Lake unless you hike to it.

You soon meet the signed turnoff to Lady Lake after climbing a low, granite-bound ridge, then jog northwest to crest another low, rocky ridge sparsely forested with lodgepole pines. A descent to the Stanford Lakes follows, and hikers are accompanied by views of impressive alpine peaks rising above the basin in the west and northwest.

Shortly after the trail levels off on the floor of the Stanford Lakes basin, you reach an unsigned junction with a rock- lined, westbound trail.

Hikers have two options at this point. They can continue down the Stanford Lakes basin on the Lillian Lake Trail, reaching Lillian Lake in one mile; or more adventurous hikers and those experienced in route-finding may elect to turn left on the rock-lined trail. This often-faint trail soon crosses Shirley Creek, and ascends northwest up the glaciated basin along the course of that creek.

The Stanford Lakes are mostly too shallow to support a trout population, but anglers will be compensated farther on at Shirley and Chittenden lakes.

As you ascend this basin, notice the evidence of past glaciation that abounds. The polished rock, gouges, striations, and step-like benches give mute testimony to the incredible grinding and scouring action of glacial ice.

One mile of mostly cross-country hiking and 400 feet of ascent along Shirley Lake's outlet creek suffice to bring you to the shores of this small but beautiful lake at an elevation of 9,200 feet. Set in a timberline, granite-bound cirque under the alpine crags of 10,552-foot-high Sing Peak and 10,693-foot-high Gale Peak, this fine lake rewards all who visit its shores with sheer beauty and an isolated location. Fishing is good here for pan-sized trout. Chittenden Lake, an easy southward jaunt from Shirley Lake around a truncated spur ridge, provides even more solitude, in addition to good fishing for brookies as large as twelve inches.

Sing and Gale peaks add to the attraction of this high basin and can be scaled via class 2 and class 3 routes, respectively.

From Shirley Lake, proceed across the basin in a northeasterly direction, soon crossing a low rise. Then descend to Lillian Lake via a steep, rocky gully.

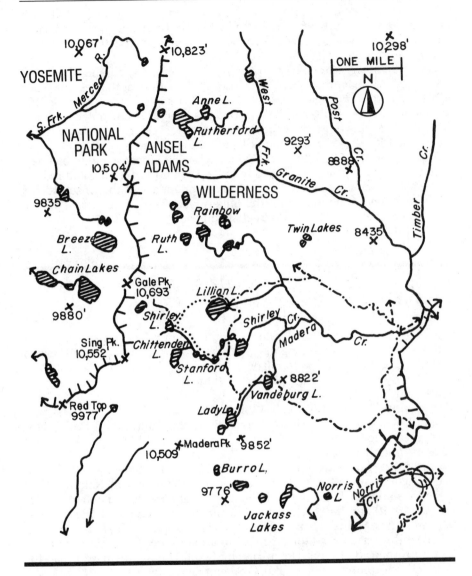

You will pick up a trail along the northwest shore of the lake—follow it to the outlet stream.

The excellent campsites you pass on this side of the lake are off-limits to backpackers. The Forest Service has closed this shore of the lake to camping due to past overuse.

Upon reaching the dam-regulated outlet creek of Lillian Lake, the largest lake in the Granite Creek drainage, you meet the Lillian Lake Trail and turn left, descending along the creek.

Soon hopping across a Madera Creek tributary, you briefly climb over a low ridge and meet the Fernandez Trail on your left, descending from the lakes in the northwest. Turning right here, you begin a thickly forested descent.

You soon break into the open along a dry ridge sparsely forested with juniper, lodgepole and Jeffrey pine, and white fir. From here, views are good back up into the Madera Creek headwaters and east across a thickly forested landscape to jagged High Sierra summits.

Your trail soon switchbacks down into heavy timber, passing the rarely used, northeast-bound Timber Creek Trail at the bottom of the descent. Your nearly level trail now leads toward Madera Creek. You soon avoid the left-branching Walton Trail, and just beyond that you are confronted with the wide, swift waters of Madera Creek. To avoid wet feet, detour downstream for about 100 yards, where you will find a log crossing.

From the south side of the creek, you begin a 500-foot ascent up boulder-dotted north-facing slopes cloaked in lodgepole and silver pine and red fir.

After this moderate ascent, you reach the boundary of the Ansel Adams Wilderness and a junction with the Lillian Lake Trail. From here, retrace your route back to the Norris Creek Trailhead.

HIKE 71 HETCH HETCHY RESERVOIR TO RANCHERIA FALLS

General description: A moderate thirteen-mile round-trip backpack (which can be completed in one long day), passing stark granite cliffs and domes and ending at a beautiful waterfall on a major Yosemite National Park stream.
Elevation gain and loss: 1,620 feet, -800 feet.
Trailhead elevation: 3,820 feet.
High point: Rancheria Falls, 4,640 feet.
Maps: Lake Eleanor and Hetch Hetchy Reservoir 15-minute USGS quads, Yosemite National Park map.
Season: March through November.
Finding the trailhead: From Oakdale, follow State Highway 120 east for about eighty-four miles. Just before reaching the Yosemite National Park entrance station at Big Oak Flat (where overnight hikers can obtain a wilderness permit), turn left (east) onto the signed Evergreen Road. Another sign here indicates Mather Camp and Hetch Hetchy Reservoir.

Follow this paved road for 7.3 miles to a road junction in Mather Camp, then turn right (east) onto Hetch Hetchy Road. Follow this paved road for nine miles to the parking area at O'Shaughnessy Dam.

The hike: Extensive areas of bare granite, most often in the form of near-vertical cliffs soaring 1,000 feet or more into the California sun, characterize the terrain traversed on this fine hike around Hetch Hetchy Reservoir.

Construction began on O'Shaughnessy Dam in 1915, impounding the Tuolumne River for San Francisco's water supply and flooding magnificent Hetch Hetchy Valley, once thought to be second only to Yosemite Valley in sheer beauty and grandeur.

Hetch Hetchy Valley was carved out of a V-shaped canyon created by the down-cutting of stream water, then widened into a broad, U-shaped valley by the massive Tuolumne Glacier, flowing tens of miles from its origin at the Tuolumne Ice Field near the Sierra Nevada crest. This ancient glacier attained a maximum depth of about 4,000 feet in the Grand Canyon of the Tuolumne River.

During repeated glacial episodes, ancient soils were removed, leaving vast areas of bare granite bedrock. Over the years, this granite has been slowly weathered and decomposed, allowing a few plant species to take hold and gather nutrients from the thin, meager soil. These plants, in turn, continue to break down the rock.

There is still much exposed solid bedrock in this area, and the combination of weathering and decomposition of the bedrock continues, enabling more and various plants to persist in establishing themselves. These plants also provide habitat for a variety of wild creatures. Such processes of weathering and plant colonization are much in evidence on this hike, and provide ample food for thought to hikers visiting the reservoir.

Wapama Falls, plunging 1,200 feet over a resistant granite precipice, is just one of many highlights on the hike around Hetch Hetchy Reservoir.

HIKE 71

HETCH HETCHY RESERVOIR TO RANCHERIA FALLS

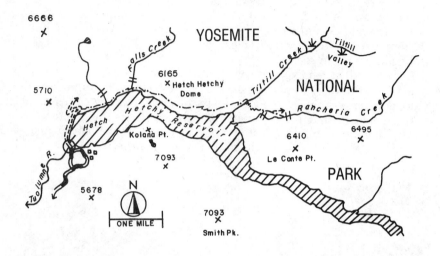

Be sure to carry plenty of water for the long, dry stretches along the way. A wilderness permit is required for overnight camping in the park.

From the parking area, proceed north across the dam, with the blue waters of the reservoir to your right and the roaring spillway feeding the lower Tuolumne River to your left. Views across the reservoir are spectacular, including the white ribbon of Wapama Falls on the north side and the sheer granite of Kolana Rock on the south side of the reservoir.

At the north end of the dam, you pass through a tunnel cut into the mountain, offering a cool, albeit brief, respite from the penetrating summer sun.

Upon exiting the tunnel, you pass a destination-and-mileage sign and continue hiking the old Lake Eleanor Road around the lower end of the reservoir, partially shaded by canyon live oak, California bay, digger pine (a California endemic), ponderosa pine, and black oak. Shrubs like mountain mahogany, manzanita, and some poison oak are also present.

After hiking .9 mile from the trailhead, leave the poor road behind and turn right onto the trail at a destination-and-mileage sign. Your trail crosses rocky, south-facing slopes and benches above the north shore of the reservoir, shaded at times by canyon live oak, black oak, digger pine, and scattered specimens of California bay and ponderosa pine. Even at this low elevation, evidence such as glacial polish attests to the activity of glaciers in the area.

You pass below Tueeulala Falls after about 1.5 miles from the trailhead. These falls tend to dry up as the summer progresses. Beyond, your trail winds its way toward the ribbon of Wapama Falls. This 1,200-foot-high falls represents the dramatic terminus of Falls Creek, a major Tuolumne River tributary which flows through the backcountry of Yosemite National Park from Dorothy Lake near the Sierra Nevada crest.

You cross the multi-branched creek below the roaring falls via excellent wood-and-steel bridges. To your south, the smooth granite of Kolana Rock plunges 2,000 feet into the depths of Hetch Hetchy Reservoir, and directly above to your northeast rises the 2,200-foot-high walls of Hetch Hetchy Dome.

Beyond the falls, you begin a shaded ascent along a bench high above the reservoir. Smooth, towering walls are ever-present to your left.

Eventually leaving the shaded bench behind, you begin a sunny, switchbacking descent. The trail soon levels off and begins a traverse into the environs of lower Tiltill Creek. You cross that cascading, gorge-bound creek via another excellent bridge, then immediately begin climbing away from the creek.

With an understory consisting primarily of manzanita, the few digger and ponderosa pines offer scant shade during this sunny, switchbacking ascent. Along this stretch you can glimpse impressive domes in the northeast, lording over the precipitous canyon of lower Tiltill Creek.

The trail levels off around the 4,400-foot level, and from here you briefly spy Rancheria Creek where it tumbles and cascades over solid granite. The rocky area below these cascades has been used as a camping area, but is barely shaded by scattered digger and ponderosa pines.

Continuing up the trail, branch right onto a faint path that leads to excellent campsites, well-shaded by ponderosa pine, black oak, and incense-cedar along Rancheria Creek and just below foaming Rancheria Falls. Fishing for good-sized trout in this creek is challenging.

After enjoying this fine area, hikers will eventually double back to the trailhead.

HIKE 72 *TIOGA ROAD TO TEN LAKES*

General description: A moderate 12.8 mile, (or longer), round trip backpack of two or more days, following the headwaters of Yosemite Creek to a lake-filled subalpine basin in central Yosemite National Park.
Elevation gain and loss: 2,180 feet; -730 feet.
Trailhead elevation: 7,500 feet.
High point: 9,680 feet.
Maps: Hetch Hetchy Reservoir 15-minute USGS quad; or Yosemite National Park USGS quad.
Season: Late June through mid-October.
Finding the trailhead: The signed Ten Lakes trailhead lies just west of the Yosemite Creek bridge on the Tioga Road (State Highway 120). To get there from the west, proceed to Crane Flat (where backcountry permits can be obtained), eighty-four miles from Merced and ninety miles from Modesto. The trailhead can be found 19.6 miles east of Crane Flat, or by traveling from the east, following State Highway 120 west, from its junction with U.S. Highway 395F or 12.6 miles to Tioga Pass, and thence another twenty-seven miles to the trailhead. Permits can be obtained at the Tuolomne Meadows Visitor Center.

The hike: Tucked against the high north slope of the Tuolumne/Merced River divide, near the geographical center of Yosemite National Park, is an exceptionally beautiful lake basin, featuring excellent fishing and outstanding high country scenery. John Muir gave the basin its name, but park rangers often refer to it as Seven Lakes, since there are only seven bodies of water large enough to be considered lakes. A host of tarns also dot the basin.

The trail touches only two of the lakes, while the others are accessible by either informal trails or cross-country hikes. This is a fine mid-elevation Yosemite hike, and it is snow-free much earlier than trails in the Tuolumne Meadows and Sierra crest areas of the Park.

Yosemite is famous for its glacier-carved and ice-scoured terrain, and hikers will see much of this kind of scenery throughout the hike. In addition, you will witness first hand the forest transition, from Jeffrey pine and Sierra juniper forest to stunted timberline stands of whitebark pine and mountain hemlock during the 2,000-foot ascent.

Primary attractions of this memorable hike include spectacular vistas of Yosemite's remote backcountry and unusually good fishing for brook trout in the Ten Lakes. The nearby Grant Lakes are stocked with rainbows, and also offer good fishing.

Deep forests, wildflower-speckled meadows, and ice-polished granite slopes are typical of the scenery in the middle elevations of Yosemite National Park.

Backcountry permits are required for camping in the park, and quotas are in effect on all park trails. The Ten Lakes are a popular destination, but not as heavily used as are many backcountry areas that lie so close to primary Park roads.

Campfires are prohibited above 9,600 feet, but much of Ten Lakes basin lies below that elevation. Nevertheless, firewood is scarce, so hikers should plan on carrying a backpack stove. If you must have a campfire, you will have to obtain a fire permit in addition to a backcountry permit and camp only in sites with an established fire ring.

The law requires that you protect your food supply from the hungry black bears that roam the Park's backcountry. Hanging your food from a tree using the counterbalance method is the best way to save your food from the remarkably resourceful bears (see the back of your permit for instructions). It is also a good idea to avoid cooking in your tent or near your campsite.

Water is available intermittently enroute to Ten Lakes. Once in the basin, it is abundant but must be treated before drinking. And of course, expect mosquitos to harass you until mid to late summer.

The trail begins west of the Yosemite Creek bridge on the north side of the Tioga Road. For .1 mile it roughly parallels the road among boulders and an open forest of Jeffrey and lodgepole pine, and Sierra juniper. After joining another trail coming up from the road, turn right (northeast) and stroll on the level amid white fir, lodgepole pine, and juniper. The moist forest floor here is grassy and bedecked with wildflowers.

This shady canyon bottom stretch, west of the infant Yosemite Creek, is dominated by lodgepole pines, but the forest is soon joined by a scattering of red firs. By contrast, the drier and rockier slopes above host Jeffrey pine and Sierra juniper.

After .5 mile you will climb the west wall of the canyon and enter that drier forest. The moderately ascending trail offers increasingly good views into Yosemite Creek's headwaters where you will see gentle, forested ridges, abundant ice-scoured bedrock and, farther on, the glacier-chiseled north face of 10,650-foot Mt. Hoffman, high above to the east. Manzanita and huckleberry oak grow thickly among trailside slabs on this sunny slope.

The grade finally eases amid some unusually large junipers, and you presently stroll easily under a shady canopy of red fir and lodgepole pine.

The trail crosses a sluggish stream after 1.8 miles, next to a fir-shaded campsite, then rises gently for another .2 mile, where you meet the westbound trail leading 5.5 miles to White Wolf. Immediately thereafter, hop across a larger creek and proceed along the forested margin of a small meadow.

A moderate but tree-shaded ascent ensues, leading past a trickling seasonal stream. The trail continues climbing through pine and fir forest, eventually approaching the corn lily-clad banks of yet another small stream at 3.4 miles.

The trail climbs alongside its flower-decked banks, then levels off on a bench boasting several large silver pines among the red firs and lodgepole pines.

Soon a brief descent leads to the edge of lodgepole-rimmed Half Moon Meadow after 3.7 miles, a georgeous spread adorned with colorful wildflowers. Among them are yampah, elephant heads, corn lily, aster, groundsel, and monkey flower. One can't help but imagine that this nearly level meadow, lying at the foot of ice-gouged cliffs, may have once been a lake.

The trail skirts the meadow, leading to its northern end, where the final ascent, an 800-foot grind, awaits. An informal trail branches off to the right

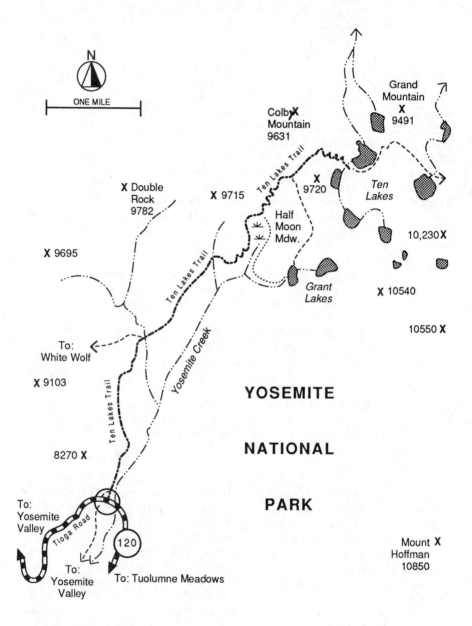

N
ONE MILE

X Double
Rock
9782

X 9715

Colby X
Mountain
9631

Ten Lakes Trail

X
9720

Grand
Mountain
X
9491

Ten
Lakes

X 9695

Half
Moon
Mdw.

10,230 X

Ten Lakes Trail

Grant
Lakes

X 10540

10550 X

To:
White Wolf

X 9103

Yosemite Creek

YOSEMITE

Ten Lakes Trail

8270 X

NATIONAL

To:
Yosemite
Valley

Tioga Road

PARK

120

To:
Yosemite
Valley

To: Tuolumne Meadows

Mount X
Hoffman
10850

at this point, leading past possible campsites east of the meadow. An alternate route to Grant Lakes, cross-country, begins here, heading south from the meadow for .5 mile to the lakes' outlet creek and thence uphill for another .5 mile, gaining 500 feet to lower Grant Lake.

To reach Ten Lakes, follow the steep switchbacking trail beneath scattered pines that offer little shade. The initial climb leads past a small, willow-clad stream, your last source of water until you reach the lakes.

Views stretch southward, where the green opening of Half Moon Meadow foregrounds more distant, heavily forested and gently rolling mountains and ridges.

The grade eventually tapers off as you rise moderately through open slopes thick with lupine, corn lily, groundsel, and monkey flower, almost attaining a ridgetop saddle before jogging northeast and rising more steeply once again. Forest cover here consists of a scattered stand of stunted and wind-flagged lodgepole and whitebark pine, and mountain hemlock.

After 4.6 miles you reach a signed junction with a right-forking trail leading one rough mile to Grant Lakes. Bearing left at this junction, the final ascent leads through sparse forest that soon gives way to open slopes, which in turn lead to the broad crest of the Tuolumne River/Merced River divide. Even the most jaded hiker will be awestruck at the vast panorama that unfolds from this 9,680-foot ridge, 5.1 miles from the trailhead. Before you is a dramatic sweep of Yosemite backcountry; from the jagged summits of the Sierra crest, from Tower Peak in the north and Mt. Gibbs in the east, to ice-polished domes, thick forests, cirque basins, and impossibly deep canyons.

Reluctantly pulling away from the unforgettable vista, follow the trail down to a saddle, then climb briefly upon the slopes of Hill 9,600. From here you will gain an incredible view into the depths of Muir Gorge, lying within the Grand Canyon of the Tuolumne River, over 4,000 feet below.

Three of the Ten Lakes are visible during the plunging descent from the hill. Finally, after 6.4 miles, you reach the north shore of the second largest of the Ten Lakes, an island-dotted lake at 8,950 feet.

Red fir and lodgepole pines are the predominant trees shading campsites at this and other lower lakes, while at the timberline lakes and tarns, whitebark pines and mountain hemlocks offer only a modicum of shelter.

The main trail climbs 500 feet over the ridge south of Grand Mountain, reaching the largest lake, at 9,400 feet, after one mile. Hikers searching for solitude can surely find it by expending a little extra effort to reach some of the higher benches and tarns in the basin, from which good fishing lakes are still only a short distance away.

HIKE 73 *TIOGA PASS TO MOUNT DANA*

General description: A strenuous 6.5 mile round trip day hike, for hikers in good physical condition, to the second highest mountain peak in Yosemite National Park.

Elevation gain and loss: 3,108 feet.

Trailhead elevation: 9,945 feet.

High point: Mt. Dana, 13,053 feet.

Maps: Tuolumne Meadows and Mono Craters 15-minute USGS quads (trail not shown on quads); or Yosemite National Park USGS quad.

Season: Mid July through September.

Finding the trailhead: Follow State Highway 120 (Tioga Road) to the Yosemite National Park entrance station atop the Sierra crest at Tioga Pass, twelve miles east of its junction with U.S. Highway 395, or 46.5 miles east of the Crane Flat Ranger Station in the western reaches of the park. An entrance fee is collected at park entrance stations. A large parking area is available along the west side of the road just south of the entrance station.

The hike: Have you ever wanted to scale a lofty Sierra Nevada peak and revel in far-flung panoramas and a sense of accomplishment that is typically enjoyed only by backpacking peakbaggers but have balked at the long approaches necessary to gain access to such summits? If so, consider the short hike to 13,053-foot Mt. Dana, perhaps the easiest and certainly one of the highest Sierra peaks accessible to day hikers, provided that they are in good physical condition and acclimated to the thin, High Sierra atmosphere. It is wise to consider spending a day or two in one of the nearby high elevation campgrounds along Highway 120 in the Inyo National Forest, or in the Park's Tuolumne Meadows campground.

There are numerous challenging routes leading to Dana's summit, but the informal trail worn into the mountainside from Tioga Pass is certainly the easiest. Hikers following this trail will, more or less, be following in the footsteps of William Brewer and Charles Hoffman, members of the famous Whitney survey who mapped much of the High Sierra in the 19th century, who first scaled the peak on June 28, 1863.

Be sure to pack along plenty of water, sunglasses, and sunscreen. Also, plan on the possibility of strong winds and cold temperatures.

The trail begins immediately east of the Tioga Pass entrance station atop the Sierra crest, heading eastward past a prominent lodgepole pine. A grand view of Mt. Dana, looming boldly on the skyline more than 3,000 feet above, is enjoyed at the start but soon fades from your view.

Proceeding eastward just north of the presently low crest, the trail leads through a forest of lodgepole and whitebark pine, past meadows adorned with lupine, groundsel, and Indian paintbrush, and along the shores of numerous small, shallow tarns. Views to the north from this glacier-excavated gap are superb, reaching into the headwaters of Lee Vining Creek and including Tioga Lake, and the colorful metamorphic peaks that lie east of the mostly granitic Sierra crest.

After .5 mile the trail crosses the crest, entering Yosemite National Park and remaining within its boundaries. Soon reaching the foot of the Mt. Dana massif

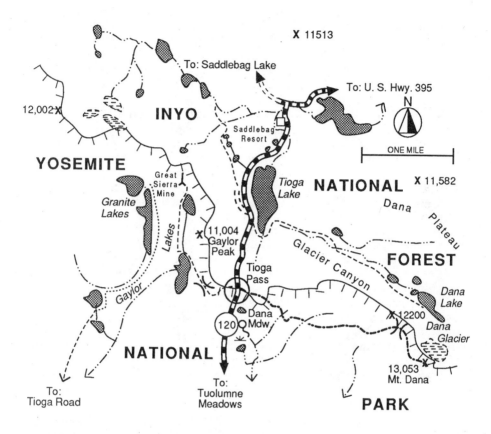

just below timberline, the well-worn path jogs southeast, climbing a west-facing slope at a moderate grade. Shortly thereafter you will cross a trickling stream where a profusion of wildflowers bursts upon the scene. Within this flower garden you will discover cinquefoil, larkspur, lupine, corn lily, aster, groundsel, monkeyflower, Indian paintbrush, and fireweed. Hikers will also be delighted by the vistas stretching across the subalpine spread of Dana Meadows to the Kuna Crest and the rugged peaks of the Cathedral Range.

Soon the trail abandons the lush flower gardens and its moderate grade, presently zig-zagging very steeply into the uppermost stand of stunted timber. This exceedingly steep grind continues, without respite, to the very summit of Mt. Dana.

Upon emerging from the timberline forest, you will notice a diverse collection of low plants and shrubs blanketing trail side slopes, including red heather, cinquefoil, yellow columbine, corn lily, gooseberry, elderberry, horsemint, sagebrush, snowberry, phlox, buckwheat, and pearly everlasting. Typical of high mountain ascents, splendid vistas are ever-increasing as you toil upward.

As you continue up the boulder-covered slopes the grade will ease briefly where you boulder-hop your way over a rock-buried stream. The stream flows on the surface just upstream and is your last source of water enroute. Beyond, the trail once again climbs steeply upon scree slopes where only a scattering of grasses grow.

After 2.1 miles, the grade once again moderates very briefly atop a grassy bench at 11,700 feet. Hikers can't help but notice the lovely perfume emanating from the prostrate lupine that thrives here. A welcome pause here next to the large trailside cairn not only allows you to catch your breath but to revel in the vast panoramas of Yosemite's magnificent backcountry.

Beyond the cairn, the path becomes increasingly obscure as it leads southeast toward the foot of the final 1,300-foot climb to the summit. The route is straightforward, however, so if you lose the trail simply choose your route up the rocky slopes to the top. The only sign of life above 12,000 feet is a fragrant purple flower, polemonium or sky pilot, that should be familiar to those who have hiked the trail to Mt. Whitney.

Hikers will be astounded by the far-ranging vistas from this lofty summit reaching across meadows, canyons, peaks, forests, and deserts. Gazing southwestward, you will see three prominent Yosemite subranges: Kuna Crest, Cathedral Range, and the Clark Range, plus Mt. Lyell, highest in the park, and its sparkling glacier. That peak and Mt. Dana are the only Yosemite peaks exceeding 13,000 feet. Westward are the vast grasslands of Tuolumne Meadows and an array of ice-polished domes surrounding it. Beyond the meadows are the rockbound upper reaches of the Grand Canyon of the Tuolumne River, and the Mt. Hoffman high country.

The Sierra crest marches northwestward in a series of lofty crags, including Mt. Conness, North Peak, and the peaks of Shepherd Crest. These granitic summits contrast with the red and gray metamorphic peaks that dominate east of the crest. Hikers may have noticed by now that Mt. Dana and nearby Mt. Gibbs, the red peak to the south, are also composed of ancient metamorphic rocks.

Northward, beyond the Sierra Nevada are the Sweetwater Mountains; to the northeast ancient Mono Lake with the relatively recent volcanic formations of the Mono Craters rising south of the lake; and beyond them 11,000-foot Glass Mountain and finally the White Mountains.

Directly below your vantage point to the east, great cliffs plunge nearly 2,000 feet into the cirque harboring Dana Lake. Above that lake broken cliffs rise to the broad tableland of the Dana Plateau, a remnant of the ancient, gentle surface of the Sierra Nevada.

Reluctantly pulling away from the tremendous panorama, hikers should carefully retrace their steps to Tioga Pass.

Other trails in the Tioga Pass area offer worthwhile day hikes to a variety of alpine lake basins.

HIKE 74 SADDLEBAG LAKE TO MCCABE LAKES

General description: A demanding 9.5 mile (or longer) round trip backpack, partly cross-country, leading to a remote lake basin in Yosemite National Park. This trip is suitable for hikers with ample cross-country and route-finding experience.

Elevation gain and loss: 1,400 feet; -1,080 feet.

Trailhead elevation: 10,150 feet.

High point: Sierra crest, 11,300 feet.

Maps: Tuolumne Meadows 15-minute USGS quad; or Yosemite National Park USGS quad; or Hoover Wilderness map (topographic).

Season: Mid-July through September.

Finding the trailhead: Follow State Highway 120 either two miles northeast from Tioga Pass, or ten miles west from U.S. Highway 395 to the signed turnoff to Saddlebag Lake. Follow the narrow and rough dirt road for 2.4 miles to the signed trailhead parking area south of the lake. Hikers who choose to ride the boat to the head of the lake rather than hiking the shoreline trail should continue up the road for another .2 mile to the parking lot at the Saddlebag Lake store.

The hike: This lofty excursion is an immensely rewarding trek, but due to the trailless alpine terrain near the Sierra crest, it should be attempted only by seasoned backpackers. Offering quick access into the Yosemite backcountry via an obscure route, this trip avoids the crowds typically encountered along trails beginning at Tuolumne Meadows.

The convenience of an inexpensive boat ride ($2 one way; $4 round trip) across the gull-dotted waters of Saddlebag Lake shortens the distance to McCabe Lakes by 1.7 miles. Hikers choosing this option can make arrangements for the boat ride and a pickup time of their choice at Saddlebag Resort, located .2 mile beyond the trailhead parking area opposite the campground entrance .

A national forest wilderness permit is required for overnight camping, since the initial segment of the hike leads through the Hoover Wilderness. Permits can be obtained at the Lee Vining Ranger Station, 1.25 miles from Highway 395, or at the Saddlebag Resort.

Water is easy to find along much of the route, and mosquitos should be expected until about mid-August. Wood fires are prohibited between Greenstone Lake and the Sierra crest, and in the Yosemite backcountry above 9,600 feet, which includes the entire McCabe Lakes basin.

From the trailhead parking area, cross the Saddlebag Lake Road and follow an old road downhill to Lee Vining Creek below the lake's dam. From there, the road quickly climbs to the dam where the trail begins. Already above timberline, the trail undulates above the lake's west shore over the crunchy red and gray metamorphic rocks that dominate the landscape east of the Sierra crest. Only a scattering of krummholz whitebark pines dot the trailside slopes, while red heather, a common alpine plant in the Sierra, is the most prevalent wildflower passed enroute.

About midway around the lake, the granite crags of the Sierra crest come into view, contrasting in color and in character with the metamorphic peaks and ridges nearby. It is obvious why John Muir so aptly named the Sierra Nevada the "Range of Light", since the nearly white peaks along the crest not only reflect the intense alpine sunshine but almost seem to radiate a light of their own.

The lowest point visible on the crest, to the northwest, lies above a grassy slope. That is your pass, and you can already begin visualizing a route up to it. Approaching the head of the lake, the pointed summit of 12,242-foot North Peak and its permanent snowfield come into view on the western skyline.

After 1.5 miles, the trail fades into obscurity in an alpine meadow above and west of Saddlebag Lake. However, ducks lead you the short distance to the meandering creek emanating from nearby Greenstone Lake, where a search for a log crossing helps you to avoid wet feet.

Once beyond the creek you will soon intersect a trail leading west to the shoreline of that lake, one of many alpine gems in the 20 Lakes Basin. Turn left onto that trail and proceed to the lake's north shore where the trail and the old mining road, .3 mile from Saddlebag Lake's upper boat dock, nearly

From the rocky shores of glacier-gouged Steelhead Lake, hikers enroute to McCabe Lakes in Yosemite National Park pause to absorb the breathtaking beauty of the High Sierra.

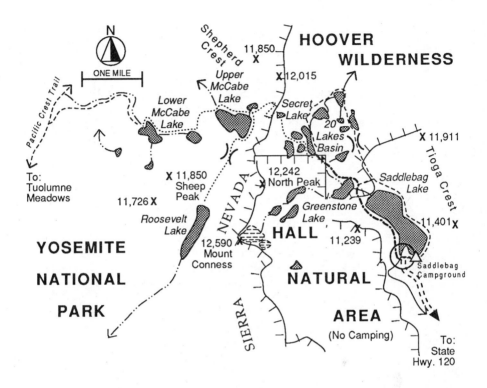

coalesce. At this point, leave the trail, which ultimately leads to Conness Lakes basin beneath the towering crag of Mt. Conness, presently visible to the southwest and begin following the old road uphill toward the northwest.

Tree cover in the basin is sparse, but there's a much thicker stand of trees than that surrounding Saddlebag Lake, consisting of lodgepole and whitebark pines.

Beyond Greenstone Lake, you will pass a tarn before beginning a moderate ascent, leveling off near the trickling outlet of "Z" Lake. The old road then jogs west, and at 2.1 miles from the trailhead a sign declares that you are entering the Hall Natural Area where camping and open fires are prohibited.

You will soon notice that trailside slopes are littered with scattered granite boulders—glacial erratics—resting upon the metamorphic rocks from which the basin was carved.

The brief westward course ends above the rocky, irregular shore of Wasco Lake where you presently head northwest, passing a shallow tarn and leaving the Hall Natural Area. Quite soon the road leads past another small tarn and begins descending, now in the Mill Creek drainage.

At the north end of this tarn, 2.5 miles from the trailhead and one mile from the upper boat dock on Saddlebag Lake, you will notice another old mining road branching left. Follow this road downhill to the south end of lovely Steelhead Lake, largest in the 20 Lakes Basin.

From here, the old Hess Mine can be seen above the lake's northwest shore in a mineralized area at the contact zone between granitic and metamorphic rocks.

Upon reaching the deep lake, the road leads west before climbing a south-trending gully. A cascading creek is seen nearby, plunging into Steelhead Lake from presently invisible Potter Lake. At this point you leave the road and begin following an obscure route, climbing over a bedrock knoll just south of the cascade.

You will quickly reach 10,300-foot Potter Lake, 2.75 miles from the trailhead, hop across its outlet creek above the cascade, then head northwest over bedrock and grassy pockets to slightly smaller Towser Lake. Imposing North Peak and its snowfield provide an exciting backdrop to the lakes in this high basin.

From here, the route to Secret Lake is readily apparent. Climb northwest along a small creek that spills down the grass and whitebark pine-dotted slope.

After .7 mile of steady but easy climbing, you arrive along the shores of 10,900-foot Secret Lake. The lake is unusual in that it is perched on a small, hanging bench rather than in a large, glacier-carved bowl.

From Secret Lake, hikers can ponder a choice of routes to reach the Sierra crest. The easiest and most obvious route follows an uphill-sloping ledge to the south-southwest. To reach the ledge, scramble up steep slopes behind the lake and follow it for about .1 mile. At this point, ducks will lead you over bedrock directly to the Sierra crest, which you then follow north to the crest's low point. Vistas from the crest are superb.

A ducked route leads down loose rocky slopes and past snow-flattened whitebark pines to a shallow alpine lake at 10,500 feet. From here follow the course of that lake's outlet stream to the northeast shore of upper McCabe Lake. Campsites are only fair where a strip of whitebarks hugging the north shore offer only a modicum of shelter.

Ample opportunities for side trips can extend your stay in the area for several days. After enjoying the high country excursion, hikers should retrace their steps back to the trailhead.

HIKE 75 *GREEN CREEK TO SUMMIT LAKE*

General descrition: A moderate 15-mile round-trip backpack in the eastern Sierra Nevada, leading into a sub-alpine lake basin, in the Hoover Wilderness.
Elevation gain and loss: 2,100 feet.
Trailhead elevation: 8,100 feet.
High point: Summit Lake, 10,200 feet.
Maps: Matterhorn Peak 15-minute USGS quad, Toiyabe Naitonal Forest map.
Season: July through early-October.
Finding the trailhead: From U.S. 395, 4.3 miles south of Bridgeport and 85.75 miles north of Bishop, turn southwest onto the signed Green Lakes Road. Bear left after one mile where a sign points to Green Creek. After another 2.5 miles, turn right; the Virginia Lakes Road continues straight ahead. Proceed another 5.8 miles to the trailhead at the end of the road.

The hike: Visiting a number of sub-alpine lakes, this interesting eastern Sierra backpack surveys a landscape of colorful peaks, differing in color from the "typical" white or grey granite found in most east-side canyons. The hike should appeal to angler, photographer, and anyone else who enjoys majestic mountain scenery.

Finding water is no problem along the entire route.

A wilderness permit is required and should be obtained at the Bridgeport Ranger Station.

The trail begins at the northwest end of the parking area and heads southwest through a forest of lodgepole and Jeffrey pine, aspen, and juniper. Ahead lie the conical alpine peaks encircling the upper West Fork Green Creek and Glines Canyon.

You soon begin negotiating a series of elevation-gaining switchbacks. A pause during this ascent offers over-the-shoulder views down the U-shaped trough of Green Canyon to the Bodie Hills in the eastern distance.

Entering the Hoover Wilderness at a Toiyabe National Forest sign, your trail edges close to Green Creek, which is dammed at this point by aspen-gnawing beavers.

Continuing up the canyon, you soon notice the East Fork Green Creek opening up to the south, exposing the massive red flanks of Dunderberg Peak which, at 12,374 feet above sea level, is the highest summit in the Green Creek area.

Your trail follows the course of the West Fork Green Creek in a forest of aspen and lodgepole pine. Hikers in October will be rewarded not only with solitude but with a colorful display of turning aspens.

The trail crosses several creeklets issuing from the lower slopes of Monument Ridge, where you are treated to a variety of colorful wildflowers in season.

After two miles of steady ascent from the trailhead, you reach a junction with the right-branching trail to West Lake. Turn left, soon crossing the dam-regulated outlet of Green Lake. You may have to search for a log to get across this swift creek.

Excellent opportunities for camping exist around this large lake 8,900 feet above sea level, and the trout population is abundant and hungry. In the

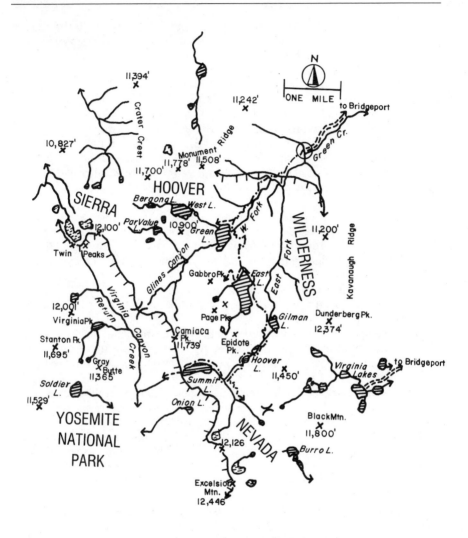

northwest, a white ribbon of water falls over a band of red rock on the flanks of Peak 10,900; and Glines Canyon, with its willow-clad meadows and sparse timber, sweeps steadily westward from the lake to Virginia Pass, blocked by semi-permanent snow and a 200-foot high wall. Experienced backpackers may be enticed to tackle that pass, then descend into Virginia Canyon and loop back via Summit Lake. However, most hikers will be content following the trail to Summit Lake.

From Green Lake, the trail jogs south, begins a series of short swithchbacks, and soon fords the outlet stream of East Lake. As you continue climbing under the shade of lodgepole pine and mountain hemlock, you ford this creek twice more (and crossings will be difficult in early season) before reaching East Lake at the 9,500-foot level. Just before the last ford, avoid a right-branching trail going around the west side of East Lake.

Your trail skirts the eastern shore of this fine lake, and provides superb views across its deep waters to the triad of Gabbro, Page, and Epidote peaks. These colorful 11,000-foot-high peaks offer a change of pace to hikers used to the usual white granite found in most eastern Sierra canyons.

Soon leaving East Lake behind, your trail passes tiny Nutter Lake, then climbs around a low, rocky ridge and traverses above secluded Gilman Lake. You then ford the East Fork Green Creek below the Hoover Lakes, and ascend toward those lakes amid rapidly thinning and increasingly stunted whitebark pines and mountain hemlocks. Scattered willows and red mountain heather add to the alpine feeling of the area.

The trail skirts the east shore of the lower Hoover Lake, and you then hop across the outlet of the upper Hoover Lake before heading around its rocky western shore directly under precipitous Epidote Peak.

A ford of the East Fork is required above upper Hoover Lake, and wet feet here are difficult to avoid.

The sparse, stunted timber, red-and-grey rocky slopes, alpine peaks, and numerous semi-permanent snowfields all combine to make the upper East Fork quite spectacular.

You soon hop across an East Fork tributary after passing the southeast-bound trail leading to the Virginia Lakes Trailhead. Turning west, your route crosses the outlet of Summit Lake, and soon reaches the east end of this sub-alpine gem. To the west, across the low gap of Summit Pass, you are treated to excellent, sky-filling views of the white granite peaks of 11,365-foot-high Grey Butte and 11,695-foot-high Stanton Peak, providing an interesting contrast with the multi-hued peaks in the Green Creek drainage.

Surrounded by alpine peaks and numerous snow fields, this magnificent lake has a number of campsite possibilities among its stunted lodgepole and whitebark pines, and mountain hemlocks that crowd its north shore.

From the Yosemite National Park boundary at Summit Pass west of the lake, views are superb into the densely forested Virginia Canyon and northwest to the soaring, snow-streaked red crag of 12,001-foot-high Virginia Peak.

After enjoying this fine area, return the way you came.

HIKE 76 *GIANELLI CABIN TO UPPER RELIEF VALLEY*

General description: A moderate sixteen-mile round-trip backpack into the incomparable Emigrant Wilderness, where landscapes of granitic and volcanic rocks form some of the most dramatic contrasts to be experienced on any hike.
Elevation gain and loss: 1,750 feet, -1,110 feet.
Trailhead elevation: 8,560 feet.
High point: 9,200 feet.
Maps: Pinecrest 15-minute USGS quad, Stanislaus National Forest map.
Season: July through early-October.
Finding the trailhead: Proceed east from Sonora on State Highway 108 for

about thirty miles, then turn right where a sign indicates Pinecrest and Dodge Ridge. After driving .5 mile, turn right again and follow signs to Dodge Ridge Ski Area. Turn right once again after another 2.9 miles; a sign here points to Aspen Meadow, Bell Meadow, and Crabtree Camp. This turn is located just before a large sign designating the Dodge Ridge Ski Area.

After turning right here onto Forest Road 4N06Y, you turn left after you reach the stop sign .5 mile ahead. Your road, Forest Road 4N26, climbs steadily eastward and turns to dirt at the pack station, after you have driven 1.7 miles from the stop sign. You bear right .8 mile from the pack station, still on Forest Road 4N26. A sign here points to Gianelli Cabin. After driving two miles from that junction, stay to the left where a right-branching spur road leads down to Crabtree Camp. You are now on Forest Road 4N47 and you continue another 3.9 miles, then bear right where another road joins on the left. Descend less than .1 mile to the trailhead parking area.

The hike: Long before the ancestral Sierra Nevada was uplifted to its present height, volcanic eruptions from the east flowed over much of the landscape north of Yosemite National Park. These flows buried most of the exposed granitic bedrock in the region.

When the glaciers formed, they began to carry away much of the volcanic debris that buried the landscape, re-exposing the granitic bedrock.

Beyond the northern end of the High Sierra, this glacially re-exposed granite gives way to deep volcanic deposits that weren't completely removed by glaciation, thus forming a landscape much different than areas farther south in the Sierra. The contrasts between the two rock types is often striking, making this hike not only scenic, but offering insights into the geologic history of the region.

Mule deer are quite common in this area.

Be sure to carry plenty of water—no reliable source is available during the first 4.7 miles.

A wilderness permit is required for overnight camping, and can be obtained at the Summit Ranger Station, where you turn off of State Highway 108.

The trail begins at the south end of the parking area and heads east across a small creek to the remains of Gianelli Cabin. From here the trail climbs quite steeply for 600 feet to Burst Rock. Pausing to catch your breath along the way, you obtain good westward views across the heavily forested western Sierra foothills.

At the top of this stiff climb, superb vistas unfold atop 9,161-foot-high Burst Rock, some of the most far-ranging on the entire hike.

The view north across the South Fork Stanislaus River, with its glacially re-exposed granite, provides a marked contrast with the volcanic peaks rising in odd forms north of the river. These volcanic peaks include 9,603-foot-high Cooper Peak, 9,600-foot- high Castle Rock, and The Three Chimneys.

Soaring alpine peaks of the Sierra Nevada crest rise to the east, and in the southeast a low, heavily glaciated rocky plateau extends toward the eastern boundary of Yosemite National Park.

In the south, thickly forested, gentle west-slope terrain contrasts vividly with all the exposed granite lying immediately to the east.

These vistas will accompany hikers through most of this ridgetop journey.

A descent of 250 feet through sub-alpine forest follows. At the bottom of this descent, you pass an unmarked trail on your left leading a short distance

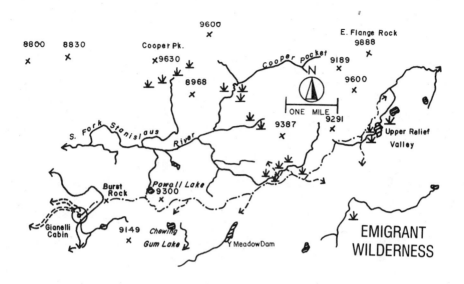

north to an elevation of 8,800 feet and Powell Lake. Surrounded by bare granite and scattered timber, and with good northward views to volcanic pinnacles, this lake makes a pleasant and quite scenic rest stop.

You next climb 250 feet over a north-south ridge 9,200 feet above sea level, in a mixed forest of mountain hemlock, red fir, lodgepole and silver pine, then descend 350 feet to reach a junction in Lake Valley, 2.8 miles from the trailhead. The signed southbound trail leads to Chewing Gum Lake .7 mile away and continues beyond to the trailheads at Crabtree Camp and Bell Meadow.

Bearing left at that junction, you soon leave tarn-dotted Lake Valley behind and begin climbing moderately under a canopy of lodgepole and silver pine and past wildflower-filled openings, dominated by lupine and senecio.

Nearing the top of this ascent, you traverse an open, grassy ridgetop offering great views north and east. This ridge is capped by volcanic deposits, unlike the initial segment of the hike that passed over granitic rock exclusively. You will also notice the difference in vegetation on granitic and volcanic slopes. A fairly lush grass and wildflower-type of vegetation thrives in the volcanic-enriched soils, whereas only sparse grasses and wildflowers are able to take hold on the meager soils of granitic slopes.

A greater water-holding capacity and the fact that these volcanic rocks have decomposed into a fairly deep soil (contrasting with the often-thin layer of decomposed granite and its lesser water-holding capacity) helps contribute to these variations in vegetation.

Soon passing back into the realm of granite, you begin another descent of 350 feet, and reach a junction with a southbound trail leading to Y-Meadow

Dam, after hiking 4.3 miles from the trailhead.

Bearing left here where a sign points to Y-Meadow Dam, you proceed northeast through a gradually thinning forest. Soon you break into the open and head east across aptly-named Whitesides Meadow, meeting the northwest-bound trail to Cooper Meadow near the east end of this large grassland. Staying right at this junction, your trail soon leaves that spread, skirts the edge of a small meadow filled with lupine and senecio and meanders up to a junction with a right-branching trail leading to Salt Lick Meadow and the lake-filled terrain in the heart of the Emigrant Wilderness.

Bearing left here, your trail begins an easterly course, first on the north side, then on the south side of the ridge, alternating between volcanic and granitic terrain.

About 1.25 miles from the Whitesides Meadow you pass the small meadow and trickling stream forming the headwaters of Relief Creek, and begin descending.

You soon are skirting the western edge of Upper Relief Valley's sub-alpine grassland, gloriously brightened by lupine, senecio, and mountain helenium. You pass a southbound trail leading to Salt Lick Meadow after a short jaunt into the valley. Good campsites can be found around the valley and near the two small, shallow lakes at its northern end.

Water isn't as plentiful here as in other areas in the Sierra; and wherever you do obtain water in this area, purification is recommended.

The view across the valley to barren, alpine Sierra Nevada crest peaks, including Sonora Peak, add to the scenic attraction of this grand meadow. In the foreground, the volcanic pinnacles of East Flange Rock point their stark fingers into the sky.

The valley itself is flanked by dissimilar glaciated slopes. To the east is a low, granite ridge, forested with lodgepole and silver pine and mountain hemlock. To the west lies a volcanic ridge, its dark brown rock contrasting with the greenery that thrives on its slopes.

Experienced cross-country hikers may consider a 2.5- to 3- mile jaunt east from Upper Relief Valley to several remote alpine lakes lying in cirques just north of 10,322-foot-high Granite Dome, the large, rounded alpine mountain rising east of the valley. The Tower Peak 15-minute USGS quad is recommended for this side trip.

Hikers will eventually backtrack to the trailhead.

HIKE 77 *DARDANELLES LOOP*

General description: A moderate seven-mile loop day hike or overnighter, circumnavigating the spectacular Dardanelles, in the Carson-Iceberg Wilderness. The route is vague in places, and should appeal to more experienced hikers.
Elevation gain and loss: 1,150 feet.
Trailhead elevation: 7,200 feet.
High point: 8,100 feet.
Maps: Dardanelles Cone 15-minute USGS quad (road to trailhead and trail not shown on quad), Stanislaus National Forest map.

Season: Mid-June through early October.

Finding the trailhead: About seventeen miles west of Sonora Pass on State Highway 108, and about 55.5 miles east of Sonora, turn north where a sign indicates Clark Fork. This paved road quite soon crosses the Middle Fork, then the Clark Fork Stanislaus River. After driving .9 mile from the highway, turn left onto Forest Road 6N06 where a sign indicates Fence Creek Campground. You now follow this dusty dirt road west, avoiding the right-branching spur road to Fence Creek Campground after .2 mile. After driving 6.4 miles from the highway, avoid right- branching Forest Road 6N06A, and continue another .7 mile to the County Line Trailhead at the roadend.

The hike: This scenic hike loops around the intriguing Dardanelles, a striking volcanic formation rising well over 1,000 feet above the surrounding heavily forested landscape.

The Dardanelles are part of the lava flows that buried this region millions of years ago. Since much of the volcanic material has been removed by repeated episodes of glaciation, the Dardanelles stand like a volcanic island in a "sea" of granite.

Carry plenty of water for this mostly dry hike.

A wilderness permit is required for overnight camping, and can be obtained at the Summit Ranger Station at the Pinecrest Lake-Dodge Ridge turnoff from State Highway 108, about thirty miles east of Sonora.

From the trailhead, you pass amid stumps and other scars of past logging, and after 150 yards branch right onto the McCormick Creek Trail, a closed jeep route, and head northeast through a forest of Jeffrey pine and white fir, obtaining occasional tree- framed views of The Three Chimneys and Castle Rock in the southeast.

The Dardanelles typify the volcanic material that buried this region of the Sierra Nevada millions of years ago. Although much of the volcanics was removed by repeated glaciation, the Dardanelles were resistant enough to withstand the glacial attacks and thus provide a vivid contrast to the surrounding granite-dominated landscape.

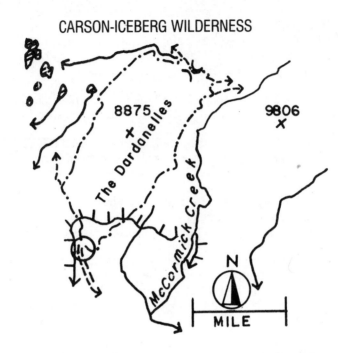

CARSON-ICEBERG WILDERNESS

After red fir joins the forest, you pass through a small meadow where your route narrows to trail width and you leave most of the stumps and logging scars behind. From this point, the Dardanelles loom boldly on the northern skyline, their dark volcanic cliffs contrasting with the greenery that thrives in the rich volcanic soil of their lower slopes.

Continuing on a northeasterly course, pass through small meadows that contain, among the previously mentioned forest trees, lodgepole pines and aspens.

Soon you begin a stroll across an aspen-rich meadow. The fantastic castle-like formation rising in the eastern foreground is Peak 9086, lying on the ridge one mile southwest of Dardanelles Cone.

Your trail passes through more aspen-clad meadows that host corn lilies, willows, currants, and assorted wildflowers. While crossing these meadows, early-morning and late-afternoon hikers are apt to see some of the abundant mule deer that inhabit this region.

You eventually begin climbing, soon passing an isolated stand of black cottonwood. Quite soon thereafter, bear left onto a very faint northbound trail, or if you can't find it, simply head north under a juniper-topped bench of volcanic rock. The McCormick Creek Trail continues east.

Your trail climbs steeply at first, then levels off just west of the above-entioned volcanic bench. Red-painted blazes on rocks and trees help lead the way.

Your route soon skirts a corn lily-filled meadow, and you reach a junction at the meadow's eastern end. A faint eastbound trail continues onward, marked by more red blazes, but you bear left instead onto a faint northwest-bound trail, also marked with red-painted blazes on trees.

You soon begin a series of moderately ascending switchbacks leading through a heavy red fir forest, finally topping a saddle 8,100 feet above sea level and immediately northeast of the Dardanelles.

You presently begin a northwest descent into a cow-inhabited meadow. This is where route-finding problems begin.

Take the trail that stays east of and above the meadow, following the red-painted blazes. You soon meet a well-defined cow trail that continues the northwesterly descent, but the blazes turn southwest and the trail disappears. Simply walk out into the sloping meadow and cross to its southwest margin. Pick up the alder-lined outlet creek draining the meadow and follow it downstream, soon re-locating the trail.

You now continue your trail walk through a red fir and silver pine forest. Northward views into the granitic-volcanic landscape in the Highland Creek drainage are excellent. Your trail is used frequently by deer and wandering cattle but is seldom traveled by man.

Notice that the sheltered northwest slopes of the Dardanelles are thickly forested and less imposing than the dramatic southeast slopes.

Your trail passes through several small meadows as you proceed on a southwesterly course through a forest of red and white fir and silver pine.

After 2.25 miles of pleasant hiking beyond the cow-inhabited meadow, your trail joins the north-south trail coming from Lost and Sword lakes and Highland Creek in a broad, grassy saddle.

Turning left onto this popular trail from the signed Dardanelles Spur Trail, head south toward the County Line Trailhead.

Soon passing through a stock gate (which you should be sure to close) you gain 250 feet of elevation before finally descending through pine and fir forest to your car at the trailhead.

HIKE 78 *BLUE CANYON*

General description: A moderate four-mile round-trip day hike or backpack for experienced hikers, in the Emigrant Wilderness, leading into a glaciated volcanic canyon where one of the most magnificent floral displays anywhere in California can be seen and enjoyed.

Elevation gain and loss: 1,020 or 1,280 feet.

Trailhead elevation: 8,720 feet at the lower trailhead, or 8,980 feet at the upper trailhead.

High point: Blue Canyon Lake, 10,000 feet.

Maps: Sonora Pass 15-minute USGS quad (trail not shown on quad), Stanislaus National Forest map. Also use hike No. 79 map.

Season: July through early October.

Finding the trailhead: There is no actual trailhead for Blue Canyon hikers. You must park in one of a few turnouts on State Highway 108. Thus, it is wise to use the Sonora Pass quad and/or the Stanislaus National Forest map to help you identify Blue Canyon so you know when to park.

Just before State Highway 108 passes the mouth of Blue Canyon, there is parking on the left hand (northwest) side of the road for three vehicles. This spot is just above two short switchbacks on the road. From this point you can see Blue Canyon's creek cascading into Deadman Creek just southeast of the highway.

Otherwise, continuing east on State Highway 108, you can park in one of the small turnouts on the right hand (east) side of the road just below the semi-permanent "9,000 Feet" sign. If you are approaching from the east, simply keep an eye out for the "9,000 feet" sign so you know when to park.

These parking areas are about six miles east of the Kennedy Meadows turnoff from State Highway 108.

The hike: Blue Canyon is truly one of the most scenic areas in the entire state. This deeply glaciated canyon, surrounded by striking volcanic peaks and ridges, is a natural flower garden containing a vast collection of colorful wildflowers.

At the head of the canyon, lying under impressive 11,000- foot-high peaks, are two very beautiful alpine lakes. No fish live in these lakes, but the vivid scenery is adequate compensation for the lack of a trout dinner.

Water is abundant on this hike.

A wilderness permit is required for overnight camping, and can be obtained at the Summit Ranger Station in Pinecrest. Campfires are prohibited above 9,000 feet in the Emigrant Wilderness, which includes all the Blue Canyon.

Starting just below the "9,000 Feet" sign on State Highway 108, descend steeply into Deadman Creek. After hopping across this creek, you should pick up a fairly good trail ascending into Blue Canyon just north of its creek.

If you are departing from the lower parking area, however, descend into Deadman Creek and pick up a good path that climbs along the west side of Blue Canyon's creek.

Both trails join in Blue Canyon in about .3 to .4 mile, after avoiding a narrow chasm at the canyon's mouth.

If you started at the upper trailhead, you quickly climb to a lodgepole- and whitebark pine-clad bench after crossing Deadman Creek, then enter the Emigrant Wilderness.

Follow this sometimes faint path up the canyon toward a pyramidal volcanic peak in the south.

The mountains surrounding this canyon are obviously of volcanic origin. This rock was resistant enough that glaciers were only able to carve out many deep cirques and excavate basins that contain two alpine lakes. Since most volcanic rocks are much less resistant to glacial attack than granite, lake basins are rarely gouged into a volcanic landscape. The resulting glacially sculpted volcanic peaks in this canyon are stunningly beautiful.

Tree cover in the canyon is sparse, restricted to its lower end. You pass by scattered stands of whitebark pine in the lower canyon, with a few lodgepole and silver pines on the west-facing slopes above. Whitebark pines will accompany hikers part way up this canyon, often stunted and deformed by years of savage winters.

The variety of wildflowers in this canyon, particularly in the lower half of the canyon, is truly unbelievable, putting forth a dramatic, colorful display, especially in late July through mid-August.

In these natural flower gardens you will find, among a variety of other flowers: red Indian paintbrush, aster, helenium, corn lily, red columbine, green gentian, scarlet gilia, stonecrop, mariposa tulip, monkey flower, larkspur, mule ears, lupine, wallflower, Kings smooth sandwort, yampah, buttercup, phlox, shooting star, whorled penstemon, senecio, whitehead, pennyroyal, mountain sorrel, and alpine pynocoma.

Continuing your leisurely walk amid flower gardens and clumps of stunted whitebark pines, you approach the cascading creek before climbing steeply beside it on the now-gravelly trail. Care should be exercised along this stretch—walking on volcanic gravel tends to resemble walking on marbles, and a misstep can send you flying.

Above this brief climb you have excellent views of snow-streaked volcanic crags looming boldly at the canyon's head.

Water in Blue Canyon is very abundant, issuing forth from the porous volcanic rock and spilling down steep slopes to feed Blue Canyon's creek.

You soon hop across the "east fork" of Blue Canyon's creek, draining

Blue Canyon Lake, 10,000 feet above sea level, lies at the head of magnificent Blue Canyon in the Emigrant Wilderness. Just below the barren surroundings of this lake, mid-summer hikers are treated to one of the finest displays of wildflowers in the state.

Deadman Lake and the permanent snowfields clinging to the flanks of 11,570-foot-high Leavitt Peak, highest in the Emigrant Wilderness. You can ascend this fine canyon to Deadman Lake, or from Blue Canyon Lake you can hike crosscountry to Deadman Lake, then descend via the east fork for a rewarding and highly scenic alpine hike.

Your trail soon disappears beyond the east fork, but shortly reappears as an obscure path. Continue south, passing just west of the colorful landmark pyramid that has guided you from the lower canyon, then descend steeply to cross the creek in a narrow gorge. Over-the-shoulder views from this vicinity include the Sierra Nevada crest from Sonora Peak north to Stanislaus Peak.

As you proceed up the canyon, notice that the variety of wildflowers has diminished markedly, but color is still fairly abundant.

You eventually end your climb at incomparable Blue Canyon Lake. This small, turquoise-colored lake lies in a deep cirque at the 10,000-foot level, surrounded by magnificent volcanic crags soaring more than 1,000 feet above its shoreline. The colorful pinnacle just east of the lake is especially striking.

Unfortunately, backpackers have camped too often on the grassy northwest shore of this alpine gem, and the resulting scars are much in evidence and may take a century to heal. Please, do not camp at Blue Canyon Lake. Common sense should alert hikers to the fact that camping in a highly fragile alpine environment such as this causes unacceptable damage to the delicate alpine vegetation. This trip is better taken as a day hike. If you do plan to camp in Blue Canyon, be sure to exercise minimum-impact camping practices to the fullest.

Several opportunities exist for side trips from the vicinity of Blue Canyon Lake. Immediately south of the lake, at an elevation of 10,800 feet, is a deep notch. A serious scramble to this notch via unstable volcanic slopes and snowfields yields excellent vistas into the interior of the Emigrant Wilderness.

Also, as previously mentioned, a loop back to the trailhead via the east fork of Blue Canyon is possible for experienced hikers.

From Blue Canyon Lake, hikers return to the trailhead.

HIKE 79 SONORA PEAK

General description: A rigorous five-mile, partially cross-country, round-trip day hike to an alpine Sierra Nevada peak where 100-mile vistas of awe inspiring scenery in the Carson-Iceberg Wilderness await.
Elevation gain and loss: 2,012 feet.
Trailhead elevation: 9,450 feet.
High point: Sonora Peak, 11,462 feet.
Maps: Sonora Pass 15-minute USGS quad, Stanislaus National Forest map.
Season: July through early October.
Finding the trailhead: The trailhead lies at the end of a spur road that leads north from State Highway 108 for about 100 yards, about .8 mile west of Sonora Pass. This pass is 72.5 miles east of Sonora via State Highway 108, and 7.75 miles east of the Kennedy Meadows turnoff.

The hike: Sonora Peak's volcanic slopes rise abruptly northward from Sonora Pass, and hikers scaling its alpine summit are rewarded with far-flung vistas of the northern Sierra Nevada, the Great Basin, and part of Nevada.

The first half of this fairly strenuous hike is on a closed jeep route and trail; the final half is cross-country. Although route-finding here is no problem for experienced hikers, novices should be content with views obtained from St. Marys Pass.

Carry an adequate supply of water.

A wilderness permit is required, and can be obtained at the Summit Ranger Station at the Pinecrest Lake turnoff on State Highway 108, about thirty miles east of Sonora.

Begin this hike by walking north along the retired jeep road, past the barrier which blocks it to use by motor vehicles. This route leads generally north under the intermittent shade of a scattered timberline forest of lodgepole and whitebark pine, ascending grassy slopes clothed in sagebrush and splashed with the colors of a variety of wildflowers, including gilia, Indian paintbrush, helenium, cinquefoil, lupine, mariposa tulip, wallflower, aster, dandelion, pussy paws, and pennyroyal.

The massive, reddish alpine mountain that dominates the view ahead is your destination.

The closed jeep route, quite steep at times, leads up to the cold runoff of a wildflower-decorated spring, then quickly narrows to trail width. You soon splash through the runoff of another cold spring, this one decorated by elephants heads and shooting stars.

Now ascend steep grassy slopes to the west-trending ridge emanating from Sonora Peak. This ridgetop at 10,400 feet above sea level is known to hikers as St. Marys Pass. The views that have continually expanded throughout this ascent are even more breathtaking at this point, and are surpassed only by the view from Sonora Peak itself.

The narrow path you have been following continues northward from here toward the reddish cone of Stanislaus Peak. Another faint path branches left from here, eventually leading hikers into the upper Clark Fork of the Stanislaus River. Backpackers may want to descend about 2.5 mostly-trailless miles into beautiful Clark Fork Meadow after scaling Sonora Peak.

From the pass, you leave the trail, turning right (east) and ascending steep grassy slopes, soon leveling off on a bench and passing a last, isolated clump of ground-hugging whitebark pines. At these altitudes, where high winds and deeply drifted snow are common, the whitebark grows only to shrub height. In the ground- hugging form, known as krummholz, it is protected by an insulating blanket of snow during the winter. During the extremely short growing season at this altitude, it puts forth little annual growth, but those branches that are able to grow above the snow level will be killed the following winter by the sandblasting effect of wind-blown ice and snow.

At this point, the summit lies dead ahead and from here you simply pick your way up the steep volcanic slopes to the summit. The easiest route would be to ascend the crest north of the peak, then turn southeast and follow a very faint path to the high point.

Hikers who complete the ascent to this fine mountain are rewarded with a glorious, all-encompassing, 360-degree panorama.

To the east are the Sweetwater Mountains, crowned by the bright white summits surrounding Mt. Patterson. Far to the southeast, the White Mountains

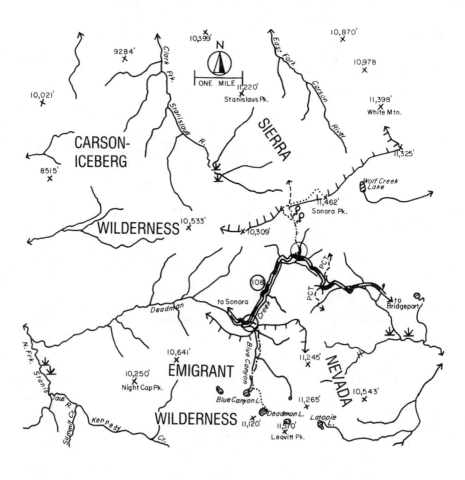

are easily distinguished from their northern terminus in Nevada southward. Peaks of the majestic High Sierra are visible as far south as Banner Peak, Mt. Ritter, and Mt. Lyell. Also visible is Mt. Dana, and closer at hand is impressive Tower Peak. To your south and southwest, immediately across State Highway 108, is a region of high volcanic peaks, clearly illustrating the depth of the volcanic flows that buried this region before the Sierra Nevada rose to its present height. In the west, the thickly forested western slope of the Sierra is interrupted by the impressive Dardanelles. In the northwest, peaks as far away as the Lake Tahoe region can be seen, and in the north you can see the Carson Valley of western Nevada lying at the foot of the Carson Range. The deep canyon immediately to your north is the East Fork Carson River. You will notice a marked difference in the topography north of Sonora Pass, compared with that south of the pass. To the north the character of the landscape is highly scenic, but is more subdued than the magnificent alpine terrain to the south. Consequently, Sonora Pass is often considered the geographical dividing point between the "High" Sierra and the northern Sierra.

From the peak, carefully backtrack to the trailhead.

HIKE 80 *DESERT CREEK TO MOUNT PATTERSON*

General description: A fairly rigorous nine-mile round-trip day hike (or backpack), in the Toiyabe National Forest, for experienced hikers, to the alpine crest of an obscure eastern California mountain range.

Elevation gain and loss: 2,773 feet, -100 feet.

Trailhead elevation: 9,000 feet.

High point: Mt. Patterson, 11,673 feet.

Maps: Fales Hot Springs 15-minute USGS quad, Toiyabe National Forest map.

Season: July through early October.

Finding the trailhead: To find the "trailhead," you must first locate the Burcham Flat Road. This signed road branches north from U.S. 395 about 14.5 miles northwest of Bridgeport and two miles southeast of the U.S. 395-State Highway 108 junction. This hard-to-spot turnoff is just beyond a highway sign designating a 50 MPH curve, and lies just east of a gravel pit.

This good dirt road heads east for a short distance after leaving the highway, then swings north past a destination-and- mileage sign. Among the information listed on this sign is the distance to Lobdell Lake Road, five miles ahead; this is your turnoff. Where the Burcham Flat Road reaches its high point after 4.2 miles before descending, turn right onto the unsigned Lobdell Lake Road.

Follow this often-narrow, sometimes-rough dirt road for 6.2 miles to a road junction at Lobdell Lake. Turn left, driving around the south and west sides of levee-dammed Lobdell Lake, then proceed north across a meadow-covered flat. The road at this point is basically a rough jeep road, but only low-clearance vehicles should have any trouble negotiating the route. After driving two rough miles from the previous junction, you meet a southeast-bound jeep route on your right, designated by a sign depicting a jeep. Turn right onto this jeep road and proceed southeast along the course of Desert Creek. After approximately .4 mile up this road (which is easier going than the previous two miles from Lobdell Lake), you reach a rough segment where large rocks protrude out of the roadbed, forcing all but high-clearance four-wheel drive vehicles to park. Those who are able to negotiate this extremely rough section should park in another .3 mile before the jeep route crosses Desert Creek.

Hikers with low-clearance vehicles should consider bearing right at the Lobdell Lake road junction and parking near Lobdell Lake. From here, they can follow a northbound jeep route for about one mile to reach the trail .5 mile above the Desert Creek trailhead.

The hike: The Sweetwater Mountains, one of the most well-watered of all Great Basin ranges, rise high above the West Walker River east of the Sierra Nevada. On their middle flanks are cool stands of lodgepole pine and aspen;

above, whitebark pines, twisted and stunted by winter's unobstructed fury, cling tenaciously to life; and still higher, conditions become so fierce that only alpine cushion plants are able to survive on the highest peaks and ridges of the range.

This moderately strenuous trip takes hikers to the apex of the Sweetwater Mountains, where far-ranging vistas of Nevada and the Sierra Nevada are enjoyed.

Water is available near the trailhead from Desert Creek, but is fouled by cattle. A more reliable source is the East Fork Desert Creek, but potability is questionable here due to an upstream mine. The best solution is to carry all the water you will need.

From the trailhead, proceed southeast along the course of Desert Creek.

Your jeep route stays west of meadow-lined Desert Creek where sagebrush, helenium, lupine, yarrow, cinquefoil, western blue flag, aster, sheep sorrel, rosy everlasting, and a number of grasses thrive. Monkey flowers will be found in the wettest areas next to the creek. The open, sagebrush- and aspen-clad slopes on your left contrast markedly with the thick lodgepole pine forest on your right.

You are soon forced either to ford Desert Creek or to search downstream for a boulder crossing. Your jeep route now angles across an open, cow-filled meadow, meets another jeep route on your right coming from Lobdell Lake, and soon crosses a small Desert Creek tributary.

You now begin ascending eastward along an open hillside. As you gain elevation, westward views begin to expand, exposing the jagged, snowy Sierra Nevada crest. You will leave most of the cattle behind during this climb.

Your eastward ascent terminates at the 10,000-foot level in a sub-alpine forest of lodgepole and whitebark pine. From here, a brief descent soon leads past a "Closed to All Motor Vehicles" sign, intended for a northbound set of jeep tracks. Bearing right, you head around a spur ridge, and are treated to your first glimpse of the glistening white peaks surrounding Mt. Patterson.

The jeep route now descends to the East Fork Desert Creek, and you soon pass a sign bolted to a whitebark pine indicating that the jeep route is closed to motor vehicles beyond this point. Unfortunately, some uninformed (or illiterate) trail bike riders have continued.

You then hop across the small East Fork and proceed upstream near its meadow-clad banks. Sparse whitebark pines survive here and there beneath the stark alpine peaks surrounding this drainage. It is possible to camp here along the East Fork, but level ground is not in abundance.

Two short switchbacks soon get you started on your climb out of the East Fork. With a moderate-to-steep ascent just west of Peak 11,431, you eventually pass the last stand of tenacious, stunted, gnarled, ground-hugging whitebark pines, the ground around them littered with the beautifully weathered remains of their ancestors.

Continuing your climb, you negotiate one last, steep switchback. Then after a moderately steep traverse, you reach the windswept alpine crest of the Sweetwater Mountains. You quite soon pass an old set of jeep tracks leading downslope to your right to the Montague Mine, and another set of tracks leading northeast.

From this point you get your first view of Mt. Patterson, rising abruptly directly ahead. A bulldozed swath, leading up the northwest flank of the peak, unfortunately detracts from the stark beauty of this alpine landscape.

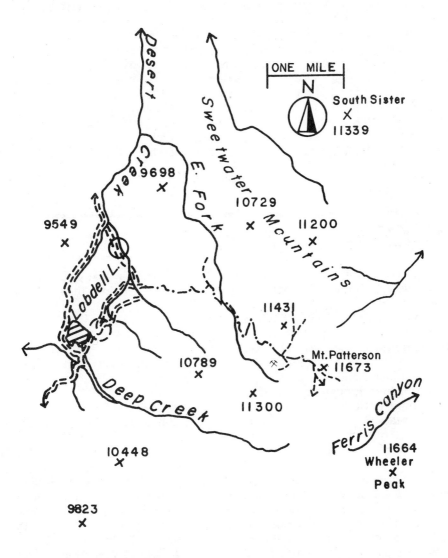

You head for that steep swath, however, and ascend toward the summit of Mt. Patterson. Nearing the peak, another jeep route branches off to your right. Bearing left, continue following the bulldozed jeep route, quite soon leaving it to scramble a short distance to the summit. You are rewarded with breathtaking scenery from this 11,673-foot-high peak.

The Sierra Nevada comprises the westward view, from the Wheeler Crest in the south to the Carson Range in the north. The impressive, glacier-clad Sawtooth Ridge, dominated by Matterhorn Peak and Twin Peaks, is especially striking.

The unmistakable, glaciated north face of Mt. Lyell in Yosemite National Park is easily distinguished in the south beyond lower, less impressive Sierra peaks.

Far to the southeast are the White Mountains, crowned by one of only two 14,000-foot peaks in California that lie outside of the Sierra Nevada. To the east, Great Basin ranges gradually dissolve into the vast Nevada desert. To the northwest, Topaz Lake straddles the California-Nevada border, and the Carson Valley sprawls out beyond.

From Mt. Patterson, return the way you came. On your way home, consider stopping by the Bridgeport Ranger Station or writing the Toiyabe National Forest Supervisor to express concern about vehicle (primarily motorcycle) access into the Mt. Patterson area. This fragile alpine landscape deserves protection.

HIKE 81 *EBBETTS PASS TO NOBEL LAKE*

General description: A moderate nine-mile round-trip day hike or backpack in the Toiyabe Naitonal Forest, leading into a sub-alpine basin in the northern Sierra Nevada.
Elevation gain and loss: 950 feet, -750 feet.
Trailhead elevation: 8,650 feet.
High point: Nobel Lake, 8,850 feet.
Maps: Markleeville 15-minute USGS quad (trail not shown on quad), Toiyabe or Stanislaus National Forest map.
Season: July through early October.
Finding the trailhead: The signed Pacific Crest Trail trailhead lies .1 mile east of State Highway 4, about .4 mile north of Ebbetts Pass. This pass is 125 miles east of Stockton and 12.75 miles west of the junction of State Highway 4 and State Highway 89.

The hike: This moderate hike utilizes a segment of the Pacific Crest Trail to reach the subalpine basin at the head of Nobel Canyon. A base camp can be made in this basin, and hikers can scale Tryon Peak, hike southeast to remote Bull Lake, or just relax and enjoy the view and the magnificent surroundings.

The trail begins at the southwest (upper) end of the parking area, and proceeds generally south for .25 mile through a forest of lodgepole and silver pine, red fir, and mountain hemlock. Views through the trees across the highway to glacially smoothed granite and the volcanic pinnacles beyond help to make this short stroll pass quickly.

Upon meeting the Pacific Crest Trail (PCT) you turn left, soon topping an open ridge at the 8,800-foot level, where you have good views north across the upper Silver Creek drainage. Then your trail contours through a timberline bowl under striking volcanic cliffs. You soon slice through a wildflower-dappled meadow, reenter a red fir, mountain hemlock, and silver pine forest, then contour around a granite spur ridge before beginning a side-hill descent. You

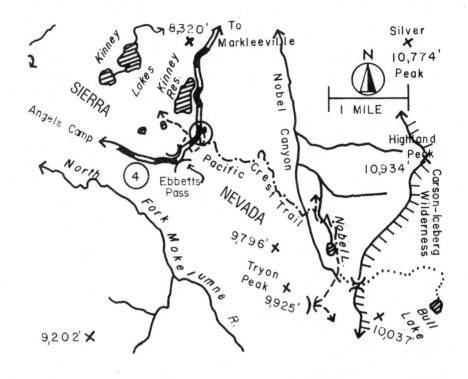

have great views along this stretch across the deep, U-shaped trough of Nobel Canyon to 10,774-foot- high Silver Peak and 10,934-foot-high Highland Peak.

Your gently descending trail leads southeast through a sparse boulder-dotted forest, crossing three small creeklets enroute. Just before reaching the bottom of Nobel Canyon, you hop across two more small creeks, and notice that the granitic landscape you have been traversing changes into one dominated by volcanic material.

You then cross Nobel Canyon Creek and swing north briefly to round a spur ridge. The trail soon jogs south around that ridge, enters the shade of red fir and silver pine, then passes an unsigned trail on your left, descending the length of Nobel Canyon.

Quite soon your trail contours into a gully containing Nobel Lake's outlet stream, and you then negotiate three long switchbacks ascending a volcanic hillside, passing an occasional stunted juniper enroute.

Above this climb, you begin hiking along the outlet of Nobel Lake in increasingly alpine terrain dotted with a few stunted mountain hemlocks and whitebark pines, soon reaching the northeastern shore of Nobel Lake. This fine lake lies in a truly "noble" setting, surrounded by a grassy landscape decorated with a variety of wildflowers and scattered stands of whitebark pine and mountain hemlock, with a backdrop of craggy volcanic peaks. This lake can be a good producer of pan-sized golden trout.

Good campsites are located throughout this high basin, which lends itself to cross-country exploration due to its open, gentle terrain.

Cattle are sometimes present in this basin, so water purification is advised. From Nobel Lake, return the way you came.

HIKE 82 *SCHNEIDER CAMP TO SHOWERS LAKE*

General description: A moderate 8.1-mile loop day hike or overnighter circumnavigating a section of the northern Sierra Nevada crest while obtaining panoramic vistas of the Lake Tahoe region, within the Lake Tahoe Basin Management Unit.
Elevation gain and loss: 1,450 feet.
Trailhead elevation: 8,300 feet.
High point: 9,200 feet.
Maps: Silver Lake and Fallen Leaf Lake 15-minute USGS quads (most of trail not shown on quads), Eldorado National Forest map, and/or Lake Tahoe Basin Management Unit map.
Season: July through early October.
Finding the trailhead: From State Highway 88 above the north shore of Caples Lake, about 102 miles east of Stockton and three miles west of Carson Pass, turn north where a sign indicates the CalTrans Caples Lake Maintenance Station. Drive past the maintenance station, and after .4 mile, turn right (north) where a sign points to Schneider. The road turns to dirt at this point. Follow this occasionally rough and dusty road for 1.7 miles to the upper end of a cow-filled meadow and park. The road continues on beyond a stock gate, but is disguised as a jeep route.

The hike: Anyone who has hiked in the Lake Tahoe area knows how popular this region can be. In fact, some hiking areas in the region are downright overcrowded, and for good reason. The scenery here is often spectacular, and the hiking is generally easy.

This hike, traversing sub-alpine terrain for the entire distance, is by far the least-used trail in this area, save the Showers Lake environs. Sub-alpine Showers Lake is often crowded, especially on summer weekends. Solitude-seeking hikers may have to consider locating their campsites in the Upper Truckee River basin, in one of the west-side bowls along the latter part of the hike; or they may establish a dry camp on the Sierra crest for utter solitude and a glorious sunrise.

Water is available, but isn't overly abundant, and cattle are present in some areas.

From the east end of the large meadow labeled Schneider Camp on the quad, your trail leads eastward past a sign indicating that the route is closed to motor vehicles. You quickly pass through a stock gate and begin ascending volcanic slopes clothed in sagebrush and a variety of wildflowers.

As you near the top of your climb, you pass a few stunted whitebark pines, and after hiking 1.1 miles from the trailhead, you reach your high point atop the alpine Sierra Nevada crest. Vistas from this point are excellent. Below to

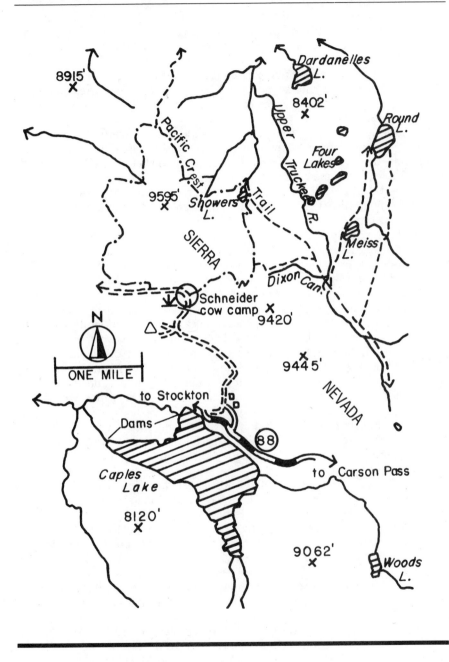

the east lies the wide valley of the Upper Truckee River. Meiss Lake glistens in the middle of that sub-alpine valley and beyond are the southernmost summits of the Carson Range—Red Lake and Stevens peaks—both of which rise to 10,061 feet above sea level.

Views from here also include the American River drainage in the west, the Freel Peak environs in the north, and the jagged peaks of the Ebbetts Pass region in the southeast, with higher peaks fading into the distance beyond.

Just after reaching your high point, you pass an eastbound trail descending Dixon Canyon and proceed north along the wildflower-clad east slopes of the Sierra Nevada crest. Quite soon, Round Lake and the Four Lakes come into view in the Upper Truckee River basin; beyond, Lake Tahoe begins to dominate your northward gaze.

Your briefly contouring trail now begins a descent toward Showers Lake, visible in a shallow basin in the north. Soon entering sub-alpine timber, your steep, gravelly route joins the Pacific Crest Trail (PCT) before reaching Showers Lake. You turn left and soon begin skirting the numerous east shore campsites set amid a forest of mountain hemlock, red fir, and lodgepole and silver pine. On any given summer weekend, unoccupied campsites around this lake may be hard to find.

This fine lake is surrounded by glacially-smoothed granite, lying just below the contact zone between the granitic rock and the volcanic material that buries that bedrock. Fishing here is poor, but the scenery is superb.

You soon pass a sign pointing to Echo Summit and then descend northward to cross the dam-regulated outlet creek below Showers Lake before doubling back up that creek and jogging west into a willow-cloaked meadow.

Your trail, the northbound PCT, soon passes another sign pointing to Echo Summit, then begins traversing a timberline bowl flanked by volcanic mudflow boulders on the left and glacially re-exposed granite on the right.

Exiting this bowl, the trail passes into a drier forest of mountain hemlock and lodgepole pine, with a few whitebark and silver pines added for diversity. It then passes through one of the many stock gates (which you should be careful to close) encountered along this hike.

You soon meet the homebound segment of your loop on the wildflower-speckled Sierra crest, about 1.75 miles from Showers Lake. Turn left here and part company with hikers on the Pacific Crest Trail. A sign here points south to Schneiders Cow Camp.

You quite soon obtain an excellent northwestward view across a meadow (often occupied by cattle) at the head of Sayles Canyon to Pyramid, Jacks, and Dicks peaks in the Desolation Wilderness.

The trail passes drift-bent lodgepole pines and shelter-giving stands of mountain hemlock before you encounter a sign bolted high on a lodgepole pine informing northbound motorcyclists (which are rarely seen on this trail) that the terrain north of the sign is closed to motorized forms of recreation.

Your southbound course leads through two timberline bowls west of the Sierra crest. Avoid drawing water from the northernmost bowl—cattle are sometimes present.

Occasional views, northward into the Desolation Wilderness country, westward across the conifer-clad western slope of the Sierra, and southward to the volcanic divide separating the American and Mokelumne rivers, help pass the time during your southbound trek.

You eventually break into the open upon beginning an eastward traverse, enjoying superb vistas of the Carson Pass region, Elephants Back, impressive Round Top, and Caples Lake. This view clearly displays the vivid contrast between the character of the bedrock granitic rocks and the deep volcanics that bury them.

Descending amid thickening timber, you soon amble out onto a jeep road, turn left, and hike one-half mile back to the trailhead.

HIKE 83 LUTHER PASS TO FREEL MEADOWS

General description: A moderate 7.25-mile semi-loop day hike or overnighter in the Carson Range, leading to two beautiful, seldom-visited, subalpine meadows within the Lake Tahoe Basin Management Unit.
Elevation gain and loss: 1,754 feet.
Trailhead elevation: 7,716 feet.
High point: 9,280 feet.
Maps: Freel Peak 15-minute USGS quad (Tahoe Rim Trail not shown on quad), Tahoe or Eldorado National Forest map.
Season: Late June through early October.
Finding the trailhead: The trailhead lies on the north side of State Highway 89, near the west end of a very large meadow, about 1.75 miles west of Luther Pass and about 6.6 miles southeast of the junction of State Highway 89 and westbound State Highway 50. Park in the turnout on the south side of the highway at the west end of the above-mentioned meadow. Then walk east along the highway for about 100 yards and turn onto the westbound trail on the highway's north side.

The remote Freel Meadows along the Tahoe Rim Trail offer hikers considerable solitude, a precious commodity in the often-crowded Lake Tahoe region.

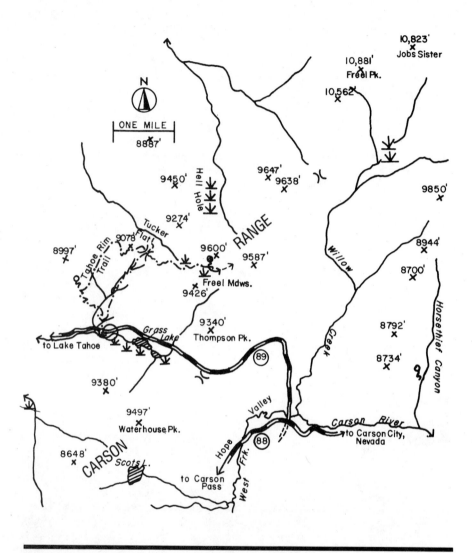

The hike: Utilizing the initial segment of the Tahoe Rim Trail, this Carson Range hike leads to two lovely meadows, seldom visited by hikers. A return via the old Tucker Flat Trail offers an alternative to hikers not wishing to retrace the entire route.

The isolated character of the Freel Meadows-Tucker Flat area offers a welcome change-of-pace from the crowded trails of the Lake Tahoe region.

Water is usually available at west Freel Meadow until late summer, and a more reliable source is found at Tucker Flat.

The trail begins by following blazed trees west as it parallels the highway before bending north in a forest of Jeffrey pine and red and white fir. You soon cross a small alder-lined creek, noticing the Tucker Flat Trail branching right and ascending along the course of that creek. That trail forms the homebound segment of this hike.

Continuing along the Tahoe Rim Trail, you eventually cross a larger stream before switchbacking up toward Peak 8997 in a pleasant pine and fir forest.

When the trail levels off, cross a small creek hidden under large granitic boulders below an aspen-covered meadow. Soon thereafter your route bends into another gully and crosses its small creek amid aspens, lodgepole pines, and red firs.

After hiking 1.8 miles from the trailhead, you top a boulder- strewn ridge amid silver pines and red firs, briefly glimpsing Lake Tahoe in the northwest and snowy Sierra Nevada summits in the southeast.

The trail now leads generally east while climbing up and around Peak 9078, almost touching its rocky summit. Occasional openings in the forest reveal the Crystal Range and other Desolation Wilderness peaks in the northwest.

East of Peak 9078, the trail descends to Tucker Flat Saddle at the 8,800-foot level. The old Tucker Flat Trail crosses the Tahoe Rim Trail at this point branching right and descending to State Highway 89 (your return route), and branching left and descending into Tucker Flat, where backpackers may elect to spend the night.

You, however, now work your way east along the wide lodgepole- and silver pine-forested ridge, and after hiking .75 mile from Tucker Flat Saddle, you begin traversing above west, or lower, Freel Meadow. This small but beautiful spread is dotted with boulders and brightened by a variety of wildflowers. Its margins are forested with lodgepole and whitebark pines and a few mountain hemlocks. The small creek flowing through the southern edge of the meadow, the headwaters of Saxon Creek, usually contains water until late in the summer.

Proceeding east, your trail passes over a low divide and skirts the northern margin of upper, or east, Freel Meadow.

Conical, 10,023-foot-high Hawkins Peak is framed by the forest in the southeast across this vividly green grassland. The trail traverses above the meadow, providing good views as far south as Stanislaus Peak.

Secluded camping is usually the rule in these seldom-visited meadows, but the new Tahoe Rim Trail will undoubtedly increase foot traffic in this area which was once all but unknown.

Eventually, hikers retrace the route back to Tucker Flat Saddle, turn left, and begin a steep southbound descent. About .4 mile below the saddle, just before crossing a small tributary creek on your left, you are treated to southward views of Sierra Nevada crest Peak 9595 and the Showers Lake basin.

Your route follows the main creek downstream, crossing it twice before leaving it behind to angle through a meadow-floored flat where the trail becomes muddy at times.

Aspen soon joins the pine and fir forest as you begin descending along the course of a small creek, which quickly leads you back to the Tahoe Rim Trail, where you turn left and backtrack to the trailhead.

HIKE 84 *GROUSE RIDGE TO GLACIER LAKE*

General description: A moderately easy nine-mile round-trip day hike or backpack in the Tahoe National Forest, into a glacier-carved, lake-filled sub-alpine basin in the northern Sierra Nevada.

Elevation gain and loss: 650 feet, -600 feet.

Trailhead elevation: 7,500 feet.

High point: Glacier Lake, 7,550 feet.

Maps: Emigrant Gap 15-minute USGS quad (Glacier Lake Trail not shown on quad), Tahoe National Forest map.

Season: July through early October.

Finding the trailhead: From Interstate 80, seventy- three miles northeast of Sacramento, take the westbound State Highway 20 exit and proceed west for about 4.1 miles, then turn right (north) where a sign points to Bowman Lake. (This turnoff can also be reached by following State Highway 20 east from Marysville for sixty miles.)

Your road, Tahoe National Forest Road 18, has a good paved surface. As you proceed, follow signs at all junctions pointing to Grouse Ridge Lookout. After driving 6.2 miles from State Highway 20 turn right where a sign indicates that the Grouse Ridge Lookout is six miles ahead. Presently on Tahoe National Forest Road 14 (dirt surfaced), you proceed east, and after 1.3 miles bear right where a sign indicates Grouse Ridge Campground. After another four rough and dusty miles, bear left, passing the campground entrance, and follow signs pointing to Trail Parking Area. You reach the parking area after another .2 mile, just beyond the left-branching spur road leading up to the Grouse Ridge Lookout.

The hike: An abundance of glaciated, sub-alpine scenery awaits hikers who complete this easy hike to the Glacier Lake area. Side trips to Five Lakes Basin and/or Byers Lakes offer some cross-country challenge and a chance for solitude.

Carry plenty of water—no reliable source is available until Glacier Lake.

From your ridgetop trailhead, you are treated to a superb, sweeping panorama, encompassing the North Coast Ranges in the west, Lassen Peak in the northwest, the craggy Sierra Buttes in the north, English Mountain in the northeast, Black Buttes in the east, and the peaks of the Granite Chief-Lake Tahoe region in the southeast.

Your route, closed to motorized vehicles, immediately begins descending northeastward through scattered silver pines. The trail from the campground quickly intersects your route on the right, and as you continue descending, red firs join the silver pines along this open ridge. Passing just east of Milk Lake amid thickening timber, you presently pass a westbound trail leading to Milk, Island, and Feeley lakes. Bearing right at that junction, you continue wandering through the forest, now joined by an occasional lodgepole pine. In early summer, pine drops add a dash of red to the mostly lupine understory found along this forested stretch of trail. At times, spiraea is also a fairly common understory plant.

You shortly pass a northbound trail leading to Sawmill Lake via the lake-filled basin to the north, and bear right onto the Glacier Lake Trail. Soon

264

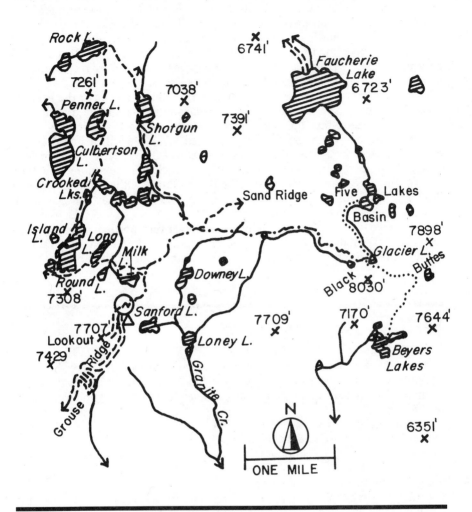

thereafter, avoid the Sand Ridge Trail on your left, proceeding instead east through a small lodgepole pine-rimmed meadow. The somber Black Buttes loom on the skyline ahead.

Your gently ascending trail presently heads east through a meadow-floored forest of red fir and lodgepole and silver pine while passing rocky, glacially smoothed knolls at the foot of Sand Ridge.

Enroute you pass above a small lake that is in the advanced stages of transition from lake to meadow. Lodgepole pines, willows, and corn lilies are rapidly invading its shores.

Your route continues through lodgepole pine and red fir forest decorated by various wildflowers, and you steadily work your way toward the Black Buttes via increasingly rocky, glaciated terrain.

After hiking about four miles from the trailhead, the trail levels off on a subalpine flat before climbing briefly over an open rocky hill. From this locale, you can gaze northeast to the rounded mass of 8,373-foot-high English Mountain, contrasting with the stark black crags of the Black Buttes to your immediate south. Snow patches cling to the Buttes long into summer.

Soon winding up and over another low hill, this one well-forested, you quickly reach Glacier Lake at the 7,550-foot level. This small but deep glacial tarn, set in a rockbound cirque at the very foot of the Black Buttes and fed by lingering snow patches, has excellent campsites shaded by red fir, mountain hemlock, and silver pine above its rocky west shore.

A few rewarding side trips are possible from Glacier Lake. For the average hiker, a .75 mile descent along Glacier Lake's outlet creek via a faint path suffices to get one into the scenic, rockbound Five Lakes Basin.

For the more adventurous and experienced hiker, a southeastward ascent of 350 feet, over steep rock and grass slopes, above Glacier Lake to the obvious mountain hemlock-clad saddle on the skyline includes the scaling, via class 3 rock, of the 8,030-foot-high point of Black Buttes. Otherwise, hikers can descend, first southeast, then southwest, for 1.25 miles from that saddle to remote Beyers Lake.

From Glacier Lake, return the way you came, or turn north onto the Sawmill Lake Trail (1.7 miles from the trailhead), looping back via Penner, Crooked, Island, Long, Round, and Milk lakes for a grand tour of the area.

HIKE 85 *FEATHER FALLS*

General description: A moderate seven-mile round-trip day hike (or backpack) in the western Sierra Nevada foothills, suitable for novices and veterans alike, in the Plumas National Forest, leading to the third-highest waterfall in the nation.

Elevation gain and loss: 500 feet, -1,000 feet.

Trailhead elevation and high point: 2,500 feet.

Maps: Big Bend Mtn. 15-minute USGS quad (trail not shown on quad), Plumas National Forest map.

Season: March through November.

Finding the trailhead: From State Highway 70 in Oroville, turn east onto Oroville Dam Boulevard (State Highway 162), and after 1.4 miles turn right onto Olive Highway. After driving 6.5 miles on this road, turn right onto Forbestown Road. A sign here points to Feather Falls. After another six miles turn left onto Lumpkin Road, where another sign indicates Feather Falls. After driving 10.8 miles on this paved but narrow and winding road, turn left just before reaching the small village of Feather Falls. A sign here indicates that the Feather Falls Trailhead is two miles north. After .2 mile of northbound travel, turn right and proceed 1.5 miles to the trailhead at the roadend where there is adequate parking space under the shadow of towering Douglas-firs and ponderosa pines.

The hike: This foothills hike on the western slope of the northern Sierra Nevada leads hikers through well-watered ponderosa pine forests and oak woodlands. The excellent trail maintains a gentle grade throughout.

With a drop of 640 feet, Feather Falls is surpassed in height in the U.S. only by 1,612-foot Ribbon Fall and 1,430-foot Upper Yosemite Fall, both in Yosmeite National Park, California.

Climbers will be attracted to the numerous possible climbing routes on Bald Rock Dome. Due to the remoteness of these impressive cliffs, climbs in the area are rarely attempted.

Be sure to carry an adequate supply of water.

Your hike into the 15,000-acre Feather Falls Scenic Area begins at the information sign at the trailhead and leads north through an open forest of ponderosa pine and Douglas-fir, mixed with specimens of canyon live oak, black oak, and madrone.

As you proceed along the gradually descending trail, you obtain occasional forest-framed views of the southeast face of Bald Rock Dome. Its sheer granite face rises impressively above Bald Rock Canyon on the Middle Fork Feather River and beckons adventurous climbers.

Among the trailside wildflowers that add their color to this foothills jaunt are Indian pink, yarrow, larkspur, and iris. The cool, shady forest of ponderosa pine, incense-cedar, Douglas-fir and black oak reflects the seventy inches of average annual precipitation this relatively low-elevation area receives.

Take notice of the numerous patches of poison oak growing alongside the trail—the plant is unmistakable with its three- lobed, oak-like leaves.

Feather Falls, on the western slope of the Sierra Nevada, is the third-highest waterfall in the nation, the Fall River plummeting 640 feet into the Middle Fork Feather River.

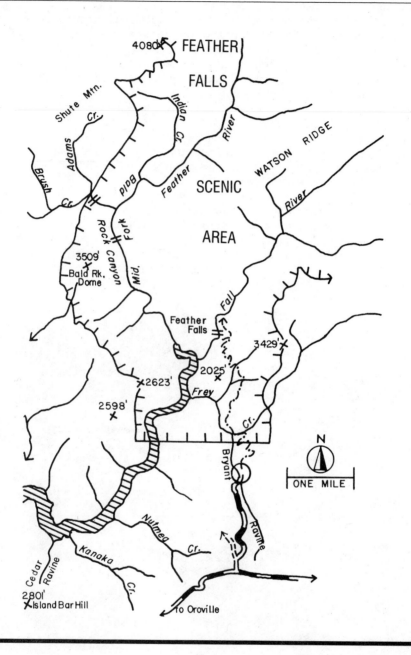

As the trail makes its way into the Frey Creek environs, thimbleberry and bracken fern join the understory of this north- slope forest. There are handrails along this switchbacking section to remind hikers not to shortcut the trail.

Just beyond the one-mile marker, the trail descends to the banks of Frey Creek, soon crossing above its boisterous waters via a wooden bridge. The trail then parallels the creek downstream above its east bank and, now on a southwest-facing slope, the hiker will notice that canyon live oak begins to dominate the forest.

Soon, Bald Rock Dome comes into view again, and in spring, an impressive waterfall can be seen just north of the Dome.

As you continue descending high above noisy Frey Creek, you may notice the introduction of Indian paintbrush, monkey flower, and penstemon among the trailside flora.

After curving northeast, the trail descends into a shady Frey Creek tributary canyon where ponderosa pine and incense-cedar rejoin the forest. In moist areas such as this small canyon, large banana slugs, reaching lengths of seven inches or more, will sometimes be seen making their way across the trail.

The trail soon crosses two small creeks, then ascends through an area labeled "Wagner Valley" on some Forest Service maps. This climb is shaded by ponderosa pine, tanbark-oak, and black oak. Manzanita, lupine, and monkey flower constitute the understory.

The trail appears to be headed for a low, forested saddle on the northwestern skyline. As you ascend the last small gully toward that saddle, you may notice a few specimens of the seldom- seen California nutmeg. This interesting tree, sometimes confused with a fir, has sharply pointed, fir-like needles.

Just before the trail attains the above-mentioned saddle, it veers eastward and begins traversing sunny, southeast-facing slopes. The trail soon switchbacks west on this open, live oak- clad hillside. The surrounding forest covered mountains come into view and the trail becomes increasingly rocky.

A few digger pines (a California endemic) are seen just above, attesting to the hot, dry conditions that prevail on this sunny slope. The contrast between this slope and the forested slopes traversed previously provides a good example of the way slope aspect (the direction in which a slope faces) influences vegetation types at this low elevation.

Soon your trail bends northeast and, because of the precipitous nature of this rocky slope, becomes lined with handrails.

The large Middle Fork Feather River and a major tributary, the Fall River, shortly meet your gaze as you progress northeastward. You soon round a bend and are confronted with the awesome spectacle of roaring Feather Falls. This magnificent 640- foot falls plunges over a resistant granite precipice on its way to the Middle Fork Feather River and its impoundment in Lake Oroville.

However, Feather Falls does tend to dry up considerably as the summer wears on.

Following the handrail-lined trail, turn left where a faint trail continues ascending along the course of Fall River, passing just above the brink of the falls. Backpackers will want to continue along this trail for pleasant riverside campsites and often-good trout fishing.

After turning left, descend via one switchback and a wooden stairway to the fenced-in overlook platform precariously perched above the near-vertical gorge of the lower Fall River. This platform offers a head-on view of the impressive falls.

To the southwest, you can see the upper end of the Middle Fork arm of Lake Oroville, .75 mile below. Adventurous boaters can view the falls from that point.

From Feather Falls, either return to the trailhead or ascend the Fall River for about two miles to trail's end.

HIKE 86 *LAKES BASIN*

General description: A moderately strenuous 9.2-mile day hike in the Plumas National Forest, looping through one of the northernmost glacial lake basins in the Sierra Nevada.

Elevation gain and loss: 1475 feet.

Trailhead elevation: 6,600 feet.

High point: 7,500 feet.

Maps: Sierra City 15-minute USGS quad (some of the Lakes Basin trails not shown on quad), Plumas National Forest map.

Season: July through early October.

Finding the trailhead: From State Highway 70, about twenty-four miles east of Quincy, turn right (southeast) onto State Highway 89. After driving about 2.5 miles, turn right (south) onto the Gold Lake Road, where a sign indicates that Gold Lake is seven miles ahead. Follow this good paved road generally south for about 7.5 miles. Just before cresting a low summit on this road and just before leaving Plumas County and entering Sierra County (at the signed boundary), turn southwest onto an unsigned paved road. Follow this road a very short distance to the parking area opposite the access road to the Gold Lake Lodge. A southbound road just beyond the parking area leads to Gold Lake.

The hike: This hike through Lakes Basin, an area set aside for day-use only, surveys one of the northernmost glacial lake basins in the Sierra Nevada. Ranging from lake shores to windswept ridges with sweeping vistas, this trip allows hikers to experience the contrasting landscapes found in the northern Sierra. Fair fishing and cool swimming are always close at hand in the basin, and easy side trips to numerous lakes are made possible by the network of trails in the area.

This network of trails linking numerous lakes close to the road make the area ideally suited for families or anyone else who isn't looking for a hike as strenuous as the one described here.

Carry plenty of water, as none is readily available during the first 7.5 miles.

From the parking area, proceed west toward a barrier across a jeep road and a sign showing a map of the area. Begin hiking west along this jeep road under a canopy of red fir, soon passing outlying buildings of the Gold Lake Lodge on your right.

After hiking .25 mile, you meet the return leg of your loop on the right, leading to Big Bear Lake and beyond. Bearing left here, you proceed along the abandoned jeep trail through a forest dominated by red fir, at times passing grassy, wildflower- speckled clearings. You sometimes have tree-framed views

of Mt. Elwell across the basin in the northwest which, at 7,812 feet above sea level, is the highest point in the Lakes Basin area.

Your route becomes increasingly rocky as you work your way up the basin, and you soon pass the old Round Lake Mine.

Presently passing a right-branching trail leading down to Round Lake, the route finally narrows to trail width as you approach the Lakes Basin crest, passing scattered silver pines, mountain hemlocks, and a few red firs and Jeffrey pines. As you continue climbing, you get your first glimpse of immense Long Lake spreading out at the foot of Mt. Elwell.

Soon glacial Gold Lake meets your gaze in the southeast, the largest natural lake in this region of the Sierra.

After hiking barely less than three miles from the trailhead, you reach a ridgetop junction with the Pacific Crest Trail. Note how abruptly the forest has thickened on the deeper soils of this slope, in comparison with the sparse forest growing on the meager soils in the glaciated basin you have been hiking through.

You presently turn right (north) onto the Pacific Crest Trail. From here, you have a superb view east across island- dotted Gold Lake, and in the south, the serrated Sierra Buttes thrust their toothy crags skyward. In the southeast lie distant Interstate 80 peaks, and beyond are summits as far as the Lake Tahoe region.

This view gets even better as the trail nears the summit of Peak 7550, high on the crest above Lakes Basin. In addition to the above-mentioned landmarks, the view now includes Snake and Little Deer lakes below to your west, the North Coast Ranges beyond the western slope of the Sierra Nevada, and far-off Sierra crest peaks in the northeast.

The trail contours around the north side of Peak 7550 just above the head-wall of Lakes Basin, and from here the entire lake- filled basin spreads out before you. Far to the northwest, snow- streaked Lassen Peak rises above all else.

You soon cross over to the west side of the crest and after two descending switchbacks, a trail from Oakland Pond joins your route on the left. Conti-nuing on a gentle northwestward traverse through red fir and silver pine forest, that trail soon branches right from your route, the Pacific Crest Trail.

You then enter a dense mountain hemlock forest and reach another ridgetop junction five miles from the trailhead. Turning right here, you descend north-east through the often-dense forest. After .6 mile, you pass a right-branching trail leading to Silver Lake and beyond, and shortly thereafter you pass a left-branching trail, a northbound segment of the Pacific Crest Trail.

You continue descending northeastward along the open ridge, spying several Lakes Basin waters in the east before reaching a three-way junction. A few hikers will be tempted to tackle the steep mile-long climb to Mt. Elwell for boundless vistas of the surrounding countryside, but most will turn right and descend toward Mud Lake, avoiding the middle trail leading to Long Lake and Graegle Lodge.

Your sometimes-brushy route begins descending, soon levels off, and then re-enters a conifer stand where you notice an unmarked trail branching left and leading to Long Lake.

After hiking around the west shore of small Mud Lake, you begin laboring up grass- and tree-covered slopes, soon edging close to a trickle of water originating from the small lake just above, whose north shore the trail soon skirts. Shortly after passing this small tarn, incorrectly signed Helgramite Lake, a westbound trail joins your route on the right as you descend to Silver Lake. This fine lake, whose shores are shaded by scattered timber, has a backdrop of rugged cliffs that help to make this one of the most scenic spots in Lakes Basin.

At the north end of Silver Lake, avoid a southbound trail leading to Round Lake and proceed east along a ridge lined with manzanita and huckleberry oak, briefly sighting Long Lake directly below to your left.

Soon, you pass a northbound trail leading to Lakes Basin Campground on your left, and you continue past Cub, Little Bear, and Big Bear lakes, all lying just south of the trail and whose shorelines are easily accessible to anglers and swimmers alike.

Stay right at the north end of beautiful Big Bear Lake, avoiding another north-bound trail to the campground. From here, a pleasant .6-mile jaunt through the forest brings you back to your jeep route, where you turn left and backtrack .25 mile to the trailhead.

HIKE 87 *HAY MEADOW TO LONG LAKE*

General description: A moderately easy, 7.8-mile loop day hike or backpack in the Caribou Wilderness, leading through peaceful forests and passing several pleasant lakes where generally good fishing and late-summer swimming are major attractions.

Elevation gain and loss: 650 feet.

Trailhead elevation: 6,400 feet.

High point: Posey Lake, 7,000 feet.

Maps: Chester 15-minute USGS quad (road to trailhead not shown on quad), Lassen National Forest map.

Season: Mid-June through early October.

Finding the trailhead: Follow State Highway 36 to its junction with southbound Plumas County Road A-13, five miles east of Chester and twenty-nine miles west of Susanville. From this junction, turn onto a northbound road directly opposite Plumas County Road A-13 and proceed north, turning left onto signed Lassen National Forest Road 10 after .2 mile, avoiding the eastbound road to the Chester Landfill. Drive west for another .5 mile and then turn right, staying on Forest Road 10. The pavement ends after another 2.7 miles. Continue north on Forest Road 10 (obviously the main road) and avoid several signed and unsigned, well-graded spur roads. At major junctions, signs point to Caribou Wilderness. After driving 9.8 miles from State Highway 36, turn left, leaving Forest Road 10, where a sign points to Caribou Wilderness two miles ahead. Proceed northwest on this good dirt road for 1.6 miles to the roadend at the Hay Meadow Trailhead.

The hike: The Caribou Wilderness is an area of gentle topography interrupted by numerous volcanic cones lying immediately east of Lassen Volcanic National Park in the southern Cascade Range. It is a thickly forested area that contains dozens of lakes. The lakes that are able to support fish are stocked with rainbow and brook trout. The numerous shallow lakes unable to maintain trout populations are often good swimming holes, especially in August when their waters have warmed to comfortable levels.

Except during the spring snowmelt period, the only water available to hikers in this area is directly from the lakes. Thus, you should carry as much water as you will need or else plan on purifying any water you obtain in the Caribou Wilderness.

Mosquitoes are abundant in early summer. Mule deer are likely to be seen throughout the area.

The trail heads northwest from the roadend past an information sign and skirts the eastern margin of lush, forest- rimmed Hay Meadow. After a short jaunt through a lodgepole pine and red fir forest dotted with an occasional silver pine, you reach a junction at the south end of wet, cattle-occupied Indian Meadows. The right fork is the homebound segment of your loop.

Stay left here, passing the Caribou Wilderness sign and spying South Caribou in the northeast as you walk around the south end of Indian Meadows. Your trail shortly jogs west and begins a moderate ascent along a seasonal stream that is usually dry by late summer.

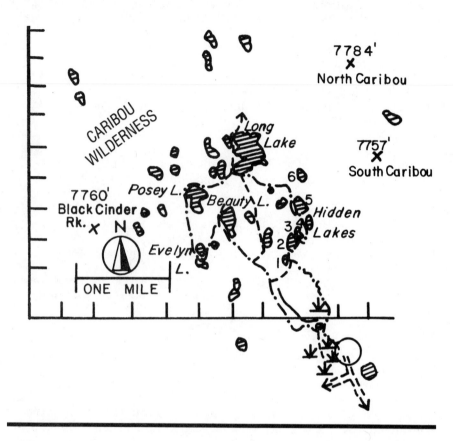

After a pleasant stroll through pine and fir forest, you pass an unmarked northeastbound trail leading to the Hidden Lakes, and .3 mile beyond that you pass a signed trail on your right leading past Long Lake to Cone and Caribou lakes.

Staying left, you are soon traversing above the southwest shore of forest-rimmed Beauty Lake. The trail swings away from the lake after passing a right-branching trail leading to lakeshore campsites.

The trail presently heads southwest and soon begins traversing above the east shore of forest- and rock-fringed Evelyn Lake. With a backdrop of volcanic cliffs, this is one of the more scenic spots on the hike; but just as at Beauty Lake, campsites are somewhat scarce here.

After hiking around the south shore of Evelyn Lake, be sure to avoid a well-worn path that hugs the west shore of the lake, staying left on the less obvious main trail.

Another pleasant stretch of walking shaded by fir and pine brings you to the meadow-lined shores of Posey Lake. Campsites around this fine lake are fairly abundant, and fishing for pan-sized trout is usually good.

A mild descent beyond Posey Lake for .5 mile gets you to the shores of Long Lake, the largest lake in the southern Caribou Wilderness. From this lake you are treated to your first good view of the red cone of 7,784-foot-high North Caribou and 7,757- foot-high South Caribou peaks in the northeast. Campsites around this large lake are numerous.

At the lakeshore junction, turn right, very soon passing an unsigned southbound trail and immediately thereafter reaching a signed junction with another southbound trail, where you bear left and proceed toward the Hidden Lakes.

You soon pass a pond lily-smothered tarn, then jog east to briefly skirt the south shore of Hidden Lake No. 5, where fishing is unpredictable. Garter snakes are fairly common around this and other meadow-fringed lakes in the wilderness.

The trail leads generally south past the lower four Hidden Lakes, of which No. 4 is the deepest. The lower three lakes are ideal for cool dips in August.

At Hidden Lake No. 1, you meet a southwest-bound trail on your right, turn left, and begin a descent. In addition to the previously cited forest trees, white fir joins the forest as you negotiate this moderately steep descent.

Leveling off, you shortly reach the upper end of Indian Meadows, where your trail promptly disappears at the meadow's edge. Walk southeast across this narrow arm of the meadow and find the trail in the lodgepole pines on the other side.

The trail then turns south along the east edge of Indian Meadows, soon intersecting the initial segment of the hike, where you turn left and retrace your steps for .25 mile to the trailhead.

HIKE 88 LASSEN PEAK

General description: A moderate five-mile round-trip day hike to the alpine summit of the southernmost volcano in the Cascade Range, where an all-encompassing vista of northern California unfolds, in Lassen Volcanic National Park.

Elevation gain and loss: 1,982 feet.

Trailhead elevation: 8,475 feet.

High point: Lassen Peak, 10,457 feet.

Maps: Lassen Peak 15-minute USGS quad, Lassen Volcanic National Park map.

Season: Mid-July through early October.

Finding the trailhead: From Red Bluff, follow State Highway 36 east for forty-seven miles to the northbound State Highway 89. Turn left and drive north into Lassen Volcanic National Park, paying the five dollar fee at the Park entrance station. Just west of the road's high point in the Park, and about a mile beyond Lake Helen, you reach the signed Lassen Peak Trailhead on the north side of the road.

You can also reach the trailhead by driving east from Redding via State Highway 44 for forty-eight miles. Then turn right onto southbound State Highway 89 and drive twenty-two miles through Lassen Volcanic National Park to the well-marked trailhead.

The hike: Lassen Peak, a landmark for emigrant guide Peter Lassen, is easily attainable and frequently climbed. A well-graded 2.5-mile trail leads hikers to its rewarding summit for remarkably far-ranging vistas of northern California. Although this hike is fairly strenuous, families with children are often seen treading the easy path to the peak. There is no water available along the trail, so carry an adequate supply. Although it may be warm at the trailhead, the exposed summit is frequently buffeted by strong, cold winds.

The trail heads north from the parking area, switchbacks into a timberline stand of mountain hemlock, then levels off briefly on a sub-alpine flat. The deep snow drifts clinging to this slope, some remaining all year, attest to the severe winters and very deep snows that visit this region annually.

Soon passing a lateral trail to a pair of restrooms, your trail proceeds into a realm of prostrate whitebark pines. If the wind is right, the thin air during the first few hundred feet of ascent will be permeated by hydrogen sulphide fumes from Little Hot Springs Valley, Bumpass Hell, and the Sulphur Works where there are hot springs and fumaroles.

As you gain elevation, views continue to expand. The high peaks of southwestern Lassen Volcanic National Park are among the first to meet your gaze. Eagle and Ski Heil peaks, Mt. Diller, and Brokeoff Mountain form a ridge of impressive alpine peaks a few miles to the southwest.

Brokeoff Mountain, the high ridge between it and Lassen Peak, and Mt. Conard in the south are all remnants of the former rim of Mt. Tehama, thought to have been 1,000 feet higher than present-day Lassen Peak, was a composite volcanic cone that existed hundreds of thousands of years ago but eventually collapsed.

Lassen peak is the southernmost volcano in a chain of largely volcanic mountains extending north from Lassen Peak through Oregon and Washington and into British Columbia.

The summit region of Lassen Peak, the southernmost volcano in the Cascade Range, was re-shaped by eruptions during the period 1914-1917. And this popular mountain, offering extensive vistas of northern California, is still considered an active volcano.

Near the one-mile point on the trail, a sign points out a terminal moraine just downslope to the southeast. That terminal moraine figures prominently in geologists' estimations that Lassen Peak is approximately 11,000 years old. If Lassen Peak were older, geologists say, it would be extensively glaciated. But since the last ice age began to subside approximately 10,000 years ago, this small path of glaciation was all that the waning glaciers excavated.

Eventually rising above the last wind-tortured whitebark pines, you begin switchbacking up the narrow southeast ridge. Along this stretch the trail edges close to several dark crags protruding from the talus that mantles the slopes of the peak. These cliffs are composed of dacite, and are thought to be part of the original dacite plug dome of Lassen Peak, which was extruded as partially solidified lava from one of Brokeoff Cone's still-active vents. The fracturing and crumbling of the dome produced the talus slopes you see today.

Above timberline, hikers are treated to the pungent blue flowers of the showy polemonium as they ascend alpine slopes via continuous switchbacks, passing another pair of restrooms within .75 mile of the peak.

Eventually the trail levels off on the summit ridge just west of the peak. Notice Davidson's penstemon and showy polemonium here, demonstrating that life forms exist even in this incredibly harsh environment.

The trail then continues east to the craggy summit of Lassen Peak. Views from the top are breathtaking, encompassing a vast sweep of northern California scenery. In the northwest stands the gargantuan sentinel of northern California, 14,162-foot-high Mt. Shasta, the largest of Cascade Range volcanoes. In the foreground between Lassen Peak and Mt. Shasta lie the numerous and various volcanoes of the southern Cascade Range, mantled in dense conifer forests. The Modoc Plateau country lies to the northeast, and beyond are the Warner Mountains in extreme northeastern California. To the south, the northern Sierra Nevada marches off toward the Lake Tahoe region, punctuated in the foreground by Lake Almanor. The North Coast Ranges line the western horizon, highlighted by Snow Mountain in the south, the South and North Yolla Bolly mountains in the north, seen across the broad plain of the upper Sacramento Valley, which is often obscured by an orange haze second in California only to that infamous pall that so frequently blankets the Los Angeles Basin.

Lying to the north of the North Coast Ranges are the perpetually-snowy Trinity Alps and beyond, the Scott Mountains march off to the northeast. Below to your east is the thickly forested terrain of Lassen Volcanic National Park and the Caribou Wilderness, interrupted by numerous volcanic features such as cinder cones, composite volcanoes, and lava flows. The impressive dacite domes of the aptly-named Chaos Crags lie below to your north. And the interesting Devastated Area lies immediately below the peak on the northeast flank of the mountain.

The Devastated Area is a result of eruptions that took place in the vicinity of the peak between 1914 and 1917. On May 19, 1915, for example, molten lava flowed about 1,000 feet down the west side of the mountain before solidifying; simultaneously, hot lava and ash flowed down the northeastern slope, where it encountered and melted deep snowpack, thus creating a disastrous mudflow that avalanched down the mountain, destroying the forest in its path and burying the area under mud and ash. Then on May 22, 1915, a terrific explosion sent a giant ash cloud 30,000 feet skyward. A portion of this hot blast of gases and ash settled over the devastated area, regenerating the

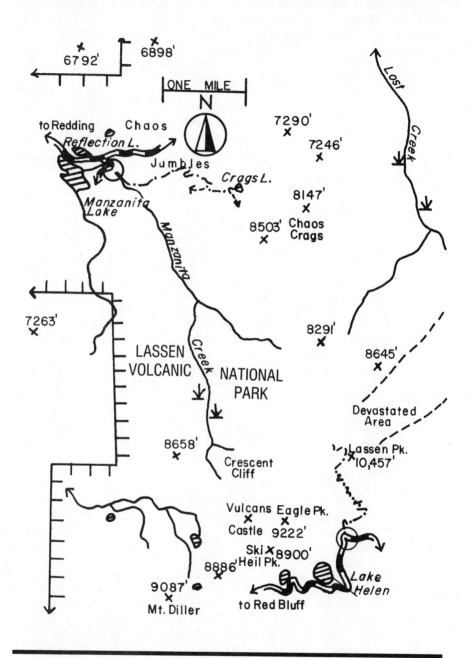

6792'   6898'

ONE MILE
N

7290'
7246'

to Redding   Chaos
Reflection L.
Jumbles   Crags L.

Manzanita
Lake   8147'
                     8503' Chaos
                            Crags

7263'   8291'

                              8645'

LASSEN
VOLCANIC   NATIONAL
              PARK
                            Devastated
                              Area

                         Lassen Pk.
                          10,457'
8658'
        Crescent
        Cliff

        Vulcans Eagle Pk.
        Castle 9222'
        Ski 8900'
        Heil Pk.
8886'   Lake
9087'   Helen
Mt. Diller   to Red Bluff

mudflow and completing the destruction begun three days earlier. Today young trees are slowly reforesting the area.

On the summit region of Lassen Peak, the features you see are largely the result of the volcanic activity that took place between 1914 and 1917. During 1914 and 1915 alone, 150 eruptions of varying intensities were recorded, eruptions which altered the topography of the summit region. Lassen Peak is still considered an active volcano.

A trail just below the summit leads to the north rim of the mountain through an area of small craters and dacite flows. The dacite flows occurred during 1915, and the craters were formed between 1915 and 1917.

The northward view from the north rim is unobstructed and worthy of investigation.

After enjoying this magnificent and fascinating mountain, hikers eventually return to the trailhead.

HIKE 89 *CRAGS LAKE*

General description: A moderately easy five-mile round-trip day hike, suitable for novices and veterans alike, in Lassen Volcanic National Park.
Elevation gain and loss: 850 feet, -50 feet.
Trailhead elevation: 5,920 feet.
High point: 6,720 feet.
Maps: Manzanita Lake 15-minute USGS quad, Lassen Volcanic National Park map. Also use hike No. 88 map.
Season: Mid-June through early October.
Finding the trailhead: From Redding, follow State Highway 44 east for forty-eight miles, then turn right onto State Highway 89 and enter Lassen Volcanic National Park. Proceed past Manzanita Lake and then Reflection Lake, and after 1.1 miles turn right (south) where a large sign indicates Manzanita Lake Campground. Follow this road about .1 mile to the signed Chaos Crags Trailhead on the south side of the road, just before the road crosses Manzanita Creek, a signed spawning stream.

The hike: This easy hike leads to the depression at the foot of Chaos Crags labeled "Crags Lake" on the quad. Hikers in late summer, however, are likely to find the "lake" bone-dry. Nevertheless, the area is highly scenic.

Carry plenty of water.

From the trailhead, you head south on the level through a park-like forest of Jeffrey pine. The trail passes just west of a cluster of buildings comprising the Manzanita Lake Lodge. The lodge area was closed in 1974 because of the probability of massive rock avalanches emanating from the Chaos Crags.

White firs join the forest as you begin hiking along the course of Manzanita Creek, surrounded by dense brush including manzanita and tobacco brush.

The trail soon jogs east into thick forest, shortly crossing the cold runoff from an upslope spring. Presently you bridge a small spring issuing from beneath the trail, and continue east through an increasingly open forest, occasionally spying the bulk of the somber gray Chaos Crags.

Soon the trail nears the Chaos Jumbles area indicated on the quad. This is an interesting area consisting of loose angular boulders and dotted with small conifers. The Chaos Jumbles originated from the Chaos Crags. Some geologists theorize that a sequence of volcanic explosions near the base of the Chaos Crags loosened a large quantity of material that was transported northwest to the flanks of Table Mountain by a succession of avalanches. Scientists believe that these rock avalanches moved at great velocities on a cushion of compressed air, which enabled the rock mass to travel about two miles northwest from the base of the Chaos Crags and then approximately 400 feet up the south slope of Table Mountain.

The Chaos Crags are dacite plug volcanoes similar to Lassen Peak, but are composed of four or more plug domes.

After negotiating the second switchback on the trail, you meet a well-worn westbound path on your right. Bearing left, you continue ascending through a red fir, white fir, and Jeffrey pine forest. The adjacent slopes are smothered with manzanita. Straight ahead loom the bold Chaos Crags, towering almost 2,000 feet above you.

Soon after lodgepole pines join the forest, you crest a ridge above Crags Lake basin. A faint trail branches right from here and ascends toward the crags, but this detour should be attempted by experienced hikers only due to the unstable volcanic slopes.

From this ridge the Chaos Crags rise in bold relief directly above, and you have an excellent view down across the Chaos Jumbles.

From here the trail drops steeply via rock and sand slopes into the boulder-filled depression of Crags Lake. Only early season hikers are likely to find water in this bowl.

The Chaos Crags in Lassen Volcanic National Park are actually very young (1,200 years old) volcanic plug domes, similar to Lassen Peak. Volcanic plug domes (the Chaos Crags are composed of dacite) are formed as partially solidified plugs of lava are pushed upward above the earth's surface.

A sparse forest of lodgepole, Jeffrey, and silver pine dots the rocky slopes of the basin, with bitterbrush, spiraea, chinquapin, and manzanita forming a brushy understory. The loose rock and often-deep sand makes travel slippery and hazardous in this area.

This basin may appear at first glance to have been glaciated. But considering the age of the Chaos Crags—less than 1,200 years—and the fact that glaciers disappeared approximately 10,000 years ago, glaciation could hardly be responsible for the basin's characteristics. This bowl was formed instead by the same volcanic explosions and resulting avalanches that created the Chaos Jumbles.

From Crags Lake basin, return the way you came.

HIKE 90 *BUTTE LAKE TO SNAG LAKE LOOP*

General description: A moderate 13.5 mile loop in Lassen Volcanic National Park, suitable for a backpack of two to three days, visiting two large lakes and circumnavigating one of the youngest lava flows in the Park.
Elevation gain and loss: 1,010 feet.
Trailhead elevation: 6,060 feet.
High point: 6,440 feet.
Maps: Prospect Peak 15-minute USGS quad; or Lassen Volcanic National Park and Vicinity USGS quad.
Season: Late June through mid-October.
Finding the trailhead: Follow State Highway 44 east from Redding for 73 miles, or west from Susanville for 40.5 miles,
and turn onto the southbound dirt road signed for Butte Lake, Forest Road 32N21. This road is wide but usually has a rough, washboard surface. As you drive south, avoid various right and left turns, all signed.

After 6.5 miles, you reach the self-pay station at the Park boundary and the Butte Lake Campground entrance. Bear left at this junction and after .1 mile you will reach the large trailhead parking area above the north shore of Butte Lake.

The hike: Along the eastern margin of Lassen Volcanic National Park, cinder cones, large lakes, lava flows, and thick forests of pine and fir dominate the landscape. Lacking the exciting backdrop of snowy peaks and crowds of hikers that are prevalent in the western reaches of the Park, this fine loop trip takes hikers through a more peaceful landscape. The gentle grade of the trail, ample campsites, and delightful scenery make this trip a fine choice for a weekender for any hiker, even for families with children.

The area was not always as peaceful as it seems today. Numerous cinder cones, the tall shield volcano of Prospect Peak, and the Fantastic Lava Beds, a stygian jumble of broken rock, all attest to the region's origin as a land born of fire. Most of the cinder cones you will see along this hike are old and no longer active, now cloaked in forests of pine and fir. But Cinder Cone and the Fantastic Lava Beds are nearly devoid of vegetation, and the nearly symmetrical aspect of the cone, lacking any obvious effects of erosion, attests to the youthfulness of these features. Geologists believe that Cinder Cone may be less than 2,000 years old.

The Fantastic Lava Beds consist of numerous lava flows that emanated from the cone during this 2000 year period. One of these flows dammed Grassy Creek, thus forming Snag Lake. Snag Lake, then, is an unusually youthful lake, compared with most mountain lakes that were created by the effects of glaciation 10,000 or more years ago.

The most recent volcanic activity in the Cinder Cone area may have taken places as late as 1850-51, although some geologists believe the last eruption occured about 400 years ago.

The final leg of the loop trip traces Nobles Emigrant Trail, a route that played an important role in the settlement of northern California. This route was pioneered in 1852 by William H. Nobles, who came to California from Minnesota in quest for gold.

Vast lakes, cool, peaceful forests, and gentle volcanic terrain typify the scenery in the far northeastern reaches of Lassen Volcanic National Park.

Backpackers should bear in mind the following restrictions when selecting a campsite. Camp at least 100 feet from lakes, trails, and streams. Camping within .25 mile of Butte Lake, excepting its south shore is prohibited. Campfires are prohibited. There are bears in this country, so protect your food supply. And finally, be sure to obtain a backcountry permit at the Butte Lake Ranger Station if you intend to stay overnight on the trail.

From the parking area, ignore the northbound trail to Bathtub Lake (route of Nobles Trail) and head east, briefly following a service road, to the trail proper. Soon passing a destination and mileage sign, you enter a park-like forest of pine and fir on a smooth tread of volcanic sand. Soon a moderate grade leads you up the slopes of Knob 6272. Rewarding vistas greet hikers atop the knob, but quickly fade from view as the trail switchbacks down to an easy log crossing of Butte Creek at the north end of Butte Lake.

Beyond the crossing, the trail hugs the lake's east shore where rainbows leaping from its cold, clear waters may invite anglers to linger. Don't be surprised to see an osprey diving for trout in this lava-rimmed lake. Vistas from the lakeshore stretch across the lava beds to the smooth gray slopes of Cinder Cone and to snowy Lassen Peak.

Approaching the south end of the lake, lodgepole pines and aspens join the forest of pine and fir, accompanying you to a signed junction 2.3 miles from the trailhead. Bear right here toward Snag Lake and begin climbing gently southward. This stretch begins in a grassy lodgepole pine forest along an often-dry streabed, but soon climbs onto drier slopes, where currant and mule's ears join the grassy understory. These drier slopes also begin to host pines and firs, which ultimately dominate the forest by the time you reach the top of the ridge ahead. As you gain elevation during this gradual 300-foot ascent, numerous colorful wildflowers join the large yellow blossoms of mule's ears on trailside slopes, including penstemon, coyote mint, Indian paintbrush, and aster.

You will probably not realize you have gained the ridge until you begin descending the other side. This gentle descent leads .5 mile through thick forest, ending near the east shore of immense Snag Lake, rimmed on three sides by low, forested ridges, and on the other by the lava beds that created it. Rainbows and brookies inhabit the lake's vast waters.

Presently the trail heads south, across a grassy, aspen-clad slope above the east shore. Where the trail curves west, you enter heavy conifer forest, passing beneath benches where campsites might be located.

After 5.75 miles, you enter a small but wet grassy pocket and cross a trickling stream where the trail briefly becomes obscure.

Helping to pass the time on your trek around the park's second largest lake are tree-framed views of the Fantastic Lava Beds, Cinder Cone, and Prospect Peak. You will cross another small stream .6 mile from the last, where campsites could be located on grassy, tree-sheltered benches upstream.

After another .5 mile, presently high above Snag Lake's south shore you should bear right where another trail joins on your left bound for Juniper and Jakey lakes. Your trail heads southwest, crosses four springs, and reaches the bridged crossing of Grassy Creek after .1 mile. Willows, cottonwoods, lodgepole pines, and white firs hug the banks of the creek, its abundant moisture nurturing colorful blossoms such as monkey flower, leopard lily, yarrow, aster, and groundsel.

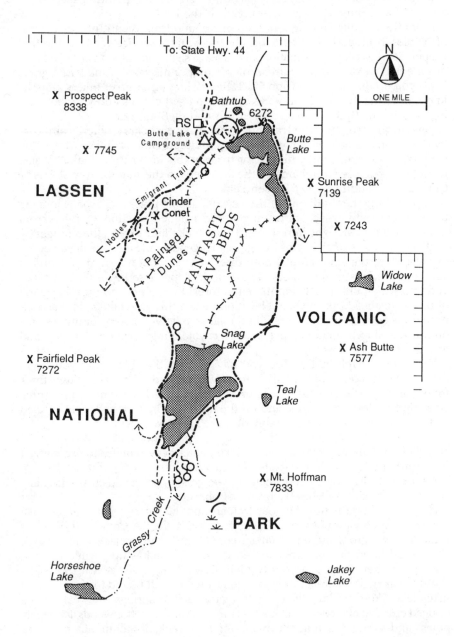

To: State Hwy. 44

N

ONE MILE

X Prospect Peak
8338

*Bathtub
L.* 6272

RS ☐
Butte Lake
Campground

*Butte
Lake*

X 7745

X Sunrise Peak
7139

LASSEN

X 7243

*Cinder
Cone*

Emigrant Trail

Nobles

F A N T A S T I C   L A V A   B E D S

*Painted
Dunes*

*Widow
Lake*

VOLCANIC

*Snag
Lake*

X Fairfield Peak
7272

X Ash Butte
7577

*Teal
Lake*

NATIONAL

X Mt. Hoffman
7833

Grassy Creek

PARK

*Horseshoe
Lake*

*Jakey
Lake*

Beyond the crossing, a level stint through lodgepole forest (ample opportunities for campsites) leads to another southbound trail heading for Horseshoe and Juniper lakes. Turning right, another pleasant .5 mile jaunt leads to yet another junction with a left-branching trail bound for more backcountry lakes.

But you stay right, continuing north well above the west shore of Snag Lake. Quite soon you will enter a charred forest. Lightning in the summer of 1987 ignited this small fire, which fortunately burned itself out at the shore of Snag Lake and along the edge of the lava beds. Here, at the southern edge of the burn many trees are charred but still living. As you proceed, you will notice that most of the forest was consumed by the blaze, and this ghost forest of blackened poles lends an eerie feeling to the landscape. Most of the trees that succumbed to the blaze were thin-barked lodgepole pines, while the thicker-barked white firs and Jeffrey pines survived.

After .6 mile from the last junction you cross a small stream then skirt the sandy lakeshore before climbing above a steep, rocky shoreline. Blackened trees frame good views across the lake to red-topped Ash Butte and the prominent cone of Mt. Hoffman.

You reach the head of the lake opposite the lava beds 1.5 miles from the last junction. Charred forest will accompany you for the following .75 mile as you skirt the lava flow, composed of a jumble of jagged, red, grey, and black basalt boulders, barren of vegetation save for a few spindly pines.

Presently flanked by intact forest, the trail dips in and out of a small depression, then descends gently over grey sand hills sparsely forested with lodgepole pines. Soon, bulky Cinder Cone fills your view as the trail drops into another, deeper depression. The trail is now quite sandy, and thus progress is much slower.

After strolling 1.75 miles from Snag Lake, a trail joins your route on the left, entering on a slightly higher contour. A sign here advises you to stay on the trail to avoid tracking the cinder fields. Avoiding the visual affect of your passing is a good practice in minimizing your impact on the backcountry.

Bearing right at the junction, your trail begins climbing the cinder fields opposite the colorful Painted Dunes. With a view of prominent Cinder Cone ahead of you and snow-streaked Lassen Peak behind, you reach an unsigned junction after .3 mile. Hikers can either turn right to climb the steep southern slopes of Cinder Cone, its summit offering exceptional views over the Fantastic Lava Beds, Painted Dunes, and much of the route you have travelled thus far, or bear left, climbing .25 mile to the wide track of Nobles Emigrant Trail.

A fine panorama unfolds upon reaching that trail, stretching across the lava beds to Red Cinder Cone, Mt. Hoffman, Mt. Harkness, and Fairfield Peak. Turning right onto Nobles Trail, you climb easily toward a low saddle, flanked on the left by Jeffrey pine forest, and on the right by the smooth, nearly barren slopes of Cinder Cone. Ochre-flowered buckwheat is the only plant seen growing on the cinder fields along the edge of the trail, its yellow blooms brightening the landscape during August.

A .25 mile stroll along the trail leads to a junction with a trail climbing out of the cinder cones fields below. Staying to the left, you proceed through the long saddle at the forest's edge, and here a profusion of round black boulders litters trailside slopes. Known to geologists as volcanic bombs, these rocks were ejected in a molten state, probably from the main crater atop Cinder Cone.

Descending northeast from the saddle, you reach a junction with the trail that climbs .5 mile to Cinder Cone's summit, .4 mile from the previous junction.

Bearing left at that juncture your trail descends into a forest of large Jeffrey pines, from which fine views over the lava beds and Painted Dunes are briefly enjoyed. Soon thereafter, the trail once again skirts the edge of the lava flow amid pine forest, reaching the left-branching trail to Prospect Peak after another 1.25 miles.

Prospect Peak, 2.8 miles distant and 2,000 feet above, offers a commanding view and is a worthwhile side trip if time and energy allow.

Continuing ahead, you quite soon reach a signed spur trail leading 100 yards to the edge of the lava, from which issues trickling Cold Spring. The remainder of the hike continues along the edge of the lava beds, soon passing below the campground. You should avoid the use trails leading up to it. Reaching the road end near the ranger station, .3 mile from the Prospect Peak Trail, follow it uphill for the final .2 mile to the parking area.

HIKE 91 *TAMARACK TRAILHEAD TO EVERETT AND MAGEE LAKES*

General description: A moderate 12.9-mile semi-loop backpack comprising a grand tour of the best of the Thousand Lakes Wilderness, one of the few wild areas in California's southern Cascade Range.
Elevation gain and loss: 1,485 feet.
Trailhead elevation: 5,900 feet.
High point: Magee Lake, 7,215 feet.
Maps: Manzanita Lake 15-minute USGS quad (road to trailhead not shown on quad), Lassen National Forest map.
Season: Late June through early October.
Finding the trailhead: From State Highway 89 in the Hat Creek Valley, turn west onto a dirt forest road signed for "1000 Lakes Wilderness." This easy-to-miss turnoff is fourteen miles south of State Highway 299 and four miles south of the Hat Creek Work Center (USFS); it is also seven miles north of Old Station and the junction with eastbound State Highway 44. The turnoff is .1 mile north of the signed Wilcox Road.

Proceed generally west on this good dirt road, which is quite steep at first. After .8 mile, you reach a three-way junction; take either of the two left forks which rejoin ahead quite soon. Follow signs labeled "Wilderness" at major junctions, and avoid several spur roads, many unsigned. Follow the "main" road—the one that appears much more used than others—at unsigned junctions. The only truly confusing unsigned junction is 4.1 miles from the highway, where two well-graded roads branch right from the "main" road, one leading west and the other south; bear left here.

After driving 5.6 miles from the highway, turn right (west) where a sign points to the trailhead. This road is steep and rocky and immediately becomes very rough. After .3 mile you reach a point where large rocks begin to protrude from the roadbed, and all but four-wheel drive and high-clearance vehicles will have to park here, where there is room for at least five cars. Parking here will add a total of 2.4 miles and 180 feet of elevation gain and loss to the hike.

Above that rocky area, the road levels off but continues to be quite rough for the remaining 1.2 miles to the trailhead.

The hike: This interesting semi-loop hike leads through hushed forests, past four major wilderness lakes, and ends in an impressive cirque surrounded by near-vertical cliffs and alpine peaks.

The central feature of the Thousand Lakes Wilderness is a large lake-dotted bowl, glacially excavated from the north slopes of Magee Peak, an andesite volcano.

For hikers on the summit of Lassen Peak, Magee Peak and its satellite summits appear unimpressive—simply another sloping, steep-sided features so typical of the southern Cascade Range. However, only the north slopes of the mountain were glaciated, and the hiker who ascends the steep trail to Magee Peak's 8,550-foot summit can experience these contrasting perspectives firsthand.

Except during the spring snow-melt period, the only water available in the area comes directly from the lakes. Thus, pack all the water you will need or plan on purifying any that you obtain in the wilderness.

Mule deer are quite common in the area.

From the trailhead on the eastern boundary of the Thousand Lakes Wilderness, head west past an information sign and enter a red fir, white fir, and Jeffrey pine forest. As you begin ascending just north of Hill 6300, you enter a dense stand of white fir. After leveling off, the trail skirts the edge of a lava flow, the forest thins, and manzanita and tobacco brush begin to invade sunny openings.

After a brief climb, you reach a ridgetop junction just south of invisible Eiler Butte. The right fork is the homebound segment of the hike.

Bearing left, you descend and enter the Thousand Lakes Valley under a canopy of lodgepole and Jeffrey pine, red fir, and white fir.

Ancient glaciers carved a huge bowl out of the north slope of volcanic Magee Peak. Today this lake-dotted bowl forms Thousand Lakes Valley, the destination of most hikes into the Thousand Lakes Wilderness in the southern Cascade Range.

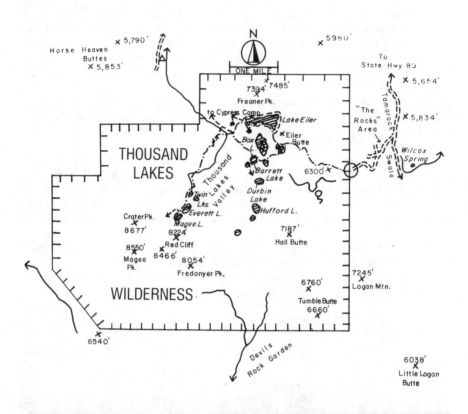

Proceeding southwest, nearly on the level in a forest becoming increasingly dominated by lodgepole pines you pass north of a shallow pond before skirting the north shore of Barrett Lake. Spying the high summits of Crater Peak, Magee Peak, and Red Cliff soaring skyward at the head of Thousand Lakes Valley, you presently stroll around the west shore of this shallow lake, soon reaching a junction with a southbound trail leading to Durbin Lake and beyond.

Turning right, you amble .8 mile northwest to reach a four- way junction. The right fork leads northeast to Lake Eiler, and after exploring the lakes at the head of Thousand Lakes Valley, you will return to this junction and hike past Lake Eiler on the way back to the trailhead.

The middle fork at this junction leads northwest to a trailhead at Cypress Campground.

You take the left fork, signed for Everett and Magee lakes. You soon cross a bone-dry streambed (which flows only during the early runoff season) draining the upper lakes, and quickly meet another right-branching trail leading to Cypress Campground.

Bearing left, you begin a series of switchbacks ascending a shady northfacing slope. As you gain elevation, brushy Freaner Peak comes into view, the northern sentinel of the wilderness. The massive andesite volcano of Burney Mountain meets your gaze in the northwest, and beyond rises the bold, snowy cone of Mt. Shasta.

After the trail levels off in a sparse pine and fir forest, you cross the same bone-dry streambed encountered 1.5 miles below. Notice the mountain hemlock joining the sub-alpine forest.

After a brief climb, the trail passes small, shallow Upper Twin Lake, spectacular with its backdrop of precipitous Red Cliff crags. These cliffs are largely gray, but streaked with the red volcanic rock (rich in iron) that gave the mountain its name.

Presently in a sub-alpine forest of silver and lodgepole pine, red fir, and mountain hemlock, you wind your way up to beautiful Everett Lake, where fishing is good for pan-sized trout. Behind the lake rises majestic Red Cliff and the impressive glacial cirque at the head of Thousand Lakes Valley. Campsites are numerous around the shores of this fine sub-alpine lake.

A short jaunt beyond Everett Lake brings you to a junction with the right branching trail leading to Magee Peak. The left fork proceeds around the shores of Magee Lake, the highest lake in the wilderness. Lying at the very foot of Red Cliff, this lake has numerous excellent campsites shaded by red fir, mountain hemlock, and silver and lodgepole pine; and like Everett Lake, it is deep enough to support a healthy population of pan-sized trout. Most of the campsites around the west shore of the lake are too close to the water, however, and should not be used.

From Magee Lake, retrace your route for three miles to the above-mentioned four-way junction, this time taking the middle (northeast) fork to Lake Eiler. After .5 mile of very gentle descent, you reach the west end of 6403-foot-high Lake Eiler, lying at the foot of Freaner Peak's volcanic slopes. Turn right here and walk around the south shore of the largest lake in the wilderness. Campsites are numerous and trout fishing is good.

After hiking a mile around the lake, you reach a junction at its southeast end—turn right. Quickly topping a short, steep rise, the trail levels off and passes a few ponds in various stages of transition from lake to meadow. After walking .5 mile from Lake Eiler, you rejoin the initial segment of the hike, turn left, and backtrack 1.6 miles to the trailhead.

HIKE 92 NORTH YOLLA BOLLY MOUNTAINS LOOP

General description: A moderately strenuous 11.3-mile loop day hike or backpack, involving some moderate cross-country travel, touring the high country of the northern Yolla Bolly-Middle Eel Wilderness.
Elevation gain and loss: 2,700 feet.
Trailhead elevation: 6,000 feet.
High point: 7,700 feet.
Maps: Yolla Bolly 15-minute USGS quad (road to trailhead and most of trail not shown on quad), Shasta-Trinity National Forest map.
Season: Late June through mid-October.
Finding the trailhead: From Red Bluff, follow State Highway 36 west for thirty-eight miles, then turn left (southwest) onto signed Tedoc Road, Forest Road 45. Or from Eureka, drive south on U.S. 101 for twenty-two miles then proceed east on State Highway 36 for ninety-six miles to the Tedoc Road. This turnoff is about 9.6 miles east of the Harrison Gulch Ranger Station, where wilderness permits can be obtained.

Follow this road, mostly dirt with remnant sections of oiled surface, for 12.2 miles to a multi-signed junction at Tedoc Gap. Turn right here; a sign indicates that Stuart Gap is seven miles ahead. Bear left in less than .25 mile where the signed right hand road heads toward Stuart Gap.

Continuing on Forest Road 45, avoid several signed spur roads as you proceed. After driving 5.3 miles from Tedoc Gap, you reach a multi-branched road junction and the signed trailhead at Rat Trap Gap.

The hike: The North Coast Ranges, bounded by the Pacific Ocean on the west and the Sacramento Valley on the east, march northward from the San Francisco Bay region to their confluence with the Klamath Mountains in northwestern California. The Mendocino Range is one of many independent ranges that comprise this mountain complex. It is the highest of the North Coast Ranges, reaching above 8,000 feet in the South Yolla Bolly Mountains.

The northward location of the Mendocino Range and its proximity to the coast gives rise to considerable precipitation that nurtures healthy conifer forests.

Its western flanks drain the Middle Fork Eel River, and eastside streams eventually empty their waters into the Sacramento, California's mightiest river.

The unusual name Yolla Bolly is derived from the language of Wintun Indians, and means "snow-covered high peak."

The Yolla Bolly-Middle Eel Wilderness lies near the northern terminus of the Mendocino Range high country. Only the highest peaks in the area ever hosted glaciers. Although quite small, they were nevertheless able to excavate small basins that add to the attraction of the area. Some of the finest examples of this minor glaciation can be seen in the vicinity of the North Yolla Bolly Mountains.

The highest peaks in the wilderness stand at or just above timberline. The remainder of the region is characterized by ridges and canyons covered with thick conifer forest.

Many trails in the area are faint, owing to light use by backcountry enthusiasts. Here in this highly scenic area, hikers can roam for days and are likely to see few other hikers.

Water can be scarce in the summer, and hikers are often forced into canyon bottoms or must rely on the numerous springs emanating from the slopes of the highest peaks.

A wilderness permit is required.

The trail heads south from Rat Trap Gap, very soon passing the homebound segment of your loop on the right. The route then climbs moderately steeply under a shady canopy of Douglas-fir, red fir, and white fir.

You soon negotiate a few elevation-gaining switchbacks and pass just above a reliable spring after leaving the last Douglas-firs behind.

Another moderately steep ascent follows, bringing you to a small creek draining the area labeled Barker Camp on the quad. Campsites can be located here, and this is the last reliable water source until Pettijohn Basin, more than 4.5 miles ahead.

Beyond Barker Camp, you enter the Yolla Bolly-Middle Eel Wilderness at a Shasta-Trinity National Forest sign, and just beyond that sign, an opening in the forest allows hikers to view the Sacramento Valley and Lassen Peak in the east. Soon thereafter, you reach a junction on a major east-west ridge at the 7,027-foot level. Hikers not wishing to tackle the partially cross-country route ahead can take the left fork that contours along south-facing slopes below the North Yolla Bolly Mountains, rejoining the main route on the saddle just east of Black Rock Mountain.

Most hikers, however, will turn right onto the faint North Yolla Bolly Trail.

This route heads west through a corridor in the red fir forest and soon breaks into the open on grassy, south-facing slopes interrupted by scattered stands of stunted red fir. On these open slopes, you are treated to unobstructed southward views into the heavily forested interior of the Yolla Bolly-Middle Eel Wilderness. The trail is often faint on these grassy slopes, where lupine and pussy paws add color during mid-summer.

A rewarding hike over the North Yolla Bolly Mountains delivers solitude and challenge in the seldom-visited Yolla Bolly-Middle Eel Wilderness in northern California.

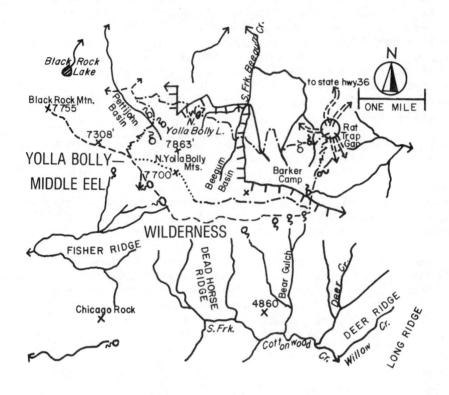

Your trail briefly re-enters a red fir stand. Beyond that, you may notice some foxtail pines joining the sparse forest just southwest of Peak 7531.

Your ridgecrest route presently passes above the glaciated valley of Beegum Basin. Soon the trail disappears altogether, and you continue your grassy, ridgeline jaunt where occasional ducks (piles of stones used as markers) help guide you.

Vistas improve as you progress, soon including the Sacramento Valley, Mt. Shasta, and the glacier-clad peaks of the Trinity Alps. Lassen Peak meets your gaze in the east, and south of it the west slope of the Sierra Nevada fades away into the distant haze. In the southeast across the deep, forested canyon of South Fork Cottonwood Creek, the South Yolla Bolly Mountains rise to their highest point at 8,092-foot-high Mt. Linn. And in the west, heavily forested ridges of the North Coast Ranges march off toward the distant, invisible Pacific Ocean.

Your trail briefly re-appears long enough to get you into a stand of foxtail pines just east of the south summit of the North Yolla Bolly Mountains before disappearing for good.

The foxtail pine is endemic to California. It is found in two general areas separated by more than 300 miles. The southern population occurs from the high elevations surrounding the Kern River drainage north into Kings Canyon National Park, where it often forms extensive timberline forests. The northern population occurs here in the Yolla Bolly Mountains, in the Marble Mountains, and in the Trinity Alps-Scott Mountains area, where it most often occurs in mixed stands with other conifers at high elevations.

From the foxtail pine stand, scramble a short distance west to the rocky high point of the south summit of the North Yolla Bolly Mountains, Peak 7700. The north summit, Peak 7863, lies due north, separated from the south peak by a low gap, and is an easy .3-mile cross-country jaunt. Vistas here from the south peak are excellent—from this vantage point, the Trinity Alps are especially striking.

To the northwest rises the summit of 7,755-foot-high Black Rock Mountain, crowned by a lookout tower and separated from the south peak by a low saddle. You presently head for that saddle, first scrambling down steep and often-loose rock west of the south peak. Once that obstacle is behind you the going is easier, although you are still forced to go over or around some rocky sections on the ridge.

Upon reaching the saddle after less than a mile, you can continue west up the ridge via a faint trail to Black Rock Mountain for more boundless vistas, or you can turn right and descend a series of switchbacks into Pettijohn Basin.

As you descend, you will notice the black crag of the north peak of the North Yolla Bolly Mountains soaring impressively above the basin. You soon pass several springs forming the headwaters of the East Fork of South Fork Trinity River, then jog northwest and begin traversing high above meadow-floored Pettijohn Basin, where secluded campsites can be located. You then splash through the runoff of several cold, reliable, cattle-trampled springs, and within .25 mile you should begin watching for an unmarked right-branching trail. When you locate this trail, turn right. From this point, you can see impressive Black Rock Mountain and its associated cliffs rising above Pettijohn Basin in the west.

After turning right, proceed east through fir forest while steadily ascending to the ridge above the deep, cliff-bound cirque containing North Yolla Bolly Lake. From this ridge you have an unobstructed view east to the Sacramento Valley and the west slopes of the Sierra Nevada.

You presently negotiate numerous switchbacks before leveling off and reaching the lake. This small, fishable lake, with a backdrop of precipitous 700-foot-high cliffs, makes an excellent rest spot or campsite, although the latter may be somewhat scarce in the red fir and white fir forest.

The trail traverses to the east side of the lake, crosses its seasonal outlet, and descends into another small basin lying below a group of striking black pinnacles.

As you continue through that basin, you will notice the presence of silver pines and a few sugar pines—if you fail to notice the trees themselves, you will at least notice their large cones littering the ground.

Your route soon curves south to reach a hop-across fork of South Fork Beegum Creek. A cross-country scramble up the course of this creek leads to rarely-visited Beegum Basin and isolated camping in the shadow of the North Yolla Bolly Mountains.

Beyond that crossing, Douglas-fir joins the forest consisting mostly of red fir and white fir as you contour along north-facing slopes toward another small creek. You then pass a spring issuing from beneath a large boulder, cross another small creek, and soon reach the initial leg of your loop, where you turn left and stroll back to the trailhead.

HIKE 93 *LIGHTNING TRAILHEAD TO KINGS PEAK*

General description: A moderate 5.75-mile round-trip day hike or overnighter leading to a remote Coast Range peak towering above northern California's Lost Coast, in the King Range National Conservation Area (administered by BLM).
Elevation gain and loss: 2,053 feet; -150 feet.
Trailhead elevation: 2,184 feet.
High point: Kings Peak, 4,087 feet.
Maps: Honeydew and Shubrick Peak 7.5-minute USGS quads; or King Range National Conservation Area BLM map (topographic).
Season: April through October.
Finding the trailhead: Follow U.S. Highway 101 either 63 miles south from Eureka, or 91 miles north from Ukiah to the Redway exit. Proceed into the small town of Redway and turn west onto the Briceland Road, heading toward Briceland and Shelter Cove. After a long mile from Redway you bridge the Eel River and proceed through the Whittemore Grove of redwoods.

Pass through the small town of Briceland 5.7 miles from Redway, and after another 4.2 miles, avoid a right turn signed for Honeydew and Petrolia. Ignore a signed left turn to Whitethorn 12 miles from Redway, and continue along the steep and winding paved road, avoiding the signed left-branching road leading to Nadelos and Wailaki campgrounds 17.1 miles from Redway.

Presently the road climbs to another ridge, and just before attaining the summit, avoid a left-forking paved road. At the summit, the paved road continues ahead for four miles to Shelter Cove, but hikers should turn right onto a dirt road, indicated by a large BLM sign. Almost at once avoid a paved road that forks right, instead follow the steep, narrow, and winding dirt road northwest, passing the entrances to Tolkan Campground after 3.7 miles, and Horse Mountain Campground after 6.4 miles. Be sure to avoid an unsigned, left-branching dirt road .1 mile before reaching Horse Mountain Camp.

After 9.3 miles from the pavement, or 26.8 miles from Redway, you will reach a prominently signed junction. Turn left here on to King Range Road. This wide and smooth dirt road is a noticeable improvement from the past 9.3 miles. Stay to the right where a signed spur forks off to the Saddle Mountain Road after two miles, then curve into and out of several drainages to the signed Lightning Trailhead after 6.4 miles. Parking space is available for several cars just north of the trailhead.

The hike: The Coast Ranges of California typically thrust abruptly skyward from the shores of the Pacific Ocean making them seem much higher than their modest elevations would suggest. One such mountain chain, the King Range, located along northern California's coast, boasts the greatest relief in the shortest distance of all the state's Coast Ranges. Its chaparral-clad slopes soar from the ocean's edge to more than 4,000 feet in a lateral distance of only three miles.

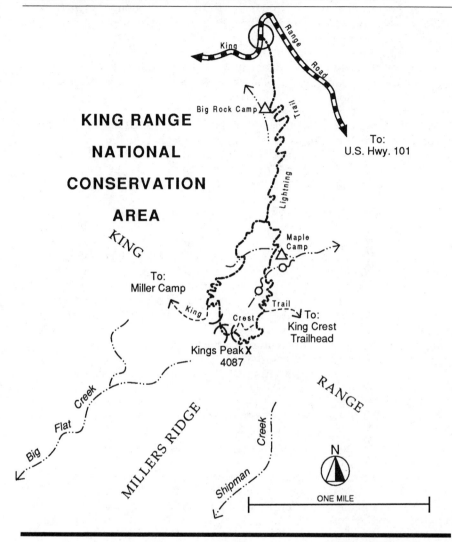

Despite the dry appearance of the brush-clad seaward slopes of the range, this region is one the wettest in the continental U.S. The small hamlet of Honeydew in the Mattole River valley northwest of Kings Peak, averages 100 inches of moisture annually. November through March brings heavy rains to this region, while in summer, fog blankets the coastline.

The shoreline beneath the King Range is known as the Lost Coast, the wildest and most remote coastal strip remaining in California. The Lost Creek Trail is a superb hiking route along this coastline, stretching more than 50 miles from the mouth of the Mattole River in the north to Usal Creek in the south. Much of this trail passes over public lands administered by the Bureau of Land Management and Sinkyone Wilderness State Park.

This hike follows the Lightning Trail, a steadily climbing spur to the 16 mile long King Crest Trail, which you follow to the apex of the Kings Range. Enroute, the hiker passes through coastal forests of Douglas-fir, madrone, and tanbark-oak, and coastal chaparral. Two delightful trail camps along the way invite hikers to stay overnight. Despite the elevation gain, the trail is wide and smooth, making the hike a fine outing for almost any hiker.

From the crest of the King Range, vistas of much of the Lost Coast, and access to an extensive trail system in the BLM's 60,000-acre King Range National Conservation Area, and the 6,000-acre Sinkyone Wilderness State Park south of Shelter Cove, will likely give hikers ample incentive for planning future hiking vacations in this remote coastal region.

From the destination and mileage sign at the trailhead, the smooth tread of the Lightning Trail climbs quickly past a register box, then switchbacks at a moderate grade to a ridgeline. Climbing steadily southward, salal soon joins the understory, and after .75 mile you meet a signed spur trail branching right to Big Rock Camp. There is only one campsite here, just a few feet off the main trail, next to a small stream.

Beyond the trail camp, hikers will enjoy occasional tree-framed views to the rolling hills of the lower Mattole River Valley to the northwest, and eastward over the vast forested hills of the North Coast Ranges, as they switchback steadily for one mile among stately Douglas-firs to a signed junction. Here trails fork right and left, both leading to Kings Peak and forming a pleasant loop.

Maple Camp lies along the left-branching trail which descends for 150 feet from the junction. Once the trail begins to rise you enter Douglas-fir forest, soon reaching signed Maple Camp, two miles from the trailhead. Backpackers will find seven campsites carved into the steep trailside slopes. A spring issues from the draw just below the camp. This spot is a fine choice for an overnight stay, and it lies close enough to Kings Peak that hikers can scale the summit after dinner and enjoy a memorable sunset over the ocean. Be sure to bring a flashlight for the return trip.

Beyond Maple Camp, the trail climbs up the draw before leaving it to ascend brush-clad slopes, gaining the shoulder of a minor ridge after .5 mile. The trail then winds for .1 mile, reaching the crest of the King Range and a junction with its namesake trail.

A .1 mile traverse across slopes thick with manzanita and scrub oak brings you to another junction. The crest trail continues the traverse, but to reach the peak you must take the left fork, which climbs steeply and is noticeably rougher than previously hiked trails. Just below the peak another trail branches right, leading back down to the King Crest Trail. You will use that trail for your return trip. First climb the final few feet to the summit, passing a crude shelter just below the high point, .4 mile from the King Crest Trail.

The far-reaching vistas from Kings Peak are breathtaking, encompassing mountains, forest, valleys, and the ocean. Hikers can reach that stretch of Lost Coast beneath the King Crest Trail by following the crest trail and the Smith-Etter Road northwestward to Telegraph Peak, and thence down the steep trail to the ocean, ten miles distant. (Consult the BLM's King Range NCA map.)

Eventually hikers must abandon the memorable vistas and begin the trek back to the trailhead. First descend to the aforementioned trail and turn left, switchbacking through brush for .1 mile to the juncture with the King Crest Trail, where you bear left once again. Presently the King Crest Trail drops slightly to another saddle before climbing the east slopes of a minor summit. It then switchbacks steadily downhill to another junction .6 mile from the peak. You should bear right here to the end of the loop at the juncture with the trail to Maple Camp after .4 mile. From here turn left and retrace your steps for 1.75 miles to the trailhead.

HIKE 94 *CANYON CREEK LAKES*

General description: A 16.2-mile round-trip backpack into the heart of northern California's majestic Trinity Alps, in the Trinity Alps Wilderness.
Elevation gain and loss: 2,606 feet.
Trailhead elevation: 3,000 feet.
High point: Lower Canyon Creek Lake, 5,606 feet.
Maps: Helena 15-minute USGS quad, Trinity Alps Wilderness map (topographic).
Season: Mid-June through mid-October.
Finding the trailhead: From State Highway 299 in Junction City, eight miles west of Weaverville and ninety-five miles east of Arcata, turn north onto the unsigned Canyon Creek Road. This turnoff lies .3 mile west of the Junction City Forest Service Guard Station (where wilderness permits can be obtained) and just east of the Canyon Creek bridge on State Highway 299.

Proceed north on the paved Canyon Creek Road, (County Road 401), bearing right after 1.9 miles where a westbound shortcut road to State Highway 299 joins your road on the left. Continuing up the Canyon Creek Road, avoid a left-branching road after another eight miles. The road turns to dirt after another 2.3 miles, just beyond the Ripstein Campground, and continues .8 mile to the large parking area at the trailhead.

The hike: Characterized by precipitous granite peaks and numerous lake-filled glacial basins, the Trinity Alps Wilderness includes portions of the Salmon and Scott mountain ranges. Along with the Marble and Siskiyou mountains, these rugged ranges in the northwest corner of California are known collectively as the Klamath Mountains.

The dominating feature of this wild area is the Trinity Alps, a cluster of high, jagged peaks whose flanks host numerous permanent snowfields and small glaciers. The highest peak in the region, 9,002-foot-high Thompson Peak, forms the centerpiece of the Trinity Alps.

Canyon Creek, a major drainage originating from several alpine snowfields in the heart of the Trinity Alps, tumbles southward for seventeen miles through a remarkably straight canyon to contribute its waters to the Trinity River.

Although well-used, this hike takes you into one of the most awe-inspiring regions of northwestern California, where blazing white granite peaks soar skyward from glacier-carved, sub-alpine lake basins.

Trout fishing is unpredictable in the lakes but is usually productive along Canyon Creek below the lakes.

Campsites are scarce at the lakes. It is best to pitch camp on one of the benches below the lakes and make day-hiking excursions into upper reaches of the basin.

Although the lower portion of the canyon can be quite hot during the summer, the upper canyon is cooled by the downslope movement of air from high peaks in the evening.

Water is easy to find except during the first four miles of the hike.

A wilderness permit is required.

From the east side of the loop at the roadend, the trail leads briefly eastward, then curves north as you part company with those hiking the Bear Creek Trail.

The northeast-bound trail leads you through a shady forest of ponderosa pine, incense-cedar, and Douglas-fir. To your west, a high ridge soars more than 4,000 feet above the canyon floor.

The almost-level trail soon bends into Bear Creek, which you boulder-hop beneath the shade of Pacific dogwood and big-leaf maple. The trail then jogs west for a traverse above Bear Creek, then leads above Canyon Creek after it jogs north once again.

Among the many outstanding features of the Trinity Alps is the rare weeping spruce, a tree found only in isolated locations in northwestern California and southwestern Oregon. This specimen is at Lower Canyon Creek lake. Photo by John Rihs.

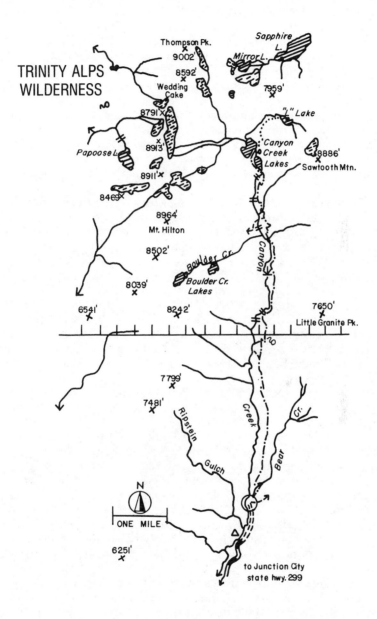

TRINITY ALPS
WILDERNESS

Thompson Pk.
✕ 9002'

Sapphire L.

Mirror L.

8592'
✕
Wedding
Cake

7959'

8791 ✕

"L" Lake

Canyon
Creek
Lakes

8886'
✕
Sawtooth Mtn.

Papoose L.

8913'
✕

8911'✕

8469✕

8964'
✕
Mt. Hilton

8502'
✕

Boulder Cr.

Canyon

8039'
✕

Boulder Cr.
Lakes

6541'
✕

8242'
✕

7650'
✕
Little Granite Pk.

7799'
✕

7481'
✕

Ripstein

Creek

Bear Cr.

Gulch

N

ONE MILE

625l'
✕

to Junction City
state hwy. 299

You presently begin a protracted northward course high on the east wall of the canyon in an oak-dominated forest mixed with some madrone, Douglas-fir, and ponderosa pine.

After eventually leaving most of the oaks behind, you are treated to occasional views up the canyon toward impressive granite crags and pinnacle-ridden ridges towering thousands of feet above.

Part-way up the canyon, you will be hiking through a mixed conifer forest consisting of white fir, incense-cedar, ponderosa pine, and Douglas-fir.

After hiking three miles, you pass a left-forking trail leading down to fair campsites along Canyon Creek in an area known as The Sinks.

You soon negotiate two switchbacks while splashing through the runoff of a cold, reliable spring.

Above the spring, you get a glimpse of lower Canyon Creek Falls, but your attention is quickly diverted to the striking mass of pinnacles that comprise 8,886-foot-high Sawtooth Mountain near the head of the canyon.

The canyon above the falls has the typical U-shape of a glacially excavated canyon, distinguishable from the V-shaped profile of the stream-carved lower canyon.

Your trail soon approaches Canyon Creek below the upper cascade of Canyon Creek Falls. This upper falls plunges over a low granite ledge into a deep, green pool, an excellent spot for a cool dip on a hot summer afternoon.

You then begin hiking next to the wide creek, soon passing the first, rare weeping spruce. These interesting trees are similar to Douglas-firs but have drooping branchlets and bark similar to that of the familiar lodgepole pine.

Weeping spruces are fairly common above the lakes.

The trail becomes hemmed in by tall ferns as you stroll along the eastern margin of lush Upper Canyon Creek Meadows, passing lateral trails leading to numerous good campsites.

After hiking just over a mile from the meadows, you pass a left-branching fork which leads to the Boulder Creek Lakes. Good campsites are located on this conifer-clad bench.

The trail climbs briefly to another bench just below the lakes. Because camping is limited at the spectacular Canyon Creek Lakes, the best choice for camping is on one of these benches.

The Canyon Creek Lakes are encircled with awe-inspiring white granite peaks dotted with numerous permanent snowfields. Scattered stands of red fir, Jeffrey pine, and weeping spruce cling to the slopes around these lakes. Fishing is fair to good at the lakes, especially in early summer and early autumn, for rainbow, brown, and eastern brook trout.

A recommended side-trip to the highest lake in the basin, "L" Lake at an elevation of 6,529 feet, is a worthwhile excursion. Although campsites may be difficult to locate around this high lake, the views obtained during the cross-country climb above upper Canyon Creek Lake are superb. One can gaze across the beautiful Canyon Creek Lakes to the rockbound upper basin of Canyon Creek. Several peaks approaching the 9,000-foot level are visible, as well as Thompson Peak; and the numerous permanent snowfields clinging to the sheltered flanks of these alpine crags combine to make this area reminiscent of the High Sierra.

From this magnificient area, hikers eventually retrace their route back to the trailhead.

HIKE 95 *LONG GULCH TO TRAIL GULCH LOOP*

General description: A moderate nine to 9.8 mile loop, suitable as a day hike or backpack, visiting two subalpine lakes nestled under the crest of the Salmon Mountains in northwestern California's Trinity Alps Wilderness.

Elevation gain and loss: 2,395 feet.

Trailhead elevation: 5,600 feet.

High point: 7,440 feet.

Maps: Coffee Creek 15-minute USGS quad (part of the trail not shown on quad); Trinity Alps Wilderness map (topographic).

Season: July through September.

Finding the trailhead Follow State Highway 3 to the small town of Callahan on the Scott River, fifty-eight miles north of Weaverville and fourty-five mile south of Yreka. Hikers can also reach Callahan from Interstate 5, taking the Edgewood-Gazelle exit 3.5 miles north of Weed, just north of the bridge over the Shasta River. Proceed west from the freeway, following signs to Gazelle, located 7.5 miles northwest of I-5.

Turn left (west) in the small town of Gazelle where a sign points to Callahan and Scott Valley. Follow the winding Gazelle-Callahan Road over the mountains for 26.5 miles to Callahan. Hikers who have not yet obtained their wilderness permit may do so (on weekdays) at the Callahan Work Center (USFS).

At the north end of town, just before bridging the South Fork Scott River, turn west onto a paved road signed for Cecilville, Somes Bar, and Forks of Salmon. Follow this road as it steadily climbs for 11.6 miles to unsigned Carter Meadows Summit on the Salmon Mountains crest. Continue west for .75 mile downhill to a left-branching dirt road (Forest Road 39N08) signed for Carter Meadows Trailheads. This is a fair dirt road, narrow in places, and a rough washboard surface throughout much of its length. After 1.8 miles you will reach the Long Gulch Trailhead, just west of a streamside campsite.

The hike: West of Interstate 5 and north of State Highway 299 lies a rugged stretch of mountainous terrain known to geologists as the Klamath Mountains province. The region actually consists of several mountain ranges interconnected by high divides. Proximity to the Pacific Ocean and a climate not unlike the Pacific Northwest nurtures dense, cool forests that blanket the deep river valleys, mountain slopes, and high divides with a diversity of tree species unmatched in the state. The southern end of one such Klamath Mountains range, the Salmon Mountains, is embraced by the boundaries of the Trinity Alps Wilderness, and is the location of this memorable hike. Here the range trends east- west, and evidence of glacial excavation abounds on the range's north-facing slopes.

Contrasting cool virgin forests of fir and hemlock with craggy peaks and lake-filled basins, this fine circuit is suitable for either a day hike or a backpack of two to three days. The trail passes through two amazingly straight, north-trending U-shaped glacial valleys, visits two subalpine lakes, and crosses over the lofty crest of the Salmon Mountains where far-flung vistas reward hikers for their efforts.

Water is abundant along much of the trail, but should always be treated before drinking.

A wilderness permit is required to hike in the Trinity Alps Wilderness and can be obtained in several locations. Hikers traveling from the north can get one at ranger stations in Yreka, Fort Jones, or Etna, while those traveling from the south should stop at the Weaverville Ranger Station in that town on State Highway 299.

From the trailhead parking area just west of Long Gulch's creek, a destination and mileage sign points the way south up the long-closed logging road that serves as the initial segment of the trail. Following this corridor through white fir forest, you soon pass a small clearcut replanted with ponderosa pines. Beyond, the way is lined with a narrow thicket of young white firs, the result of natural reforestation along the disturbed roadway.

Ice-gouged cirque basins and valleys, and shady forests of hemlock and fir in the Salmon Mountains offer California hikers a slice of the Pacific Northwest that lies virtually in their "backyards."

HIKE 95 *LONG GULCH TO TRAIL GULCH LOOP*

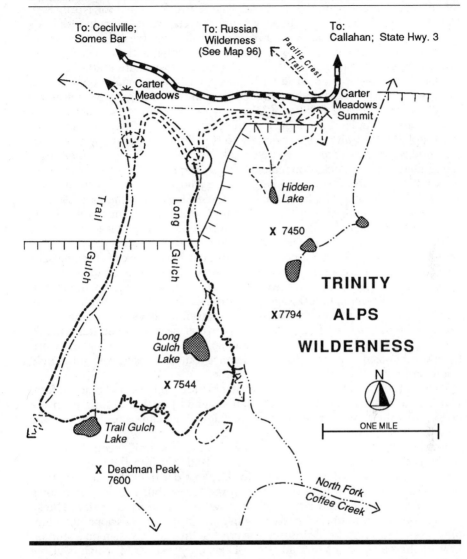

To: Cecilville; Somes Bar

To: Russian Wilderness (See Map 96)

To: Callahan; State Hwy. 3

Pacific Crest Trail

Carter Meadows

Carter Meadows Summit

Trail Gulch

Long Gulch

Hidden Lake

X 7450

TRINITY

X 7794   ALPS

WILDERNESS

N

ONE MILE

Long Gulch Lake

X 7544

Trail Gulch Lake

X Deadman Peak 7600

North Fork Coffee Creek

Alternating between gentle and moderate grades for .75 mile, a sign announces your entry into the Trinity Alps Wilderness at the northern margin of a boulder-dotted, wildflower-speckled meadow. Jagged pinnacles and the cliff-bound headwall of the Long Gulch cirque meet your gaze for the first time as you proceed through the lovely meadow, presently on a trail.

At the meadow's upper end you reach Long Gulch Creek and either hop across its shallow waters or utilize the log crossing just upstream. Beyond that crossing the trail rises through a meadow before entering a cathedral-like forest of giant white firs.

At 1.25 miles hop across another small creek then begin meandering rather steeply uphill along a rocky moraine amid small white firs, many of which have been killed by gypsy moth infestation. This ascent brings you to a signed junction 1.75 miles from the trailhead. The left fork, signed for North Fork Coffee Creek, climbs to the Salmon Mountains crest, while the right fork leads .4 mile to Long Gulch Lake. That trail leads through fir forest, crosses a small, wet meadow, and reaches the lake just beyond its small outlet creek. Pleasant, boulder-strewn red fir and white pine-shaded campsites are scattered along the lake's northwest shore. The lake is deep, clear, and usually boiling with hungry brookies and rainbows. Broken gray cliffs soaring 1,000 feet above the south shore of the 6,390-foot lake provide an exciting backdrop.

To continue the loop, walk back to the aforementioned junction and turn right, uphill. The trail rises moderately to steeply under a canopy of red firs to a muddy crossing of an alder-lined creek. As the trail becomes increasingly rocky, mountain hemlocks dominate the forest, where snow patches may linger into July. Views enroute are excellent but are enjoyed to their fullest atop the 7,000-foot crest, one mile from the Long Gulch Lake Trail junction. A short jaunt westward along the crest reveals a birds-eye view of Long Gulch Lake, and a pleasing vista of the discontinuous forest and hillside meadows on the Salmon Mountains crest to the north, beyond the headwaters canyon of the East Fork of South Fork Salmon River. Russian Peak, apex of its namesake wilderness area, is the prominent tree-covered knob in the center of your view.

The trail descends southward from the crest for about fifty yards, then forks. You should take the right fork, signed for Trail Gulch Lake. Descending gently to moderately, first south then southwest, occasional views into the vast wilderness of high peaks and deep, forested canyons, seen between tall trailside firs, help pass the time enroute. The trail splits a few times into paths worn by hikers choosing the line of least resistance, but these pathways ultimately rejoin farther on.

Upon entering a sloping meadow clad in alders, corn lilies, and bracken fern, you hop across a small creek and reach a signed junction .6 mile from the crest, along the forested margin of the meadow. Fine campsites surround the meadow, and there is water nearby.

Turning right here and re-entering the meadow, the trail becomes obscure in the grassy spread. Widely spaced ducks lead you into the southwestern lobe of the meadow where you begin to skirt an alder thicket, first west, then northwest. The trail briefly reappears in the forest, but it fades again for a short time as you ascend a sloping meadow in a westerly direction. Ducks will lead you up into the red fir forest where the trail becomes apparent, climbing steeply to your high point atop the crest of the range. A sign on a stunted trailside hemlock points to Trail Gulch Lake, only a sliver of which is visble in the basin far below.

Vistas from this point are outstanding, including the high country of the Russian Wilderness to the north, and the deep, arrow-straight trough of Trail Gulch below to the west. Granite boulders litter the crest here, one mile from the last junction, and a jaunt either north or south offers more fine vistas and a chance to scale 7,600-foot Deadman Peak, .75 mile to the south.

Presently the trail descends very steeply, switchbacking amid red fir, mountain hemlock, and white pine forest. Near the bottom of this knee-jarring descent, the trail reaches the head of a sloping, alder-choked opening, where it once again becomes obscure amid fallen trees. But with ducks to lead the way, most hikers have no trouble reaching a rock-strewn meadow that slopes down to the northeast shore of the lake. Here the trail fades entirely, but the way to the lake's north-trending outlet is obvious.

After hopping across the outlet stream, you may see some lodgepole pines mixing with the red and white fir forest. From here, follow the trail westward along the 6,450-foot lake's shore. Rainbow and brook trout are abundant in this deep lake. You will pass several good campsites, but most are located too close to the shore. However, there are satisfactory sites nearby. Remember that you must select a campsite at least 100 feet from the lakes, trails, and streams in the Trinity Alps Wilderness.

The trail skirts the foot of a talus slope beyond the lake and hikers reach a signed junction, .5 mile from the lake's outlet and 1.5 miles from the crest. The left fork climbs to the divide, bound for Coffee Creek, but you take the right fork angling downhill. Much of the trailside terrain is sloping, but potential campsites can nevertheless be found. Hikers will notice that mosquitos are more of a nuisance in Trail Gulch than they are in Long Gulch.

You exit the wilderness 1.5 miles from the previous junction and continue descending, presently on a long-closed logging road. Another .5 mile brings you to small Trail Gulch Creek, which you step across and quickly rise to a bouldered meadow. The old road, descending once again, hugs the east side of the gulch. The Trail Gulch trailhead is .5 mile past the meadow at 5,290 feet.

To complete the circuit, turn right and stroll along the road, gaining 310 feet in .7 mile to your cars at the Long Gulch trailhead.

HIKE 96 *FOREST ROAD 39N48 TO BINGHAM LAKE*

General description: A moderate 12.1 mile round trip backpack of two or more days, following the Pacific Crest Trail along the Salmon Mountains in the Russian Wilderness.
Elevation gain and loss: 1,240 feet; -810 feet.
Trailhead elevation: 6,720 feet.
High point: 7,300 feet.
Maps: Coffee Creek and Etna 15-minute USGS quads (trail not shown on quads); Klamath National Forest map.
Season: Late June through September.
Finding the trailhead: Follow driving directions of Hike 95 to Carter Meadows Summit. The PCT crosses the highway here, heading south and northwest. A trailhead parking area lies 100 yards up the steep spur road just south of the summit (6,200 feet). Hikers choosing to begin here should add 1.1 miles and 520 feet of elevation to the hike.

Immediately west of the summit, Forest Road 39N48 forks rights, climbing. A sign here warns: Dead End Road; Not Maintained for Travel. Despite the lack of maintenance, the road remains passable even to low clearance passenger cars. It is a little rocky and rough at the start but smooths out farther on.

Turn right here and follow the switchbacking road up a forested hillside, first right, then left for .4 mile. The PCT crosses the road 75 yards short of the second switchback. After another .2 mile, the road switchbacks a third and final time. The PCT is visible just downslope to your left. Some hikers may wish to begin here, as there is parking space for about five vehicles. But this starting poing will add 320 feet of elevation gain and .7 mile to the hike.

To reach the highest starting point, continue along the presently smooth road, avoiding two rough, lesser-used spur roads farther on, one climbing steeply to the left, and the other contouring to the right. After the road exits a shady hemlock forest it almost touches the Salmon Mountains crest. Here a very short spur road forks left, where you will find parking space to accomodate five vehicles.

The hike: The small 12,000-acre Russian Wilderness embraces the high backbone of the Salmon Mountains and is separated from the Marble Mountain Wilderness to the north and the Trinity Alps Wilderness to the south by only two lightly used mountain roads. Altogether, these three wild areas protect much of the Klamath Mountains high country.

The Russian Wilderness is dominated by a relatively young body of granite intruded into much older metamorphic rocks. These two rock types are of interest to hikers primarily due to their weathering and erosional characteristics which form very different and contrasting landforms throughout the course of this hike. The initial segment of the hike passes along metamorphic-dominated terrain, where smooth but steep slopes harbor discontinuous forest, grass and wildflower-clad openings, and scree-covered hillsides. But upon entering the Russian Wilderness, hikers may believe they have just entered the Sierra Nevada, where jagged peaks, U-shaped canyons, an abundance of glacier-smoothed bedrock, and nearly two dozen lakes lie in cirque basins carved from this resistant rock.

Few hikers are disappointed by a trek along the famous Pacific Crest Trail, and this hike should be no exception. Far-ranging panoramas and long traverses near the Salmon Mountains crest offer easy access to numerous 7,000-foot peaks, and once within the Russian Wilderness side trips to a half-dozen lakes, many full of hungry trout, could keep hikers and anglers busy for several days.

One notable disadvantage typical of the PCT is lack of water. Hikers will need to carry a full day's supply to reach the lakes, where water is abundant. This wilderness is not heavily used, so solitude is the rule rather than the exception. A wilderness permit is not required.

From the ridgetop parking area, the PCT is visible just downslope to the south. But to avoid damaging fragile vegetation, restrain your urge to scramble down to it. Instead, return to the forest road and stroll 150 yards west, intercepting the PCT and turning right, or west. Rising at an easy grade, the trail parallels an upslope jeep route just south of the crest.

A variety of conifers clothes the slope at this point. Incense-cedar, Jeffrey pine, and white fir thrive on these south-faciung slopes, while red fir and mountain hemlock hug the crest and the cooler north-facing slopes just over the ridge.

Vistas are superb from the start and will accompany hikers for miles to come. Particularly notable are the U-shaped troughs of Long Gulch and Trail Gulch to the south, above which rise a host of rocky timberline summits.

The jeep route soon crosses the PCT twice, beyond which you begin a traverse beneath Peak 7,040, alternating between white fir forest and grassy openings, resplendent with wildflowers that slope away steeply into the forested canyon of the East Fork of South Fork Salmon River.

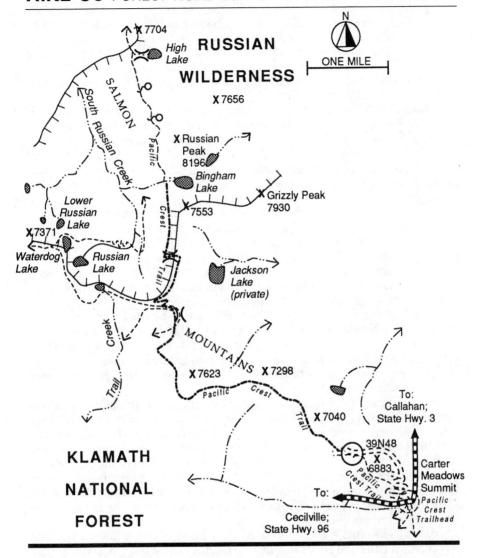

The trail undulates along the southern slopes of several 7,000-foot peaks, and as you proceed near the 7,000-foot contour, red fir joins the forest. Occasional sun-drenched openings host a variety of mountain shrubs, including manzanita, ceanothus, chinquapin, and ocean spray.

After 2.25 miles, just before the trail curves northwest around a shoulder of Peak 7,623, observant hikers may notice several foxtail pines growing among the firs a few feet upslope. The foxtail pines of the Klamath region are a subspecies of those found more than 300 miles distant in the southern Sierra (see Hike 92).

Presently the trail heads north, then west, and north again, descending steadily. Views now include the deep trench of Trail Creek, below to the west.

After 3.25 mile, a long-abandoned logging road and the PCT coalesce for fifty yards. The trail then proceeds under a canopy of red fir and mountain hemlock, crosses a gravelly slope below a grasssy saddle, then quickly climbs to another old road at 3.75 miles.

Your trail angles uphill beyond the road on a northwesterly course passing through a lovely sloping meadow just below the crest. Enroute you will cross two small, alder-lined streams, but the presence of grazing cattle makes treatment advisable before drinking.

After four miles, you reach an important junction on yet another old jeep road. Hikers have the option of turning left here to reach a half-dozen high lakes, all but one of which lie within the Russian Wilderness.

Siphon Lake, 7,250 feet, is the first lake, only .6 mile west. It is unusual in that it lies in a cirque carved into the south side of the crest rather than on the more typical north side. Hikers will find several suitable, tree-shaded campsites here.

Following the trail past the lake, hikers will reach Waterdog Lake after another 1.5 miles. That 7,000-foot lake boasts numerous fine campsites. Russian Lake, the largest in the basin, lies just over the ridge to the southeast, where the granite cliffs of Peak 7,731 soar 650 feet directly above.

A more difficult cross-country hike, mostly downhill, is required to reach the isolated Lower Russian Lakes and Golden Russian Lake, lying in the basin just over the low ridge north of Waterdog Lake.

To reach Bingham Lake, follow the PCT beyond the road, climbing northeast past a Russian Wilderness sign. The trail initially rises through firs, then switchbacks onto a grassy slope, angling uphill toward the ridge above where you pass beyond metamorphic rocks and onto granitic terrain.

Ahead the slope becomes brushy, but it is enlivened by the yellow summer blosssoms of buckwheat.

Topping out after 4.5 miles on a 7,300-foot ridge, breathtaking vistas will cause hikers to linger. Southward your gaze extends over miles of lofty Trinity Alps Wilderness summits, crowned by glacier-clad Thompson Peak, at 9,001 feet, the tallest peak in northern California's coast ranges. Looming boldly on the eastern horizon is the immense, snowy bulk of majestic Mt. Shasta.

Presently the trail descends northward across boulder- littered slopes under a shady canopy of red fir and hemlock for .5 mile to a 6,730-foot saddle beneath a low but imposing summit. The trail switchback once below the saddle before resuming a northerly course.

Soon you will cross a boulder-choked gully beneath which flows a trickling stream. Ahead, the trail bends slightly into another similar gully, but with a more vigorous flow, emanating from Bingham Lake, six miles from the trailhead.

There are two ways to reach the lake; either scrambling up this gully and alongside the flower-decked stream for .1 mile to the lake, or follow the PCT a short distance ahead to a faint, ducked route climbing steep loose slopes, a slightly longer alternative.

The deep, oblong lake harbors an abundance of pan-sized trout but campsites along the rocky, forested shore are few and must be searched for. Soaring almost 1200 feet above the lake to north is Russian Peak.

After exploring this remote and spectacular high country, backtrack to the trailhead.

General description: A moderate 9.4-mile round-trip day hike leading through a Coast Redwood forest to an inviting northern California beach, in the Prairie Creek Redwoods State Park.

Elevation gain and loss: Ninety-five feet, -245 feet.

Trailhead elevation: 155 feet.

High point: 250 feet.

Maps: Orick and Fern Canyon 7.5-minute USGS quads, Prairie Creek Redwoods State Park map.

Season: All year (avoid stormy periods).

Finding the trailhead: From U.S. 101, six miles north of Orick and thirty-four miles south of Crescent City, turn west at the signed entrance to Prairie Creek Redwoods State Park Campground and Headquarters at the north end of large Elk Prairie. A three-dollar day-use fee is charged for parking here.

Some hikers arrange to have a vehicle waiting in the parking area at the end of the hike on Davison Road. This road branches west from U.S. 101 about three miles north of Orick and leads eight miles to its end near Fern Canyon.

The hike: This leisurely hike through forests of towering Coast Redwoods and sitka spruce follows the James Irvine Trail, formerly a route to a mining camp near the Gold Bluffs. The region is characterized by heavily forested coastal mountains cut deeply by numerous streams and rivers. One of the highlights of the hike is spectacular Fern Canyon, a narrow gorge whose walls are encrusted with ferns and mosses. Beyond Fern Canyon lies Gold Bluffs Beach, and hikers with ample time will surely want to explore this rugged coastline.

One of the herds of Roosevelt Elk (wapiti) that inhabit Prairie Creek Redwoods State Park can often be seen along Gold Bluffs Beach.

Due to harvesting of Coast Redwoods on private lands, the Redwood state parks and Redwood National Park in California will soon contain the only remaining old-growth redwood forests within the original range of the species.

The Coast Redwoods (and their close relatives, the Giant Sequoias) were once widespread throughout much of the northern hemisphere. Changes in climate over several million years (a relatively recent span on the geologic time scale) have resulted in the elimination of the species from vast areas of its former range. Thus, the Coast Redwood *Sequoia sempervirens* is presently restricted to the outer Coast Ranges, from sea level to elevations of 2,000-3,000 feet, ranging from extreme southwestern Oregon discontinuously southward to Santa Cruz County, California. A few isolated groves exist as far south as Monterey County, California.

Rainfall within the range of the Coast Redwood is variable, with annual averages ranging from thirty-five inches in the south up to 100 inches in the north. The Elk Prairie area receives approximately seventy inches per year, and along the coast as much 100 inches of rain or more falls annually. The climate in Prairie Creek Redwoods State Park is cool and moist. Average temperatures vary only about fifteen degrees annually, generally remaining between forty-five and sixty degrees.

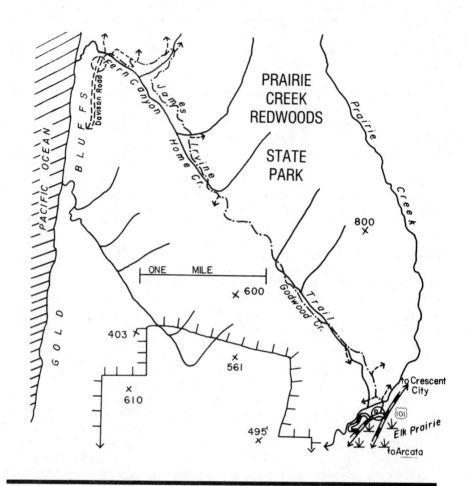

Coast Redwoods are among the tallest trees on earth. Their forests are usually quite dense, with trees often exceeding 250 feet in height. The considerable shade cast by these trees, and the deep layer of plant debris that accumulates on the forest floor, tends to reduce the number and variety of herbaceous plants in Coast Redwood forests. Most common are evergreen huckleberry, salal, rhododendron, wax-myrtle, sword fern, redwood sorrel, inside-out flower, and trillium. These species are typically found in all Coast Redwood forests, but in varying degrees of concentration depending on environmental influences.

Be sure to carry plenty of water for this hike. If you intend to backpack in Prairie Creek Redwoods State Park, contact the visitor center at the trailhead for details.

The trail begins just northeast of the visitor center at a large destination-and-mileage sign, and soon crosses Prairie Creek via a redwood bridge. This creek is the major watershed of the state park, draining about 25,000 acres, and is a productive fishery for coho and chinook salmon, steelhead, and smaller numbers of cutthroat trout. The salmon and steelhead begin their migrations from the sea to spawn in Prairie Creek in the fall. The creek is closed to fishing during the spawning season.

You reach the first of many trail junctions beyond Prairie Creek. All are well signed, so at each junction simply follow the signs indicating the James Irvine Trail and Fern Canyon.

You proceed through a forest of majestic, towering Coast Redwoods and their understory of ferns, evergreen huckleberry, and redwood sorrel. The trail ascends an almost imperceptible grade in a northwesterly direction along the course of tiny Godwood Creek.

Salal, a major understory component of Coast Redwood forests, soon joins the lush, fern-dominated understory as you progress. Cross Godwood Creek several times in the shadow of Coast Redwoods and later of a few sitka spruces. Large banana slugs are fairly abundant along the entire route, some reaching eight inches in length.

After leaving Godwood Creek behind, you continue your trek through a hushed forest of towering giants, and soon you unknowingly cross the divide into the Home Creek drainage.

Your route presently descends into Home Creek, and at a point about three miles from the trailhead, after passing a lateral trail to Cozzens Grove, the forest becomes dominated by sitka spruce, a coastal species found from this area northward along the Pacific coast into Alaska.

After bearing left where the Zone 5 Grove Trail branches right, you continue descending through sitka spruce forest accompanied by understory plants typical of Coast Redwood forests (although there are no Coast Redwoods at this point).

About .2 mile past the Zone 5 Grove Trail, you leave the James Irvine Trail and turn left, descending into Fern Canyon. You soon enter the narrow gorge of Fern Canyon, surrounded by near-vertical walls more than fifty feet high, matted with sword ferns, lady ferns, five-fingered ferns, and mosses. The continuous seepage of water from these walls helps maintain the lush vegetation. During winter and following periods of heavy rainfall, Home Creek often floods the floor of Fern Canyon, forcing hikers to wade their way through the narrow gorge.

You soon exit the red alder-shaded canyon, crossing Home Creek one last time before reaching the parking area at the end of Davison Road. From here you can plow through the alders to get to the beach about .25 mile west, or hike north to explore Gold Bluffs Beach via the Beach Trail.

Hikers who did not arrange to have a vehicle waiting here will retrace their route through primeval forest back to Elk Prairie and their cars, or choose from a variety of scenic trails to loop back to the trailhead.

HIKE 98 KELSEY RIDGE TRAIL TO BEAR LAKE, LITTLE BEAR VALLEY

General description: A moderate 6.2-mile round-trip day hike or overnighter to a remote sub-alpine lake in a seldom- visited northwestern California mountain range, in the Siskiyou Wilderness.

Elevation gain and loss: 850 feet, -800 feet.

Trailhead elevation: 4,750 feet.

High point: 5,600 feet.

Maps: Dillon Mtn. 15-minute USGS quad (road to trailhead not shown on quad), Klamath National Forest map.

Season: June through early October.

Finding the trailhead: To locate the trailhead, you must first locate Forest Road 15N19, marked by a small sign, on the west side of State Highway 96, about 49.4 miles north of Weitchpec and 10.5 miles south of Happy Camp. This hard-to-spot turnoff lies .4 mile south of the Clear Creek bridge on State Highway 96.

After locating the turnoff, proceed west on Forest Road 15N19, a good paved road, avoiding several numbered spur roads. After driving three miles, bear left onto Forest Road 15N24, staying on the pavement. Now-dirt Forest Road 15N19 continues ahead to eventually rejoin your paved road.

The pavement ends after another 3.4 miles at a four-way junction. Proceed straight ahead, taking the middle fork where a sign indicates Bear Lake and the Kelsey Trail. Head west on this good dirt road, and five miles from the end of pavement turn right where a sign indicates Bear Lake and Kelsey Trail, then climb steeply for .1 mile to the trailhead, where there is room for at least five vehicles.

The hike: The southern Siskiyou Mountains rise abruptly westward from the low hills of the North Coast Ranges to a crest of mile-high peaks before plunging eastward into the very deep canyon of the Klamath River.

The Klamath River, born in the mountains of southern Oregon, makes a long arc around the east, south, and southwest flanks of the Siskiyou Mountains, effectively delineating the boundaries of the range.

Conifer forests in the range are well developed, owing to its proximity to Pacific Ocean moisture. Several glacial lakes at rather low elevations dot the cirques that cling to the flanks of many of the peaks.

Lying far from major population centers, this little-known region sees few hikers. The vast Marble Mountain Wilderness rising eastward beyond the Klamath River is much better known and attracts the majority of hikers visiting this region.

There is no water available along the route until you reach Bear Lake.

If you intend to build a campfire, you must obtain a campfire permit, available at the ranger station in Happy Camp, or at the USFS work centers at Somes Bar or Ti Bar along State Highway 96 in the Klamath River canyon.

Your trail, an old jeep route, heads northwest from the trailhead, quickly leading you into a forest of white fir, Douglas-fir, mixed with a few incense-cedars. After a brief climb, your route promptly narrows to trail width.

After slogging through the mud below seeping Elbow Spring, you head north,

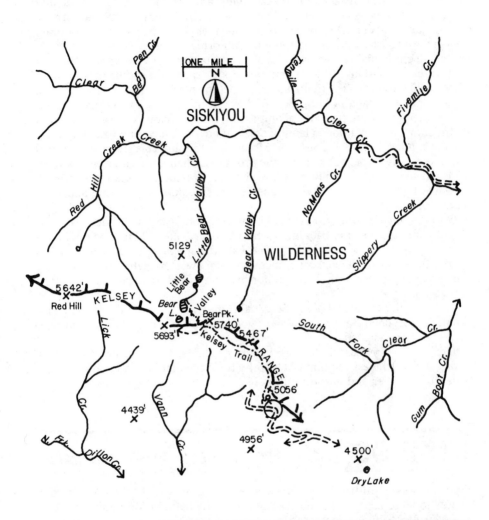

with occasional views northwest to brushy Bear Peak and west to the somewhat-rocky east slopes of the Siskiyou Mountains crest, crowned by 5,850-foot-high Harrington Mountain. Among the varied understory vegetation along this stretch of trail are deer oak, huckleberry oak, manzanita, beargrass, tobacco brush, wild rose, Oregon grape, and bracken fern. After passing above the range of incense-cedar, you may notice an occasional western white pine mixed into the forest.

The trail soon bends northwest while traversing the southwest slopes of Peak 5467, and hikers are treated to excellent vistas of the wild Siskiyou crest in the west and the glacier-clad crags of the Trinity Alps in the southeast.

You soon reach a saddle at the 5,200-foot level, immediately east of Bear Peak, and are rewarded with superb northward views. Directly below to your northeast lies meadow-bottomed Bear Valley, and beyond rises the spectacular crag of 7,309-foot-high Preston Peak, the highest summit in California's Siskiyou Mountains. On the far northeastern skyline are Siskiyou Mountain peaks rising just south of the Oregon-California border.

As you climb higher, the vast Marble Mountains meet your gaze to the east across the deep Klamath River canyon. Upon reaching a saddle west of Bear Peak, 2.25 miles from the trailhead, you meet the northwest-bound trail leading down to Bear Lake and Little Bear Valley. At this point, a truly magnificent vista emerges, even more all-encompassing than previous views. In addition to the previously-mentioned landmarks, you now see, to your north and northwest, countless impressive Siskiyou Mountain summits. This is a view reserved for hikers only. From left to right, the prominent high points include: sparsely forested and aptly-named Red Hill; Peak 5631; Prescott Mountain; Peak 5629; massive Bear Mountain; Twin Peaks; Youngs Peak; and towering above all else, Preston Peak.

Turning right at that junction and entering the Siskiyou Wilderness, you begin your steep, switchbacking descent to Bear Lake, 800 feet below in the deep cirque of Little Bear Valley. The varied but sparse tree cover consists of red fir, white fir, Douglas-fir, incense-cedar, western white pine, and the rare weeping spruce, found only in northwestern California and southwestern Oregon.

You spy lily-covered Lower Bear Lake midway during this descent and finally reach deep Bear Lake, where good campsites shaded by fir, spruce, and cedar are located.

During the dry season, there is usually no inflow to or outflow from Bear Lake. It nevertheless maintains a healthy trout population, and fishing is best in early summer and early autumn.

HIKE 99 SHACKLEFORD CREEK TO SUMMIT LAKE

General description: A moderate 11.9-mile semi-loop backpack, offering access to large lakes and good fishing under the Salmon Mountains crest in the Marble Mountain Wilderness.
Elevation gain and loss: 2,200 feet.
Trailhead elevation: 4,400 feet.
High point: 6,600 feet.
Maps: Scott Bar 15-minute USGS quad, Klamath National Forest map.
Season: July through early October.
Finding the trailhead: From Interstate 5 just south of Yreka, turn west onto State Highway 3 and drive 15.2 miles to the westbound Scott River Road, just south of Fort Jones. The Scott River Ranger Station is located at this junction, and campfire permits for open fires can be obtained there.

Proceed west on the Scott River Road for seven miles, then turn south onto the Quartz Valley Road. Follow this road south through forests and farmlands for 3.9 miles, then turn right (west) where a sign indicates Shackleford Trailhead. Proceed west on this dirt road, following signs at all major junctions indicating the Shackleford Trailhead. After seven miles of dusty travel on this often-narrow road, you reach the trailhead parking area just north of large Shackleford Creek.

If you are approaching from the west, follow State Highway 96 east for eleven miles from Seiad Valley. (Seiad Valley is 152 miles northeast of Arcata.) Then turn south onto the Scott River Road, following it 23.2 miles south, then east, to the Quartz Valley Road. Then follow the above-mentioned directions to reach the trailhead.

The hike: The Salmon and Marble mountains form a vast region of rugged grandeur in northwestern California, a region protected as the Marble Mountain Wilderness. Due to its remoteness from major population centers, backcountry trails are seldom overcrowded, thus allowing an enjoyable and satisfying wilderness experience.

Owing to the area's northerly location and proximity to Pacific Ocean moisture, timberline in the wilderness is rather low, compared with regions farther south and farther inland. Although the highest peak in the area barely exceeds 8,000 feet, there is an abundance of sub-alpine scenery.

Shackleford Creek and its headwaters presents one of the most spectacular landscapes in the Marble Mountain Wilderness. Its two large, fish-inhabited lakes, rugged cliffs and peaks, sub-alpine forests, and numerous other lakes accessible by lateral trails all combine to make this area an excellent choice for hikers with less than five days to spend in the backcountry.

Finding water is no problem on this hike.

Your trail, a closed jeep road during the first .5 mile, heads west from the parking area, and leads hikers into a forest of white fir, Douglas-fir, incense-cedar, and Jeffrey pine, staying within sight and sound of noisy Shackleford Creek. Upon reaching a large wilderness information sign, your route becomes the Shackleford Creek Trail, where you enter the Marble Mountain Wilderness.

This gentle creekside ascent continues, passing numerous possible campsites, hopping across several small streams issuing from the flanks of Red Mountain, and leading through a few small meadows whose margins are being invaded by lodgepole pines. The two-needled lodgepole pine is found in a variety of life zones. Typically, it flourishes on dry, well-drained sites within sub-alpine forests. Not requiring much oxygen, this tree tends to occur where the local soil and climatic conditions are unsatisfactory to development of other conifers. Thus, one often finds lodgepole pines invading the water-logged environs of meadows, well below their normal elevational range.

Soon after hopping across Long High Creek, you obtain a stimulating up the canyon to precipitous, rocky crags.

After hiking 2.8 miles from the trailhead, your route leaves the main fork of Shackleford Creek and begins a moderate ascent along the Summit Lake creek tributary, passing a left-branching trail leading up to Campbell lake in one mile. After another .5 mile, you pass a signed junction on your right where a northeast-bound trail leads to Calf and Long High lakes, nestled in a cirque high on the flanks of Red Mountain. Just below that junction, the trail passes

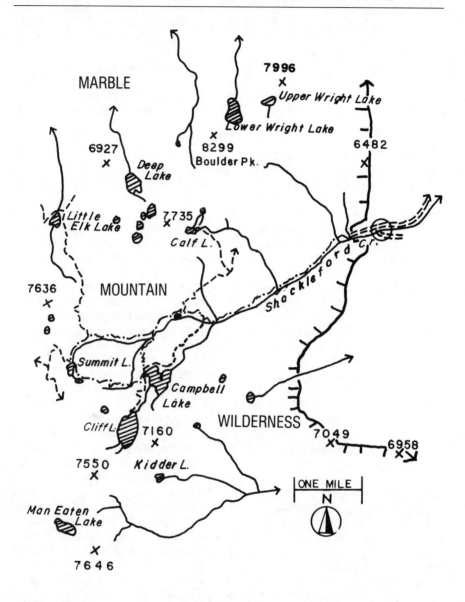

MARBLE

7996
X

Upper Wright Lake

Lower Wright Lake

6927
X

Deep
Lake

8299
X
Boulder Pk.

6482
X

Little
Elk Lake

7735
X

Calf L.

Shackleford Cr.

7636
X

MOUNTAIN

Summit L.

Campbell
Lake

WILDERNESS

7049
X

6958
XX

Cliff L.

7160
X

7550
X

Kidder L.

ONE MILE

N

Man Eaten
Lake

X
7646

between campsites on the right an aptly-named Log Lake on the left. This shallow, log-filled, pond lily-covered tarn offers good fishing for rainbow trout.

From Log Lake, the spectacular high country along the crest of the Salmon Mountains fills your southwestward gaze, and you shortly pass through the cattle-trimmed turf of a meadow infested with sneezeweed.

After hiking .6 mile from Log Lake—just before the trail crosses seasonal, multi-branched Summit Lake creek—you may not notice the return leg of your loop, which branches right and invisibly makes its way across the meadow in a westerly direction. You then cross a creek that will be swollen with runoff in early summer, often-dry by late summer, and begin a series of moderately ascending switchbacks.

After .6 mile of climbing, your trail levels off as you enter a realm of red fir and mountain hemlock, and silver and lodgepole pine, soon reaching the northwest shore of beautiful Campbell Lake. A shoreline trail soon joins on your left, and you may wish to follow that route in search of campsites. Fishing in Campbell Lake for rainbow, eastern brook, and brown trout is best in early summer and early autumn.

Bearing right at that lakeside junction, the trail curves around the west side of this fine lake and joins another trail within .2 mile. This hard-to-spot junction is indicated by an old, small sign bolted to a log. Bear right here, and after about 100 feet another log-bound sign points left to Cliff Lake.

Cliff Lake is the second largest lake in the Marble Mountain Wilderness and the deepest. Hikers who pack in a raft and fish from the middle of the lake will probably have good luck during the mid-summer slowdown, when the water has warmed and the fish retreat into the depths. Shoreline anglers will find fishing is best in early summer and early autumn for rainbow, brown, and brook trout.

Fall turnover, a common phenomenon affecting the water temperature in lakes, occurs when the water temperature cools and the colder water at the lake bottom and the warmer water near the surface circulate until the lake attains a uniform temperature throughout. At that point, the fish begin feeding in earnest. Fishing can also be productive just after the ice breaks up in late spring or early summer.

You can reach Cliff Lake by turning left at this junction and hiking .7 mile. At this popular lake and at Campbell Lake rangers advise hikers to camp no less than 200 feet from the lakeshore.

To complete the loop, bear right at the junction, soon skirting the eastern margin of a small sub-alpine meadow. You shortly meet yet another trail leading to Cliff Lake on your left. Views improve as you gain elevation, soon encompassing the precipitous, rocky crags that soar above Campbell Lake.

Your route tops a pass at the 6,600-foot level, then descends westward, soon passing just north of shallow Summit Meadow Lake, shaded by mountain hemlocks and lying at the foot of dark, 800- foot high, metamorphic cliffs.

Blue gentian and aster brighten the grassy opening below the lake, and a short jaunt beyond finds hikers traversing above the east shore of sub-alpine Summit Lake. Beyond the lake in the northwest soars the reddish crag of Peak 7636, providing a vivid contrast to the waters of Summit Lake and the dark green conifer forest that surrounds it. Fishing is good for brookies, and as with most lakes in the area, is best in early summer and early autumn.

After crossing Summit Lake's outlet creek, you meet a left- branching trail leading to the Pacific Crest Trail on the crest of the Salmon Mountains. Turn right. Proceeding northeast, you soon amble across a lovely sub-alpine meadow, passing the invisible, unmaintained trail leading to Little Elk Lake. Careful scouting is necessary to find that trail—it crosses the saddle immediately east of Peak 7636 and descends through a sub-alpine, glacial basin to Little Elk Lake at the 5,400-foot level, where fishing is only fair for rainbow trout.

Your trail continues east, descending through occasional meadows amid mixed conifer forest, and soon fades out entirely just before rejoining the trail to Campbell Lake. Turn left here and backtrack to the trailhead.

HIKE 100 *PATTERSON LAKE VIA THE SUMMIT TRAIL*

General description: A moderately strenuous 11.2-mile round-trip backpack in the South Warner Wilderness to a deep, sub-alpine lake in California's northeasternmost mountain range.
Elevation gain and loss: 2,300 feet, -150 feet.
Trailhead elevation: 6,850 feet.
High point: Patterson Lake, 9,000 feet.
Maps: Warren Peak 7.5-minute USGS quad, Modoc National Forest map.
Season: July through early October.
Finding the trailhead: From U.S. 395 at the south end of Alturas, turn east onto Modoc County Road 56. This road quickly passes through the city park and proceeds toward the Warner Mountains, soon skirting the west and north shores of Dorris Reservoir. After driving 6.5 miles from U.S. 395, bear right where Modoc County Road 58 branches left and heads northeast to State Highway 299. The pavement ends after thirteen miles from Alturas, replaced by a good gravel-surfaced road. After another .4 mile, immediately before entering the Modoc National Forest in the foothills of the Warner Mountains, bear left where the sign indicates Pepperdine (7 miles), Parker Creek (3 miles), and Cedarville. Bear left after another 3.2 miles. After driving twenty miles from Alturas, turn right where a sign points south to Summit Trail 1—this turnoff is at the northeast end of a corn lily and aspen-clad meadow. Proceed south on this dirt road, soon passing marshy Porter Reservoir. Just beyond a muddy spring after .3 mile, a right-branching road leads west to Pepperdine Camp. The trailhead and a campground lie another .3 mile up the left fork.

The hike: The South Warner Wilderness, crowning the Warner Mountains in extreme northeastern California, is one of the least-visited wilderness areas in the state. It is so seldom visited, in fact, that the Modoc National Forest abandoned wilderness permit requirements in the early 1980s.

This backpack on the aptly-named Summit Trail leads hikers to the largest and highest lake in the range, nestled in an impressive, cliff-bound cirque at timberline. In addition to sometimes excellent fishing for large trout, a base camp at Patterson Lake allows hikers to scale Warren Peak for far-ranging vistas encompassing portions of three states. There is no water available during the first five miles of the hike.

From the trailhead, the trail rises moderately through an open forest of white fir and ponderosa pine. You soon break into the open in a rocky area sparsely vegetated with mountain mahogany. From this point, you are treated to the first of many inspiring panoramas that continue to develop as the hike progresses. To the west, seen across the Modoc Plateau, lies Mt. Shasta, and to the east are the milky-gray Alkali Lakes sprawling across Surprise Valley. Several miles to the south along the crest of the Warner Mountains rises the snowy northeast face of 9,710-foot-high Warren Peak, towering above your destination.

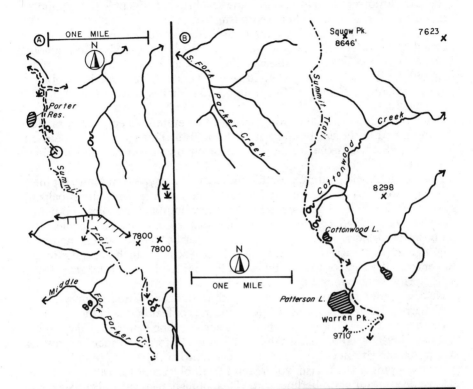

After a long level stretch of walking, you enter the South Warner Wilderness at a Modoc National Forest sign, proceed beneath the partial shade of scattered white firs, and avoid a right-branching path within .25 mile of the wilderness boundary.

The trail soon begins ascending an open, sagebrush-clad slope from which expansive westward vistas emerge.

After hiking a mile from the wilderness boundary, you ascend one switchback (avoiding the short-cut trail) and meet the signed Squaw Peak Trail branching left. Eastward views are good from here, into the Surprise Valley and beyond to distant northwestern Nevada ranges.

Continuing south along the Summit Trail, you soon spy the snowy cone of Lassen Peak in the southwest. During your mild but steady ascent, the trail alternates between stands of weather-tortured limber pines and open slopes clothed in grasses, sagebrush, some mountain mahogany, and many colorful wildflowers in season. You are often hiking along the very crest of the range, accompanied by continuous panoramic scenes.

Nearing Warren Peak, you glimpse an inviting green meadow in Cottonwood Creek basin immediately downslope to your left (east), and soon thereafter climb over the crest of the range amid stunted limber pines and enter the upper reaches of that drainage.

Avoiding a left-branching trail just above a reliable spring, your contouring trail crosses slopes covered with lupine, horsemint, helenium, and other colorful wildflowers, in addition to some sagebrush. Lodgepole pines join the limber pine forest in this sheltered basin.

The trail proceeds through wildflower-sprinkled meadows and stands of sub-alpine timber. After a short climb, you reach small but attractive Cottonwood Lake. This fine lake has no inflow or outflow and is too shallow to support fish, but the stunted timber and vivid wildflowers that surround it, combined with a backdrop of dark, 600-foot-high cliffs, makes this a beautiful spot nevertheless.

Beyond Cottonwood Lake, you ascend a moderately steep grade to reach the south end of the eastbound Squaw Peak Trail. This route could be used to loop back toward the trailhead. It is strenuous, however, and involves considerable climbing.

Bearing right, you continue south amid stunted lodgepole and limber pines. Limber pines are quite similar to whitebark pines, both of which are subalpine species present in the Warner Mountains. They both have needles in bundles (fascicles) of five and are almost indistinguishable except by their cones. The limber pine bears a cone that is open at maturity, is three-to-ten inches in length, and is characterized by tips of the cone scales which are quite thick. In contrast, the cone of the whitebark is 1.5 to three inches in length, closed at maturity, with pointed tips on the scales of the cone.

Nearing Patterson Lake, your view takes in the contrasting scenery of the near-barren desert of Surprise Valley, thousands of feet below to the east, and the sub-alpine forest and snow- clad cliffs surrounding Patterson Lake a short distance south. Nowhere else in the West but in California do such contrasting environments so often appear in such close proximity to one another.

After topping a slight rise, you reach incredibly beautiful Patterson Lake, set in a deep cirque at timberline, with 700- foot-high, near-vertical cliffs soaring above it. Campsites are numerous amid stunted timber. Colorful wildflowers garnish the shoreline, including helenium, blue lupine, yarrow, red Indian paintbrush, green gentian, aster, corn lily, shooting star, and elephant head.

Unfortunately, careless backpackers in the past have left their marks at this fine lake in the form of numerous blackened fire rings, trampled campsites too close to the lake, and the like. Please tread lightly and employ minimum-impact camping to the fullest to protect this fragile alpine landscape. Camp-fires in sparse timberline forests such as this should always be avoided.

Fishing for large trout in Patterson Lake can be excellent but highly variable. The lake is quite deep, and during the heat of summer the trout are lurking in the depths and may be hard to catch from the shoreline. Thus, fishing from the banks is best just after ice-off in the spring and after the fall turnover.

The upper Cottonwood Creek drainage lends itself to exploration. Adventurous hikers will want to investigate the glaciated basins of this drainage, characterized by several benches dropping eastward in stepladder fashion from Patterson Lake. These basins have abundant water, are lush with grasses and wildflowers, and scattered stands of timber offer sheltered camping.

From Patterson Lake, one can proceed south on the Summit Trail for .5 mile to an east-trending ridge emanating from Warren Peak, where hikers are rewarded with sweeping vistas. In the northwest lies the Modoc Plateau country, punctuated by massive Goose Lake straddling the Oregon-California border. The Warner Mountains stretch far to the north, plunging eastward for thousands of feet into the Surprise Valley. Within that valley, from north to south, are Upper Alkali Lake, farmland surrounding the town of Cedarville, and the Middle and Lower Alkali lakes. Beyond the Surprise Valley, Great Basin ranges extend eastward into the distant Nevada haze. To your immediate south lies the headwaters bowl of Owl Creek, and beyond, the crest of the Warner Mountains, mantled with whitebark and limber pines, stretches southward to the apex of that range, 9,892-foot-high Eagle Peak. Far to the southwest rises Lassen Peak, soaring out of the dense conifer forest that covers the southern Cascade Range.

Adventurous backpackers are urged to hike the Summit Trail south to its end at the Patterson Ranger Station, a total of twenty-two miles from the Pepperdine Camp Trailhead.

Peak-baggers will want to ascend to Warren Peak's lofty crown for an all-encompassing vista. To get there, head west from the above-mentioned ridgetop viewpoint along the knife-edged ridge, often passing next to the brink directly above the blue oval of Patterson Lake. You soon reach a point just east of the peak, and scrambling the final pitch to the summit involves some class 2 climbing.

Leaving this magnificent and uncrowded area behind, hikers eventually backtrack to the trailhead.

A BASIC HIKER'S CHECKLIST

Too many of us hike into the backcountry and discover we've forgotten something. No one will always take everything in the following list, but checking it before leaving home will help ensure that some essential item has not been forgotten.

- ☐ day pack or backpack
- ☐ sleeping bag
- ☐ foam pad or air mattress
- ☐ ground sheet, plastic or nylon
- ☐ dependable tent
- ☐ sturdy footwear
- ☐ lightweight camp shoes
- ☐ sunglasses
- ☐ maps and compass
- ☐ matches in waterproof container
- ☐ toilet paper
- ☐ pocket knife
- ☐ sunburn cream
- ☐ good insect repellent
- ☐ lip balm
- ☐ flashlight with new batteries
- ☐ candle(s)
- ☐ first aid kit
- ☐ survival kit
- ☐ small garden trowel or shovel
- ☐ fifty feet of nylon cord
- ☐ water filter or purification tablets
- ☐ one-quart water container
- ☐ one-gallon water container for camp use (collapsible)
- ☐ plastic bags (for trash)
- ☐ soap
- ☐ towel
- ☐ toothbrush
- ☐ cooking pots

- ☐ spoon and fork
- ☐ backpack stove and extra fuel
- ☐ aluminum foil (as windscreen for backpack stove or candle holder)
- ☐ pot scrubber
- ☐ enough food, plus a little extra
- ☐ fishing license
- ☐ fishing rod, reel, flies, lures, etc.
- ☐ camera and film
- ☐ binoculars
- ☐ waterproof covering for pack
- ☐ watch
- ☐ dependable rain parka
- ☐ rain pants
- ☐ wind garment
- ☐ thermal underwear (polypropylene is best)
- ☐ shorts and/or long pants
- ☐ wool cap or balaclava
- ☐ wool shirt and/or sweater
- ☐ jacket or parka (fiberpile is excellent)
- ☐ extra socks
- ☐ underwear
- ☐ lightweight shirts
- ☐ bandanas
- ☐ mittens or gloves
- ☐ belt
- ☐ sewing kit
- ☐ hat

IF YOU NEED ADDITIONAL INFORMATION

For additional information regarding California's wildlands, don't hesitate to contact the following agencies:

Hikes No. 1 & 2: Anza-Borrego Desert State Park, Park Headquarters, Box 299, Borrego Springs, CA 92004, (619) 767-5311.

Hike No. 3: Palomar District Headquarters, 1634 Black Canyon Road, Ramona, CA 92065, (619) 788-0250; or Cleveland National Forest, Forest Supervisor, 880 Front Street, Room 5-N-14, San Diego, CA 92188, (619) 557-5050.

Hike No. 5: Mt. San Jacinto Wilderness State Park, P.O. Box 308, Idyllwild, CA 92549,(909) 659-2607; or Palm Springs Aerial Tramway, (619) 325-1440; or, for recorded information, (619) 325-4227.

Hikes No. 6, 7, & 8: Superintendent, Joshua Tree National Park, 74485 National Park Drive, Twentynine Palms, CA 92277, (619) 367-7511.

For information on the following hikes within San Bernardino National Forest, contact Forest Supervisor, San Bernardino National Forest, 114 N. Mountainview Ave., San Bernardino, CA 92408, (714) 383-5588 or the appropriate district ranger:

Hike No. 4: Idyllwild Ranger Station, P.O. Box 518, Idyllwild, CA 92349, (714) 659-2117.

Hikes No. 9, 11, 12, 13, 14, & 15: San Gorgonio District Ranger, Route 1, P.O. Box 264, Mentone, CA 92359, (909) 794-1123.

Hikes No. 10, 16, & 17: Big Bear District Ranger, P.O. Box 290, Fawnskin, CA 92333, (909) 866-3437.

Hikes No. 18 & 20: Cajon District Ranger, Star Route, Fontana, CA 92335 (714) 887-2576.

For information on the following hikes within Angeles National Forest, contact Forest Supervisor, Angeles National Forest, 150 S. Los Robles Ave., Pasadena, CA 91101 (818) 577-0050 or the appropriate district office:

Hikes No. 19, 20, 21, 22, 23, & 25: Mt. Baldy District, 110 North Wabash Avenue, Glendora, CA 91740, (818) 335-1251.

Hikes No. 21, 22, 24, & 25: Valyermo District, P.O. Box 15, Valyermo, CA 93553, (805) 944-2187.

Hike No. 26: Saugus District, 30800 Bouquet Canyon Road, Saugus, CA 91350, (805) 296-9710.

For information on the following hikes within Los Padres National Forest, contact Los Padres National Forest, Supervisor's Office, 6144 Calle Real, Goleta, CA 93117, (805) 683-6711 or the appropriate district:

Hikes No. 27 & 28: Mt. Pinos District, Star Route, Box 400, Frazier Park, CA 93225, (805) 245-3731.

Hikes No. 29, 30, 31, & 32: National Park Service, Mojave National Preserve, Barstow, CA 92311, (619) 255-3400; Bureau of Land Mangement, Needles Resource Area Office, P.O. Box 888, Needles, CA 92363, (619) 326-3896.

Hikes No. 33, 34, 35, 36, 37, & 38: Death Valley National Park, Death Valley, CA 92328, (619) 786-2331.

Hike No. 39: Santa Lucia District, 1616 N. Carlotti Drive, Santa Maria, CA 93454, (805) 925-9538.

Hike No. 40: Big Sur District, Pfeiffer-Big Sur State Park, Big Sur, CA 93290, (408) 667-2316.

Hike No. 41 & 42: Monterey District, 406 South Mildred, King City, CA 93930, (408) 385-5434.

Hike No. 43: Park Superintendent, Pinnacles National Monument, Paicines, CA 95043, (408) 389-4485.

Hike No. 44: Big Basin Redwoods State Park, 21600 Big Basin Way, Boulder Creek, CA 95006-9050, (408) 338-6132.

Hike No. 45: Park Superintendent, Pt. Reyes National Seashore, Pt. Reyes, CA 94956, (415) 663-1092.

Hike No. 46: Stonyford Ranger District, Stites Lodoga Rd., Stonyford, CA 95979, (916) 963-3128; or Forest Supervisor, Mendocino National Forest, 420 East Laurel Street, Willows, CA 95988, (916) 934-3316.

Hike No. 47: Bureau of Land Management, Caliente Resource Area Office, 4301 Rosedale Highway, Bakersfield, CA 93308, (805) 861-4236.

The following hikes are within Sequoia National Forest:

Hikes No. 48, 49, 50: Cannell Meadow Ranger District, P.O. Box 6, 105 Whitney Rd., Kernville, CA 93238, (619) 376-3781.

Hike No. 52: Forest Supervisor, Sequoia National Forest, 900 West Grand Avenue, Porterville, CA 93257, (209) 784-1500.

Hike No. 55: Hume Lake Ranger District, 35860 East Kings Canyon Road, Dunlap, CA 93621, (209) 338-2251.

The following hikes are within Sequoia-Kings Canyon National Parks:

Hikes No. 54, 55, 56, & 57: Sequoia-Kings Canyon National Park, Three Rivers, CA 93271, (209) 565-3341.

The following hikes are within Inyo National Forest:

Hikes No. 51, 53, & 58: Mt. Whitney Ranger Station, P.O. Box 8, Lone Pine, CA 93545, (619) 876-6200. (Note concerning Hikes No. 53 and 58: There is a commercial shuttle service based in Lone Pine serving most trailheads in the Mt. Whitney Ranger District of the Inyo National Forest. Contact the Mt. Whitney Ranger Station in Lone Pine for more information.)

Hikes No. 60, 61, 62, 63, 64, 65, & 67: White Mountain Ranger District, 798 North Main Street, Bishop, CA 93514, (619) 873-2500.

Hikes No. 68 & 69: Mammoth Ranger District, P.O. Box 148, Mammoth Lakes, CA 93546, (619) 934-2505.

For information on the following hikes within Sierra National Forest, contact Forest Supervisor, Sierra National Forest, Federal Building, 1130 "O" Street, Fresno, CA 93721 or (209) 297-0706 or the appropriate ranger district:

Hike No. 59: Pineridge Ranger District, P.O. Box 300, Shaver Lake, CA 93664, (209) 841-3311.

Hike No. 70: Minarets Ranger District, North Fork, CA 93643, (209) 877-2218.

The following hikes take place within Yosemite National Park:

Hikes No. 71, 72, 73, & 74: Yosemite National Park, P.O. Box 577, Yosemite National Park, CA 95389, (209) 372-4461.

Hike No. 74: Inyo National Forest, Mono Lake Ranger District (Lee Vining Ranger Station), P.O. Box 429, Lee Vining, CA 93541, (619) 647-6525.

The following hikes are within Stanislaus National Forest:

Hikes No. 76, 77, 78, & 79: Summit Ranger District, 1 Pinecrest Lake Road, Pinecrest, CA 95364, (209) 965-3434.

The following hikes are within Toiyabe National Forest:

Hikes No. 75, 80, & 81: Bridgeport Ranger Station, P.O. Box 595, Bridgeport, CA 93517, (619) 932-7070; or Toiyabe National Forest, Supervisor's Office, 1200 Franklin Way, Sparks, Nevada 89431, (702) 331-6444.

The following hikes are within the Eldorado National Forest:

Hike No. 82: Amador Ranger District, Star Route 3, Pioneer, CA 95666, (916) 622-5061; or Eldorado National Forest , Information Center, 3070 Camino Heights Drive, Camino, CA 95709, (916) 644-6048.

The following hikes are within the Lake Tahoe Basin Management Unit:

Hikes No. 82 & 83: Lake Tahoe Basin Management Unit, 870 Emerald Bay Rd., South Lake Tahoe, CA 96150, (916) 573-2669.

Hike No. 84: Tahoe National Forest, Nevada City Ranger District, Highway 49 and Coyote Street, Nevada City, CA 95959, (916) 265-4531.

The following hikes are within the Plumas National Forest:

Hikes No. 85 & 86: Forest Supervisor, Plumas National Forest, P.O. Box 11500, 159 Lawrence St., Quincy, CA 95971, (916) 283-2050.

For information on the following hikes within Lassen National Forest, contact Forest Supervisor, Lassen National Forest, 55 South Sacramento Street, Susanville, CA 96130, (916) 257-2151, or the appropriate ranger district:

Hike No. 87: Almanor Ranger District, Box 767, Chester, CA 96020, (916) 258-2141.
Hike No. 91: Hat Creek Ranger District, Box 220, Fall River Mills, CA 96028, (916) 336-5521.

The following hikes are within Lassen Volcanic National Park:

Hikes No. 88, 89, & 90: Park Superintendent, Lassen Volcanic National Park, P.O. Box 100, Mineral, CA 96063-0100, (916) 595-4444.

For information on the following hikes within Shasta-Trinity National Forest, contact Forest Supervisor, Shasta-Trinity National Forest, 2400 Washington Ave., Redding, CA 96001, (916) 246-5443, or the appropriate ranger district:

Hike No. 92: Yolla Bolly Ranger District, Platina, CA 96076, (916) 352-4211.
Hike No. 94: Weaverville Ranger District, P.O. Box T, Weaverville, CA 96093-1190, (916) 623-2131.

The following hike is within the Arcata Resource Area:

Hike No. 93: Bureau of Land Management, Arcata Resource Area Office, 1125 16th Street, Room 219, Arcata, CA 95521, (707) 822-7648.

The following hike is within Prairie Creek Redwoods State Park:

Hike No. 97: Prairie Creek Redwoods State Park, Orick, CA 95555, (707) 488-2171.

For information on the following hikes within Klamath National Forest, contact Forest Supervisor, Klamath National Forest, 1312 Fairlane Road, Yreka, CA 96097, (916) 842-6131, or the appropriate ranger district:

Hike No. 95, 96, & 99: Scott River Ranger District, 11263 North Highway 3, Fort Jones, CA 96032, (916) 468-5351.
Hike No. 98: Happy Camp Ranger District, P.O. Box 377, Happy Camp, CA 96039, (916) 493-2243.
Hike No. 100: Warner Mountain District, P.O. Box 220, Cedarville, CA 96104, (916) 279-6116; or Forest Supervisor, Modoc National Forest, 441 Main Street, Alturas, CA 96101, (916) 279-6116, 6117, or 6118.

For more information on wildlife statewide, contact California Department of Fish and Game, Resources Building, 1416 Ninth Street, Sacramento, CA 95814.